SERVICE ON A PLATE

The Story of Contract Cate

D1514582

Published by H2O Publishing Ltd and Dine Contract Catering Ltd.

British Library Cataloguing in Publication Data: a catalogue record for this title is available in the British Library.

Library of Congress Catalogue Card Number: on file

First published: 2016

ISBN: 978-0-9935236-0-1

Design and typesetting by: H20 Publishing Ltd

Cover design by: Jim Lyons

Printed by: Samson Druck

H2O Publishing | Joynes House, New Road, Gravesend, Kent, DA11 0AJ | T: 0345 500 6008 | F: 0345 500 6009

FOREWORD

What an industry contract catering is! It gives service 24 hours a day, every day. It affects every corner of the modern economy – from the staff restaurant to the boardroom dining room, from the local primary school to the largest NHS hospital, from infancy to old age.

It feeds our armed forces, day in, day out, in peacetime and in war.

It provides greater value for money to the customer than any other sector in the hospitality industry.

And it offers a memorable career which can lead to wealth and great happiness to those with even the most modest education.

And yet, it is seen as far less glamorous than the commercial hotel and restaurant sector. Colleges tend to ignore contract catering; careers lecturers know too little about it and too few students see the opportunities it presents.

So we wanted to shine a light on an industry now called, more accurately and rather more grandly, food and service management (because, now, it provides many other services than just catering). In doing so, we trace its fascinating history and highlight the many personalities who have built it to what it is today: a £4bn business that, in one way or another, touches us all throughout our life.

And, at the end, we wanted to take a look at the future.

With the help of my company, Dine Contract Catering Limited, and of my son, Ian, who is now the very able managing director, I was very pleased to be able to sponsor *Service on a Plate*. I was even more delighted that Miles Quest agreed to undertake much of the research and writing.

Our 18 months of interviews and research have taken us to distant places in the UK and Ireland, meeting 80 or so extraordinary people who have helped drive the industry into the 21st century. I hope we've captured some of their stories in this book. We can only thank them for their time and support.

My own career, spanning some 50 years, is not unlike many of those we highlight – from apprentice chef to owning my own company – and all the time enjoying the ride and making a very good living.

So, in its own way, this book is a big thank you to an industry which has personally given me a career of long-lasting interest and excitement and my family great good fortune. I believe the same opportunities continue to hold true for all those who are committed, have talent and who are willing to take a calculated risk or two. There are examples aplenty in these pages and we dedicate this book to all those who have helped us write it – they made the industry.

I hope you enjoy reading it as much as we did writing it.

Jim Cartwright
Chairman,
Dine Catering
Co Ltd

February 2016

CONTENTS

ACKNOWLEDGMENTS

When we embarked on the story of contract catering, we envisaged that there would be plenty of written archive to help us along the way. Alas, this was not the case. The one company which we thought would have a library of written material, Gardner Merchant – it is, after all, the oldest and had produced a highly readable centenary booklet in 1986 – inadvertently disposed of all its historical material at the time of its acquisition by Sodexo. Office moves by other companies accounted for much other destruction that would have proved so helpful to us. Few executives at times of great events and drama think of the needs of future historians. So we have been reliant on the trade press, individual collections of material and oral history.

Here, thanks go to *Caterer* magazine and *Cost Sector Catering* for their help – often unwitting but hopefully acknowledged whenever used. Without access to their sources, this book would have been impossible to write – and, we suggest, much less interesting to read. Thanks must also go to Janine Mills, librarian at the Institute of Hospitality, for her ever-patient assistance.

Particular thanks also go to Alan Sutton, who spent over 30 years writing about industrial and welfare catering for *Caterer and Hotelkeeper* (as it was then called – we have called the magazine by its present title throughout), *Catering Times* and latterly for *Cost Sector Catering*; his private collection of material proved priceless and shows, once again, that good journalists know how to hoard valuable material.

There have been a number of books which have proved helpful and from which we quote: Professor Rik Medlik's *The British Hotel and Catering Industry* (1961) Pitman, and *Profile of the Hotel and Catering Industry* (1978) Heineman; William Kay's biography of Sir Gerry Robinson, *Lord of the Dance* (1999) Orion Business Books; *Food for Work* (1961) by Robert Heller (Sutcliffe); *The Food of the People* (1949) by Sir Noel Curtis-Bennett (Faber and Faber); *Hunger* (2007) by James Vernon (Harvard University Press); *Managing to Serve* (2002) by Sally Heavens and John Childs (RH Business Books); *Winning at Service* (2003) by Waldemar Schmidt, Gordon Adler and Els Van Weering (John Wiley); *I've Had a Lot of Fun* (2007) Pierre Bellon (Sodexo). Gardner Merchant's centenary publication – *A Century of Catering Excellence* (1985) provided much valuable information on the early days of industrial catering.

There are many other people to thank. All have given help in different ways: in time spent in meetings and interviews, in providing written recollections and memories; in checking passages for accuracy. Some were kind enough to entertain us; others we have gladly entertained. One or two – they will know who they are – have been pestered for information and have patiently responded well beyond the call of duty. In telling the story of contract catering, their help was invaluable. Without it, this book could not have been written. The following list of names acknowledges their help but they will all know exactly how much they contributed – some massively – to this story:

Anthony Adams, Lord Allen of Knightsbridge, Peter Aldrich, Nigel Anker, Trevor Annon, Mike Bailey, Jane Baker, Del Bampton, David Barnes, David Bateman, William Baxter, Martin Bell, Trevor Briggs, Ian Carswell, Tony Coles, Tim Cookson, Chris Copner, Bob Cotton, Martin

Couchman, Richard Cousins, Mike Day, Don Davenport, Peter W. Davies, Simon Davis, Ian Doughty, Pam Evans, John Forte, James Stirling Gallacher, Howard Goodman, David Greenwood, John Graveney, Dr Juliet Gray, Ian Hall, Geoffrey Harrison, Sir Garry Hawkes, Chris Hind, Phil Hooper, Philip Houldsworth, John Houston, Robyn Jones, Vic Laws, Hilary Lewis, Sir Francis Mackay, Jack Mathews, Noel Mead, Arthur Meakin, Gillian Medcalf, Philip Morley, David Osterhout, Chris Page, Vince Pearson, Peter Roberts, Alan Robinson, Sir Gerry Robinson, Ian Sarson, Julia Sibley, Peter Smale, Clive Smith, John V Smith, Mike Stapleton, Graham Stone, Alistair Storey, John Symonds, Derek Taylor, Mike Taylor, David Thomson, Bill Toner, Ian Tritton, Marc Verstringhe, Bill Vickers, Hilary Ward, Tony Ward-Lewis, Tim West, Frank Whittaker, Lou Willcock, Gordon Wishart, Debbie White, Dan Wright.

Needless to say, while these contributions, so generously made, have made this book a far more worthwhile project than would otherwise have been possible, any errors or omissions are entirely of our own making.

Miles Quest & Jim Cartwright

CHAPTER ONE

Where it all began

John Toulson Gardner was born in 1858, the son of a beer-shop keeper. He died in 1920, the founder of a catering empire.

John Toulson Gardner, the butcher who founded a catering empire.

At the time when John Gardner was born, most youngsters wanted to enter a trade by being apprenticed to a master. Gardner wanted to become a butcher – a much admired profession with its own Livery Company. In 1872, aged 14 and with little education, he took up an apprenticeship with a master butcher, Morris in Leadenhall Market. It was a tough seven years. He had to be at work by 6am six days a week with regular visits to the slaughter house to learn about killing, evisceration and practising cutting up and dressing the joints. The powerful odour pervaded his clothes long after he came back to his home in Southwark at night.

At Morris, sides of beef and lamb were hung up on large hooks suspended from rails either in the shop ready to be cut up for customers or in an ice-safe which was kept cool with ice supplied by the ice man. Fresh sawdust on the floor and shining tiles on the walls ensured the shop was kept clean. At the end of every day, Gardner and other apprentices had to scrub down the chopping boards with scrapers and wire brushes and wash them with hot water. Cleavers and knives had the same treatment. In the evening, the sawdust was swept up from the floor and new sawdust was put down ready for trade the next day.

The apprenticeship was both long and comprehensive and involved learning on the job with tuition from the more experienced butchers employed by the shop. Part of the training was front-of-house, serving the customers on the shop floor.

Into his apprenticeship, Gardner learnt how to serve customers, all of them rich enough to be able to afford to buy the beef and lamb, the rabbits, the game and the poultry that Morris sold, though working clerks and others came in for the cheaper cuts and the scraps that could be made into stews and soups. But it was a time of rising prosperity and London's population had grown from one million in 1801 to four million in 1881. Morris took full advantage of this rising demand and John Gardner was swept along with the general excitement of the times.

He was friendly and personable, encouraging customers to buy a bit more of this, a bit more of that, and got to know them well, delivering meat to many of them in their home. He had a good business head on him, too, and made sure he understood the ins and outs of the shop's trade, from the purchase and preparation of the meat to the payment of the bills, from organising the staff rotas to the stock taking.

He finished his apprenticeship and

Morris, the butcher's shop in Leadenhall Market where John Gardner worked his apprenticeship – and which he eventually owned.

became a Master Butcher – something he was proud of all his life – and in 1886, at the age of 28 and 14 years after entering his apprenticeship, the opportunity came for him to take over the running of the Morris shop. It is not known why the business became available but, most likely, it was because the owners were retiring. Gardner took on the lease, the rent payable weekly in cash and was encouraged in the move by the rising consumption of meat in Britain (it soared by almost 50 per cent between 1870 and 1900). Mrs Beeton, who first published her *Book of Household Management* in 1860 and who no doubt was a major influence on the rise in meat-eating, wrote:

"In the metropolis, on account of the large number of its population possessing the means to indulge in the best of everything, the demand for the most delicate joints of meat is great."

When Gardner took over Morris, he wrote in his ledger: "We must get better before we get bigger!" It showed his business acumen as well as his ambition. It was clear, at the outset, that he had grander ideas.

It was a good time to be a butcher. The City of London employed many thousands of people who worked in banks, insurance companies and other trading businesses, most of them commuting from other parts of London. Some brought their own lunch but many patronised the eating houses and coffee shops that sprang up during this time, such as Baker's Chop House in Change Alley and Simpson's in Cornhill.

Morris supplied meat to many of the clubs, chop houses, restaurants and shops in the City as well as banquets in the Livery Halls. Business boomed to such an extent that in 1890 Gardner took over a London eating house, Wilkinson's in Coleman Street, which typically offered on its menu a plate of beef with carrots and potatoes and half a pint of porter for 9d. Wilkinson's was 'food on the run', as this contemporary account relates:

"Mostly, from 12 o'clock until two, the eating houses of the City are crammed with hungry clerks. You no sooner are seated in one of the snug, inviting little settles with a table laid for four or six, spread with a snowy cloth still bearing the fresh quadrangle marks impressed by the mangle and rather damp, than the dapper, ubiquitous waiter, napkin in hand, stands before you and rapidly runs over a detailed account of the tempting viands, smoking hot and ready to be served up. Beef boiled and roast, veal and ham, loin of pork, cutlet, chops and steaks, greens, potatoes and peas."

With the purchase of Wilkinson's, Gardner had moved from retail and into catering. It was the beginnings of a trail that led directly to the development of contract catering.

* * *

If Gardner was the forerunner of contract catering he was not by any means a pioneer in industrial catering. Some argue that industrial catering stretches as far back as the Middle Ages or before, when the king had to feed his followers, and the knights and barons in their manor houses had to feed their many staff and retainers, the larger houses running into several hundred people. In fact, the medieval manor was a highly engineered industrial unit living off the land and providing food and shelter for the whole community. Huge wood-fired

Robert Owen, an enlightened employer, took over the management of his father-in-law's spinning works near the Falls of Clyde in 1799, marking the beginnings of modern industrial society.

kitchens cooked enormous quantities of meat and fish for everyday use as well as for banquets; dining tables were equally vast, one Lord's table was said to be six yards long. Staff included cooks, bakers, brewers and candlemakers (candles were made from mutton and deer fat). In the larger houses, galleries were built for minstrels to entertain diners – a kind of medieval Music While You Eat.

This kind of catering provision in manor houses and castles lasted well into the early 20th century; indeed, it still exists in some great houses today though less lavishly and with greater sophistication. But it also began to appear in other areas of society.

In the 18th century, factories and other places of work began to emerge throughout the country employing men, women and children, frequently in dire working and living conditions. Food for the workers was poor or non-existent. Those in the

workhouses (made famous by Oliver Twist's famous request but introduced as far back as 1679) fared better; here, food was generally considered to be reasonably good "and better than the most industrious labourer could afford himself at his own habitation", commented one account.

The emergence of Robert Owen, an enlightened employer who took over the management of his father-in-law's spinning works near the Falls of Clyde in 1799, marked the beginnings of modern industrial society. Owen is widely credited as the pioneer of industrial welfare, which included the provision of food for his workers. It was industrial catering as we call it today. He recognised that those working in factories and their families at the time were "a collection of the most ignorant and destitute from all parts of Scotland, possessing the usual characteristics of poverty and ignorance. They were generally indolent and much addicted to theft, drunkenness and falsehood and all their concomitant vices and strongly experiencing the misery which these ever produce."

Such unpromising material was not uncommon for factory owners to face in those days as compulsory education was many years away, but they did little to put the situation to rights. Often workers were treated with some cruelty and with little pay, while women and children were abused and exploited.

Owen took a different view, introducing measures to turn layabouts into (in his words) 'honest, industrial, sober and orderly' workers; he also believed that their children should be given a modicum of education. In this, Owen was an enlightened employer but he was also a businessman and the measures he introduced were not entirely altruistic. They also aimed to increase profits by making the

workforce better skilled, better fed, better housed and thus more employable and more productive. He introduced large kitchens and a dining hall of 4,400 sq ft at the factory in which to feed his staff. He built places for children to play 'where their young minds may be properly directed' and toilets 'calculated to give children such habits as will enable the master of police to keep the village in a decent clean state,' adding grimly 'and this is no small difficulty to overcome.' Facilities for education, including a course for girls 'to learn to cook cheap, nutritious food and to clean and keep a house neat and in order' were also installed.

The cost of this was significant – £6,000 (about £700,000 in today's money), made even more remarkable by the fact that Owen's ideas were pioneering. Few other employers took such a benevolent attitude towards their staff. But the fact that the measures worked was proof that they made good business sense as well. Owen claimed that during his management, the company was able to pay five per cent interest on the £50,000 capital invested, while productivity increased five times with a reduction in costs of £6,000 per annum. It was a convincing argument in favour of improving working conditions.

Owen went on to be a significant force in the introduction of the Factory Laws which were originally opposed by many factory owners but which paved the way for altogether more enlightened attitudes towards employment.

By the end of the 19th century, these attitudes were manifested in the approach of a number of large, well-known companies, including the three Quaker companies of Cadbury, Fry and Rowntree, co-incidentally all cocoa and chocolate manufacturers. Other companies, such as Lever Bros of Port Sunlight and Colman's, the mustard producer based in Norfolk, were also introducing new concepts of employee welfare.

Cooking or reheating food that was brought in by employees was a feature of many of the early catering facilities operated by companies, Cadbury's later expanded to become a major industrial caterer. By 1902, it provided 40,610 sq ft devoted to catering accommodation (a rise from 17,820 sq ft in 1886) with the workforce increasing from 700 to 3,600 over the same period.

In an account published in 1905, the facility at Bourneville was described as 'the most extensive dining accommodation in the United Kingdom, seldom surpassed anywhere in size and nowhere in provision, where tables for 2,000 of Messrs Cadbury's girls are in regular use in a fine hall. Food may be brought in from home, and either cooked in the kitchen or heated in unique steam cupboards in the room, or it may be purchased at wholesale prices at the counter. To provide the very best, wholesale buyers are employed by the firm.'

In the best places, the provision of cooked meals proved too tempting for employees to resist. According to the same account, at Lever Brothers in Port Sunlight, two dining halls had been erected, the bigger one costing £18,000 (worth around £1.7m in today's money) with seats for some 1,500 girls:

"Here again, there is the fullest liberty to bring food and have it warmed or cooked free, all the necessary utensils being provided; but the price and quality of the bill of fare prove too tempting to most, as well they may, to judge from the following specimens: meat and potatoes or hot pot 2d, pudding, soups, tarts etc – 1d; tea etc ½d."

In an adjoining dining room, however, it was reported that the men usually brought food from home to be cooked on the

---

> ## *Few employers provided cooked meals*
>
> At the outset, few employers provided cooked meals for their staff. Bringing food in to be cooked or reheated on the company's premises was typically more prevalent and most companies only provided facilities for re-heating or cooking food brought in from home.
>
> In Saltaire, the industrial village in south Yorkshire founded in 1853 by Sir Titus Salt, a dining hall was provided where food was cooked for operatives who brought it in but cooked meals were also provided at cost, or less. Some of these dining facilities were vast. At Brunners in Mond, a factory that later became part of ICI, a dining room was provided with heating apparatus for food and water for 3,000 men.
>
> At the North Eastern Railway works at Gateshead, two rooms sitting 1,100 were fitted with long deal tables nearly two feet wide, each with a division 10 inches high running down the centre so that, says one account written by Budgett Meakin, a lecturer in industrial relations, "without rising or leaning over, no-one can see what his vis-à-vis has brought and all can go home with the comforting hallucination that their neighbours supposed them to fare better than they did".
>
> This kind of class-driven privacy was prevalent throughout industrial catering at the time but it hardly survived the first world war when sexes and classes were thrown together. Even so, segregation both of the sexes and the workers continued well into the 1950s, particularly in heavy industries where those in dirty overalls were separated from blue and white collar workers. At Cadbury's, only red badge men of exceptional trustworthiness and integrity were allowed to enter workrooms where girls were employed.

---

premises (free tea was provided for all those working overtime).

In all of these accounts, the companies themselves introduced and operated the catering facilities but there is an early example in the late 1800s of an unnamed contractor being employed to provide a catering service at Tangye's, a Birmingham engineering company employing some 3,000 men in its Great Cornwall Works. The mess room was able to seat 1,000 people and the contractor charged a penny a week for each user of the room, for which he provided hot water or warmed food if required; with that kind of turnover it must have been a sure-fire money spinner. He also supplied cooked food such as hot meat and two vegetables (6d), chop and steak to order (4d), bacon and eggs (3d), boiled ham or beef per ounce (1d), tea, coffee or bun (½d). No alcohol was served but smoking

was permitted in the latter half of the dining hour.

Almost all catering facilities were demarcated by gender – women and girls ate in separate areas to men and boys – but also by status. At Tangye's, free dinners were served to 60 of the leading clerks and managers in comfortable rooms attached to the offices. Nor was food the only nourishment to be provided. To maintain and uplift the moral standards of employees, instructional addresses on a wide variety of subjects were delivered in the mess room during the last half hour, when the men could smoke.

In some companies, waitress and self-service operations existed side by side. In Cadbury's Bourneville factory, for example, a self-service cafeteria system was in operation together with restaurants where waitresses served the meals for an extra charge. Even the waitress service area was on a significant scale, seating 600 people (both men and women) compared with 5,000 in the self-service area – the so-called dining rooms, which were gender segregated.

In all these developments, the scale of some of the catering facilities is extraordinary. Montagu Burton's multiple-tailor factory opened in Leeds in 1900, although its first canteen was introduced only in 1922, providing seating accommodation for 2,000. This very soon proved to be too small and a dining room was subsequently built to seat 4,000 people. Even this proved inadequate and a new canteen, completed in 1934 and covering 100,000 sq ft (the kitchens at 5,124 sq ft) was opened by royalty; it seated 8,000 in one sitting. Burton's subsidised the entire operation except for the cost of the food.

Even here, hot cupboards were provided for workers who wanted to bring their own food to be re-heated. The company offered other employee benefits including extensive welfare, medical and health facilities which were far ahead of their time but they followed Robert Owen's pioneering concepts.

How these huge canteens were manned, especially in wartime conditions when labour was scarce, is something to be marvelled at but their operating cost was sometimes cut by a special programme of volunteering. At Burton's, the meals were provided directly from the kitchens. This was made possible by the recruitment of relays of helpers from the works' staff to assist in the service. The helpers stopped work 10 minutes before the lunch hour and were given a free meal for their help. The system clearly kept the catering wage bill

down even if it raised the catering cost by providing free meals for hundreds of helpers.

Other firms, including Hartley's jam factory in Liverpool and Huntley and Palmer in Reading, operated canteens for their workers, though at Huntley and Palmer only about a fifth of workers used the facility 'owing to the large number of eating shops in the vicinity and partly because a large proportion of employees are able to get home for their midday meal.' Competition from nearby commercial catering outlets is clearly nothing new.

* * *

As he tentatively entered the catering industry with the purchase of Wilkinson's in 1900, John Gardner was fortunate to be living at a time when working conditions

Lunch is served: some canteens accommodated well over 1,000 diners at one sitting.

Colman's introduces hot delivered meals

Colman's in Norwich was an enlightened company. It provided several dining rooms with a kitchen that offered meals at 2d or 4d per dish, either served in the dining rooms or sent out to workers in double tins, the outer compartment of which was filled with hot water – an early example of hot delivered meals.

Budgett Meakin describes how Colman's had pioneered an early form of merchandising its menus:

"A most ingenious form of menu is adopted, namely a glass showcase hanging on the wall by the factory gate, that all may inspect it, wherein are displayed each day, as in a cook shop window, priced specimens of the viands to be obtained. So practical an advertisement must decide many where to dine."

were gradually improving and when there was a growing understanding of the importance of nutrition and its place in the work environment. More than a century after Robert Owen had proved the connection, the general realisation that food and nutrition had an impact on worker output and productivity was beginning to take firm shape.

In 1913, the chief inspector of factories noted: "It is gradually being realised that the physical fitness of the worker has an important bearing on the output of the factory and it is found that dining rooms and restaurants are slowly becoming more general, more especially in the modern, up-to-date factories."

Later, in wartime 1916, a report in *The Times* said that "provision of proper meals for the workers is, indeed, an indispensible condition for the maintenance of output on which our fighting forces depend, not only for factory but for their very lives". And later that year, a government booklet entitled *Feeding the Munition Worker* stated that there was now an overwhelming body of evidence and experience which proves that productive output "is largely dependent upon the physical efficiency and health of the worker".

In the same year, Dorothea Pound, a scholar in sociology, noted that mess rooms, in which workers brought their own food, were often unsatisfactory because they were unattractive, bare and ill-kempt but that in restaurants 'the arrangements are usually much superior and the food is supplied at a wonderfully cheap rate'.

It was not until 1943, when the Hot Springs United Nations Conference on the Food Requirement of Nations was set up, that it was laid down that all industrial workers should be given full opportunities to obtain a third of their total daily calories required for maintaining health and

Lunch at the George and Vulture, George Yard, Lombard Street; John Gardner bought the ancient inn after his purchase of Wilkinson's chop house – his first foray into catering.

efficiency in their respective employment through their midday meal.

The Hot Springs Conference report meant, however, that the onus was being placed firmly on employers throughout the world to take steps to ensure that adequate nourishment was provided at the place of work for every worker. Not every country took note of course, but the British government did. Indeed, well before, in 1940, it had already forced larger employers to introduce works canteens and encouraged local authorities to set up Community Feeding Centres through grants, popularly called British Restaurants, to feed people in need of a nutritious and well cooked meal. Many of these still existed well into the 1950s.

* * *

In the 1900s, however, John Gardner was more concerned with growing his business. He was nothing if not an opportunist.

Earlier, in 1904, the Russian Fleet, at war with Japan, left the Baltic without making adequate arrangements for re-provisioning. Anchored off Hull, it had to send two sailors to London to arrange for new supplies. The Russians, who could speak no English, met John Gardner, who could speak no Russian but knew a man who did. As a result, two trains later left London for Hull laden not only with meat but with other provisions, all provided by John Gardner.

The beginnings of a complete supply chain took root in Gardner's mind; if he could supply the Russian Fleet, why not a chain of restaurants? Which is exactly what he next acquired – first, the George and Vulture in Castle Court, London, an early 18th century inn with literary connections,

John Gardner took over the White Swan laundry in 1916 to cope with all the laundry requirements of its growing empire.

The growth of canteens

When the First World War broke out, it was estimated that there were barely 100 regular factory canteens; by the end of the war there were over 1,000. No munitions factory was without a canteen. By 1918, over one million meals a day were being served in factory canteens and the practice of bringing food in to be reheated was being discouraged because it defeated the aim of improving the quality of food being consumed (assuming that the canteen did actually supply better quality food).

In 1921, in *The Health of the Industrial Worker,* the authors, two government medicos, suggested that the midday meal should provide at least 1,000 calories for women and 1,250 for men.

They concluded that a factory canteen, apart from its primary object of "supplying wholesome food under favourable conditions, has in it great possibilities as a social institution, where workers meet, make friends and learn to be part of, and take part in, the life of what should be a valuable humanising influence, their industrial home".

Grand though this conclusion is, it remains relevant to this day.

John Gardner's ships' stores department provisioned many of the Cunard liners in the heyday of transatlantic travel, including the RMS Berengaria, 56,000 tonnes, which entered Cunard's service in 1920.

including Charles Dickens, who sited many of Mr Pickwick's activities in the hostelry. He also bought Groom's Coffee Houses, the best known branch being opposite the Law Courts in Fleet Street. Eventually, Gardner's restaurants spread all about the City.

John Gardner's organisation – his motto was Do it Now! – thus became a mixture of catering and retailing and proved a fertile training ground for his four sons, John, Percy, Charles and Harold, all of whom came into the business which extended into bakery, wine and spirits; even a laundry came into the growing empire in 1916.

He died in 1920 at the age of 62. Trained as a butcher he had laid the foundations of a significant catering business. His death spurred his sons on to develop it further, the youngest, Harold, joining in 1926. They were aided by Sam Smith, a newcomer who had started his career in insurance but who wanted to escape from the office-bound nature of the job. Smith joined in the same year as Harold and stayed as long, eventually becoming managing director before retiring in 1966.

The 1920s, however, were not auspicious. The slump, the general strike in 1926 and the Wall Street crash in 1929 all had an impact on business, yet the company survived the economic gloom, taking advantage of a new mode of travel that took off in the 1920s and reached its heyday in the 1930s. Sea travel was dominated by a succession of Cunard's massive liners. John Gardner had already set up a special ships' stores department in the mid-1920s but this was further enhanced by the establishment of a cigar department to complement the wine and spirit sales of the company. Victualling the major cruise lines became big business. It set the company on the way to becoming the country's biggest contract caterer.

A John Gardner canteen: most catering workers were female – few photographs of the day showed male catering workers.

CHAPTER TWO

*Between the wars
and catering in wartime*

*The Second World War gave contract
catering the boost it needed and business
boomed.*

The impetus given to industrial
catering generally by the 1914-18
war did not, in the words of Sir
Noel Curtis Bennett in his book
The Food of the People, 'bear the fruit
which might have been hoped'.

The First World War had encouraged
the concept of industrial feeding and by
1918 the number of factory canteens had
grown from barely 100 in 1914 to over
1,000, excluding all munitions factories.
Professor Rik Medlik, in his book *The
British Hotel and Catering Industry*,
published in 1960, ascribes this growth
not so much to a revival of the medieval
responsibility but to a new recognition of
the need of the worker for adequate food.
Nevertheless, as soon as the First World
War ended this new-found social and
nutritional consciousness fell away
and many of the canteens that had been
so enthusiastically opened in the war
were closed.

According to Sir Noel, there were a

*The depression following the General Strike of 1926 discouraged major improvements in welfare as companies
struggled to survive.*

number of reasons for this. Canteen managers then were not a very enterprising or professional lot and didn't see, or want to see, much of a future in industrial catering in peacetime, largely because their background was not in catering. Because of this they didn't campaign for staff catering to continue. Companies themselves were unenthusiastic, believing that staff canteens were both expensive and difficult to provide. Worse, the workers themselves showed little enthusiasm for the idea. The apathy was exacerbated by the difficult economic times – the depression followed by the General Strike of 1926 discouraged major improvements in welfare as most companies struggled to survive, let alone improve working conditions. In Medlik's words "industrial catering remained almost stagnant in the twenties".

Another reason may have been the fairly basic standard of food that was then being provided in industrial canteens. Compared with today's offerings, food for workers then was decidedly utilitarian. Only the larger companies, influenced by trends and practices in the United States, began to appreciate that new investment in machinery and equipment and new methods of management and organisation, could financially benefit both workers and the companies that employed them. Included in this new approach was a renewal of the recognition, widely accepted in the war but forgotten afterwards, that nutritious meals were a key factor in worker productivity and in their health and welfare.

It was left to those companies that had successfully led the way earlier and which were now adopting new (often US-based) methods of management, such as market research, work study, personnel management and other innovative ideas that were designed to lead to lower costs

and higher profits. Looking more closely at the organisation of work and motivational techniques helped to keep the industrial catering flag flying.

At the same time, the growing industrialisation of the economy was encouraging new industries to emerge. The early pioneers of industrial feeding, such as the major chocolate companies, were being joined by major car manufacturers such as Morris at Cowley, the Austin factory in Birmingham and Ford at Dagenham, each employing thousands of workers.

The introduction of these new industries and the growth of industrial Britain in the 1930s began to impinge on the catering industry. This was a gradual process and it was made more difficult by the growing realisation that if a canteen was to be introduced, it needed a professional caterer to operate it. Previously, canteen managers were often works or staff managers who had been given the job of running the canteen because no-one else was available. Companies began to realise that, to run a canteen successfully, expert management was needed. Catering was not a subject in which they had any skill. As in the 19th century, most of the emerging industries chose to provide the catering themselves but some felt that they did not have the expertise to provide it cost-effectively. Nor, even in those early days, did they want to divert management and organisational time away from the main activity of the business.

In Sir Noel's words, "the industrial canteen, run by an expert caterer, either within the firm itself or from outside it, began to emerge as an essential welfare service – based not on philanthropy but on a scientific realisation of the needs of the industrial worker if he was to make a full contribution to industry."

As a result, firms began to appoint

trained caterers to organise their catering facility rather than let it be run by the works manager. Some appointed contractors. Many set up a Works Canteen Committee to try to involve shop floor workers and unions in the way the canteen was run, the food it offered and the service it provided.

Once again, the industrial canteen began to emerge as an essential welfare service and one – going back to Robert Owen again – based on the recognition of the physical needs of the workers and the relevance of balancing those needs with the efficiency of the company they worked for. The new management theories were having their impact and the canteen was again beginning to be seen as an asset of the company, not a liability. The fact that great strides were being taken in the field of understanding nutrition hastened this development.

* * *

In 1929 the Gardner brothers decided to form a limited company. The 1920s had been a difficult decade and it was thought prudent to limit the family's liabilities but, with Harold Gardner as chairman, the company's first annual report showed a healthy trading profit of £33,968 (£1.8m in today's money) which was over £1,000 (£53,000) more than had been forecast in the prospectus. A dividend of 7½d (£1.60) was paid. John Gardner had ridden the storm of the General Strike and the Wall Street crash, wisely taking note of developments in the catering industry both in the US and in the UK.

In the US, the growth of popular eateries was beginning to influence catering in the UK. With some foresight, Harold Gardner had travelled to the US in the 1920s and came back with an idea.

Cafeterias – mainly self-service eateries – had become popular in the US in the early part of the century and were now an accepted part of the catering scene. Not so in the UK. Indeed, Lyons' Corner Houses, which were first established in 1909 and went on to become popular well into the 1970s, relied on waitress service with the Lyons 'Nippy' becoming synonymous with fast, friendly service providing well cooked, well presented food in stylish art deco surroundings. Each Corner House typically employed over 400 staff and with Lyons still wedded to waitress service, self-service had not yet become established.

This did not stop Gardner bucking the trend. Harold Gardner opened what was the UK's first cafeteria in 1929 at 55 Moorgate. Fewer staff meant lower costs, lower costs meant lower prices, lower prices meant more volume and more volume meant higher profits. The concept worked and the outlet prospered until it was destroyed in the Blitz in 1940.

It was just at this time, in 1929, that John Gardner moved into contract catering when the business took over a bankrupt WJ Pollard, an outside caterer of sorts. Pollard, who had much flair and flamboyance but little business acumen (something which John Gardner could provide) brought several staff with him together with some equipment, the latter providing the beginnings of Gardner's outside catering business. Pollard also had useful contacts and one of his contracts was for the officers' mess at Aldershot – the earliest known Ministry of Defence contract.

The merger was John Gardner's introduction to contract catering, opening the door to an aspect of catering that the company had not previously considered but by the time war was declared in 1939,

the company was a thriving contract caterer operating some thirty contracts – its first being the British Legion poppy factory – as well as supplying companies such as Ford (since 1930) and units of the armed forces with food and other items. It was the beginning of a long association with Ford that went well into the Gardner Merchant era thirty years later. It was also running some half a dozen restaurants and it had developed an outside catering arm which catered for such major events as the Royal Naval review at Spithead and the Aldershot Military Tattoo which was attended by over 500,000 people – a gigantic achievement.

Clearly, great opportunities now appeared on the horizon for those with catering expertise. John Gardner was not alone. Another contractor – D Ellis and Co – had been established in 1919 and claimed to be "one of the pioneers of this great social experiment in industry and its aim is to raise the standard of works catering to the highest possible level". Ironically, this was a company owned by Jack Bateman's first mother-in-law and was acquired in

1950 by Gardner Merchant. Other contractors also appeared, the most prominent being Barkers.

Early in the 1930s Herbert Merchant started a cigar business in London and, anxious to expand, recruited John Pepys and Robert (Bob) Stent as directors, both of whom were familiar with the London club and social scene and could help to promote the sale of Merchant's cigars and other tobacco products in key outlets.

One of these outlets was a company run by a man called Barker who had a hand in catering by supplying cakes and buns to

The Lyons' 'Nippy' became synonymous with fast, friendly service in the company's Corner Houses.

John Gardner celebrated its 50th anniversary in 1936 and in the same year catered for the Aldershot Military Tattoo attended by over half a million people.

Assortment of Dishes (according to Season) provided in their Canteens by

BARKERS (Contractors) LIMITED

SOUPS

Tomato, Potato, Thick Gravy, Thick Kidney, Vegetable, Scotch Broth, Barley Broth, Mutton Broth, Cream of Onion, Lentil, Oxtail... ... ... **2d.**

FISH (Special day, Friday).

*Fried Filleted Cod and Chips (6oz. por. of fish) ... ... **7d.**
*Fried filleted Plaice and Chips (4oz por. of fish) ... ... **9d.**
Fish Cake (1) and Chips ... ... **5d.**
Fish Cakes (2) and Chips ... ... **8d.**

JOINTS (including 2 Vegetables).

Roast Leg of Pork ... ... **10d.**
Roast Leg of Lamb, Mint Sauce ... **9d.**
Roast Beef and Yorkshire Pudding ... **9d.**
Roast Leg of Veal and Stuffing ... **10d.**
Roast or Boiled Mutton ... ... **9d.**
Boiled Silverside of Beef and Dumplings **9d.**
Roast Loin of Lamb and Mint Sauce **9d.**

ENTREES (including 2 Vegetables).

Steak and Kidney Pie ... ... **9d.**
Individual Steak and Kidney Pudding **9d.**
Braised Sheep's Heart ... ... **9d.**
Chop Toad in the Hole ... ... **8d.**
Sausage Toad in the Hole ... ... **8d.**
Liver and Bacon ... ... **9d.**
Veal and Ham Pie ... ... **8d.**
Irish Stew ... ... **8d.**
Savoury Roll ... ... **7d.**
Shepherds Pie ... ... **9d.**
Cottage Pie ... ... **9d.**
Savoury Rissoles (2) ... ... **7d.**
Lancashire Hot Pot ... ... **9d.**
Haricot Mutton ... ... **9d.**
Stewed Neck of Lamb ... ... **9d.**
Grilled Lamb Chop ... ... **10d.**
American Hash Cake & Tomato Sauce **7d.**
Shrewsbury Steak ... ... **9d.**
Stewed Steak & Carrots & 1 vegetable **9d.**
Sausages 2, & Mashed Potatoes & 1 veg. **7d.**
Stewed Lamb Chop & Peas & 1 veg. **10d.**
Steak & Potato Pie & 1 veg. ... **9d.**

HOT SWEETS

	Per portion.	
	Without Custard	With Custard
Baked Jam Roll	—	2½d.
Boiled Jam Roll	—	2½d.
Boiled Fruit Roll	—	2½d.
College Pudding	—	2½d.
Fresh Fruit Pudding ...	2½d.	3d.
Fresh Fruit Pie ...	2½d.	3d.
Apple Dumpling	2½d.	3d.
Apple Prior Tart	2½d.	3d.
Bakewell Tart	—	2½d.
Open Jam Tart	2½d.	3d.
Apple Pudding	2½d.	3d.
Devonshire Roll	2½d.	3d.
Boiled Sultana Roll ...	—	2½d.
Boiled Dundee Roll ...	—	2½d.
Macaroni Pudding ...	2½d.	3d.
Rice Pudding	2½d.	3d.
Sago Pudding	2½d.	3d.
Apples and Rice	2½d.	3d.
Vermicelli Custard ...	2½d.	—
Tapioca Custard	2½d.	—
Mixed Fruit	2½d.	3d.
Cabinet Pudding	2½d.	3d.
Bread and Butter Pudding...	2½d.	3d.
Savoy Pudding	2½d.	3d.
Queen's Pudding	2½d.	3d.
Ginger Pudding	—	2½d.
Manchester Pudding ...	2½d.	3d.
Date Roll or Pudding ...	—	2½d.
Victoria Pudding	2½d.	3d.

COLD SWEETS

Fruit Jelly, per portion ...	2½d.	3d.
Blancmange and Jam ...	2½d.	—
Sponge Trifle	2½d.	3d.
Fruit Trifle	2½d.	3d.
Fruit Salad	—	6d.
Prunes	2½d.	3d.

CHOCOLATES and CONFECTIONERY.

All popular varieties.

CIGARETTES and TOBACCO.

All popular brands.

*The price of these dishes is liable to fluctuation according to the season and prevailing market costs.

BEVERAGES

Tea, per cup ... ... **1d.**
Coffee, per cup ... ... **2d.**
Cocoa, per cup ... ... **1½d.**
Oxo ... ... **2d.**
Milk, hot ... ... **2d.**
Milk, cold ... ... **1½d.**
Hot Chocolate ... ... **3d.**
Horlicks, plain ... ... **3d.**
Horlicks with milk ... ... **4d.**
Lemonade, per glass ... ... **1½d.**
Orangeade ... ... **1½d.**
*Minerals ... ... **2d. and 3d.**
Pot of Tea, 3d. for one, 5d. for two.

BREAD, CAKES, ETC.

Roll with Butter ... ... **1½d.**
Bread and Butter (2 slices) ... **2d.**
Buttered Toast (1 slice) ... **1½d.**
Ham Rolls ... ... **3d.**
Salmon Rolls ... ... **3d.**
Cheese Rolls ... ... **2½d.**
Sandwiches, etc., various ... **3d.**
Cut Cake, per slice ... ... **1½d.**
Assorted Cakes & Pastries **1d., 1½d. and 2d.**
Bread and Margarine (2 slices) ... **1½d.**

SALADS AND COLD MEATS, ETC.

*Tomato Salad ... ... **4d.**
*Mixed Salad ... ... **4d.**
*Egg Salad ... ... **5d.**
*Potato Salad ... ... **4d.**
*Beetroot Salad ... ... **3d.**
*Green Salad ... ... **4d.**
Ham, per plate ... ... **8d.**
Brisket, per plate ... ... **6d.**
Brawn, per plate ... ... **6d.**
*Boiled Egg, each ... ... **4d.**
*Poached Egg on Toast ... ... **5d.**
*Scrambled Egg on Toast ... ... **6d.**
*Egg on Chips ... ... **5d.**
*Egg on Bacon ... ... **7d.**
Baked Beans on Toast ... ... **5d.**
Welsh Rarebit ... ... **5d.**
Omelettes, various ... ... **7d.**
Butter, per portion ... ... **1d.**
Pickles, per portion ... ... **3d.**
Jam, per portion ... ... **2d.**
Biscuits, per packet ... ... **1d. and 2d.**
Packet Chocolates ... ... **1d. and 2d.**
*Boiled Sweets, Bananas, Oranges and Apples

May 20th, 1940: The price list for Barkers (Contractors) for a client, William Beardmore and Co, showing the range of dishes available. Even though the country was well into the Second World War, the number of dishes would not disgrace a staff restaurant today.

workers on building sites. Unfortunately, Barker failed to pay his bills so Merchant took him over, combining it with a small business being developed by Pepys and Stent that supplied cab drivers with refreshment huts in various parts of London. Thus the catering side of the Herbert Merchant business began to develop as Barkers (Contractors) Ltd.

Through contacts with Pepys' eldest brother, a motor racing driver, Barkers obtained contracts to cater for employees in the car industries that were beginning to expand in the Midlands in the mid- to late-1930s. In 1940, Barkers recruited a hotelier, Stanley Woodhead, to the board to oversee the company's actual operations; he was the only member of the board who had had any catering training. A year later two more directors, Walter Cardy and Reginald Staines, both from Ever Ready, one of Barkers' contracts, also joined. In 1942, they formed a subsidiary company, Practical Catering Systems, a competitor of sorts to Barkers but which was offering a catering service on the basis of a fixed annual fee. A startling innovation in those days, it was designed to prevent criticism that the contractor was profiteering from feeding workers during the war. In 1944, Barkers Equipment Company was established to plan industrial canteens and other catering facilities and the company went from strength to strength.

Even after the creation of Westminster Technical Institute and between the wars, catering education was largely non-existent. There were domestic science and housekeeping courses run almost exclusively for ladies, but these had little relevance to industrial catering though many of their students later went into the sector, particularly during the Second World War. It was not until May 1938 that the Institutional Management Association (IMA and now part of the Institute of Hospitality) was formed, mainly as a result of pressure from the Association of Teachers in Domestic Education. Branches of the IMA were quickly established and during the war many of its members were active in industrial feeding. By 1943, it was suggested that the IMA should become the national examining body for institutional management and three years later, in 1946, it held its first examinations.

A year earlier, catering education began to take off when the government set up the Catering Trades Education Committee; this became the National Council for Hotel and Catering Education which, in 1949, was taken over by a new organisation, the Hotel and Catering Institute (now the Institute of Hospitality.) It was only after this that the number of colleges offering all types of catering education began to expand, from craft to management, with the introduction of City and Guilds examinations, national diplomas and,

Who was doing the training?

Where were the catering professionals to come from in order to staff the burgeoning industrial feeding industry?

Even by the late-1920s, there was only one catering college, Westminster Technical Institute (later Westminster Technical College), which was formed in 1910 largely through the efforts of Sir Isidore Salmon, the chairman of J Lyons, the owner of London's Tea Shops and Corner Houses as well as other large catering and bakery enterprises.

Before Westminster, catering had not been considered a subject for a college education; if you wanted to become a hotel or a catering manager, or a chef or a waiter, you had to learn on the job, from dishwashing upwards. As few British youngsters were keen to do this, the catering industry was largely dominated by French and other continental personnel the most famous of whom must be Escoffier, the Savoy hotel's legendary chef de cuisine (in his book *The Golden Age of British Hotels*, Derek Taylor claims that Escoffier was dismissed for his failure to achieve acceptable financial results; a similar fate was enjoyed by the Savoy's then general manager, Cesar Ritz.)

Little wonder, then, that despite Sir Isidore's interest in popular catering, Westminster's cookery courses were concerned solely with haute cuisine while anyone wishing to become a waiter aimed to be a maitre d'hotel.

The hotel and restaurant sectors dominated college educational thinking. It's a situation which some in the contracting industry would suggest continues to this day.

Credit National Portrait Gallery, London

Sir Isidore Salmon – a pioneer in catering education.

eventually, degree courses.

Between the wars, however, there is no doubt that industrial catering was the poor relation of the industry, with hotels and restaurants attracting the most skilled staff despite the long hours and hard work they involved. Pay in general was not particularly good although waiters and other front of house staff picked up good tips in the best restaurants and hotels and the industry provided meals for workers on duty.

Yet, there is little evidence that contractors like Ellis, Barkers and John Gardner, all very active in the period, were held back by lack of skilled manpower. They did their own training. If they were to attract people to work for them, the recruits had to be trained on the job which involved long apprenticeships and other periods of training at work, very rarely at college. Barkers, Ellis and John Gardner all trained their own staff or poached from each other or from other, smaller caterers. But when Taylorplan, Midland Catering and Bateman Catering were launched from scratch in 1940, with no pool of employees, the search for trained staff, many of whom had been called up, must have been desperate.

The numbers employed in industrial catering had exploded in direct proportion to the number of units being operated but with most able bodied men at the front line, it could only cope by recruiting as many women as it could. As the majority were untrained, they all had to learn on the job with very few at the outset having any experience of mass catering – or of catering at all.

Industrial catering during the war years was thus manned mostly by amateurs and very largely by women who had to become catering professionals within a matter of weeks, if not days. Despite the fact that the meals provided were unsophisticated – which reflected the standard and style of home-cooking at the time – it is extraordinary that industrial catering could find and nurture a sufficient number of workers with the necessary skills to be able to expand as it did. The fact that wastage had to be avoided because of food shortages and nutritional standards had to be maintained because of government edicts, meant that workers had to acquire cooking skills quickly.

By the late 1930s, there was a growing realisation that the lessons of the 1914-18 war would have to be re-learned. Nutritious food was again recognised as a key element in worker productivity and efficiency; some of the larger companies, like Burton's, had already acknowledged this by opening canteens for their staff. Sir Noel Curtis Bennett cites an unnamed food manufacturer (but possibly J. Lyons) with 11 staff restaurants, medical and dental services, extensive playing fields, youth clubs, schools and a large entertainment hall (a venue, perhaps, for one of BBC radio's famous *Music While You Work* programmes) all within the factory area. Sir Noel claims many other firms had similar extensive welfare facilities.

A SCHOOL FOR PAGE-BOYS IN THE WEST END

A lesson at the first school for page-boys, which has just been started in a West End hotel. There is a right and wrong way of carrying a salver, and the instructor is here seen showing the boys how it should be done.
"*Daily Sketch*" photograph.

Almost until after the war years, employers had to train their own staff rather than rely on catering college education – one (unnamed) hotel even started a school for page boys.

It was in 1939, with war on the near horizon, that industrial expansion to meet the war effort opened up new opportunities for industrial catering. New factories, particularly for munitions and other war *materiel*, were built.

In 1940, when the Factory Canteens Act was introduced, every company employing over 250 workers in manufacturing or repairing munitions, was required to provide a dining area where wholesome meals could be provided. Within a very short space of time the number of Gardner-operated canteens had grown to 300-plus. Barkers, too, prospered, as did contractors like Ellis. It became a boom time.

Earlier, in 1939, Hugh Taylor and his brother Roy, seeing the opportunities that contracting presented, had launched Taylorplan Catering (see Chapter 6). On

6th June 1941, Jack Bateman founded a company called Factory Canteens Ltd – an accurate, if a not very inspiring name. Six days later, Roland Webb founded Midland Counties Industrial Catering Ltd. The Taylors, Bateman and Webb were among the entrepreneurs who recognised the opportunities being presented by the war effort; John Gardner and Barkers were already taking full advantage of them – indeed, John Gardner acquired the Kenya Coffee Company in 1942, giving the company access to a ready supply of coffee (inhibited though the supply was by wartime conditions) and a number of coffee houses in London.

The munitions factories were running a 24-hour, seven day a week operation and contractors hardly had to look for business. So much were their services in demand that all of them had to turn business away.

Men were now being called up in the forces with the result that female workers predominated. Few, if any, photographs of wartime kitchens show a male catering worker. Worse, the shortage of normal supplies and the need to locate some factories in remote places for security or strategic reasons, meant that ingenuity was the name of the game.

Shortages of meat, sugar, fat, flour and other key ingredients gave rise to numerous ingenious recipes, including the famous (or infamous) Woolton pie named after the Minister of Food, Lord Woolton. Vegetables were one item that could be largely home grown and didn't need to be imported. Woolton pie was thus an inexpensive dish of vegetables created in the Savoy hotel by its then head chef, Francis Latry, and was one of a number of recipes produced by the Ministry of Food to encourage the preparation of nutritious war-time meals. Consisting of diced potatoes (or parsnips), cauliflower,

Lord Woolton: "The appeal I make to you is that you will today raise the whole standard of industrial catering in this country. You will be doing war work of the greatest importance."

swede, carrots and turnip, with rolled oats and chopped spring onions added to the thickened vegetable water, and topped with potato and grated cheese (itself difficult to obtain) and served with vegetable gravy, it became an iconic dish. However, Woolton pie was not universally well received. *The Times* commented:

"When Woolton pie was being forced on somewhat reluctant tables, Lord Woolton performed a valuable service by submitting to the flashlight camera at public luncheons while eating, with every sign of enjoyment, the dish named after him."

Apart from carrot cake, none of these dishes in their original form has survived to the present day, though many of them, being meatless, form the basis of today's vegetarian menus.

While the Factory Canteens Act gave a huge boost to the number of industrial

Woolton pie - the iconic wartime vegetable dish created in The Savoy hotel kitchens.

canteens in operation, this number was increased when a clause in the Essential Works Order Act, 1941 obliged the Ministry of Labour to ensure that workers in building and civil engineering sites, docks and mines should be provided with suitable welfare facilities, including a canteen. In the case of miners, a suggestion that they should be given extra food rations compared with other workers was rejected. Nevertheless, because of the nature of their work, it was thought that they needed to be provided with food to sustain their efforts. By September 1941, an expansion of canteen facilities for the coal industry was put in place. Within a very short period of time, canteens in over 90 per cent of the country's mines employing more than 50 people had been established at a cost of over £2.6m (nearly £115m in today's money).

At its peak, catering turnover in over 1,000 collieries reached £5m a year (£216m today). Most of the colliery canteens were organised by joint councils of employers and employees on a non-profit making

In September 1941, legislation was brought in to introduce canteen facilities for miners.

The rise and fall of British Restaurants

The first British Restaurant opened in October 1940 and the number soon spread, reaching a peak of 2,160 in 1943 serving 619,000 meals a day, which were produced largely by voluntary labour recruited by local authorities. Many used improvised facilities such as village halls, shops, clubs, even houses, though some were in customised buildings and the vast majority were self-service. Perhaps surprisingly, in view of the voluntary and fairly haphazard nature of their creation, surveys showed that most people who used a British Restaurant liked them and sociologists certainly had a field day extrapolating their widespread use to a new democratic revolution in which customers rubbed shoulders with each other and ate together, whatever their social class or standing. But, as Professor James Vernon explains in his book *Hunger* (Harvard University Press), in the socialist dawn that emerged after the war, the democratic dream began to fade. Rather than creating a socialist paradise, British Restaurants were criticised for regimenting men and women into communal feeding and giving them food that 'was good for them'. By 1947 only 850 British Restaurants were left, although some survived well into the 1950s. They had served their purpose and were largely judged a success but their unchanging menus and basic standard of cooking, combined with their communal ambience, meant that they were no longer relevant for the changing times in which they now found themselves.

Credit: IWM (D 10673)

At their peak, British Restaurants, largely run by volunteers, served over 600,000 meals a day.

basis although contractors were involved in some of the larger collieries where as many as 4,000 people required feeding. Later legislation extended the Factory (Canteens) Order 1943 to factories supplying civilian needs.

Canteens thus became a vitally important part of the wartime industrial scene. A government booklet published in 1944 entitled *Man Power*, praised their contribution during the war years:

"There can be no doubt about the role of this great canteen movement both to the war effort and to the community. It has meant that vast numbers of workers, with the minimum of trouble to themselves, can

LEAN BUT NEVER HUNGRY...

By John Smith

This article, written by John Smith and published in the 2012 annual bulletin of the Minchinhampton Local History Group, was sparked off when the author found an old notebook written when he started working for John Sutcliffe in 1951, the founder of Factory Canteens (West of England) Ltd, with its offices at 40/41 London Road, Stroud.

When I joined him after seven years in the Army and university I was then twenty-five years old and without a penny to my name, so I was eager to start.

The government gave extra allowances to those in industry, so eating in the canteen was an excellent supplement to the basic rations available to everybody at home, and that is why Sutcliffe did well.

What were those basic rations? Every week each adult was entitled to the following:

Potatoes, vegetables, fruit, chicken, fish and rabbits were 'off ration' and so was the offal so generously given in *Dad's Army* by L/Cpl Jones; I quite liked chitterling.

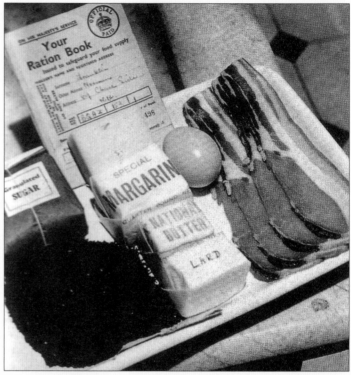

January 1940	Bacon, ham or meat	4oz
	Margarine	4oz
	Butter	2oz
	Milk	3 pints
July 1940	Tea	2oz
	Lard	4oz
March 1941	Preserves	1lb every two months
May 1941	Cheese	2oz
June 1941	Eggs	1 only
	Dried egg	1 packet every four weeks

In October 1939, the 'Dig for Victory' campaign produced home-grown vegetables. Allotments were at a premium. Villages formed their own pig and poultry clubs and with the availability of orange juice and cod-liver oil and extras for nursing mothers and children, the country was arguably fitter in many ways than today. Certainly I recall no mention of the word obesity.

On my notebook's first page is this recipe for plum and rhubarb tart for 350 people. It was costed by me at the Rotol and Dowty canteens near Staverton (Metric equivalents have been added.)

Thus each of the 350 portions cost 2.28d and to this was added custard at 0.3d per portion with the total portion at just over 2½d.

The plum and rhubarb with custard was the most expensive pudding, closely followed by fruit jelly and cream and jam tart with custard, both at 2d per portion. Black-cap pudding was next and

	£	s	d	£	p
8 tins (each 7lbs) plum jam	2	2	4	2	12
40lb rhubarb		6	8		33
12lb sugar		4	6		22
8lb margarine		8	2		41
3lb sugar		1	2		6
18lb flour		3	9		19
	£3	6s	7d	£3	33p

cost 1½d, followed by macaroni, rice and sago puddings all at 1¼d. Along with them came baked date sponge. Finally, at around 1d per portion, were Dundee marmalade pudding, bread and butter pudding, steamed jam roll and spiced bread pudding – all with custard. Nothing was wasted and the end product was called leftover pudding and because it was cheaper, and tasted good, it always found a buyer. As for the preparation, any waste in the kitchen went as pigswill and there was always a local pig keeper on hand to clear up, and be pleased to pay for it.

Every factory had its mid-morning break. We used five-gallon containers and sold tea in half-pint cups for 1d. The basic cost of each container was 6s. 8d using 5oz tea at 3s a pound, 12ozs sugar at 5½d a pound, 4 pints of milk at 3s 1d a gallon and 4-5 gallons of boiling water. Water was not metered and sugar was included at source as it was largely home-produced from sugar beet and the nearest beet factory was in Worcestershire.

I recall that it was the manager's job to ensure that staff when cutting bread got twenty slices from a loaf and that was a difficult task with new bread. No wonder the expression 'the best thing since sliced bread' came into common parlance.

What canteens did Sutcliffe operate in Stroud district? Not one of these companies exists any more and it is a story repeated all over the country.

During the war years, kitchens were not always big affairs. The Small Canteen (OUP, 1947 published under the auspices of the Empire Tea Bureau) showed workers collecting their meal and taking it back to their place of work to eat.

have at least one substantial and wholesome hot meal a day."

And noting the canteen's role as a social meeting place, it commented: "It has brought together in companionable ease, workers of all kinds – and our factories are now filled with people formerly belonging to many different classes – and given them an opportunity to develop a new and wider social life. Finally, it is helping to make us a more gregarious and perhaps more truly civilised people."

Such high-flown sentiments were backed up by the growing number of canteens. Before the war, the number was under 1,000 – reliable figures are not available. By April 1942 the figure was 9,509 but this had grown to 11,635 within seven months with 4.4m meals served weekly. By January 1945, the number had risen to 12,888

including those on building sites. By then, over 50 million meals were being served every week, including meals which were served in British Restaurants. *Man Power* stated that at the end of 1943, there were 4,270 canteens in factories with more than 250 workers and 5,700 in factories with fewer than 250 workers, with a further 700 canteens in building and civil engineering sites and 180 in docks.

The canteens, said the booklet, ranged widely in scope and nature. "The canteens themselves vary enormously from little places serving cups of tea and odd snacks to the gigantic establishments in the big factories with meals for three-shift workers on a 24-hour service, vast electrified kitchens and properly equipped stages for ENSA or works concerts or other shows and dance bands."

Even so, in spite of this provision, which clearly involved a prodigious organisation on the part of the government and industry, some workers were reluctant to take advantage of what was available. Only 16 per cent of the meals provided for miners were full meals, the majority (65 per cent) were snaps (food packets taken below ground for consumption in the pit) and the remainder were snacks (light meals served and eaten at the pithead). Nevertheless, by the end of June 1946, 570 collieries had canteens providing hot meals for over 510,000 workers while 339 collieries provided snap or snack meals for 180,000 workers.

Sir Noel Curtis-Bennett puts the reluctance to make use of the meals provided down to prejudice and conservatism which was strong in the mining industry:

"The average married miner can easily be understood... to prefer to return to his wife and family for a meal than remain behind to eat, however attractive the food and the service."

In all these catering arrangements tea assumed extraordinary importance as did the appearance of the ubiquitous tea trolley and the tea lady. During the war, a special ration of tea was issued to all factories and the Empire Tea Bureau produced several handbooks on tea distribution to workers under the title of *Tea for the Workers,* which encouraged the use of tea trolleys in factories and offices. In the larger factories, tea bars or tea points were introduced.

Tea was the nation's favourite cuppa and its almost mythic importance lasted throughout the war and well into peacetime. In fact, many worker disputes, then and subsequently, revolved around the provision and the price of tea and other items, which frequently became intricately involved in union wage negotiations. The size and make up of sandwiches and bread rolls and their price, for example, were often used as bargaining chips and all too often the contractor or the catering manager found himself (frequently herself) to be the piggy in the middle between employer and union negotiators. But if price was important for the workers, the time that workers took to have their break was also critical to the employer.

Geoffrey Harrison (now chairman of Harrison Catering), in the 1970s and working for Gardner Merchant in charge of the catering at Ford's Paint, Trim and Assembly Plant at Ford in Dagenham, tried to save Ford some £3,000 by cutting out one of the tea bays in the factory. This got nowhere. The fact that workers would have had to walk further for their tea, and take longer over it, would have cost Ford far more than Harrison's saving.

Mike Stapleton, another who began his career, like many others, at Ford (eventually to become UK corporate affairs director at Compass), tells the story of an altercation between an assembly line worker who, in rage at some incident, threw a cup of tea over the tea lady. The resulting altercation shut down the production line for seven minutes and Gardner Merchant received a bill for £28,000.

Mike Stapleton: an altercation between a worker and a tea trolley lady stopped the Ford production line for 20 minutes. "We had a bill for £28,000 for the stoppage."

The popularity of tea – and the importance of the tea break – was certainly boosted by the Tea Bureau. Established to promote the sale of tea from Ceylon and other parts of the Empire in the 1930s, it actively promoted the brew during the war, producing a number of booklets, leaflets and short films on how to make a good cup of tea. It even boasted that it had advised 3,000 employers on the importance of the tea break to workers and the benefit that the break brought to productivity. A 10-minute short, *Tea Making Tips,* widely distributed during the war and still available today though now risibly old-fashioned, laboriously went through the 'six golden rules' for making a good cup of tea, and included a tea expert advising viewers on how to store and dispose of it.

The popularity of tea – and the importance of the tea break – was boosted by the Empire Tea Bureau, throughout the war, though this was hardly necessary. The tea break was an institution. In large factories, as many as 100 girls could be employed on their daily rounds.

In fact, the Bureau, which continued well into the 1950s, ventured much further afield than tea. In 1947 it published a surprisingly comprehensive, well written and well illustrated 106-page book, *The Small Canteen,* which gave practical advice on the design and operation of canteens as well as on nutrition and other factors involved in planning and operating a catering facility. It is curious that, in its acknowledgments, no contractor was invited to advise on its contents. Four years earlier, the Bureau had published another booklet – *Canteens at Work* – which covered similar ground but with an emphasis on larger units. Quite why a tea promotion agency should be involved in publishing a major volume on a subject that was way beyond its primary focus is not clear. However, the advice it gave, which was clear, detailed and sensible, illustrated the desire of the government and other official bodies to encourage the development of industrial catering during and after the war. As the Bureau's commissioner, R L Barnes, wrote in his foreword to *The Small Canteen*: "We can hardly emphasise too strongly that from every point of view, it is better to have a small, even a crude canteen rather than no canteen at all."

Earlier, he had noted that between 1939 and 1945, the number of industrial canteens had increased 30-fold – "and there is every reason to believe that the policy of providing the worker with a good meal on the job will form a permanent part of our industrial system". There is little doubt that Mr Barnes was speaking not only for the Bureau but for the government as well.

Although the number of industrial feeding units had multiplied hugely during the war there were also clear concerns about the quality of the food being served.

Despite the caterers' best efforts there were many complaints about the standard of food being served which might have been another reason for the lack of uptake at the colliery pit heads. So concerned was the government about standards of industrial feeding that it set up a special inspectorate in 1943 to make sure that improvements in food could be implemented and sustained; at the same time it wanted to encourage improvements in the storage and quality of the all-important tea, as well as in the equipment used.

Lord Woolton, announcing the formation of the inspectorate to both the Industrial Catering Association and the National Council for Caterers in Industry (see next chapter) at a special meeting in 1943, said that the inspectors would visit industrial canteens at will. As told in *Caterer and Hotelkeeper (The Caterer)*:

"His Ministry had taken great care to give them raw food to feed the men on the job; but the thing that was equally important was that the food should be properly prepared and in the right proportions... Raw food should not be damaged in the process of cooking."

To press home the point, there was no shortage of written advice. As well as the Tea Council's *Planning for Industrial Catering* (later taken over by the Gas Council with new designs and plans), the Industrial Welfare Society produced a booklet in 1940, *Canteens in Industry*, which ran to six further editions by the end of the war. The British Medical Association had already published best-

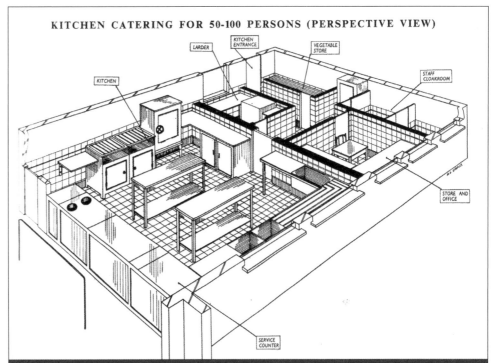

KITCHEN CATERING FOR 50-100 PERSONS (PERSPECTIVE VIEW)

The Small Canteen (OUP, 1947) was a very well illustrated book that, among other things, provided sample plans for kitchens of different sizes. Produced under the auspices of the Empire Tea Bureau, it eschewed advice from any contractor.

selling manuals – *Family Meals and Cookery* and *Doctor's Cookery Book*. There were also numerous government and other commercial publications. Professor Vernon in *Hunger* lists six books on canteen management and cookery that were published during or immediately after the war, two by Practical Press, publisher of *Caterer*. Dennis Coates' *Industrial Catering Management*, published in 1971, was a late runner though, by then, most of the earlier publications were out of print.

In 1944, Miss D Johnson, superintending inspector of factory canteens for the Ministry of Labour, in her annual report, said that the previous year had seen a 37 per cent increase in the number of small factory canteens which were successful in attracting workers to eat a main meal – "they often serve a much higher proportion of the total numbers employed than do some of the very large modern canteens", she wrote. The report also recorded steady progress being made to encourage the owners of factories to raise the standards of their catering operation. The Ministry's 37 factory canteen advisers (it is unclear where they had been found or what their qualifications were) reported "general efforts to give better balanced menus with a wider variety of choice and to retain the nutritional content of food by suitable cooking. They have also observed improvements in service and successful efforts to avoid the pre-plating of meals."

The report went on: "While most menus cling to the meat and two vegetables and pudding idea, much has been done to encourage the provision of attractive snack services."

The cooking of meals for workers on night shifts was regarded as a particular concern although the report noted an improvement:

"But the improvements still necessary in night meals are those needed in canteens at all times. There is still not enough variety within the main meal pattern and there is a need for more choice of dishes and more provision of snacks."

Miss Johnson admitted that skilled staff shortages were a challenge:

"The acute shortage of suitably trained and experienced cook supervisors and managers is a disturbing factor," she wrote. Woolton himself publicly acknowledged that the rapid development of industrial catering during the war had outstripped the supply of trained labour though his answer was to encourage more training of existing personnel than to raise any hopes of more people being made available to work in the sector. How much training could be undertaken during wartime conditions, however, was a moot point.

In these conditions, it is not surprising that the uptake in many canteens was only 30 per cent even though the number of canteens was accelerating. Professor Vernon suggests that one reason for the poor quality of the food may have been because "the enormous expansion of the service had encouraged racketeering by small, commercially-run companies that were profiteering from wartime conditions; others blamed the workers themselves who were also on the make, pilfering supplies and equipment (one Midlands factory allegedly lost a third of its china in the first two months it was open)."

These are valid suppositions. Wartime breeds black market and other conditions though there is no suggestion that any of the larger contractors indulged. At the same time, food rationing and food shortages would have created many temptations for both customers and catering workers (even twenty or so years later, it was customary for area managers and other senior staff of contractors to

---

Never mind the quality . . .

Unsurprisingly, the quality of the food provided in factory canteens did not escape the attention of the workers.

The Labour Research Department, a left-leaning research organisation that continues to provide unions with practical information today, produced a booklet *Canteens in Industry* in 1943 and subsequently *Works Canteens and the Catering Trade*, both of which were critical of the food and service that was being offered.

As quoted in Professor Vernon's *Hunger*, a litany of complaints including "cold and unpalatable food, cramped conditions, long queues, glacial service, shortages of crockery and cutlery (which were, in any case, only half washed) and no hours of opening during Sunday and night shifts" all contributed to an unhappy and even mutinous clientele which led to a boycott by staff in one engineering firm.

This was gleefully reported in the Labour Research Department's *New Propellor* magazine:

"Main complaint came from the nightshift who were served on most occasions with food left over from days and heated up. Matters came to a head when bad pies were served. The stewards went with the management to the kitchen and choosing a pie at random from a pile, cut it open, revealing the maggots that were thriving on the meal."

check that joints of meat did not find their way on Fridays to the Sunday dining tables of catering workers.)

But there were more fundamental problems in providing high quality food other than the almost intractable difficulty of attracting trained staff. Just as significant was the non-availability of the right ingredients. Food shortages and restricted availability of key ingredients were everyday problems and there are numerous references in *Caterer* to food rationing and the difficulty of obtaining even the most basic ingredients.

Not only ingredients were in short supply. Industrial caterers were getting short of crockery among other items. A three-man ICA delegation visited the Pottery Manufacturers Association in Stoke-on-Trent to plead for more crockery for industrial canteens – a plea that received fairly short shrift. *Caterer* reported:

"The pottery manufacturers, however, informed them that the labour situation was very serious and that unless pressure could be brought on the Minister of Labour to make that position easier, we should be suffering from a much greater shortage of crockery in the near future than we had in the past."

These shortages, however, were never accepted by the government nor by Lord Woolton, to be a reason (let alone an excuse) for poor standards of cooking. With the appointments of Magnus Pyke and Jack Drummond as scientific advisers to the Minister of Food, the importance of nutrition had rapidly gained ground.

Woolton was a frequent speaker at Industrial Catering Association meetings and in 1942 he told it straight to members of the southern branch. They should regard the food they served as a 'sacred trust', he said, pinpointing some concerns

No turkey for Christmas - official

In both the 1943 and 1944 Christmas festivities, caterers weren't allowed to serve turkey between 22nd and 30th December; in 1944, caterers' milk allowance was reduced to two pints per 100 hot beverages (rations of evaporated milk were doubled), while caterers' fish allowance for one four-week period was reduced to 2lbs per 100 meals or 1lb per 100 subsidiary meals, whichever was the greater. Caterers had to juggle the availability of sugar and preserves.

Elsewhere, experiments had been undertaken to quick freeze or dehydrate herrings – there had been plentiful landings of the fish in the summer of 1944 and methods of preservation were then in their early stages and untested. Caterers were promised a supply if the experiments were a success.

But it wasn't all bad news. In the same year, the Ministry for Food announced that more apples from Canada and sardines from Spain would shortly be available and there would be a 50 per cent increase in the bacon ration for caterers (if only for an eight-week period) from four to six ounces a week. Restrictions on the availability of fish were removed for the 1944 Easter period.

Nor was there a shortage of potatoes – "the supply prospects for the coming potato season are very good indeed", said the Ministry of Food official at the weekly press conference on food availability, reported in *Caterer*.

Another piece of good news that year came with the announcement that caterers were to be allowed to serve traditional accompaniments (for example, sugar, jam or custard) with puddings or other flour confectionary served as the sweet course of a meal.

The complexity of these official guidelines and rules are well illustrated by *Caterer's* explanation:

"The Ministry draws a distinction between the addition of a substance to flour confectionery and the serving of two or more substances as a sweet course. Thus, a caterer is not regarded by the Ministry as being prohibited from serving as the sweet course such dishes as stewed fruit with pastry, with or without custard or other sauce, or fruit flan, fruit pie or jam tart with custard or other sauce.

"But it would be a different matter if, for example, an artificial cream decoration were added after the baking to cakes, gateaux or similar articles of flour confectionery which, although sometimes served as the sweet course of a main meal, are also served as pastries or cakes at other meals, particularly teas."

Clearly, caterers had to understand, and interpret, arcane official rules and regulations as well as being able to cook.

Nevertheless, while rationing imposed severe problems of ingredient supply and menu fatigue, there was a side benefit; it enforced an extremely strict cost regime which benefited caterers immensely. Rationing significantly controlled costs and led to little food wastage.

With his colleague Jack Drummond, Magnus Pyke, who later became a lively speaker on the lecture circuit, did much to encourage a wider understanding of the importance of nutrition.

about standards:

"You are responsible for serving 1.5m workers in this country. That is a very grave responsibility for you. Forgive me for being plain. I hope you are facing up the gravity of that responsibility. I hope you are looking at the meals and asking yourselves whether they represent the very best in the light of all the knowledge of the world of feeding people, and with all the intelligence with which you have been endowed.

"Before the war, we used to think very little of nutritional value of the foods we used. But I do beg you to think now.

"I have seen vegetables in canteens... which were just filling the stomach because all that was good about those vegetables was on its way down the drain.

"The appeal I make to you is that you will today raise the whole standard of industrial catering in this country. You will be doing war work of the greatest importance."

However, it was not all bad news. Miss Johnson, the superintending inspector of canteens, said in her 1944 report that 1943 had been a year of steady progress in the development of canteens "principally in the standard of food and service given... Some reports note that there is now arising a healthy competitive spirit among firms in the same district in efforts to provide something better than their neighbours."

This seems rather fanciful but her report a year later continued her rather upbeat message though she seemed to be more concerned about the cheerfulness of canteen decor which, admittedly, in most cases was dire, than with the quality of the food.

* * *

But it wasn't only factory workers that concerned the government. School children comprised another sector of society that needed feeding during the war and afterwards.

School meals, however, became synonymous with inedible food, and rightly so in many cases; anyone attending school (particularly a boarding school) even as late as the early 1950s would have experienced such fruits of unskilled labour as greasy mince, grisly meat, foul smelling greens, lumpy custard – all passing for nutritious food. Only steamed spotted dick with custard, a favourite for most children, seemed at all edible.

In 1941 nutritional standards for school meals were introduced and it took a further three years before the 1944 Education Act introduced the post of school meals organiser for local authorities, at which point school meals began to be taken seriously. Nevertheless, the same factor that inhibits standards today was in place then, but even more so – principally a lack of skilled staff.

As Professor Vernon puts it, even after the universal provision of school meals was introduced in that year, "school food continued to be experienced by many people more as a form of social punishment than as an entitlement". Thankfully, from the contractors' point of view, this generally negative perception of school meals did not rub off on them to any great extent as few of them were involved in their provision at the time. Three decades later, however, the situation had changed and school meals, including catering at independent schools, had become a legitimate market, and a niche market for some contractors.

Although it is likely that Lord Woolton's plea for better standards of cooking was resented by caterers, there is little doubt that the standard and style of catering during the war years was truly basic with little if any refinement. But it was, after all, a time of survival. With hindsight, the organisation of the country's scarce food resources was a triumph of administration and innovation and the people who were involved in providing the meals that fed the nation can justifiably be called heroes.

The miracle of industrial feeding during the war lay in the fact that, despite the parlous state of the nation's larder and the chronic lack of professionally trained catering staff, the nation survived in remarkably robust health – healthier, even, than today in many respects. It had been brought about by prodigious efforts on the part of the country's catering managers and its workers and, indeed, of the government itself.

Rationing, although not perfect by any means, not only ensured an even distribution of essential food supplies but also helped to emphasise the vital importance of food and nutrition. The nation took note. Rationing foodstuffs educated the populace and led to a greater understanding of the value of food which, in the plenty of today, is now largely lost. In the 1940s, it was a matter of survival.

Despite the shortages and setbacks, the health of the population was preserved, even enhanced, by the ability and commitment of those who worked in the wartime catering industry.

The war had imposed five years of hardship but in doing so, it had firmly established in business the likes of John Gardner, Bob Stent, Jack Bateman, Roland Webb, Hugh Taylor and others. They had all prospered during the conflict. Now they were about to reap the rewards of their wartime efforts in peacetime.

Nutritional standards for school meals were first introduced in 1941 but it took a further three years before local authorities were able to appoint school meals advisers.

CHAPTER THREE

The rise (and fall) of the Industrial Catering Association

With the growth of industrial catering during the war came the emergence of the Industrial Catering Association (ICA) – but people working for contractors were excluded for many years.

The ICA was launched in December 1937 when *Caterer* sponsored its formation at the Hotel, Restaurant and Catering Exhibition (the forerunner of Hotelympia). Industrial and welfare catering was seen as a growth sector of the industry and was one which did not have an association to represent its interests. With the Second World War two years away, it was a prescient move. The ICA, with its members feeding workers in key sectors of the economy, was to play an important role in public health and nutrition.

At its inaugural meeting, 120 people attended and the catering manager of Leyland Motors, C.T.H. Gilbert, was elected its national chairman. Its laudatory aim was "to raise the standard of industrial, institutional and welfare catering generally and to promote the interchange of knowledge, information and ideas on all matters of general interest to those already engaged in industrial organisations." One of its other aims was to encourage training, which in the early days and during the war years, had taken something of a back seat. Underlying the creation of the ICA was the wish to raise the status of people working in industrial catering. *Caterer* became its official journal and it is instructive to read how the association dominated its news pages during the war years. Hardly a month went by without new branches being set up and new members recruited. In 1942, there were 226 new members with six new branches – figures that continued in the later years of the war. In addition, it attracted the attention and support of senior government ministers, Lord Woolton, the then minister for food, being particularly involved.

The ICA was led by Cliff Overend as honorary general secretary. He originally worked for the Ministry of Food and allegedly suggested to the Minister the slogan 'carrots are good for your eyes' because there had been a glut of them and they needed to be used up. He quickly took on the mantle of protector of the ICA's interests.

At the outset, the association was something of a closed shop. Its membership form specifically excluded any manager working for a contract caterer – "full membership is open to all persons holding an active managerial position in industrial or communal feeding of a non-commercial nature..." The same stipulation applied to associate members. Just to ram the point home, a footnote added: "Membership in any grade is not open to persons engaged in industrial catering contracting or employed by industrial catering contractors."

There is no doubt about the significance of the ICA in the early development of industrial catering but its initial decision to exclude contractors (rescinded in 1971), despite its aim to improve the status and professionalism of its members, necessarily deprived it of the large pool of knowledge that contractors were beginning to build up. As a result, the ICA was seen by many as more of a protection society for in-house caterers against the inroads of contractors into industrial catering than as a society of caterers anxious to advance the professionalism of the sector.

The ICA's opposition to contractors was clear: contractors were competitors to in-house caterers. If a contractor took over a contract, the job of the catering manager was in jeopardy unless the contractor wanted to employ him (or, more typically, her). Even if it did, the manager would have to cope with a new boss operating new systems and procedures. The threat that contractors posed was understandable but the wise catering managers recognised that it would not go away.

The chairman of the West Midlands ICA branch, at its 1943 AGM, replying to one member who complained that contractors were still sending out sales letters to firms, suggested that in-house caterers had to face the fact that they were up against competition and had to be prepared to meet it. The only way they would succeed in killing the competition would be if members of the ICA ran their canteens efficiently, he said.

This sensible viewpoint was not widely supported. The fear was rife that, given half a chance, contractors would take over all in-house catering operations and thus cause incumbent managers to lose their job or, at the very least, introduce new more commercial ways of working. Contractors were thus both feared and distrusted and the columns of *Caterer* are replete with arguments between the two parties during the war years.

This conflict was made worse by the formation in 1942 of the National Society of Caterers to Industry (NSCI), which consisted entirely of contractors and people working for them. Serving some 2m meals a day, nearly 1,000 managers "operating a canteen in, or in the immediate vicinity of, a factory or group of factories under contract with the factory owners", formed the initial membership. Contractors then were not much interested in providing a catering service for offices and other institutions.

With offices in Pall Mall, the NSCI was well financed and well organised, with a council consisting of H J R (Bob) Stent of

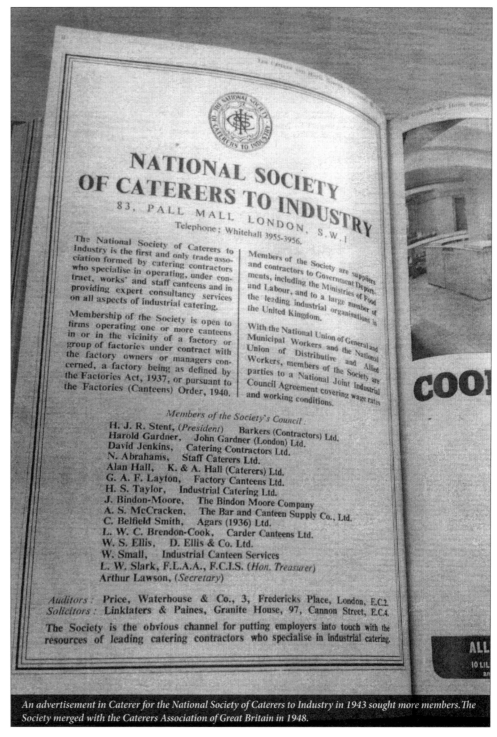

An advertisement in Caterer for the National Society of Caterers to Industry in 1943 sought more members. The Society merged with the Caterers Association of Great Britain in 1948.

Ernest Bevin: Minister for Labour and National Service during the war; he introduced a wages board for industrial catering.

Barkers (Contractors) Ltd, (the company was to become Peter Merchant and Stent went on to be managing director of the company and, ultimately, Gardner Merchant) as president and with Harold Gardner (of John Gardner), Nat Abrahams (Staff Caterers Ltd) and representatives from Jack Bateman's company, Factory Canteens, as well as others. It also had a full-time secretary in Arthur Lawson. Price Waterhouse was its auditor and Linklaters & Paines its solicitors – no slumming it there. Financed by the contractors, it clearly could afford the best. The ICA, on the other hand, was a purely voluntary organisation and had little money. But what it lacked in heavyweight backing it made up in Overend's personal commitment to the in-house cause. No association could have had a stouter defender.

Throughout the five years of war, when it might be thought that those involved had more urgent topics to occupy their mind, the two associations were at personal war with each other. Even a cursory glance through past copies of *Caterer* indicates that the two associations were forever locked in a battle led by Cliff Overend on the one side and by Arthur Lawson on the other.

Almost as soon as it was established, the NSCI formed a national joint council for the voluntary negotiation of wages and conditions of employment with several trade unions – perhaps in the hope that if agreement could be reached centrally wages throughout the contracting industry could be regularised and would not be a factor in companies poaching staff from others. Voluntary agreement would also tend to inhibit statutory legislation in setting wage rates. The attempt to head off the formation of a wages board failed, however. A year later, in 1943, the government decided that industrial catering should have a wages board – the Industrial and Staff Canteen Undertakings Wages Board – the first for the hospitality industry and one with a slightly wider remit than boards for other sectors of industry. The idea of a voluntary joint council was abandoned.

The initial reaction of the ICA to this move by Ernest Bevin, the Minister for Labour and National Service, was to oppose it but the association fairly quickly fell into line although its plea that Overend should be appointed a member of the board was turned down on the grounds that the ICA was neither an employers' nor an employees' organisation – a decision that must have riled Overend particularly as Arthur Lawson was appointed as one of the two employer representatives, together with W.C. Crozier, canteen manager for the Scottish Wholesale Society and the immediate past chairman of the ICA.

The arguments between the two associations continued more or less throughout the war. In one letter to the editor (who must have been eternally grateful for some contentious issue to rear its head among the dreary wartime news of rationing, meatless recipes and food shortages), Overend argued, not for the first time and certainly not for the last, that private enterprise sat uneasily with the provision of a catering service:

"The contractor, must, by virtue of the very nature of his business, be primarily concerned with the profit motive and, as such, must sell at a higher price or else in some degree, skimp quality, service and quality – any or all of which are detrimental to the welfare of the factory employee."

This will be a familiar argument today and, certainly in the public sector, is still put forward by unions and other interested parties to block outsourcing.

Arthur Lawson replied: "There seems to be a curious inconsistency in Mr Overend's argument. While he and his fellow managers are salaried servants of firms themselves

Credit: IWM (D 10680)

Canteens frequently came under attack during the war for poor standards of cooking and service though the conditions in which food was prepared and served often left much to be desired.

with work under contract, they are opposed to the well established practice in respect of industrial catering. Making use of their employers' canteens for the purpose, they engage in propaganda attacking a fundamental principle of private enterprise."

Lawson challenged Overend to name six "concrete instances from him or his association's experiences involving members of my Society justifying the general charge he makes."

Overend lost no time in replying – but came back with the same argument:

"As direct management aims at maximum amenities, quality, service and quantity at the lowest possible economic price, a contractor cannot offer precisely the same and yet maintain directors' salaries, head office organisation, and area supervision. Something must, of necessity suffer, and directly and indirectly, the customer finances the organisation. It does not require specific instances to prove – it is simply logic."

Lawson was not one to let that escape:

"Mr Overend denies engaging in propaganda attacking a principle of private enterprise. Surely he has said enough to make clear his dislike of a principle and practice accepted by employers of members of his association, by industry generally and by the State in peace and war – that is, the principle and practice of contracting for work to be done and services rendered on terms fundamental to private enterprise."

Earlier, a letter from Patricia Rolfe, catering officer for the Borough of Southgate, explaining that she was trying to form a British Restaurant section of the ICA, prompted Lawson to end his letter with a broadside on the Ministry of Food, showing how sensitive the relations were between the two associations. The Ministry had, apparently, 'warmly approved' a scheme which encouraged staff of British Restaurants to join the ICA,

---

Canteens under attack

During the war, there were recurring criticisms of the quality of food provided by industrial caterers. A noted doctor, speaking at a Nottingham Rotary meeting, labelled the food 'appalling' and implied that it was the cause of increased absenteeism in industry. Cliff Overend was having none of this and flew to the industry's defence, calling it 'thoughtless tattle.'

In *Caterer* he said: "I am firmly convinced from personal experience and contact with canteens throughout the country that the average standard of canteens today is considerably higher than it was at the beginning of the war." This may not have been saying much and Overend did admit that the demand for skilled staff had greatly exceeded supply and that there were 'variances' in standards throughout the country.

The Trade Unions then got into the act. At a union conference for women, it was alleged that good canteen food was being spoiled and dished up 'in a manner not fit for pigs' – an accusation that led to outrage. A somewhat defensive letter in *Caterer* said:

"A works canteen attempts to please the majority and there is a growing section who continually grumble and deplore in unreasonable fashion that the food, tea, cakes, etc., are nowhere near as good as they ought to be. It is because so many different types of people use any large canteen that there must automatically be complaints, as similarly the same set of people make mistakes in their respective office or workshop," wrote Mr F.A Dovey, an ICA member, whose position was not specified.

A letter from Arthur Lawson of the NSCI in the following week's edition of *Caterer* explained that the delegate who was quoted making the remark denied ever saying it. But, as Lawson pointed out:

"Miss Horan's denial has not been seen by newspaper readers who doubtless believe she said what she was reported to have said and that there is some substance in the very serious allegation."

Mr Dovey replied: "I wonder if this an opportune moment for the ICA and NSCI to reach an agreement on one point – the undying determination to defend canteens against unfair criticisms from very doubtful sources and to secure adequate publicity wherever possible for canteens and the good work generally performed by our staff."

Although a common cause, there is no record that this was ever agreed between the two associations.

"I have yet to learn that parliament has authorised the Ministry of Food or any other department of government, as part of its wartime duties, to engage in such a recruiting campaign," Lawson wrote.

Overend denied the ICA was opposed to private enterprise. He wrote: "The unwarranted statement that members of the ICA are opposed to the principle of private enterprise is utterly ludicrous. Support of the principle that a canteen should be an integral department of the factory just as much as is the accounts department, welfare department, a tool room, cannot be construed as an attack on private enterprise."

Lawson's criticism of the Ministry's

encouragement of British Restaurant managers to join the ICA prompted a tart reply from Rolfe: "I am not interested in catering contractors or their opinions on my efforts to get British Restaurant managers together," she told *Caterer's* readers.

Other contractors joined in the belligerent chorus of vituperation:

"It seems inconceivable that presumably intelligent people should make such ridiculous statements, both in print and in public, which in the main, are directed at catering contractors," wrote William Small, a director of Industrial Canteen Services.

"It is only by virtue of the fact that the average catering contractor operates a number of canteens that he is able, from the small income derived, from each to meet his overheads and make a reasonable profit, out of which he has to pay his share of taxation.

"Catering contractors seldom criticise the individual caterer or the ICA, which is a splendid organisation, but many of its members continually and unduly criticise catering contractors."

Mr Small's plea fell on deaf ears. An anonymous canteen manager waded in with a startling conclusion that was not to be borne out by events:

"What other business has such a huge turnover from such a small amount of capital invested... What do contractors give for their handsome net profit? A visit once a week for a few hours from a group supervisor... No canteen manager needs to fear competition from catering contractors. So many men and women will have been trained in practical catering within the next two years that there will be no need for contractors."

At this boastful conclusion, the editor closed this particular correspondence but the ill-feeling between the ICA and NSCI did not abate.

Relations became increasingly acrimonious, particularly in 1943 after Bevin refused to apply the Essential Work Order to contractors' canteens, a measure which meant that contractors' employees were liable to be transferred to other industries unless the catering was taken out of their hands and placed under the direction of the factory owners. This was a blatant piece of discriminatory legislation which was roundly attacked by Arthur Lawson:

"Mr Bevin has suggested that the factory owners should run the canteens themselves. We should like him to know that hundreds of factory owners have asked contractors to take over the responsibility from them, because they want to concentrate on production."

Another spat came about when Lawson told Roy Snell, chairman of the newly-formed Catering Trades Education Committee, that the NSCI was withdrawing from its discussions. The sticking point was unions:

"As the Committee is so clearly disinclined to accept our proposal that the trade unions, which represent catering workers be cordially invited to join the committee, my council believes that we cannot usefully continue membership of it."

In fact, the Committee wasn't entirely against the idea – it just didn't want to be swamped by a representative for each of the eight or so (even Lawson did not seem to know the number) unions involved in industrial catering; it said it was happy to accept a nomination from the TUC. The matter was resolved.

In 1945, a more serious row erupted about transforming the ICA into an Institute of Industrial Catering.

"If we are to raise the standard of industrial catering,' Overend told a meeting of ICA members, 'we must raise the standard of the canteen manager to the same level as that of the heads of other departments in the factory.

"The canteen manager would then be someone with qualifications and someone who is recognised as having a status equal to that of any other officer of his company."

A proposal was made by the Manchester branch which suggested that members of the Institute would come from both the in-house catering sector and from contractors, but this was roundly condemned by the ICA's chairman, C.T.H. Gilbert.

"The ICA is in danger – and unless we hold together as an essential unifying body, we shall go under," he wrote to *Caterer*, pleading for unity. "For reasons best known to themselves members of one area have given notice of a proposal which strikes at the very principles on which the ICA was founded but there is still considerable hope of reconsideration." He did not elaborate on the grounds on which he objected to the proposal but instead veered off into another familiar attack on contracting. But his appeal succeeded. A sub-committee was established to consider the proposal and it was later reported that, although there was some merit in the Manchester proposal, it had received only luke-warm support. The proposal was tempting. However, the idea of forming an Institute, with the additional status that it would confer on industrial caterers, had to be balanced against the need to admit contractors into membership. The sub committee came up with a compromise: introduce grades of membership and a slight increase in membership fees designed both to provide additional funds for further expansion and to ensure (with the aid possibly of examinations at a later date) a high standard of professional competency within the membership.

Overend, who quit as honorary general secretary in 1945 to join British Steel as catering manager, admitted that there needed to be clarification. The ICA was neither a trade association nor a professional body. "We have come to the stage when we must identify ourselves with one side or the other," he told a London branch meeting.

In fact, the issue was never resolved and the ICA remained, in Professor Rik Medlik's words, a personnel association which accepted members without examination who worked in industrial catering, but not working for contracting companies; no qualifications were required. It was not until 1949 that the Hotel and Catering Institute (HCI) was formed (but mainly driven by A.H. Jones, managing director of Grosvenor House, and E.W (Ted) Collinson, who had been the chairman of the Catering Trades Education Committee), which demanded examination qualifications for membership. Initially, however, membership for senior people – the great and the good – was obtained through experience and job status. In 1969, nine associations including the ICA, established a working party to explore the possibility of a single professional body for the industry. It produced a report which led to the merger of the HCI and the Institutional Management Association to form the HCIMA, but mergers between the other seven associations came to nothing. As the HCIMA represented all sectors of the industry, including hotels, restaurants, industrial and welfare catering, lecturers and students (which has turned out to be both a weakness and a strength), there was no stomach for setting up a separate rival body to attract those exclusively in industrial and welfare catering.

There can be little doubt that the ICA's high profile in the industry during the war and immediately after it was largely due to Cliff Overend's terrier-like qualities. These were well publicised in *Caterer*. Even into the mid-1960s Harold Skipper (Skipp), who was *Caterer's* industrial catering editor and who religiously attended all ICA events, was reporting Overend's views and activities; Overend remained a key figure in the ICA

until his retirement in the 1970s.

Nevertheless, despite its record and the high level of support it received during the war years, the association's influence began to fade once the exigencies of the war had disappeared. During the conflict it had been seen, with the NSCI, as a valued and invaluable partner in the struggle to maintain the nation's health. It boasted of close ties with the government but this was an imperative that did not continue once the fighting was over. By 1946 it was back to normal business again though its members were still much constrained by food shortages and continued rationing until the 1950s. Its wartime sparring partner, the NSCI, merged with Caterers' Association of Great Britain (CA) in 1948 which, as a result, set up its Industrial and Staff Canteen Division. The CA, in turn, merged with the British Hotels and Restaurant Association in 1976 to form the British Hotels, Restaurants and Caterers' Association (which became the British Hospitality Association in 1992).

* * *

The ICA continued as an independent organisation, still well supported, and in 1970 it boasted 2,000 members, holding impressively attended conferences. In the same year, it also opened its door to contractors though not, apparently, overwhelmingly. The motion to allow contractors to join was carried by 'a reasonably substantial majority,' said *Catering Times*. At the next meeting of the ICA London branch, the same newspaper reported that the decision had been a major topic with concern expressed that principals of contracting companies might be able to join; the danger of a unit manager, being a member, bringing along his sales director as a guest was also deemed a danger. Contractors clearly remained under

suspicion which probably never disappeared. However, the association was not afraid to court some controversy.

In 1971, a young Bob Cotton, fresh out of Surrey University but later to join Gardner Merchant and become chief executive of the British Hospitality Association, had taken over as assistant secretary of the North West London branch of the ICA; he was working as assistant to John Brown, group catering controller at Hawker Siddeley. He told that year's ICA national conference, in an under 30s session, that what was needed was a confederation of industrial, hospital, school meals and welfare caterers – a proposal that the report in *Catering Times* said received widespread support, though it was never to be implemented. A couple of weeks later, the same newspaper reported a proposal by the ICA – after three years of discussion – to endorse a code of professional conduct for members. These were serious topics. With an office and a full-time secretariat, the ICA now saw itself as a significant organisation in catering politics with a wish to influence the direction of the industry, as it had during the war. Overend, who had now become a vice president and who had managed to be appointed an observer to the newly-established Hotel and Catering Economic Development Committee, was even reported to be seeking a link with the CBI.

By then contractors had been gaining some strength in the association, though Jim Cartwright remembers that antipathy still existed between in-house caterers and contractors, well into the 1980s. "I went to an ICA meeting in Glasgow and I was the only contractor there and you could feel the hostility," he says.

However, Jack Matthews, catering director at Tesco who became ICA chairman in 1985 and then vice president, and who joined the association in 1968, remembers amicable meetings attended by Gardner Merchant,

Bateman and Midland people. Indeed, the issue had become clouded because many of the most prominent members of the ICA, who were in catering advisory positions in major companies, were already engaging contractors. George Wall at Ford, Reg Stinton at ICI, Brian Ball at BP, John Brown at Hawker Siddeley (later BAE Systems) were keen supporters of the association and were well known industry personalities; all of them had engaged contractors in some or all of their outlets.

Stinton and Ball went on to be elected presidents of the Hotel and Catering International Management Association (now the Institute of Hospitality). Others, such as Sheila Mitchell at Sterling Winthrop, John Neish at British Steel, Tony Beach at Kodak, David Hibbert at Chloride, Harry Sullivan

(head of local authority catering at Haringey) continued to play a prominent role in the ICA's development.

Jack Matthews believes that the ICA was at the forefront of the catering industry, dealing as it did with very large industrial feeding outlets. He says:

"We were the first to have cashless systems in Girovend, induction cookers and industrial microwave ovens. We at Tesco helped companies like McCain Foods experiment with microwave oven chips and other products. Many of our members helped in researching products and equipment. All in all, I think the ICA was a great asset to the catering industry and helped to make it what it is today."

Indeed, for as long as British industry was dominated by large factories and industrial complexes, in-house caterers remained powerful personalities running very large catering operations. London Transport had opened a central food production centre in Croydon in 1950 which was still going strong into the early 1980s under Eric Gazelle, director of catering at London Transport. An article in a London Transport pensioners' magazine shows that it was producing over one million cook-freeze items every year, along with three million cakes and nearly three million bread rolls and using 23,000lbs of tea. It was a formidable facility that also produced food for home sale to London Transport staff.

But the NSCI's merger with Caterers' Association was, perhaps, more significant than it first appeared in 1948. While the ICA attracted individual managers, the CA and then the BHRCA attracted companies rather than individuals into membership. In 1973, the BHRCA created its Industrial Catering Panel with Philip Thornton of Philip Thornton Catering Services as chairman (later to sell out to ARA) and two vice chairmen: R.C. Hall of Meal

Service Co, Brighton and Graham Lewis of Bateman. The panel comprised most of the industry's heavyweight contractors and had a number of chairmen subsequently, including Garry Hawkes of Gardner Merchant, Jim Cartwright (then at Shaw Catering), William McCall (Aramark), Bob Cotton (Gardner Merchant) and latterly Phil Hooper (Sodexo). In 1995, under the chairmanship of Jim Cartwright, it changed its name to the Contract Catering Forum (and later to Food and Service Management Forum which recognised the extension of contractors' activities towards support services other than catering) and was already taking steps to raise the profile of contracting by publishing its annual contract catering survey – first published in 1990. As the trend to outsourcing gathered pace,

Jack Matthews: "All in all, I think the ICA was a great asset to the catering industry and helped to make it what it is today."

Marc Verstringhe, a contractor, became the last chairman of the ICA before it became the ECA. The ICA's founders would have rejected his appointment out-of-hand.

with the closure of more large industrial sites and the decline in the number of in-house caterers, membership of the ICA declined. In 1985 Ron Barwood, from William Hill the bookmaker, was appointed as general secretary with a brief to increase membership and prepare the ground for the ICA to play a bigger role in industry affairs. But when Jack Matthews retired in 1987 as national chairman and Marc Verstringhe (a contractor!) took over, there were barely 500 members. It had become a shadow of its former self.

However, there was still life in the association. Sheila Mitchell, catering manager at Sterling Winthrop, was one of the ICA's most vocal supporters. She had joined in 1961 and was chairman from 1974 to 1977. In 1974, together with Harry Andrews, she launched the Catermind competition with one heat between West London colleges using the BBC's Mastermind format as the basis of the competition; from 1977 onwards, Magnus Magnusson, the Mastermind host, was chairman of the Catermind London finals. One aim was to boost the profile of industrial catering as a career in catering colleges. By the time the competition closed in 1994 it involved 206 colleges in 14 heats throughout the UK. For her efforts, Mitchell (who died in 2013) was awarded the 1986 Industrial Caterer of the Year Catey; she was appointed MBE in the 2004-2005 Honours List.

In 1983, under the chairmanship of Tony Beach, head of catering at Kodak, the ICA was incorporated as a company limited by guarantee. The aims and objectives of the association were very similar to those that were adopted at its formation in 1938 except that now contract caterers were welcomed into membership.

Always interested in strengthening links between industry and education, Verstringhe had already participated,

BRITISH HOSPITALITY Association

FOOD and SERVICE MANAGEMENT SURVEY

2010

Nestlé PROFESSIONAL.
Creative Food & Beverage Solutions

From 1989 to 2010 the British Hospitality Association produced an annual survey of contract catering (latterly Food and Service Management), tracing the growth of the sector and trends within it.

Mair Davison took over the ECA secretariat.

part of the ECA International, with Mair Davison responsible for ECA International's secretariat – a position she held until 2001. Subsequently, together with Robert Perry from Thames Valley University (now West London University), Mair organised the ECA's Student of the Year competition which ran from 1992 to 2004. This involved students from each of the 16 ECA International member countries and the USA, and was held in a different European city every year. The successful European Mise en Place Cup, based in Maastricht, followed – a competition with similar aims and still supported by Verstringhe as a member of the advisory council.

There was further change in 2006 when ECA (GB) became the Association of Catering Excellence. "Membership includes a cross section of managers, chefs, consultants, students, suppliers from the hospitality and food service sector, providing a forum for networking for all levels of staff within the catering industry through a series of informal and fun related events," explains its website.

But there is no mention of the ICA. Ironically, the majority of ACE's current patrons and council members are catering contractors and many of its corporate members are contract catering companies. It is as if the ICA had never existed.

through Catering & Allied, in a student sponsorship apprenticeship scheme initiated by Brian Watts, then the catering adviser to the Bank of England. This led to Watts being named Industrial Caterer of the Year in the 1987 Catey awards – an award which Verstringhe himself gained in 1989. The aim of the scheme was to give opportunities to young catering professionals who lacked the means to go to college and, simultaneously, to promote careers in industrial catering to students and their lecturers. The scheme was so successful that it was decided to incorporate it into the ICA.

The ICA then looked to form a catering association within Europe but one already existed in the shape of the European Catering Association formed in 1964 in order to establish a European platform for catering affairs taking in employers, employees, suppliers and both in-house and catering contractors. The proposal was accepted and in 1989 the ICA became the European Catering Association (GB),

Bateman market research unpopular with caterers

ICA claims survey may be espionage

ACCUSATIONS that a survey into industrial catering, currently being made by the Bateman Catering Organisation, is "at best a gimmick to tout for business and, at worst, sowing the seeds of doubt in the minds of company directors that their catering managers are inefficient," have been made by Industrial Catering Association secretary, James Groves.

A questionnaire, with a covering letter from Bateman managing director, Trevor Barber, has been sent to company directors, says Mr Groves, and not to the people who can really help.

"I do not believe that this

James Groves: "Survey is a gimmick."

document is what it purports to be. Bateman's should have sought the co-operation of people like ourselves, and the British Hotels, Restaurants

and Caterers Association, for this information."

A number of ICA members are reported to be upset by the document, and have already told their employers to dispose of it in their wastepaper basket.

A spokesman for Bateman told *Caterer:* "We have not heard directly from the ICA and cannot, therefore, comment.

"Whilst respecting ICA's role in the industry, we are carrying out a piece of industrial market research geared to Bateman's specific present and future marketing plans, and this research is a follow-up to our 'Leisure at Work' study completed several years ago."☐

Even as late as the late 1970s, suspicions were rife between contractors and ICA members, as this extract from Caterer shows. In-house caterers were very sensitive to overtures by contractors to their employers.

CHAPTER FOUR

Roland Webb launches
Midland Catering

Roland Webb was not the only entrepreneur to take advantage of wartime legislation by creating a successful business. But he was among the first.

In 1940, R.A (Roland) Webb, an accountant by training and a Government inspector by profession, recognised that the war offered profitable opportunities. With no background in catering but with a good business brain, he formed a partnership with James Wallace, at the time a well-known Birmingham caterer, who was already providing a catering service to some of the factories in the Midlands.

The partnership proved successful. Wallace's catering expertise, combined with Webb's accounting, commercial and sales experience, was a perfect fit, consolidating the business and enabling the company to secure more contracts in the region. The next year they formed The Midland Counties Industrial Catering Co – 'specialists in Industrial Catering and Canteen Consultants' is how they described it. The business grew. Indeed, given the circumstances, it would have been difficult for the company to fail

given the fact that a catering provision for workers in large factories was mandatory – 'a canteen in every factory' was the then Ministry of Labour's motto. This suited Midland just fine. It also encouraged the development of Bateman Catering, Taylorplan and other catering companies long-since departed.

Midland grew in the wartime environment, as did all other caterers. In 1942, Eric Vaughan, who was in charge of catering for a major car plant in the Midlands, joined Webb to supervise the company's canteens in the Birmingham-Wolverhampton area; later, as business continued to expand, he moved to Leicester to take charge of all the contracts in the east of the region. He continued working for the company, eventually becoming controller of the eastern division; by the end of the war Midland was catering for some 100 contracts throughout the region.

There was a setback in 1946, however, when Wallace died leaving Webb to take detailed control by himself of what had by then become a large industrial catering company. His other directors – all Webb's near relations – took no part in the running

of the business. Help eventually came in the form of his eldest son, Bruce, who joined in 1949 aged 25, after a career in the navy, served in part with Lord Mountbatten. It is not known whether Bruce was keen to give up the navy and take up a new career in the catering industry at the behest of his father but it is unlikely that he approached it with much relish. He never lost his love of the sea but he nevertheless threw himself into the day-to-day operational demands of building up the Midland Catering business.

* * *

It was the combination of father and son that ensured the post-war growth of the company. Webb (always referred to as Mr R.A) became chairman and managing director and Bruce (known as Mr Bruce), took up the role of director and general manager after some hasty on-the-job training on the shop floor. The company expanded in its two main regions, West Midlands and East Midlands, and later, in the 1960s, to Lancashire and Yorkshire and south to Gloucestershire and Essex.

In 1963, by the time of the opening of new

offices in Bristol South Road, Longbridge, Birmingham (which coincided with a major supplement in the *Birmingham Mail*), the total number of contracts approached 400.

This expansion was not achieved alone. Richard Pitts, for 13 years Birmingham's Civic Catering Officer, joined the company as controller of the Western Division, but lasted only a few months. Others took his place – one from Berni Inns – but none of them matched Bruce Webb's high expectations; he was not someone who tolerated fools gladly. Not being able to recruit from outside, he decided to promote from within and Mike Taylor, who had joined the company in 1956 as a relief chef and trainee supervisor, was promoted to the position of catering controller to assist Bruce Webb in the running of the company. Two others who joined Midland at the same time – Bill Burrows, who went on to become Midland's sales director, and Eric Williamson, who became divisional controller – remained with

Mike Taylor joined Midland in 1956 and remained with the company until the Compass buy-out.

The architect for the new building and associated work was Mr. John S. Scott, and the main contractors were William Sapcote and Sons Ltd., of Birmingham.

tise for staff and engage them at short notice without any opportunity to assess their competence under working conditions.

The cost of this policy does,

person for each job: of those interviewed about a third find the firm's standards are too high and another third are not up to the required level of proficiency.

Personal Contact Maintained in Growing Family Firm

AT the outset Midland Catering was a partnership between the present chairman, Mr. Rowland A. Webb, and a well-known Birmingham caterer, Mr. James Wallace. The link was formed in 1940 when Mr. Wallace was already catering for some of the factories that had been dispersed as a war-time measure around the city's boundaries.

The combination of Mr. Wallace's practical ability and Mr. Webb's wide accounting, commercial and sales experience proved to be a successful one and the partners secured contracts for more canteens.

Company Formed

In 1941 they formed the Midland Counties Industrial Catering Co. Ltd.

A year or so later Mr. Eric Vaughan, who had catered for one of Britain's largest car factories, joined the company to supervise a number of canteens in the Birmingham-Wolverhampton area. Later he moved to Leicester to take charge of a small number of contracts in the eastern division, of which he continues to be controller.

In 1946 Mr. Wallace died and Mr. Webb had to take over the detailed control of canteens and cafés in the West Midlands. Three years later, however, he was joined by his eldest son, Bruce, who had been serving with the Navy. After a period of training the latter took charge of the western division and is now the company's general manager.

The latest member of the management team is Mr.

Richard Pitts, who for 13 years was Birmingham's Civic Catering Officer and, as such, augmented a wide experience that he is applying to his new role as controller of the western division.

Through all the years of effort that made the company the remarkable organisation it is to-day Mr. Webb has had considerable support from his wife and from his three sons, all of whom served in the Forces during the war.

In the 23 years since the company was founded the number of contracts in the eastern division has risen to nearly 200 and the total in the western division is also approaching that figure.

Further, the firm has extended its activities geographically to take in an area extending from Lancashire and Yorkshire in the North to Gloucestershire

Mr. Bruce Webb, general manager and director of Midland Catering, pointing out the location of a new Midland canteen project to his father, Mr. R. A. Webb, chairman and managing director of the company.

and Essex in the South, though not so far as to reduce the important advantages of personal contact.

Midland Catering is still very much a family business, all the Webbs having been directors of the company for many years, and to-day it is the largest privately-owned concern in its field.

...crease of

staff handle invoices for payment. So far as suppliers can get their own accounting done promptly, they are paid weekly.

And one gets some idea of the magnitude of the work involved when it is realised that the purchase accounting section is clearing invoices covering more than 25,000 separate items amounting to over £20,000 a week—or more than £1,000,000 a year.

In 1963, when Midland Catering opened new offices, the Birmingham Post ran a feature on the company which, by then, had over 400 contracts.

the company until the sale of the company to GrandMet.

Mike Taylor was a striking example of the Webbs' approach to business and their desire to motivate employees and encourage loyalty. Taylor had left school at 14, went into baking and then into mobile catering, before being called up at 18 on a three-year regular engagement in the RAF. For over two years he cooked in the officers' mess in Germany. In order to co-ordinate the catering activities, he had to learn German. After demob, he spent a year working in a Birmingham restaurant and another year in a works canteen in Redditch. He joined Midland at £8 per week plus £1 per week for motorbike expenses.

"On my first day, I was taken to one of Midland's contracts at Bilston where a Mrs Phillips was in charge," he recalls. "I arrived just as they were serving lunch, which was cold mutton heated up with some hot gravy, two ice-cream scoops of mashed potatoes and a spoonful of dried peas that had been rehydrated overnight and cooked with some green dye to make them look more appetising. There was only rice pudding as a dessert and the only confectionery on offer were two kinds of Burton's biscuits – the company obviously had a deal going with Burton's."

After his experience in Germany, Taylor considered the standard of catering being provided was very basic and it stayed that way for the next 10 years or so. Even in 1956 Britain was still trying to shake off the impact of the war years and some foods were still on ration; others were difficult or expensive to obtain. Britain's culinary reputation was at its nadir – yet people had to eat, and the provision of a hot lunch at work was, for many, their main meal of the day.

Even so, change was in the air. The country's economy was gradually improving, overseas travel was in its infancy bringing

'PHONE: PRIORY 1123-4

THE MIDLAND COUNTIES INDUSTRIAL CATERING CO. LTD.

Specialists in Industrial Catering & Canteen Consultants

1197 BRISTOL RD. SOUTH
NORTHFIELD
BIRMINGHAM 31

DIRECTORS
R·A·WEBB   B·A·WEBB
A·WEBB   H·J·WEBB

27th July, 1956

RAW/EP

Mr. M.J.Taylor,
63, Clent Avenue,
Headless Cross,
Redditch

Dear Mr.Taylor,

I am very pleased to note a marked improvement in the trading results on your district and gather that really only Francis Nicholls' canteen is still a serious problem. It is disappointing that we have had to give up Ariel, but that is no fault of yours.

We shall probably be giving you one or two more canteens to look after in the near future, and in anticipation of this and as some recognition of your satisfactory progress, I have arranged for your present motor cycle allowance to be increased from £1 to £3 per week, commencing week ending 4th August. However, you will continue to receive only £1 per week of the allowance, the other £2 being held to the credit of your loan account which will be established when you buy your car, the intention being that you will repay the loan we make you at the rate of £2 per week.

I have also arranged for you to receive a full week's salary week ending 11th August, when I understand you will be away on holiday.

With best wishes,

Yours sincerely,

Managing Director.

Mike Taylor was a striking example of the Webbs' approach to business and their desire to motivate employees and encourage loyalty.

MIDLAND CATERING
COUNTIES INDUSTRIAL COMPANY·LIMITED

DIRECTORS
R. A. WEBB · B. A. WEBB
A. WEBB · H. J. WEBB
P. R. WEBB

TELEPHONE
PRIory 1123 (4 lines)
TELEGRAMS
MIDCATER, BIRMINGHAM

Canteens in the Midlands are best run by Midland Catering

1197 BRISTOL RD. SOUTH
BIRMINGHAM 31

RAW/EP

6th December, 1956

Mr. M.J.Taylor,
63, Clent Avenue,
Headless Cross
<u>REDDITCH</u>

Dear Mr.Taylor,

I have been pleased to note that the trading results in your area have been generally satisfactory and that where troubles have arisen you have investigated them very thoroughly as shown by the reports which I have been pleased to see. In addition I understand from Mr.Creek and Mr.Bruce Webb that you are making sure that our customers and contacts are satisfied also, which is of course of the greatest importance.

Now that you are taking over the Hartrick canteen and quite possibly another one in the near future, your good work deserves further recognition, and I have therefore arranged with Mr.Goodwin for your salary to be increased to £12 per week as from this week.

I was also pleased to learn from Mr. Bruce that you willingly accepted the relief duty at the Wintergarden Hotel. I gather furthermore, that although it was our intention that your wife should be there also only to keep you company and avoid you being a week away from home, she did in fact help with the work there in several ways. Please thank her from Mr.Bruce and myself and give her the pound note enclosed to buy a little present for herself.

With best wishes

Yours sincerely,

Managing Director.

A personal letter from the top. The £1 that was enclosed with the letter is worth £20 today.

with it exciting new tastes; both clients and customers began to expect more than what one company grandee calls 'hashslingers.' But it was a slow process.

For Taylor, it was the best of times. "Midland was a family-run company with R.A Webb and Bruce Webb very much at the helm. It was paternalistic, which was no bad thing, and you felt they knew everything that was going on in the business."

Within a couple of months, Taylor had a personal letter from Webb thanking him for his efforts and increasing his salary to £10 a week – "I feel you have made a very good start with the company," wrote R.A. In the next year, letters of thanks followed, raising his salary to £12, £13, £14 and then £16. Occasionally, he would receive a letter thanking him for a successful special event – "I have arranged a special bonus of £4 to be added to your next salary cheque"; another, after a client party: "Mr Creek has told me that this [event] involved quite a bit of extra work and I have therefore arranged for you to receive a special bonus of £5 enclosed herewith."

"It was that kind of company, run in a very old-fashioned kind of way," Taylor recalls. "You would get a personal letter from the top and you knew that your progress was being monitored, with extra responsibilities given to you as a result of your efforts. It was hard work but you knew all the work you were doing was being noted and appreciated. It was very motivational. Mind you, if you didn't make the figures, they would soon tell you. You knew they were *au fait* with every detail of the business."

Once, he received a short note from Webb saying: "I note cash in hand at the following canteen for the week ending 30th April was very excessive."

In his early days, Taylor used his motor cycle to collect the cash from the canteens under his control – hence the initial allowance, which was later raised to £3 per week (though the additional £2 was held in credit of his loan account which was established to buy his car – proving, if proof was needed, how business-like the Webbs really were).

"The bike had a pannier on either side and we used to collect the cash from each site and put it in a pannier to take back to the bank. We didn't have Securicor or anything like that. I remember once, I skidded in the snow and all the bags flew out of the panniers. We didn't have plastic bags in those days, just paper bags, so many of them burst open. I was very encouraged to find that people were helping me pick up the coins and stuffing them back in the bags. It was only when I got to the bank that I found out half the money had been thieved." Soon after, a car was provided.

Midland's strength in those days, and indeed later, was that it had very tight cost control systems. Every manager had to submit his figures by the end of play on Friday and by the following Wednesday, they were told the results to the nearest penny.

"If you were a pound out, they would tell you and you had to make sure it didn't happen again."

Clive Gilpin, who joined Midland a few years after Taylor in 1962, and who, like Taylor, ended his career as a divisional managing director of Compass, tells a similar story about the early days.

"The most difficult job about collecting cash from the units was trying to stay out of the tram lines, but they finally got me," he says.

Gilpin recalls that takeaways were also a regular feature of the old canteens.

"On Thursdays and Fridays, many of our female customers would bring a basin to work and we would sell them boiled ham hocks or pease pudding. The menu varied according to the part of the country you

An Australian takes over Taylorplan

Taylorplan was another company with a history stretching back to the second world war. Founded in 1939 by two brothers, Roy and Hugh Taylor, it was originally based in the south east of England and during the war was busy in both factory catering and providing meals in refugee camps. After the war, it expanded and by 1976 it had become the fifth largest contract caterer – after Gardner Merchant, Sutcliffe, Bateman and Midland – with over 200 catering and cleaning contracts in industrial catering, education and residential establishments.

By 1984 it flirted with a partnership with a Saudi company before selling out to an Australian cleaning company, Berkeley Challenge, which was keen to expand its cleaning interests in the UK with Taylorplan's catering activities as an added bonus. By then, Taylorplan had 60 or so catering contracts, plus a hotel, the Spread Eagle in Midhurst, which is still in the Taylor family through Hugh Taylor's son-in-law and later generations.

Jim Matthews, a Berkeley director, came over from Australia to take control of the business but soon found that trying to get caterers to sell cleaning contracts was a difficult proposition.

"In those days, there was huge resistance from traditional caterers to run cleaning contracts – they just didn't think that cleaning was on a par with the more highly skilled catering activities," Ian Sarson, who joined the company as a graduate trainee in 1984 and who later joined Compass and became managing director of UK and Ireland, recalls. "I didn't agree with this attitude, but it was rife at the time."

Matthews decided to exit the cost-plus catering business and in the mid-60s sold Taylorplan's catering activities to Sutcliffe keeping the cleaning business and the company's emerging defence and healthcare multi-services business, with the proviso that it couldn't re-enter the catering market within two years.

Two years later, again trading as Taylorplan Catering, Matthews re-entered the market offering both catering and other support services and by 1994 it was operating 46 contracts with an annual turnover of nearly £60m, its main wins being a three-year, fixed price catering and cleaning contract at Aldershot Garrison and the contract to provide catering to the European Commission in Brussels. It also injected £500,000 as a five-year loan to create a new 360-seat public restaurant at the Royal Preston Infirmary and grew rapidly in the hospital catering sector.

However, by 1995, rumour spread through the industry that Berkeley wanted to exit the UK market and that a management buyout, led by Jim Matthews, was on the cards – at which point, Marriott, the US-based hospitality company, stepped in. Keen to enter the UK contract catering market after what had turned out to be a disastrous foray in Italy, Marriott was willing to pay top dollar for what was a profitable and successful UK company. It clinched the deal for £28m, only subsequently realising that it had overpaid. In the words of one cautious observer, "what it bought was not entirely what it said on the label". In 1996, six months later and now desperate to acquire a company with a strong management structure, Marriott acquired Russell and Brand for £14m. Matthews quit and Tim Cookson, formerly managing director of Russell and Brand, was appointed president of Marriott Management Services (UK). But Marriott did not last long as a separate entity in the UK (see Chapter 21).

were in."

Midland's other strength was undoubtedly Bruce Webb, who gradually took more and more control of the company from his father though R.A remained as chairman until the sale of the company to Grand Metropolitan in 1968. The relationship between father and son was strong.

Although Bruce's background was in engineering and the navy, his leadership skills in the company were considerable as was his salesmanship. He had an uncanny ability to win business by persuading potential clients of the value of contracting

out and convincing them that it would be so much better for them if they installed a skilled caterer, such as Midland.

On a personal level, Bruce was tall, well built and very much the country gentleman and spoke like one. He was also the proud owner of a Citroen DS; with its hydraulic suspension, the DS was widely seen as a car of French style and great sophistication. He rarely, if ever, socialised with staff but he was a particular hit with the ladies. With three children from his first marriage to Lady Wren, a New Zealander, he married three

more times, the last to Lydia, a Russian, in New Zealand, where he lived. With a house in Jersey, after the sale of the company to Grand Metropolitan, he visited England two or three times a year to see old friends.

The sale of the company to Grand Metropolitan came as a surprise to most people. Midland had grown organically – in its entire 27-year history, it did not acquire any other company – but its success was dependent on its ownership as well as its management. R.A, however, was in his 70s. He felt it was time to put his feet up and retire to Portugal while Bruce, now 47, was

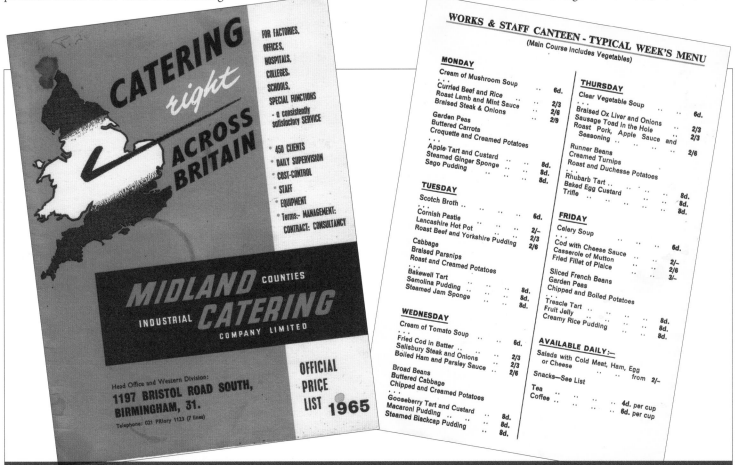

Canteens were highly demarcated in the 1950s – workers were usually separated from senior staff and had different menus, while boardrooms frequently had silver service.

SENIOR STAFF DINING ROOM - TYPICAL WEEK'S MENU

Set Luncheon at 6/6 including Roll, Butter, Serviette and Waitress Service

MONDAY
Leek and Potato Broth

...

Roast Pork, Apple Sauce and Seasoning
Steak and Kidney Pie
Savoury Meat Roll

Butter Beans
Brussels Sprouts
Roast and Creamed Potatoes

...

Apple Sponge and Custard
Chocolate Mousse

...

Cheese and Biscuits

...

Coffee

TUESDAY
Oxtail Soup

...

Roast Shoulder of Lamb, Mint Sauce
Braised Beef and Onions
Vienna Steak

Creamed Turnips
Cabbage
Parsley and Croquette Potatoes

...

Mincemeat Tart
Baked Egg Custard

...

Cheese and Biscuits

...

Coffee

WEDNESDAY
Cream of Tomato Soup

...

Fillet of Cod Mornay
Roast Leg of Mutton, Redcurrant Jelly
Braised Liver and Onions

Vichy Carrots
Garden Peas
Fried and Creamed Potatoes

...

Steamed Blackcap Pudding
Creamy Rice Pudding

...

Cheese and Biscuits

...

Coffee

THURSDAY
Scotch Broth

...

Roast Round of Beef, Yorkshire Pudding
Lancashire Hot Pot
Stuffed Lambs Hearts

Buttered Parsnips
Savoy Cabbage
Creamed and Croquette Potatoes

...

Apple and Blackberry Pie
Steamed Golden Sponge

...

Cheese and Biscuits

...

Coffee

FRIDAY
Cream of Vegetable Soup

...

Fried Fillet of Plaice
Grilled Pork Chop, Apple Sauce
Minced Beef Pie

Baked Beans in Tomato Sauce
Garden Peas
Fried and Creamed Potatoes

...

Compote of Fruit and Custard
Bakewell Tart

...

Cheese and Biscuits

...

Coffee

AVAILABLE DAILY:—
Salads, with Cold Meat, Ham, Egg or
  Cheese

Special Menus by request

A senior staff menu from the Midland brochure.

Bruce Webb was a handsome man – and a sailor by choice; he had served with Lord Mountbatten in the navy and came 20th out of 60 in the 1972 single-handed Transatlantic Race.

getting itchy feet and was keen to move on, away from the day-to-day chore of running a growing business. A keen yachtsman, he wanted to take part in the next single-handed Transatlantic Race and the 1972 event beckoned; in his yacht Gazelle, he came 20th out of 40 with 60 starting. An additional factor to his departure was that Grand Metropolitan in the previous year had bought Bateman Catering, Midland's long-standing rival, for just under £1m.

Maxwell Joseph, the chairman of Grand Metropolitan, had started out in the estate agency business in the 1930s but, in some smart property moves that foresaw the growth of tourism to London, had acquired a number of key London hotels after the war. He formed Grand Metropolitan Hotels in 1962 with a clutch of London hotels. From its hotel base, the company was at the start of becoming a major conglomerate, later buying long-established companies such as Mecca, Express Dairies, Berni Inns, the brewers

Trumans and Watneys, as well as building and buying more hotels and other interests overseas.

The Webbs found the offer of £1.2m (£19m in today's money) too tempting to resist. In a letter to employees, R.A Webb told employees that Midland had now 'joined' Grand Metropolitan, "to meet the increasing taxation handicaps imposed on family firms, but also to ensure even better service for our clients and to improve the security and prospects of employment for all our staff. Midland Catering will benefit from massive financial backing and great variety of expertise."

Bruce Webb was appointed managing director under the chairmanship of Ernest Sharp, who was joint managing director of Grand Metropolitan (Sharp was replaced in 1971 by Graham Lewis who remained chairman until 1981). Eric Williamson, Mike Taylor and Bill Burrows, the three who had joined Midland back in the 1950s, became the company's new board of directors.

'Joining', of course, was not an entirely accurate description of the GrandMet takeover and it fooled nobody; nor was R A, in his letter to employees, entirely accurate in saying that 'continuity of good management was thus ensured'; as with all takeovers, changes occurred. Nor did GrandMet intend to invest much money in Midland – rather the reverse. It saw both Midland and Bateman Catering as cash cows. However, although the Webbs' paternalistic style became a thing of the past, Grand Metropolitan interfered surprisingly little in Midland's affairs except to use its abundant cash flow to its own advantage and it happily allowed it to compete against Bateman for the next 12 years in the belief that competition between the two companies

Some of the events for which contractors like Midland provided the catering – here at the Royal Show, Stoneleigh – created huge logistical challenges.

With the appointment of Tony Walford, Midland moved into a new era. The first Midland Catering Eastern Division staff party, circa 1973, saw Robin Richter, Dennis Price, Tony Coles, Ron Fletcher and Peter Tapley on song. Tony Coles was well known in the company for his Elvis impersonations.

company's 1972 conference: "The industrial catering division is going to be in Europe if the potential to increase our business profits is there." Midland remained a predominantly England-based, B&I contractor with some long-standing blue chip clients.

* * *

Walford was a vastly different character to Bruce Webb. Whereas the latter was old school formality with an interest in country sports, Walford had climbed the greasy career pole, with a few slips on the way, through his own efforts, intelligence and engaging personality. He was keen to meet and greet the staff personally, had the knack of socialising with them on an equal footing and even played five-a-side football with them by setting up team games after work. Staff parties were introduced, even encouraged, giving the opportunity for people to let their hair down. Tony Coles, who had originally joined Midland in the late 1960s as training manager – "with the specific aim of extracting as much grant income from the Training Board as we possibly could" – looks upon Walford as his mentor. Coles had left Midland to go to Gardner Merchant but within a year was back when Walford was appointed.

"Tony turned Midland from a friendly company to a thoroughly professional company without losing the friendliness," he says. "The company hadn't changed much from the way it was run in the 1940s and Tony was a breath of fresh air."

Coles had a nice line singing *à la Elvis Presley* and many a staff party had him with others from the company, on stage, microphone in hand, band in the background. His reputation as an Elvis impersonator spread quickly throughout the company.

Walford, as did Graham Lewis, fought

made each more efficient and effective.

Nor was the sale of Midland entirely to the detriment of its employees. The Webbs, remaining true to their family values, gave several thousand GrandMet shares to all senior employees who had been with the company for more than 10 years, and cash sums to those long-serving employees who were lower down the line. Overall, several hundred benefited.

Inevitably, only two years after the Midland purchase, Bruce Webb quit his position to prepare for the 1972 Transatlantic race; after 20 years at the helm he recognised the time had come for him to take to the sea again. He left like an old soldier – he just faded away. No official ceremony marked his retirement. But it was not the end of the Midland story Bruce was replaced by Tony Walford, who joined from the Hotel and Catering Industry Training

Board where he was technical director; before that he was chief catering adviser to Trust Houses.

Walford, greatly admired in the company, remained in his post until 1978 and did much to smooth the transition of Midland from family firm to a subsidiary of a major international conglomerate, growing it to over 3,500 employees and making some key contract gains such as English China Clay in Cornwall, Toshiba in Wales, Triplex HQ in Scotland, British Rail's HQ in London, (now the Landmark Hotel), Delta Engineering in Birmingham. He doubled the size of its sales force and increased expenditure on training and development. Its efforts to enter other contracting sectors, such as hospital and school catering, were only partly successful. Nor did it gain any contracts overseas, though this was an aim of Graham Lewis, the chairman of Midland, when he told the against the perception of the industrial caterer being a second-class catering citizen. This had become a chip-on-the-shoulder issue (to a certain extent, it still is) that had long concerned people working in the sector. In their eyes, there was just as much skill in running an industrial catering outlet as there was in running a hotel but, frustratingly, neither the general public nor catering college graduates and their lecturers seemed to recognise this.

At the same conference in 1972, Walford told delegates that it was increasingly being realised that industrial catering played a role in the wider field of industrial relations. Midland was striving to improve the working environment of its employees:

"We don't take on canteens which look like tool sheds. We're trying to give our managers and manageresses units they're proud to work in," he said.

Yet at the same conference, Graham Lewis, ever the maverick, claimed that there were still too many factories in the country "where tea trolleys are manned by Fanny in her carpet slippers, serving cups of lukewarm tea and soggy biscuits". And putting a new twist on boosting sales and employee responsibility, he placed the onus squarely on the company's unit managers to persuade clients to invest in new equipment in order to enable more sales to be made.

Walford's successful reign (he left in 1978 to take over Autobar and died in 2010) was followed by the appointment of David Hutchins, previously Grand Metropolitan's HR director; for all his affability, however, he did not enjoy the confidence of his fellow directors. Two years later they summoned Lewis to a meeting to express their dissatisfaction of his leadership. It was nothing short of a directors' putsch. Hutchins left to pursue other interests and Stuart Hanson took over and remained in charge until Dick Turpin took over

the combined Midland and Bateman companies in 1981 – to be called Grandmet Catering Services.

In the 12 years in which Midland and Bateman were commonly owned, even though they had operated as separate companies, many believed that a merger between them would eventually come about – "it was inevitable," says Tony Coles.

Although competition between them had led to some efficiencies, the trend towards larger companies was well underway in industry generally and it became clear that greater value would be obtained by merging Midland and Bateman, thus saving on office space, reducing the head office and regional office head count, boosting its purchasing power and adding to client credibility. Other companies in the industry had long been mystified at the continuing competition between Bateman and Midland. In their merger was the genesis of Compass, the world's largest food service provider.

Stuart Hanson succeeded David Hutchins as managing director after Hutchins was ousted in a putsch.

Midland Caterng brochure – circa 1975.

Tony Walford: "We don't take on canteens which look like tool sheds. We're trying to give our managers and manageresses units they're proud to work in."

CHAPTER FIVE

Jack Bateman — the man who knew nothing about catering

Jack Bateman never professed to know much about catering but Bateman Catering became an industry leader.

Jack Bateman, born in 1908 and always referred to as JRB in the company, started Factory Canteens in 1941. He recognised the opportunities that the war presented to anyone with nous and enterprise. All his life, he admitted he knew nothing about catering, which was largely true – no-one ever asked him, either, and if they had, he would have referred them to his technical staff. But he did come with something of a catering background. His first wife (there were to be three more subsequently) was Beryl Ellis, the daughter of Mrs D.A Ellis whose family owned D Ellis & Co Ltd, a fair-sized catering company first established in 1919; he divorced Beryl sometime during the war. On its notepaper, Ellis & Co boasted that the company catered for the government and specialised 'in all forms of catering,' which included factories as well as weddings, birthday parties and other private functions.

A brochure it produced in 1942 shows some very large-scale works canteens in action and offered both a kitchen design and a consultancy service. Some tariffs at the time reveal that a snack, such as toad in the hole, steak pie and chips, salmon and potato pie, would cost between 6d (£1.04 today) and 8d (£1.37) and a main meal, comprising boiled leg of mutton, leek sauce, boiled potatoes, spring greens, jam capped pudding or Bakewell tart, could be had for 1s (5p) or £2.08 in today's money.

It was a firm of sufficient size to attract the interest of John Gardner who acquired Ellis & Co in 1950 when Beryl's mother appears to have hit some hard times. Gardner paid £2 for each 500 £1 Ellis shares (£30,600 today) as well as reimbursing a much larger sum – a loan of £7,161 – in total, the equivalent of £247,000 today. Whether the hard times prompted the decision of Mrs Ellis (then staying at the Hendon Hall Hotel) to sell off all the company's office furniture and equipment before John Gardner took over is not clear; it certainly led to a rather petulant letter from Gardner's company secretary, Leslie Slark, wanting to know why the furniture had been removed.

"We were distinctly under the impression that all the furniture in the offices . . . was the property of the company. In fact, it was upon this basis that we made our recent offer for the purchase of Ellis shares."

The ELLIS
INDUSTRIAL CATERING SERVICE

Whether John Gardner got the furniture back is not known. Probably not.

During Jack and Beryl's courtship, both of them worked for the Ellis family business in various capacities though Jack's commitment was not total. When the war came, he thought about his future. He was liable to call-up and, understandably, was keen to avoid it. Looking at the success

---

A slight difference

Once asked by a colleague what the difference was between Staff Restaurants and Bateman Catering, Jack Bateman allegedly replied that there was a difference: "We both serve **** but in Bateman's we put parsley on it" – a difference that neither staff nor clients would have appreciated but which might illustrate Jack Bateman's self-deprecating sense of humour.

One of Staff Restaurant's contracts was Pascall's sweet factory on the Streatham Road. As part of Philip Morley's early training, he was sent there to witness a lunch service.

"I will never forget the scary sight of 100s of workers, men and women, scrambling across tables and chairs to be first in the line for lunch. This tidal wave of humanity was frozen in time by the very loud, authoritative voice of the diminutive manageress, who screamed 'Stop!' Standing between me and the oncoming crowd she then took command. The result was two very orderly lines of people all trying hard not to be noticed and told to go to the back of the line.

"I later learned that this happened every day and it was customary for new recruits like me to be placed where I was 'just to see how bad things can get.'"

JOHN GARDNER (LONDON) LTD

BRIDGE HOUSE · LONDON BRIDGE · LONDON · S·E·1

DIRECTORS: J·E·GARDNER · P·T·GARDNER · C·W·GARDNER · H·L·GARDNER · BRIAN J·GARDNER
L·W· DE V· SLARK F·A·C·C·A, F·C·I·S SECRETARY

TELEGRAMS
TRUNKFULS SEDIST LONDON

Please reply to
CWG/KL.

TELEPHONE
HOP 8000

10th November, 1950.

Mrs. Ellis,
Messrs. D. Ellis & Co. Ltd.,
Water Road,
Wembley,
MIDDX.

Dear Mrs. Ellis,

Arising from the negotiations which have recently been carried out by Mr. Molineux of Messrs. Chantrey Button & Company, I am now formally placing my Company's offer in writing, namely:-

(1) John Gardner (London) Limited will furnish D. Ellis & Co. Ltd. with sufficient funds to enable that Company to repay your Loan which now amounts to £7,161.

(2) John Gardner (London) Limited will make payment of £2 per share for the 500 Fully Paid £1 shares issued by your Company.

My Company's Solicitor will require to have sight of your Company's Minute Book and any relative legal documents.

My Company will require from you an indemnity against undisclosed Liabilities in the Accounts of D. Ellis & Company Limited.

I understand that you have agreed to relinquish as from the 30th June 1950 the salaries and expenses payable to you by the Company as its Managing Director and that for the period from the 1st July 1950 to the 31st December 1950 you will receive salary at the rate of £500 per annum and expenses at the rate of £300 per annum.

It is my intention to call upon you on Friday afternoon when we may have an opportunity of going into any further matters which may arise out of the offer.

Yours faithfully,
For and on behalf of,
JOHN GARDNER (LONDON) LTD.,

[signature]

Managing Director.

John Gardner bought D Ellis and Co for some £8,000 (the equivalent of £247,000 today) but Mrs Ellis still managed to keep the furniture.

D Ellis & Co was a well established contract caterer, founded in 1919, but Jack Bateman had little compunction about starting up in competition to his mother-in-law.

of his mother-in-law's company and the statutory need for large factories to provide a catering service, he decided to launch himself into contracting. An added bonus was that it would enable him to argue that he was in a reserved occupation, which he successfully did. On June 6th 1941, he founded Factory Canteens Ltd, six days before Roland Webb founded Midland Counties Industrial Catering Ltd.

Inevitably, Bateman found himself in competition with his ex mother-in-law's company but that was a small matter. There was plenty of business for everyone and the contracts began to pour in. By this time, he and Beryl had already drifted apart and she and the two children – David who was born in 1937 and Carolyn born in 1935 – were sent to Scotland, well away from the very real danger of being bombed in Biggin Hill where they lived. This left Jack – a handsome fellow in his day – to concentrate on building up his company without much family encumbrance and to enjoy himself as much as the war conditions would allow, which he certainly did.

He called the company Factory Canteens Ltd, a not very original title but one that certainly made plain its business focus, and took on Frank Winter as his second-in-command – a rough diamond with a cockney accent who was also quite a ruthless operator. Not much is known about Winter except that he ran the business while Bateman enjoyed the benefits. In 1943 Jack took on John Earnshaw Sutcliffe – always Jack Sutcliffe to Jack Bateman – who had been invalided out of the Royal Marines. A year later Sutcliffe became managing director and stayed until October 1946 when he broke away (see next chapter) to form his own company. In the same year that Sutcliffe defected, Factory Canteens, with 70 contracts in the south east, was given a slightly more inspiring name –

Factory Restaurants – but four years later, in January 1950, Bateman Catering was introduced as a separate brand. This was an attempt to move the company up-market, away from the basic catering for which Factory Canteens/Restaurants had become well known. Contracts with a small turnover or of a more basic standard were assigned to Factory Restaurants while Bateman concentrated on the more refined catering for offices and some banks. Unsurprisingly, this led to some dissension in the company as the staff in the more downmarket operations resented the preferential treatment of the Bateman staff who considered themselves way superior in food, personal and business skills.

Jack had 'presence.' He was the eldest of several brothers who jointly owned Bateman's Cleaning, a business they had set up in south London before the war and which, initially at least, prospered. He was a tall man (6ft 1in), always impeccably dressed. With outstanding people skills, he

*Jack Bateman: film star looks in profile: tall and handsome – the ladies loved **him**.*

was very popular with the ladies. He loved motor cars (Rolls Royce in particular) and ate regularly at Claridge's though he never stayed for coffee. His son, David, who joined the company in 1959 after a couple of years in the City selling hire purchase with Lombard North Central, describes Jack as "not a copy book father" – but he was a very good salesman with a wonderful presence – "people felt good to be with him". He was also, in Hilary Charles' view, rather shy.

* * *

Hilary Charles had joined the company in 1964 in unit management with an IMA degree before moving to the head office and taking charge of the company's mobile relief force. She was appointed director of personnel and training in 1967 and subsequently travelled the world organising recruitment and training for the many construction camps that

Jack in later years with David Bateman, his son: "not a copy book father."

An investor in training

Bateman Catering was an early – and regular – investor in training and took it very seriously. When Graham Stone joined the company in 1966 as a management trainee from the Birmingham College of Food, part of his training was a six-month *stage* at the Bahnhofbuffet at Zurich railway station, then a top ranking establishment with over 100 chefs and its own butchery, smokery and patisserie departments; it was a *stage* that even a Savoy hotel chef would have found appropriate.

"Bateman took training very seriously and it made sure that you gained the experience which it thought was necessary – far more practical training than now, but it was all very valuable," he says.

Stone rose up through the ranks, eventually becoming regional general manager in the central region of Grandmet Catering before being made redundant in 1983. He went on to form his own company, which he sold, and then worked for West Midland Police as catering manager for 10 years - "which I loved" – before joining a catering equipment company.

Grandmet Site Services (GIS) was setting up at the time.

"As I was taking over the personnel role I thought I had better learn something about personnel management," she says. "It was also a time of much employee legislation which was sometimes very tricky for us to handle. So I enrolled on a course of personnel management and became a member of an industrial tribunal."

Of Jack Bateman she thought: "I always thought JRB was rather a shy creature – particularly in the company of women, but he was charming as well." This may have been a technique. His four marriages led to children by three of his wives. According to Hilary Lewis, the wife of Graham Lewis, Bateman's long-time managing director, you had to remember "which wife was which – it was the first thing you learnt".

In the words of Tony Ward-Lewis, who joined the company in the 1960s, Jack Bateman "was your typical paternalistic entrepreneur".

"He hardly knew anyone's name in the company but though he paid badly he

gave handsome cash bonuses at certain times which encouraged the staff to greater efforts," he says.

By the late 1960s, Bateman had grown to 300 contracts, mostly in London and the south as well as a thriving outdoor catering business based in Twickenham and at the Walls factory in north London which was run by Hilary Morris who, in 1964, married Bateman's managing director, Graham Lewis. Hilary – her father had received an hereditary peerage – was a caterer herself, having attended Yorkshire Training College of Housecraft in Leeds, her home town, on an IMA course. She joined Bateman in 1959 and rose the ranks to run the company's outdoor catering departments, taking over shows like Farnborough where Graham Lewis, on one occasion, refused to be held to ransom by the catering manageress who was demanding higher pay.

Bateman's outdoor catering department also catered for private parties, many of them Jewish, some as large as over 600 guests in marquees. One wedding party for 430 guests, with Joe Loss and his orchestra and Max Bygraves as compère, required over 40 waitresses and the food charge was £3.50 a head (about £60 today). They forgot to cut the cake and the marriage split up nine weeks later.

The business was very successful and, though it entailed very long hours was "a lot of fun" but she eventually gave it up. "There was one time when Graham and I went for 11 days without seeing each other except in bed," she says.

* * *

Graham Lewis (always known as RGL – the company was keen on using initials as monikers, Pat Lichtensteiger was called RPL) had started off as a chef, in fact, as an army cook. He came out of the army and went straight to Alfred Marks, the recruitment agency, to find a job in the catering industry but was told to go away and grow a beard. "You don't look like a chef." This Lewis did and he never shaved it off. He went back to Marks and was promptly hired, working in a hospital kitchen where Jack Bateman met him and offered him a job – initially at the Isle of Grain oil refinery as a chef.

So able was he that he was soon running the business from the Bateman head office at Brooke House, 212 Shepherd's Bush Road, while retaining the financial office above a department store in Southend, Keddies, where Bateman did the catering. Jack Bateman quickly began to rely on Lewis and left most decisions to him – "he was probably more interested in his girlfriends than in the company," admits Hilary Lewis. "He was the most striking looking man you've ever seen."

When Graham and Hilary got married, Jack paid for a first class cabin on the SS France as a wedding present, with a trip to Las Vegas and Los Angeles thrown in.

*Graham Lewis: he drove Bateman's profits with some success – **and asked Hilary Charles to massage his feet.***

"He was always very generous – but he got a great deal in return," she says.

Lewis' skill was in finance, something which Jack did not really understand. One day, Jack wanted a new Rolls Royce but was told by Lewis that it was either that or the wages payment for the week would have to be delayed. An hour later, Jack called back and said: "Cracked it, Graham! Buy two – one for you!" And he did just that.

Lewis is remembered with fondness by many in his team though he had his idiosyncrasies.

"I liked him – he had a lot to offer. I remember he always used to wear blue socks and when you went to his office he had his dog, a terrier, with him – an aggressive little creature," recalls Nigel Anker, who eventually rose to be a regional director until Gerry Robinson's buy-out of Compass in 1985. "One day the dog bit me but RGL didn't seem to care much."

Jim Cartwright says that Lewis won a major contract by seeing a potential client one day, writing the proposal on his way back in his Rolls and sending it off the next day. "The client was so impressed with the speed of the reply, we got the contract. He was always spot-on – he said once to me that there were only two things you ever had to remember – what's the gross profit and how many staff do you employ? That's not bad advice in my book."

Lewis was always very pernickety. He liked going around the units and pointing out discrepancies and other mistakes. Once, he demanded fresh orange juice at a unit, which they didn't have. On the next visit the site manager was careful to offer the juice but it was in glasses that were too tall to access from the front but Lewis insisted on helping himself and promptly got the juice down his trousers. He was not best pleased. On another visit he demanded the unit served sausage rolls.

He was, in one colleague's word, a cost manager, not a cost-cutter. He was also good with staff.

"When you dealt with RGL, you always needed a white rabbit," says Nigel Anker. "You always had to produce something new for him – some way of cutting costs or increasing profit. He was always demanding something extra."

"Very early on, I had joined as a management trainee and got a huge amount of training in many different units, but I eventually wanted to do something different and was about to leave," says Pam Evans, who became training manager.

"There was a meeting of quite a few of us trainees with RGL who asked us all if we were happy and I said, 'No, I wasn't'. He hauled me over and asked why not? I said I wanted to get out of ops and into something else – sales or personnel were the first things that came to mind. Graham took note and the next thing I knew I had a call from Hilary Charles – and the rest is history, as they say.

"Graham really did take notice and he wanted his people to be happy. And he had a wicked sense of humour."

Del Bampton tells the story of Lewis attending the opening of the Esso Terminal in Pembroke, a major contract win. After the meal, Lewis took out a sixpence and waved it at the waitress who served them. Thinking it was a tip (this was 1967) the waitress was happy but Lewis gave it to her and said. "This is a sixpence – enough for you to buy some pumice so that you can rub the nicotine off your fingers."

He enjoyed being a ladies man – "much too much; he wouldn't have got away with it today," says one contemporary. He was also considered a positive leader as well as something of an eccentric. He had an untiring sense of humour which sometimes went to dangerous lengths.

Once, driving his Rolls Royce at night, he was pulled over by a policeman and was breathalysed twice, with no result. Asked for his name, Lewis said he was the Bishop of Sunningdale.

David Bateman describes him as a cabaret act – "he could be very funny". At his first meeting, Alan Robinson, who

eventually became a director of Bateman, met Lewis in a country house acting as the butler and getting the tea, until he revealed his identity. The reason why Tony Ward-Lewis, shortly after he joined the company, had to reinstate Ward to his name – "I thought Ward-Lewis was too snobbish" – is because RGL had had a call from someone who opened the conversation with 'How are you old bugger?' "One of us will have to change our name," said Graham Lewis, firmly. "It'll have to be you." Henceforth, it was back to Ward-Lewis.

He hated telephones and used to do much of his work in the back of the car, unlike Jack Bateman who lived by the phone – "Thank God mobiles weren't around then," says Hilary Lewis. When Pat Lichtensteiger was northern director, one of his young children answered the phone on a Sunday morning – Bateman would phone any time of the day or night – and called out to Lichtensteiger: "Dad, it's Mr bloody Bateman on the phone for

Bob Botting had been with Bateman, man and boy, all his career. His retirement lunch, with past and present Bateman colleagues – some in retirement themselves - was held at the Institute of Chartered Accountants in 1988. Clockwise: David Bateman, Pat Lichtensteiger, Charles Evans (hidden - formerly managing director, Factory Restaurants), Graham Lewis, Hilary Charles, David Unwin, Kevin Birmingham, Bill Stead, Charles Allen (then managing director, Grandmet Vending), Bob Botting, Pat Beavan (head of office administration), Tony Ward-Lewis, Phil Morley and John Symonds.

you!" Unfortunately, Mr bloody Bateman heard it.

Hilary Charles admits to Lewis' eccentricities – "He used to put his feet on my lap in his office and tell me to massage them" – but says that his record spoke for itself. "The company increased its profits throughout his regime," she says.

"Graham was all right as long as you didn't believe a word he said," she adds. Being a woman probably helped; in the early 1970s she got on with the job and introduced a new technique that was then beginning to sweep through industry generally – management by objectives or MBO. It is standard management practice today but was revolutionary then.

"This was the late 1960s and MBO had become the in-thing. I thought it would help us to move from a typical first-generation family firm into a professional outfit."

An article in the *Financial Times*, extolling the impact of MBO on Bateman,

Sir Max Joseph: he bought both Bateman and Midland Catering for the cash flow.

Salary for Trainee Sales Person

January 1969   £37/8/9p   per week

Courtaulds Group fees (10th July 1969)

Fee   12 guineas +5% of income

Discount

Fees to reduce by	4.50% if total income is between	10,000 and 20,000
	4.00% on next 10K	20,000 and 30,000
	3.50% on next 10k	30,000 and 40,000
	Negotiate	over 40,000
Add	£4 Night service	
	£1 Saturday morning	
	£3 All day Saturday	
	£4 any part of Sunday	

Management fee guidelines for 1972 (ther year of decimalisation)

		Basic Fee p.w	% of turnover	Minimum fee
Bateman Catering	London	£25.00	3%	£33.00
Factory Restaurants	London	£15.00	3%	£19.00
Bateman Catering	North	£17.00	3%	£21.00
	South	£20.00	3%	£24.00
	Wales	£13.00	3%	£17.00
	Scotland	£13.00	3%	£18.00
	Midlands	£14.00	3%	£18.00
	Newcastle	£13.00	3%	£17.00

ADD

Manual weekday nights	£5.00
Saturday AM	£1.00
All day Saturday	£2.00
Any part of Sunday	£3.00

Costings for Proposals
For sale in Vending machines

Soup			1.7p
Fruit Juice			1.0p
Other Starters			3.7p
Main meal type	A	Potatoes + 1 Veg	9.0p
Main meal type	B	Potatoes + 1 Veg	10.5p
Main meal type	C	Potatoes + 1 Veg	14.0p
Main meal type	D	Potatoes + 1 Veg	17.5p
Sweet	A		1.9p
Sweet	B		2.3p
Sweet	C		2.9p
Tea			0.55p
Coffee			1.25p
Cakes			1.9p
Buttered roll			1.5p
Buttered roll	+ cheese		2.0p
Buttered roll	+ meat		2.5p
Wrapper for	Roll		0.3p
Wrapper for	main meal		0.8p

In 1969, when Bob Botting was sales manager of Bateman, he told new recruit Philip Morley to make notes in a little black book about the key facts he would need to assemble proposals to potential clients. "He said I should guard it with my life because our competitors in those days would have liked to view our fee structure and costings. I still have it."

described the company's management structure as autocratic with no formal communications and with little conscious appraisal of long-term objectives. MBO was designed to meet all these challenges. Initially, the board was very leery about the idea but Lewis and Lichtensteiger, the managing director, were eventually convinced of the need for it and the process was introduced throughout the company.

"It did work for us," says Hilary Charles. "We worked with the staff to introduce it and in the first three years, turnover rose from £6.9m to £9.2m with a 31 per cent increase in net profit. It clarified responsibilities and gave us a long-term plan. At the same time, it cut staff turnover.

'It would never have happened without Graham's and Pat's support and they really drove it through the company, to its great advantage. They were quite far-sighted."

Del Bampton, who worked with Charles for a number of years, is convinced that she was a major force in making sure that Bateman was forward looking and believes that her contribution to the company was 'tremendous', ensuring that the sometimes opposing views of Lewis and Lichtensteiger were translated into sensible company policies.

"There's no question, she was greatly admired in the company and in the world of personnel generally. I think many men were afraid of her – she was forceful, knew what she wanted, kept it logical and stuck to her guns. We were lucky to have her."

It was Hilary Charles who recognised that staff were the company's only asset – coining the phrase that was used by the company in its promotional material.

Bateman was also an early convert to bringing road shows to the catering colleges in order to recruit the best students.

"Colleges in those days were only interested in encouraging their students into hotels and possibly restaurants," she recalls. "Contract catering was the lowest of the low. We tried to do something about that and our road shows put over the story that contract catering was not just about mass feeding but operated at the top end, too. I think they did much to raise the image of contracting in the eyes of young people in the colleges – and in the eyes of the lecturers, too, who mostly had come up through the hotel sector.

"We also got heads of catering colleges together to give them the same message."

Graham Lewis supported these efforts, recognising that success depended on recruiting the right staff.

He was a canny operator. Tony Ward-Lewis recalls that when he visited clients he used to meet the area or regional manager offsite, leaving the Rolls in a secure parking place. Lewis then went on to the site in the area manager's car – "because the manager knew where he was going" – but secretly because he didn't want the client to see how much money the company was making by revealing the Rolls Royce. En route to the site, Lewis would note the relevant names of the team on the inside of his double cuff. "People were astounded and flattered that he knew their names."

To grow the business, Bateman used the outside catering side to sell his company's services by entertaining potential and existing clients at early evening cocktail parties in the dining rooms of some of the most exclusive Bateman contracts in London. The food provided at these events was very high quality not to say expensive (which the clients, knowingly or not, helped to support financially). It was a method of sales that proved to be highly successful - one *Look to Europe* evening in Wolverhampton Town Hall, attended

and opened by the Lady Mayor, yielded six confirmed contracts.

* * *

By 1967, Jack Bateman was coming up to 60 and had decided that he wanted the money to retire and to pay off some hefty debts. The first time his son, David – who had taken over the northern region in 1966 succeeding Pat Lichtensteiger who had moved to head office as managing director – heard of the deal was an urgent phone call on holiday in Menorca. He was needed back in London to sign some papers.

Looking around for a favourable exit, Bateman had approached Maxwell Joseph whom he had known as a young man. Bateman had reputedly had an offer for the business and wanted Joseph's advice as chairman of Grand Metropolitan Hotels on whether to take it or not. He met Joseph at his house, together with Grand Metropolitan's joint managing director, Ernest Sharp. Rather than giving him advice, however, Joseph made him an offer for the Bateman business which may, indeed, have been Jack's wily intention all along as the name of the other company was never revealed. Hilary Lewis tells another story about the purchase.

"Jack took Graham along to talk to Max Joseph about a deal but, as was often the case, he had a lunch date, probably with a lady friend. In the middle of the meeting, Jack suddenly said: 'Oh my God! I'll be late for lunch! Graham – you deal with it!' Graham protested but Jack said: 'I hereby grant you permission to sell the company'. Graham said: 'But what about David's 10 per cent share?' Jack said: 'That's alright. Just get on with it!' And Graham sold the company on two pieces of paper." In fact, David was not even aware that he had 10 per cent of the business.

A family business for 77 years: the Bateman Story

The Bateman family connection with catering goes back at least 77 years according to David Bateman, current chairman of Casil's parent the Bateman Group of Companies. Casil Courier offers a brief history of "one o the few reasonably-sized family businesses still in the game," says David.

David Bateman

Raquel celebrates 10 years

Just a month after being promoted to Assistant Manager at IBM Greenford, Raquel Wierzbicka, ('Vierz-bicka, I think!' she smiled) celebrated 10 years with Casil in October. 'She's proof that if you back Casil's training with hard work and loyalty you'll be rewarded," said her Manager, Ian Sinclair.

Raquel arrived from her native Spain in 1981 and ran a wine bar in the City of London, joining Casil at IBM Greenford in October 1986 as a General Assistant. By Christmas she had gained promotion, progressing to Cashier

Romance brought the Bateman family and industrial catering (as it was then known) together. In 1919, a Mrs Ellis had founded a pioneering industrial catering company, D A Ellis and Co Ltd, based in Wembley, Mrs Ellis's daughter, Beryl, met David Bateman's father, Jack, and they were married in the early thirties. So Mrs Ellis became David's grandmother. During the courtship, both helped out in the family business and became acquainted with industrial catering, still in its formative stages.

The onset of war and the Factory Canteens Order of 1940, made it compulsory for every factory with 250

David Bateman drove CASIL's growth by emphasising the long history of Bateman Catering.

So, in September 1967, GrandMet acquired all Bateman shares for £475,000 cash (£7.7m in today's money) and 910,000 Ordinary Grandmet shares worth the same again.

Thoughts of Bateman going public, to the benefit of some staff getting shares or share options, however, were dashed. All that the senior staff received from GrandMet, according to Lichtensteiger writing in the company newspaper *Feedback,* was a demand to double the profits in three years (actually achieved in two-and-a-half years). Why GrandMet, which then was purely a hotel company with a number of large London properties and an expanding hotel empire in Europe, wanted to purchase a contract catering company with no physical assets and a large number of mainly short-term contracts is something of a mystery. A history of the company, written by W.J Reader, a Cambridge don – *A History of Grand Metropolitan:*

1961-1986 – commissioned by Stanley Grinstead, the then managing director (but only completed after he had left when the publication was discontinued by his successor, Alan Sheppard) quotes Joseph as being very upbeat about the deal:

"Bateman is one of the leading firms in the field of industrial catering and we believe that in addition to the usual benefits of economies of purchasing and administration, it will provide a platform for the further profitable expansion of our interests." No doubt it was the thought of all the money that Bateman would generate with its cost-plus contracts without the need for any capital investment that attracted.

At the time of the takeover, Jack Bateman was appointed joint chairman of the company with Joseph, but the arrangement lasted only a few months and he left soon afterwards, as did David Bateman; a restriction clause prevented them from setting up a rival catering business for five years. Jack, with a need for more money to finance his somewhat chaotic domestic life-style, took over his three brothers' company, Bateman Cleaning Services, which was then losing money. He paid his brothers nothing for the company but guaranteed a life pension for them all, an arrangement which endured to 2013 when the last brother died.

Jack and David took charge of Bateman's Cleaning and brought it into profit, Jack as chairman and David as Northern director. Rebate Services (Catering Centres) was also formed in 1972. With the two companies, Rebate was part of a plan to cover the whole range of support services to industry, an early example of a full facilities management company.

Both prospered, Rebate Catering puzzlingly for a time in association with Golden Egg, a popular restaurant chain, which promised to 'offer a new deal for the

industry' but which was not successful. With offices as far north as Lancashire and Teeside, Rebate Cleaning had a slew of major contracts, such as Shell Centre, IBM, London Weekend Television, Manchester Airport and Milton Keynes Development Corporation, while Rebate Catering boasted De La Rue, BP Oil, Davy Construction as well as parts of the RAF. Initially Rebate Catering operated out of an office in Leicester and quickly gained business, claiming it was only interested in contracts with companies employing more than 1,000 people, thus setting itself up in direct competition with the bigger contractors.

At the outset, Rebate offered guaranteed fixed cost catering contracts which included take-home foods that could be made to order during the day and taken home in the evening at a competitive price (hence the Golden Egg involvement) as well as an 'almost certain' claimed reduction in the subsidy. The business grew but although it boasted of operating throughout the UK, according to *Pacesetters,* produced by *Caterer and Hotelkeeper* in 1978, turnover was £3m (£15m today) – just a tenth of the size of either Bateman or Sutcliffe Catering at the time.

Nevertheless, a year later, when Bateman was 71, Rebate Holdings was sold for £1.9m (£8.6m today) to Barrowmill, a city consortium created as a financial vehicle for acquisitions. Jack Bateman had struck another profitable deal.

Earlier, in 1972, barely outside his restriction agreement with Max Joseph, Jack had formed Catering Advisory Services International Ltd (CASIL).

* * *

In fact, CASIL was not an original idea – it originated long before in 1954 when Jack was running Bateman Catering. He had formed CASIL with the ambitious aim of advising continental companies to improve the standard of mass catering in Europe – an idea that was put on the shelf until, in 1967, it was revived by Graham Lewis, who optimistically told the *Financial Times* that "he would be very disappointed if £150,000 worth of advisory fees was not exceeded in the first 12 months" and stoutly rebuffed the accusation of taking coals to Newcastle by saying that "in many instances, bulk food on the continent is rather worse than bulk food in England."

Some work had already been undertaken – the National Bank of Belgium had already been engaged – which led Lewis to claim that if the bulk of staff catering on the continent was capable of as much improvement as that of the Bank there would be ample work for the new subsidiary. "The Bank's directors would agree with me," he added, somewhat defensively.

But Europe's companies were largely resistant to the CASIL charms and the idea never took off. After Jack Bateman revived the name in 1972, CASIL only ever operated in the UK as the catering division of a new holding company, Bateman Contract Services, which included Bateman's Cleaning Services (a successor to Rebate Cleaning) and Janitoria, a cleaning materials supplier. Again under Jack's chairmanship and David's direction, CASIL grew into a company selling both fixed term and cost-plus contracts by the time of its sale in 1998, claiming that 60 per cent of its business was fixed price – "We prefer it because it keeps us on our toes," David Bateman told *Industrial Caterer*. "It has a good effect on our staff and their attitude to work."

A surprisingly confident and punchy CASIL brochure continued this theme: "With us, the fixed price contract is more

the rule than the exception. The majority of our clients appoint us on this basis, but only because they prefer to. We are perfectly prepared to work on a cost-plus basis for any client who may prefer it."

The CASIL story was clearly persuasive. The brochure boasted that the company was the only catering contractor in the UK to be awarded a full food service contract by the US Air Force; other contracts included companies such as IBM, Lesney Toys, Black and Decker, Legal & General and Prudential. Indeed, CASIL continued to grow though Jack took less and less of an interest in the business with David eventually taking over the running of the company. Jack died in 1988 of liver disease aged 80. It had been a helter-skelter of a life and heavy drinking had taken its toll – "But he was never drunk," says David Bateman.

"My father was an extraordinary person," he recalls. "He was always full of ideas. We would groan every time he said 'I've got an idea!' and say 'What is it this time?' He once had an idea to franchise the cleaning services in Southampton, saying 'All they need is some notepaper and a lavatory brush!' He had a habit of meeting people in pubs and offering them a job."

He also had a huge sense of humour and a peculiar sense of the ridiculous.

"I can remember board meetings where we had to stop the business because my father was almost literally lying on the floor crying with laughter. The tears would be rolling down his cheeks and he would take five minutes to recover."

David carried on with the business for another 10 years until, in 1998, at the age of 61, he sold the industrial cleaning and janitorial companies for just north of £2m to David Evans who owned a company called Broadreach: two years later, it was sold on to McLennon International and disappeared from sight.

Jack Bateman was one of the industry's founders – a larger-than-life personality with considerable drive and ample charm, who lived life to the full. His death deprived the industry of one of its most charismatic leaders. Curiously, his public profile was never to the fore and there are few references to him in the press. At Bateman Catering, Graham Lewis managed the public profile and up to its sale in 1967 Jack and Graham were in perfect partnership. His company, created in the heat of the wartime years, went on to be one of the most successful in peacetime and he lived to see it become one of the founding pillars of Compass.

Jack always claimed he knew nothing about catering.

"But then," says David Bateman, "there are quite a lot of people who have done the same. They just know the right people to employ."

CHAPTER SIX

*Sutcliffe Catering:
the marines take over*

Very few of the early pioneers were catering trained; at Sutcliffe the marines organised the company, military-style.

Curiously, none of the personalities who created the early contract catering companies, except John Gardner, was in any shape or form a caterer by training. Roland Webb at Midland Catering was an accountant by profession and Bruce, his son, was ex-Royal Navy and an engineer. John Earnshaw Sutcliffe reached the rank of Major in the Royal Marines after serving in South East Asia Command but, by all accounts, was invalided out; how he met Jack Bateman on his return to civilian life is not known. Jack Bateman himself had but a tenuous connection with his mother-in-law's contract catering company, D Ellis & Co, and never professed to know anything about catering. Ken Graveney, who joined John Sutcliffe in 1951 and who went on to be managing director between 1975 and 1979, was a commando who landed on the Normandy Beaches on D Day. Mickie O'Brien, who joined Sutcliffe in 1950 and was managing director between 1965-72, was

Credit Ed Lacey/Popperfoto

John Earnshaw Sutcliffe: more interested in horses – but founded a catering empire. "We don't train people. You either sink or swim." Sutcliffe trained the horse Specify, which won the Grand National in 1971.

chief instructor of the commando assault unit of the Royal Marines and a decorated hero of the Allied landings in Normandy in 1944 where he was awarded an immediate MC. Major 'Squid' Horton, an ex-Royal Marine, who became managing director of Factory Canteens (West of England) Ltd and effectively John Sutcliffe's deputy in the early days, joined the company in 1947.

What these military characters knew about cooking could be written on the back of an envelope. Indeed, in 1951, when Sutcliffe, who had met O'Brien in 1947, asked him to run the contract of eight canteens for the Port of Bristol authority, O'Brien protested that he knew nothing

John Sutcliffe and Ken Graveney: the fact that Ken was given paid time off to spend only a day or so a week in the office while captaining Gloucestershire for two whole seasons was symptomatic of the Sutcliffe era.

about catering. "And I can't boil a bloody egg," replied Sutcliffe. It was probably true. John Sutcliffe was more interested in cricket and horses and went on to train the 1971 Grand National winner, Specify, owned by Fred Pontin.

What these characters didn't know about catering, however, they made up in their organisational and leadership skills. Tough and ready to brook no nonsense, neither from clients nor staff, they made sure they employed people (mainly women in the kitchens) who knew about catering while they busied themselves making sure the company was efficient, that the clients were satisfied and, most important, more and more clients were sold the contract catering story and the money kept rolling in so they could spend it on their own life style.

The military background of its key personalities – and particularly that of the commandos – undoubtedly had an impact on Sutcliffe's company philosophy. They believed that only small groups of trained, skilled

men, with good leadership skills, could successfully achieve objectives. Translating this philosophy to the company was the secret of its initial success. They looked after their men. When Brian Appleton, who was in his early 20s when in charge of the West Midlands region, went down with TB, John Sutcliffe kept him on a year's paid leave of absence while he recovered in a sanatorium.

* * *

Sutcliffe was appointed managing director of Jack Bateman's Factory Canteens in 1944. It was a relationship that prospered. Bateman recognised Sutcliffe's ability to lead and largely left him to it but, like many since, Sutcliffe began to think of starting up on his own. He could see the opportunities that lay ahead and in 1946 announced he was quitting. Bateman was not best pleased at the initiative but the parting of ways was sufficiently amicable for Sutcliffe to take a small handful of

Bateman canteens, employing 30 staff and worth £5,000 (£185,000 today) in Stroud, Birmingham and Cornwall, and operating from an office in Stroud. This was in return for an agreement that he would confine his activities to the West Country – hence the title of his company, Factory Canteens (West of England) Ltd, which might have been confused with Jack Bateman's company based in London.

The Sutcliffe business prospered and in 1951 a sporty J.V (John) Smith – he had won blues at Cambridge for both rugby and athletics and played rugby for England, the Barbarians and Rosslyn Park and plenty of cricket, too (something that greatly endeared him to Sutcliffe) – joined the new company as catering manager for the Port of Bristol Authority. It was the position that Mickie O'Brien was hired to take up a year later.

Like O'Brien, Smith – who had just come down from university where he had read

agriculture – knew nothing about catering but for Sutcliffe his sporting credentials were enough to give him the job of operating eight canteens providing meals for 4,000 – 'all men, no women' – every day throughout the vast site – then one of the busiest ports in the country. "Sport was very important to John Sutcliffe," Smith says.

At his interview, Sutcliffe told him to start on the following Monday. Smith baulked: "But I haven't had any training." Sutcliffe dismissed the protest. "We don't train people. You either sink or swim," he replied. "Your job is to keep 4,000 dockers happy." The salary was good – £600 a year plus £100 tax free, plus a car and no-questions-asked-expenses at a time when the average wage was nearer £400. The car was particularly attractive.

Smith's eight-month year period at the port took in the threat of strikes and the sacking of three staff working as prostitutes

on the site. After the latter imbroglio had been successfully concluded (in the process winning over the 13 site unions involved by asking them what they would have done in the same circumstances) he was given a friendly piece of advice by Jack Jones, who was then regional organiser for the Transport and General Workers' Union (TGWU) for the West of England and Wales docks (later general secretary of the union):

"You did the right thing. But never sack a woman alone without witnesses. If one of those three had ripped her blouse open and screamed you would have been out of a job."

Another to be taken on at the same time was Ken Graveney who had started at the Port of Bristol Authority a little before John Smith. Graveney, whose father-in-law was in charge of the National Union of Seamen at the port – one of the 13 unions involved – was appointed Smith's assistant.

Kenneth Richard Graveney, born in

How Sutcliffe Catering got its name

In 1952, Sutcliffe looked to expand into London. He set up a small office in Acton and told John Smith, then running the catering at the Port of Bristol, to go and 'open up in London'. Smith replied that this wasn't sensible – Jack Bateman was already operating his company with a similar name (Factory Canteens) and that would be confusing. Sutcliffe, who didn't like opposition, asked Smith what he would do.

"I told him that I would use the Sutcliffe family name. I would call it Sutcliffe Catering Group as the holding company, and I would use the Sutcliffe name for the London company. As the company expanded, the new companies could follow suit."

Sutcliffe, not welcoming arguments, harrumphed and said he would think it over. The next day he hauled Smith back into his office.

"What do you think of this, then?" he demanded, flinging a piece of paper over the table.

Looking down, Smith saw that Sutcliffe had taken his advice with a vengeance, even as far as a suggestion that the company should expand to Australia. His own name was listed as one of the directors of the London office: John Sutcliffe (chairman) 'Squid' Horton, John Smith and Margaret Arnott.

"That's how the Sutcliffe name came into use and how Sutcliffe Catering was originally created," says Smith.

John Smith suggested to John Sutcliffe a new name for Factory Canteens – which stuck.

1924 and always known as Ken, was part of a cricketing family. His younger brother Tom was an elegant Test player and his son David had a long cricket career with Gloucestershire; both captained the county. Graveney had played in a few matches for Gloucestershire in both 1947 and 1948 and then regularly in 1949, when he took 59 wickets, including all 10 wickets in an innings for 66 runs against Derbyshire. A back injury sustained on the Normandy landings with the Royal Marines plagued him throughout his career and forced him to retire from first class cricket after the

1951 season, yet 12 years later, in 1963 at the age of 39, he was appointed to lead the county side – this, in spite of the fact that he was a director of Sutcliffe's West Country company and a member of the main group board. The fact that Graveney was given paid leave to spend only a day or so a week in the office while captaining Gloucestershire for two whole seasons, was symptomatic of the Sutcliffe era. To have a well known county cricketer as a director was regarded as a positive bonus for the company, irrespective of the fact that he was able to play very little part in Sutcliffe's business.

Sutcliffe was not only interested in cricket and horse racing – the latter an underlying feature of the company – but rugby and other sports were well supported. Seats at Cardiff Arms Park were well used; they were particularly aimed at valued clients but were plentifully used by those in the company, but those who had played it at school or university were always given priority. A young trainee salesman, working for the West of England Company, who was a professional golfer in all but name, was billeted in the group office in Cheltenham and given paid release to play in

Credit Topfoto/EUFD

Hotelympia – previously called the Hotel, Restaurant and Catering Exhibition – was not only an exhibition of (mainly) kitchen equipment but a means of showing off – and testing – catering and food and beverage service skills as well.

golf competitions.

At head office in Ealing, one of the receptionists was a good enough runner to get an Olympic trial and she would have been given several months paid leave to prepare if she had been selected. One sport that didn't figure, however, was football, which might have been a touch too plebeian for Sutcliffe's tastes.

* * *

John Sutcliffe's agreement to stick to the West Country was fine on paper, but hardly stood the test of time. In 1948 he had already formed Factory Canteens (Midlands) Ltd expanding into Bristol, north into Birmingham and Coventry and south into Gloucestershire and the Forest of Dean. A key figure in this expansion was W.E (Billy) Epsom, a former chef with experience of

Mickie O'Brien MC: battle hardened, heavy drinker and an inspired leader.

catering at sea and in Canadian Pacific Railway hotels in Canada. Always wearing striped trousers and a black jacket, Epsom frequently visited the units and took a close interest in stock levels, checking on the unit's ordering; it was not uncommon to see his smart jacket and trousers flecked with flour as he delved deep into the store cupboards. He became managing director of the Midlands company in 1948 and remained there for the next 14 years building up the business with Brian Smith, who had worked for Epsom since 1958 and became managing director on Epsom's death in 1962.

Sutcliffe (Northern) Ltd opened in 1954 and Sutcliffe (Wales) Ltd in 1959 with an office in Scotland opening in 1961 with Gordon Wishart as director operating five contracts. Even in 1959, a company brochure which lists over 200 clients throughout the country still names Factory Canteens (Midlands) Ltd and Factory Canteens (West of England) as operating vehicles. It was not until 1960 that all of them were re-branded as Sutcliffe Catering.

John Smith went to London in 1953 with Margaret Arnott, who was a qualified caterer, and with Smith in charge of organisation and sales. A very capable secretary, who had previously been secretary to Sir Archibald Sinclair, the leader of the Liberal Party, completed the small office.

But the abolition of food rationing in 1954 had changed the way clients were looking at staff catering. The need to provide a hot meal to workers was not now a statutory requirement and clients were becoming more reluctant to spend money on it. It was not such an easy sell. To make matters worse, in the same year Smith's father, who ran the family animal feed business, suffered a heart attack and Smith had an ultimatum: come back and run the business or have it sold.

"I had to go back. John Sutcliffe was not pleased." John Smith's short foray into

A senior Sutcliffe team meeting at the Welcombe Hotel, Stratford: no company occasion went by without liquid refreshment and, true to form, this was one no exception. Left to right, Ken Graveney (West of England), Brian Smith (Midlands), Desmond Blackburn (North), Major 'Squid' Horton (West of England), Derek Howard (South), Eddie Crutch (Midands), Gordon Wishart (Scotland) and Marc Verstringhe (London).

catering was over.

Margaret Arnott took charge of London, a position which she held until 1968 when Marc Verstringhe succeeded her; she was with the company until 1973, latterly as a consultant to the company. By 1971, with the expansion north and into Wales and Scotland, rather than staying a small company based in Stroud, Sutcliffe had grown into a national holding company with seven regional subsidiary companies, over 700 units in the UK and a few abroad, and by 1973 employed more than 8,000 staff

Sutcliffe was convinced that the regional structure kept the company close to the client and clients close to the company. It was undoubtedly a successful strategy in its time and earned Sutcliffe a reputation for being a

---

The Sutcliffe dress code

There was a certain army conformity in the dress code. At any Sutcliffe conference most male delegates would wear more or less identical grey suits, white shirts, black shoes and short hair (women were free to wear what they liked except trousers; these were frowned upon, which, according to one contemporary, led to some extraordinary outfits.)

Brian Williams, who had been appointed group sales executive in 1970 and subsequently group sales director, once wore a new cream shirt his wife had bought him.

O'Brien spotted him and said: "Brian, why are you wearing a dirty shirt?" Williams said that is wasn't dirty – "It's new and it was clean on this morning."

O'Brien was totally unconvinced. "No – it's dirty. Now go and buy yourself a dozen white shirts on the company and let's stop this nonsense."

---

quality caterer that responded to client needs, but with so many regional autonomous companies, the company was a difficult beast to control. While it was producing an excellent cash flow, its profits were nothing to write home about. "I want to make enough money to train the horses," Sutcliffe is said to have remarked. It was a remark of some truth. Sutcliffe's first love was horses; the company was the means to achieving this end.

A year after the name change, he sold out to Olympia Ltd, famous for its exhibition hall in London, for £250,000 (£3m today). It was a curious purchase for a property and exhibition company, though perhaps no odder than Grand Metropolitan Hotels' purchase of Bateman Catering and Midland Catering: a copious cash flow and little capital investment were the most obvious attractions. It is not known why Sutcliffe relinquished the ownership of the company so soon nor why Olympia wanted to move into a sector that it knew very little about, but one reason might have been the fact that Olympia was a Sutcliffe client and John Sutcliffe knew Olympia's senior people. There may also have been a horse-racing connection. Besides, Sutcliffe could probably have done with the money; training horses was proving to be an expensive pastime. Sutcliffe became chairman and remained so until 1965, leaving him more time to attend to his horses; the ex-commando Mickie O'Brien was appointed managing director.

* * *

Albert Peter O'Brien, always called Mick or Mickie by those who knew him well but Mr O'Brien by others who feared his temper, was a short, no-nonsense, hard-drinking soldier, battle-hardened and brave, who claimed that his blood group was Johnnie Walker Scotch whisky. It was alleged that he drank a bottle

---

of Scotch a day though some who knew him well refute this. However, drink was certainly a constant among all these ex-army types.

'Squid' Horton, who became managing director of Factory Canteens (West of England) and later of Sutcliffe (West of England), was known to carry miniatures of Champagne in his briefcase every day. Marc Verstringhe recalls that he found five miniatures in Horton's case when they were staying at the Dorchester in London. Horton, impatient for Champagne to be delivered by room service, told Verstringhe to get the drink from his case. They were all heavy drinkers. Peter Aldrich, who joined the company from Bateman, recalls that there were regular invitations to Ken Graveney's office in the late afternoon to join others for a drink; they were sessions that could go on for several hours.

Peter Davies, initially based in Bristol, who had joined Sutcliffe as personnel and training director in 1973 from a career in the motor and engineering industries and latterly as lecturer and consultant at the West of England Business School (which had been attended by some senior Sutcliffe people), recalls that the Goldsmiths Arms in Acton was the regular Sutcliffe watering hole. It was there that Champagne, wine and spirits flowed in equal measure.

"The pub stocked Mickie O'Brien's favourite Champagne and poured it out as soon as he came through the door. The first time I came up for a meeting with him, Ken Graveney and Marc Verstringhe we adjourned to the pub for lunch. Innocent that I was, I really didn't realise that by the time we sat down, I would be practically legless. I spent the lunch hour in the Gent's with repeated solicitous visits by Ken to see how I was. After two hours I was fit enough to get into Ken's chauffer-driven car – the senior managers had driver/handymen in those days – to go back to Bristol. Strangely enough, rather than being disgraced, Ken and Mickie O'Brien and Marc thought it was a huge joke. It taught me a lesson."

Mickie O'Brien was either loved or feared. His father had been in the Royal Marines and the son had been brought up in army barracks so the army, as well as the Scotch, was in his blood. In 1944, he had come through a savage battle in the Normandy landings which led to the immediate award of the MC and to the subsequent liberation, a few weeks later at Fecamp, of a great deal of Benedictine – an escapade that led to his commanding officer threatening a castration with a blunt knife, a partial garroting followed by the firing squad. O'Brien said that he had always tried to remember the tirade in case he should ever need to employ it in work (which was not infrequently.) He was later posted to Burma – 'to get some sun' – where he was seriously wounded, but this did not stop him later becoming a climbing instructor in the army before quitting soldiering in 1950. Like other military types, he saw things in simple terms.

"This is a simple business," he told a young Marc Verstringhe in 1961, an area catering supervisor in London who had joined Sutcliffe a year earlier as a manager of the GEC Stoke Coventry contract.

"All you have to do is to find the right people, tell them what you want and let them get on with it – which will give you ample time for a game of golf."

Of course, much depended on the recruitment of the right people, as it still does, and Verstringhe never found time to play much golf. O'Brien was very keen on the game. Verstringhe (and others) had to send a SITREP to O'Brien every week – a term unknown to him at the time but which, in army parlance, meant a Situation Report. This was standard army procedure for field officers to tell their commanding officer what they had done each week.

But not every employee had an entirely amicable relationship with him. "If you've seen the film *Tunes of Glory*, Mickie O'Brien was Major Jock Sinclair, played by Alec Guinness, to a tee. He was army through and through," says Peter Davies.

Davies, himself noted for flamboyant outfits which went against the grain of everything that O'Brien stood for, and which subsequently did not meet with much favour from Stirling Gallacher or Don Davenport either, had been hired by Ken Graveney, then managing director of the West of England company, to visit all the Sutcliffe companies to run a one day course on personnel management, employment law and industrial relations. Graveney had realised that Sutcliffe was woefully unaware and unprepared for 'all these people issues' and recognised that the company had come to the stage, with 6,000 employees, when it needed a personnel and training director. It had only ever had a training director.

The courses were not to O'Brien's liking, however. After the last session in London, when he overheard the presentation through the doors of the conference room not as a delegate, he told Graveney that "he wasn't having that man f*** up the company." At the lunch, Graveney adroitly sat O'Brien and Davies next to each other. Davies mentioned that his father, who had been personnel director of Parkinson Cowan, had given Sutcliffe Midlands its first Birmingham contract in the 1950s; he had also forced Sutcliffe into vending after negotiating a productivity agreement with the site unions which cut out tea breaks in favour of vending machines.

"That did it! A Damascene conversion took place and a few weeks later O'Brien offered me the job of training director at £3,500 a year."

Davies refused and insisted on the title of personnel and training director, at £5,000 plus car and other perks; he joined six months later, thrilled at the prospect. He only discovered later that £5,000 a year was the rate for most of the managing directors.

Jane Baker, who was Sutcliffe's PR manager from 1974 until she was abruptly fired in 1986, recalls that O'Brien's personality was magnetic.

"I never knew anyone who I could call charismatic before – indeed, I didn't know what the word meant until I met him. He could get anyone eating out of the palm of his hand."

Despite the fact that Sutcliffe Catering consisted of largely autonomous companies, with their own cultures, structures and policies, it was seen by those working for it as a very happy ship – a culture that had been largely engendered by Sutcliffe, O'Brien, Horton, Graveney and others.

"Everybody was very committed and loyal to being a 'Sutcliffian'," Peter Davies recalls. "Whenever there were national conferences or meetings, the whole atmosphere felt like a club membership gathering and the *esprit de corps* was palpable. I had never experienced anything like it in my career and I was thrilled to be asked to join the company."

All this held together as the inevitable processes of creating uniformity, started later by Graveney as a result of the takeover by Sterling Guarantee Trust, and reinforced by Stirling Gallacher, was implemented and enforced. But it was not all plain sailing

In every way, O'Brien was a dominating personality in Sutcliffe for nigh on 30 years but his style of management, based on his army upbringing and career, was abrupt and direct; he took no hostages. After one particular military-style run-in, Peter Davies never felt comfortable with him again. "While I feared him, I didn't respect him. He was a very heavy drinker who could lose his dignity on social occasions in front of fairly junior management."

CHAPTER SEVEN

After the war

After the war John Gardner and Peter Merchant merged – and caterers began to take advantage of new technologies.

At the end of the war, contractors had their hands full. In 1945 when war ended, 50 million meals a week were being produced in industrial catering, principally in what would now be called Business and Industry (B&I) – over 2.6bn meals a year. This is almost 1bn more than the entire contracting industry serves today in all the sectors in which FSM companies now operate. However, in the years following the war most of the munitions factories were closed down together with other large factories connected with the war effort. There were other influences at work, too: John Gardner lost the London and North Eastern Railways contract because of the nationalisation of the railways. These closures and the restructuring of industry gradually deprived caterers, both in-house and contractors, of a significant section of their target market. Nevertheless, while the country was recovering from six years of war and rationing still prevailed, they were still providing prodigious numbers

of meals – in 1946 John Gardner was serving 750,000 meals a day in over 600 contracts as well as operating the restaurants that had survived the Blitz, together with a wine and spirit export business. Barkers and its sister company, Practical Catering Systems, were running 900 contracts while Bateman was operating 70 contracts. Midland Catering, too, and Taylorplan, were also prospering.

But other companies that had prospered during the war were not so long-lasting. Jack Bateman's mother-in-law's company D Ellis & Co was bought by John Gardner in 1950 and others on the council of the National Society of Caterers to Industry fell by the wayside. K&A Hall (Caterers) Ltd, The Binden Moore Company, The Bar and Canteen Supply Co, Agar's (1936) Ltd, Carder Canteens and Industrial Canteen Services were either sold or disappeared. Agar's was owned and run by Cyril Belfield-Smith whose son, John, became a prominent consultant, later joining Melvyn Greene to form Greene Belfield-Smith and Co, subsequently absorbed into Touche Ross. However, one company on the council of the NSCI, Nat Abrahams' Staff Caterers Ltd, long survived the war; in fact, it was under

Abrahams' emollient leadership that the HCI merged with the IMA in 1971 and, in the first year of the newly established HCIMA (later the Institute of Hospitality), he became joint chairman with Doris Hatfield, chairman of the IMA.

By 1950, according to the Census of Distribution, the number of industrial canteens had grown to 21,000 with the vast majority (17,000) being single unit outlets employing fewer than 10 workers, although Professor Rik Medlik, in his book *The British Hotel and Catering Industry* (1961), suggests that the real figure was probably at least 25 per cent higher. However, only 1,813 of these were operated by contractors, illustrating the steep decline in contracted outlets since the war. In a later edition of the book, published in 1972, and quoting figures from research by M Koudra, that number had grown to 25,000, of which 4,500 were operated by contractors – contracting clearly began to take off in the 1960s. None of these figures included school meals, further and higher education establishments, hospitals and other welfare outlets which, according to Koudra, comprised a further 51,000 units but only 500 of which were contracted out.

Later, in *Caterer's* 1976 *Pacesetter* magazine, the five largest contractors were credited as Gardner Merchant with 1,800 units (including 1,650 B&I outlets, 120 schools and colleges and 37 hospitals and institutions), Sutcliffe Catering with 750, Bateman Catering 500, Midland Catering 500 (including 420 B&I outlets, 70 schools/colleges and 13 hospitals) and Taylorplan Catering 200 (including 180 B&I outlets, 14 schools/colleges and seven residential units) – a total of 3,750. With many local contractors running a handful of contracts each, contracting was probably operating some 5,000 outlets. These and all other figures quoted should be viewed with caution as it is never clear (even with later BHA Food and Service Management Forum survey figures) whether the numbers refer to contracts, outlets, or individual units within an outlet: a large outlet may have several separate catering units and numerous kiosks.

A year earlier, a survey by Jordan's Dataquest had revealed that Gardner Merchant was by far the largest of the catering contractors.

Despite later claims (see Chapter 10), the 2.7 per cent margin for Gardner Merchant and the 3.0 per cent margin for Bateman were clearly behind Midland's 5.2 per cent.

The *Pacesetter* figures show that contractors were making greater headway in the B&I sector – factory and office staff restaurants – where they had already gained some 20 per cent of the total, than other sectors where their share hovered around one per cent. In fact, as contractors had also made significant inroads into private school catering, where it was estimated they had some 10 per cent of the market, their share of other sectors would have been even less. The hospital and schools market remained largely untapped and to boost its penetration, Peter Merchant, for one, began to offer what it claimed was a non-profit service. How this offer squared with the payment of a management fee it wanted to charge clients is not clear: 400 guineas per annum (£17,000 today) for up to 100 people, 540 guineas for up to 300 people and 1,000 guineas for 1,000 people. The fee was designed just to cover the costs of organising the contract.

For a commercial enterprise, this seems an unlikely scenario though Sir William Garrett, who had been HM Chief Inspector of Factories throughout the war and who had been artfully employed by Peter Merchant as a consultant adviser since 1951, tried to argue

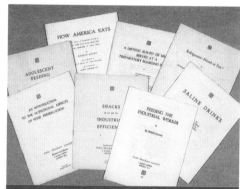

Between 1944 and 1952. Peter Merchant was a prolific publisher of research White Papers, which aimed to give the company credibility in public and government circles.

Financial results, ending October 1975		
	Turnover (£m)	Profit before tax (£m)
Gardner Merchant	67.5	1.87
Sutcliffe Catering	28.0	N/A
Bateman Catering	25.5	0.774
Midland Catering	12.3	0.647

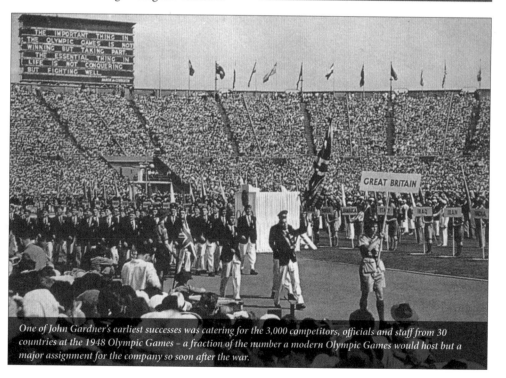

One of John Gardner's earliest successes was catering for the 3,000 competitors, officials and staff from 30 countries at the 1948 Olympic Games – a fraction of the number a modern Olympic Games would host but a major assignment for the company so soon after the war.

Sawyer's Arms

Luncheon 12 noon - 3 p.m.   **Dinner** 6 p.m. - midnight (Sunday 7 p.m. - 11 p.m.) Supper licence. Last meal orders half an hour before closing.

Steak and Plaice Bar

Aperitifs before your meal

Dry Fino Sherry	Glass 2/5	Schooner 3/8
Bristol Milk Sherry	Glass 2/3	Schooner 3/5

Chilled Fruit Juice or Tomato Juice	1/6

Prime Sirloin Steak   12/3

(8 ounces approximate uncooked weight)

Served with chipped potatoes, watercress, tomato roll and butter, and to follow, Ice Cream or cheese and biscuits.

Grilled Gammon Steak   9/6

(6 ounces approximate uncooked weight)

Served with two fried eggs, chipped potatoes, tomato, watercress, roll and butter, and to follow, Ice Cream or cheese and biscuits.

Golden Fried Fillet of Plaice   8/9

(7 ounces approximate uncooked weight)

Served with chipped potatoes, lemon, watercress, roll and butter, and to follow, Ice Cream or cheese and biscuits.

Freshly made Coffee is served in the Bars

Enjoy one of our international coffee specialities.

Wines with your meal

By the glass (one-fifth of a bottle)

Spanish Red, or White (sweet or dry)	3/–

Red

1	Spanish: Burgundy	14/9	
2	Bordeaux: Medoc	18/3	10/3
3	Burgundy: Beaujolais	19/9	10/9
4	Burgundy: Nuits St. Georges	27/9	15/–
5	Italian: Chianti	24/9	13/3

Rose

6	Rose d'Anjou	18/3	9/6

White

7	Spanish: Sauternes	14/9	
8	Spanish: Chablis	14/9	
9	Bordeaux: Graves Superieurs	18/3	10/3
10	Bordeaux: Sauternes	20/3	11/3
11	Burgundy: Pouilly Fuisse	23/9	13/–
12	Hock: Liebfraumilch	22/9	12/6
13	Champagne	45/9	24/–

We are proud of our quick and efficient service. If your time is limited you can complete your meal in 30 minutes from the time you enter the restaurant. Please tell the waitress or the Manager if you are in a hurry.
We shall be happy to welcome you at our other branches. A list of these appears on the back cover.
1/69

The staff of this Berni Inn are very pleased to serve you, and the management are anxious to maintain and further improve the standard of service. If you have any helpful suggestions or comments you would like to make, please talk to the Manager, or write, with full details please, to The Chairman and Joint Managing Director, Paul N. Rosse, Berni Inns Ltd., Berni House, Tailors Court, Bristol 1.

In the 1950s and 1960s, Berni Inns, now long forgotten, were pioneers in popular dining out. With their largely steak-based menus, served in cosy surroundings, their influence on popular catering was immense in leading the British public away from the rigours of food shortages and wartime rationing.

in a Peter Merchant White Paper published in 1952 (13 were published between 1944 and 1952) that the fee was only a means of collecting the wages for all the experts (presumably he meant staff) employed in the organisation. Needless to say, it was not made clear how supplier discounts were dealt with.

* * *

As it emerged from the war, John Gardner won a major piece of business that helped set it up for peacetime. It landed the contract for catering for competitors in the 1948 Olympic Games, held at Wembley Stadium. It was the first great post-war sporting event and nearly 400 catering staff, many of them students,

occupied the RAF Uxbridge base to provide for 3,000 competitors, officials and staff from over 30 nations. In the following 10 years the company expanded its event catering side to include the Richmond Horse Show, Henley Royal Regatta and cricket at the Oval. At its first year in Henley in 1949, it served over 4,000 lunches 7,000 teas and suppers for 350 on the last night. It was also still active in the City Livery Halls and had established a structure of regional offices to service clients like Courtaulds and Vickers, while the company's bakery was making a name for itself; it produced a special cake to mark the production of Ford's millionth car in the UK. By 1961, it was serving one million main meals a week and three million light meals and refreshments.

Even so, those meals were still basic. Though the relaxation of rationing in the early 1950s brought about an increasing availability of fats, enabling caterers to provide meals with a greater nutritional value and variety, tastes remained firmly traditional. Jack Bateman certainly had no illusions. In a brochure promoting his new company CASIL in the 1980s, he painted an unflattering picture of the quality of catering in the wartime years and soon after – the time when he himself was at his most active:

"Think back – if you can and will – to the industrial and business catering scene in the UK, say 30 years ago. Pretty grim – almost Dickensian in some cases! Today, few things contribute more to the personnel strength, well-being and image of a company than its

Credit Topfoto.co.uk : EUFD

In the early 1950s, milk bars were all the rage and many served as social meeting places.

catering standards."

If Bateman was over-egging the pudding just a little to serve his own promotional ends, he was not too wide of the mark. A survey at the time showed that a joint of meat and two vegetables was still the most popular and widely served main dish, with cabbage as the second most popular vegetable after potatoes. No survey conducted today would produce the same result. Nor was the public generally keen to explore new tastes. The introduction of whale meat and snoek (an edible fish indigenous to Australia and South Africa) after the war signally failed to excite the British appetite, despite (or because of)

government exhortations.

Not surprisingly, industrial catering took more than a decade to meet the challenges of the times but its efforts to improve have to be seen against the catering standards in the country generally. Restaurant chains hardly existed and the most popular outside London, where J Lyons predominated, comprised fish and chip shops, milk bars and privately owned cafes. It was not until the mid-1950s that Frank and Aldo Berni, one of the industry's earliest pioneers, opened their first steak restaurant in Bristol in 1956; steak was practically unknown before then. Berni Inns went public in 1962.

Now long forgotten by today's generation but continued into the present day through the Chef and Brewer brand, the Berni brothers' influence on popular catering was immense. The Berni Inn, focusing on steak and French fries served in bright, cheerful surroundings, often using open kitchens, brought a touch of excitement and luxury to what had previously been available. Prawn cocktail, steak and chips and Black Forest gateau became the dishes of the moment.

In London, a couple of years later in 1958, Mario and Franco launched La Terrazza which achieved the same result, if higher up the market, changing the face as well as the taste and social attitudes of London restaurants. Suddenly, Italian food in trendily designed Italian restaurants was all the rage; to eat in La Terrazza was the mark of someone who knew where to eat in London. Mario and Franco subsequently opened other restaurants based along similar lines to La Terrazza which reinforced their impact on the eating out scene.

Other Italian restaurants opened. Coffee bars serving real coffee from hissing Gaggia machines, not seen before in England, became widely popular. Later, Reginald and Philip Kaye launched Golden Egg, bright and brassy, offering coffee and other drinks and meals to a public that was now beginning to seek out new tastes and experiences, which included a burgeoning number of Chinese and Indian restaurants. And then came the pizza and burger bars. In all this activity and development, there is no doubt that the growth of overseas travel encouraged Britons to seek out other new foreign dishes on home soil.

While this on-going revolution was taking place, industrial catering took a little longer to recognise the shift in consumer tastes and expectations. It took another decade or so – probably into the late 1970s – for contractors to realise that they could learn plenty from

Credit Topfoto.co.uk / EUFD

Coffee bars started serving coffee from giant, hissing Gaggia machines, not seen before in England.

He *deserves*
a good meal

He should get it in the works
canteen. Managements and
administrative committees of
257 canteens, serving over
half a million workers, are
finding satisfaction
in the Industrial
Catering Service of
John Gardner
(London) Ltd.

Write for
details:—

JOHN GARDNER (LONDON) LIMITED
Specialists in Industrial Catering
13 GREY STREET, NEWCASTLE-on-TYNE TELEPHONE: 22933
HEAD OFFICE :   ADELAIDE HOUSE • LONDON E.C. 4

*John Gardner promoted its services in this 1948
Soviet-style image of the magisterial iron worker
deserving a good meal for his lunch break.*

to fight the objection; losing a well-known brand name was something to be avoided and Barkers did everything to fight for what it considered its birthright but it eventually had to withdraw from the legal fray. It agreed to change its name to Peter Merchant Ltd, after Herbert Merchant's son, and thereafter it was called Paper Merchant by those who worked for it on account of its predilection for endless reports, records and written instructions.

This setback, however, did not inhibit the company's growth – indeed, it tended to spur it on to greater things. With a new name, Stent and his fellow directors decided that it should expand by going public. To do so, it organised a reverse takeover into Lockhart Smith Ltd, an already publicly quoted company which ran a clutch of restaurants in the north of England. Lockhart Smith became the parent company and, although

the restaurants were eventually sold off, the new contracting company – which was now trading as Peter Merchant – acquired its own butchery and tea business, concentrating exclusively on contract catering and the supply of tobacco products through Herbert Merchant. By 1953, it employed over 10,000 people.

Nevertheless, the mid-1950s were inauspicious times for the British economy and Lockhart Smith (eventually shortened to Lockhart), with Peter Merchant as its contract catering arm, was still suffering from food rationing and the supply of skilled labour. John Pepys, who was chairman of Lockhart and who had succeeded to the title Lord Cottenham, complained in 1954 that it was common knowledge that the catering industry had had a difficult row to hoe in recent years, with constantly fluctuating prices, nearly always in an upward direction,

the high street with the introduction of in-house and national brands and to adopt some of the ideas and catering concepts that were then sweeping through Britain's commercial restaurants. Marc Verstringhe's oft-stated wish to make the canteen literally a *restaurant for staff* was only one manifestation which came to fruition in the 1980s and which was most clearly made manifest when Compass launched its Famous Brands concept.

* * *

Barkers, easily the largest of the wartime contractors, survived the war in good heart but immediately found itself in a controversy. In 1946, Barkers of Kensington, then one of London's leading department stores, objected to the name being used by the contractor. This was a blow because the Barker name had become so identified with food and catering. Initially Robert Stent, now its managing director, and his colleagues were disposed

The first Little Chef outside Lockhart House, Reading. Lockhart brought the brand to the UK which later grew to over 440 units.

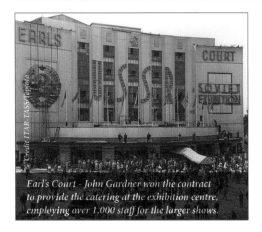

Earl's Court - John Gardner won the contract to provide the catering at the exhibition centre, employing over 1,000 staff for the larger shows.

and with the spiral of wage increases.

Things hadn't improved a year later when he told shareholders:

"The history of your company over the last six years has been one of constant fight against increasing costs... increases in wages and the cost of commodities and services without an equivalent increase in selling prices, have resulted in a smaller margin."

Such complaints continued in the following years as inflation rose, industrial unrest and strikes grew, which had a knock-on impact on turnover, and the availability of basic supplies made life difficult for caterers.

Far-sightedly, the company recognised it had to do something about the chronic skills shortage it was facing and it opened its own training centre – followed by five more. It also established a research laboratory in Oxford to examine the composition of foods and how they could be preserved. It expanded into event catering (winning the contract at Earls Court Exhibition Centre in 1957 employing a staff of over 1,000 for the large shows.) A year later it acquired a vending company, BAC, set up regional offices and then ventured into popular restaurants with Little Chef.

* * *

The boardroom never suffered

The increasingly high cost of office space, particularly in London, forced clients and contractors to rethink the design and cost of staff catering facilities with more emphasis on smarter layout, colour, ambiance and the use of modern equipment and cooking methods. Large dining rooms were being reduced to smaller, more intimate areas in order to attract custom and improve sales by means of a more enjoyable meal experience. Demarcated areas for various grades of worker were abandoned; staff catering became largely classless but catering for the boardroom remained firmly resistant to any change whatsoever.

Both in London and outside, many directors' dining facilities matched those of the most luxurious restaurants; budgets were set but money was no object; caviar and Champagne were frequently *de rigeur* and butler service was commonplace. Such facilities might have been expected in the boardrooms of City banks but even nationalised companies in the regions enjoyed the many and varied fruits of the caterer's labours. One major company in the West End spent over £1m a year on its boardroom dining facility, a figure that could easily be replicated in other companies.

Jim Cartwright, a regional director for Bateman in the 1970s, describes some boardroom facilities in the Midlands as 'phenomenal' with damask table linen, the finest china and cut glass and exceptional wines. "No expense was ever spared," he says. "The standard of catering was as high as any London restaurant – yet people still had the general impression that contractors could only serve plodge and stodge. That was never true. If the client wanted it, the client could get it – and many wanted only the finest in their boardroom."

Gardner Merchant later launched Directors' Table specifically for this market, as did Compass when it engaged Albert Roux and established Roux Fine Dining.

Standards in the City – and in many company boardrooms – were always high and frequently lavish. In 1976, Alan Robinson and Tony Ward-Lewis enjoy lunch at the Institute of Chartered Accountants, then a Bateman contract.

Little Chef was the brainchild of an American caravan manufacturer, Sam Alper. The original idea was for a chain of mobile restaurants which could be transported to venues where demand was high. Lockhart was interested in the concept and formed a company to promote it, but Alper quickly sold out his interest in the project and Lockhart decided to go it alone by setting up a special company, Lockhart Engineering, to manufacture the units. The first Little Chef was in a Portacabin-type unit, consisting of a bar and 10 stools, located outside Lockhart House in Reading, formerly the Rex cinema.

Not surprisingly, the idea of total mobility was found to be impractical for the UK market but Lockhart, recognising that no rival chain existed, believed that the Little Chef brand had potential as a popular diner on busy permanent roadside sites. Initially, Little Chef won plaudits as a convenient eatery serving popular dishes – mainly fried and grilled meat and egg dishes – and it was not long before Little Chefs began to appear across the land, eventually growing, by 1999, to 440 units but since cut back to just over 70.

For Lockhart, expanding into popular catering was a good move, but it was soon after this development, in 1961, that its two largest shareholders, Walter Cardy (now the chairman) and Lord Cottenham (ex-chairman and now acting as consultant) became concerned about the future of the company. Worried that it might pass into foreign hands they approached Trust Houses (TH) to discuss a merger. The appeal to Cardy and his board was that TH was a British-owned hotel company with no catering interests. The appeal to TH was precisely that: it had hitherto no interests in contract catering or in popular restaurants, so acquiring Lockhart (and Peter Merchant with it) broadened its base from hotels into catering. It was the fateful first step

in TH's expansion as a hotel and catering conglomerate which directly led to its merger with Forte and its eventual takeover by Granada – and ultimate dismemberment.

* * *

By all accounts, TH absorbed Lockhart and Peter Merchant without any mishap and for four years both companies prospered. But four years later, in 1964, John Gardner Ltd faced exactly the same decision as Walter Cardy and Lord Cottenham had at Lockhart.

John Gardner had died and his brother Percy was in retirement; the two remaining brothers, Charles and Harold, were both nearing retirement age. What would happen to the company on their departure or death? There were no other family members to take it over and the thought of it being acquired was as anathema to them as it had been to Cardy and Cottenham. So it was for the same reasons that Charles and Harold approached Trust Houses to discuss the formation of an alliance in a defensive move to protect their company from a hostile bid. It was clearly a marriage of convenience, as Gardner Merchant's centenary book makes clear. It was also an uncanny precursor, with the same result and using almost exactly the same language, as Gardner Merchant's alliance with Sodexo in 1995.

A complicated reverse takeover ensued. The Lockhart Group, the subsidiary of TH, was bought by John Gardner and the enlarged Gardner group became a subsidiary of TH with 56.7 per cent of the shares owned by TH; the remaining shares were acquired in 1968. In many ways, it was a merger of equals, though Gardner had by far the stronger balance sheet with assets 10 times those of Lockhart (it was a property freeholder), while Lockhart, through Peter Merchant, had undoubted strengths in its cost accounting methods and the good

Harold Gardner (right) and Sam Smith at the latter's retirement part – Sam had joined John Gardner in 1926 and retired 40 years later as managing director.

catering practices that it had developed as Britain's largest contract caterer.

At the time of their merger, Peter Merchant was considered the mass caterer and John Gardner was regarded as being more 'foodie' in the words of Garry Hawkes, who actually started his career at Peter Merchant. The combined company employed 20,000 people and made a profit in excess of £600,000 (£10.6m today). Peter Merchant had the cost control systems – stock was taken every Friday in every unit and the GP was calculated to the last penny on sites that, in some cases, catered for thousands of workers. It was catering on a mass scale with little refinement but it demanded strong control systems and accurate costing – hence the Paper Merchant moniker.

Peter Merchant's strength lay in its tight controls. Many of the sites were run by women – "The bedrock of the business," as Hawkes terms it:

"Many of these cook manageresses were highly skilled and highly successful and were often working way below their level of expertise and intelligence. They were hugely

Gardner-Merchant chefs choice

The quality of these dishes was undeniable and so was their convenience but operators at the sharp end continued to resist.

loyal. Too many people think that industrial feeding is an extension of the restaurant business. It isn't. In those days, we were feeding people so that they could live. It was often their only hot meal of the day."

John Gardner, Lockhart Group – Profit before Tax		
Year	Gardner (£)	Lockhart (£)
1959	298,265	123,108
1960	309,288	239,814
1961	389,290	190,058
1962	255,114	389,028†
1963	353,286*	303,502**

† 19 months trading due to change in accounting year
*£6.6m today **£5.7m today

Sir Geoffrey Crowther, chairman of TH, trumpeted that "the Gardner company shall retain its separate identity" – not for the first time, nor the last, would a chairman promise an unlikely outcome to a merger. Belying his words, bringing together the two contract catering arms, a total of 1,600 contracts in all, started almost immediately and was completed by September 1966, a process that forced John Howard, an accountant and an MP who had now become Gardner's chairman, to admit to shareholders that the reorganisation has "monopolised our attention to the partial exclusion of a drive for more business". Moreover, he added, overheads had risen as a result of the merger – a state of affairs that was exacerbated by the imposition of the Selective Employment Tax in 1966 which added £500,000 to the company's wage bill though, thankfully for GM, most of this was passed on to its clients.

In 1967, Peter Merchant and John Gardner were officially united under the Gardner Merchant brand. Blending the two companies

together had been a difficult process, just as merging Bateman and Midland Catering later proved in 1981 and Compass and Granada in 2000. Even GM's centenary book admitted:

"For those who had worked for so many years (and both companies had a history of staff loyalty) could not immediately become Gardner Merchant men and women. In a merger a new corporate identity has to be created and is not a process that can take place overnight, however willing the participants."

In fact, many of the participants were extremely unwilling. There had been over 500 initial redundancies, all announced in a big meeting in Earls Court, and more followed later. Merging the two cultures together was also a challenge. John Gardner was considered the higher class company in every sense of the word while Peter Merchant's reputation for basic canteen catering meant it took several years before the two cultures came together.

When they did, GM became by far the country's largest caterer with contracts in B&I, schools, hospitals (a few), event catering (including 12 racecourses), nine restaurants, 12 John Gardner coffee houses and 38 Little Chef units. Some rationalisation followed. John Gardner's Ships and Stores division was sold, as was its wine and spirits division and the Henry Wintermans Cigar Agency, while Kenco Coffee went to Schweppes.

There was change at the top, too. The old guard was on its way out. Harold Gardner, who had joined the company in 1926 and had run the catering and food production division of the company since before the war, retired in 1966. Sam Smith, who had joined John Gardner in the same year as Harold, eventually becoming managing director, retired in the same year. Charles Gardner had retired earlier. John Howard, the new chairman, retired in 1967 and Lord Cottenham died in 1968. The only member

of the Gardner family remaining, Brian (a grandson of John Gardner) took charge of the restaurants and the growing Little Chef chain; George Willerton, an ex-Peter Merchant man, took over B&I catering and Ivan Joseph took over hospitals and schools.

Even this changed when, in 1968, a report by McKinsey, the management consultants, recommended the creation of regional offices each with a regional director which set the stage for the emergence of Stirling Gallacher and Garry Hawkes, two personalities who were to play a major role in the development, not only of Gardner Merchant but of contract catering generally.

* * *

It was during this time of merger and expansion in the 1960s that contracting, too, began to change. The emergence of Gardner Merchant as the UK's largest contractor by far was accompanied by the growth of Sutcliffe Catering as well as Bateman, Midland and Taylorplan, its four nearest competitors. But in many ways, Gardner Merchant was ahead of the game. The McKinsey report gave the merged GM a new management structure with a proper board reporting to a public company parent board. GM had passed from two independent companies run by individual entrepreneurs into one company run by corporate governance; all the other major contractors were still being largely run by entrepreneurs. Jack Bateman and Roland Webb had yet to be taken over by GrandMet; Sutcliffe, even though acquired by Olympia, was really an independent entity with little overall control exercised over it until Sterling Guarantee Trust acquired it in 1973.

Contracting was also only just beginning to get to grips with some of the much-lauded management techniques that McKinsey was now extolling. GM's emphasis on sales training, one of the key factors in its future success, was not implemented nationally until Garry Hawkes became managing director in 1977 when every area manager was given sales training as a key part of his career development. GM's Eastbourne training centre was launched only in 1979. Sutcliffe took pride in *not* having a sales team and didn't appoint Simon Davis until 1980. In HR, Hilary Charles, Bateman's personnel director, was appointed to the post in 1967 but Peter Davis, her opposite number in Sutcliffe, only joined in 1972 and Ian Hall, though joining Gardner Merchant in 1969, was not appointed personnel director until 1978. It was a time when the major catering companies were beginning to recognise the importance of having skilled sales and personnel expertise on board.

There were changes, too, in the way catering facilities were being designed and equipped. Gone, or about to go, were the huge factory canteens that seated over 1,000 in one sitting that were so prevalent during the war; many factories (the car industry being an exception) had closed or had visibly shrunk. The word canteen, though still prevalent, was becoming a pejorative term but it took some years before it was replaced by the more genteel 'staff restaurant.'

To be able to have the skills it needed, industrial catering, long the poor relation in the eyes of catering colleges, recognised it had to attract the trained people it needed. It was a long process and one that, in some caterer's eyes, still leaves much to be desired. There are continuing complaints that catering colleges ignore the very real attractions of industrial catering by steering their students towards the hotel and restaurant sector even though many caterers now offer sophisticated career development programmes that match, even surpass, those offered by other hospitality companies.

The pioneering work in the late 1970s of Hilary Charles recognised the colleges'

ignorance; attempting to remedy the situation by visiting them with her team and giving talks to lecturers and students, she had something to shout about as Bateman's training programme was highly regarded. As soon as Compass became established, a management development programme was put in place that continues in a far more sophisticated form to this day with an international graduate recruitment programme focusing on a wider graduate base than purely hospitality candidates.

Mike Stapleton, who had stepped out of college lecturing to become Compass' training director, says:

"Whilst I was aware that training was also a key priority within other companies I don't think it had anywhere near the emphasis, funding or drive that it had at Compass. Having the group HR director on the main board was clearly a key driver but the whole of the main board recognised the huge cost of staff turnover, not just in cash terms but that of the whole service delivery standard and, perhaps more importantly, the consistency of it."

Later, Compass pioneered the Young Chefs' Academy and funded colleges nationally to run a Saturday Cookery Club for secondary school children through the Compass Group Foundation, which had an annual £200,000 budget. College take-up was significant.

The original purpose of the British Hospitality Association's annual Food and Service Management Forum survey, launched in 1989, was to encourage college students into the sector by emphasising the size, range of activities and the opportunities it presented, while the efforts of Compass and others to organise teacher and student visits and guest lecture facilities, providing personnel work-update programmes, made strong inroads to changing attitudes and perceptions of the sector.

Despite the fact that the current standard of industrial catering exceeds (in the opinion of many) those of the commercial restaurant sector, its most powerful attraction for youngsters is the more social hours of work it offers compared to the endless daily toil in hotels or restaurants. Almost everyone interviewed for this book suggests that this was a key factor in their own decision to work in industrial catering. In modern parlance it promised a better work/life balance for them and one that was always delivered.

Of course, the canniest recognised that contracting also offered a world of opportunity, and still does: Garry Hawkes, Stirling Gallacher, Don Davenport, Marc Verstringhe, Geoffrey Harrison, Jim Cartwright, Mike Bailey, Bill Toner, Tim West, William Baxter, Alastair Storey, to name just a handful of the successful personalities in this story, all decided to make their career in the sector after leaving catering college, though even they could not have seen quite how far this would lead them. Most trained as chefs, starting at the bottom and all worked their way up. In doing so, they either created their own companies or helped drive public corporations to extraordinary success, many of them becoming wealthy individuals in the process.

But in the 1960s, the opportunities of contracting were by no means as clear-cut as they later became, though the Gardner brothers, Jack Bateman, Roland Webb and John Sutcliffe had certainly shown that contracting was one way to enrich yourself. It would be another 20 years before Gerry Robinson led the Compass buy-out in 1985 which made him and others millionaires. Contracting was certainly seen as a sector with a future but no-one could have foreseen how bright that future was going to be.

* * *

Operating in the 1960s and 1970s was not easy. Two decades of rising food prices and higher wages, increasing National Insurance and pension costs, as well as rampant inflation, forced caterers to look ever more closely at how best to produce better quality food at less cost.

Many of the aids to the modern kitchen in terms of frozen and chilled foods were only just becoming available. It was, for example, in the late 1950s that frozen peas and other vegetables opened up new opportunities for caterers in every sector of the industry. If the time-consuming task of shelling peas could be taken out of the kitchen and into a better equipped factory, then that would save time, space and cost in the kitchen; what benefits could be reaped if other processes could be similarly transferred to a central kitchen? Many of the frozen food companies had to fight caterers' prejudice against their products, spending huge sums of money on PR and advertising trying to persuade chefs that frozen peas had more taste and tenderness than fresh peas; the pea 'tenderometer' – the device by which farmers measured the ripeness of their pea crop – became something of a talisman for the frozen food industry. Today, there is hardly a kitchen in the land that does not use frozen rather than fresh peas. Bearing in mind the continuing skill shortages and the difficulty of recruiting staff which the entire hospitality industry faced (and still does), the availability of pre-prepared items including made-up dishes, offered caterers the tempting prospect of raising standards of food without having to recruit the necessarily expensive skills required in individual units.

The arguments about the merits of cook-freeze and cook-chill started in the late 1950s and have continued ever since with hundreds of articles in the trade press trying to convince caterers of the merits of frozen and chilled food. Then, major frozen food producers such as Smethursts, Birds Eye, Ross Foods, Findus, McCain's and Alveston Kitchens all clamoured for the caterer's attention through numerous editorials and lavish advertisements; full colour food display advertising in the trade press was at its height.

The argument quickly moved on from frozen vegetables and meats to made-up dishes. These potentially offered even greater convenience and both cook-freeze and cook-chill were beginning to be seen as potential answers to the intractable problem of how to reduce the need for skilled staff and, at the same time, improve food quality. The

Rocco Forte and John Forte (seated second from right and extreme right) with the technical team at Kew, 1972, when it merged with the Forte's Spa Road Production Unit.

arguments remain particularly relevant in the provision of school meals and in hospital catering. At the time, it was also thought that both processes had a major role to play in B&I, enabling well-manned central production units to produce meals that could be frozen or chilled and then reheated at point of service without the need for skilled chefs to be employed in individual outlets.

In fact, there was nothing new about producing food centrally and transporting it to outlying sites. Cook-freeze facilities set up by companies with large, multi-unit sites with satellite kitchens, such as Ford and Rolls Royce, had originally proved successful. Eric Gazelle, director of catering at London Transport, had also been operating a food production centre at Croydon since the late 1950s which continued until the 1980s. In

John Forte, a nephew of Sir Charles, who had been general manager at Spa Road, was appointed production manager at Kew and he soon took over as general manager.

one year, 1975, it produced over one million cook-freeze portions, 2.5m bread rolls, 2.9m individual cakes and one million individual meat pies.

The facility at Ford had been introduced in 1967 before Gardner Merchant won the Ford contract and was thought to be the first central production unit to be set up to feed workers. But by 1980 its equipment was considered to be out-of-date and the use of frozen products was having "a demotivating effect on unit management tending to result in dull menus," reported *Catering Times*. The whole concept of cook-freeze was doubtful for the future, added Chris Grater, Ford's employee services manager, announcing the closure of the facility: "The limitations of the process are a serious handicap to its long-term survival. It limits the range of products and you still need some skills at unit level."

But it was the introduction of Ford's cook-freeze facility in 1967, of which Gardner Merchant had intimate knowledge, that may well have encouraged Bob Stent, by now GM's managing director, to sanction a food research and development facility at Kew in 1968 with a renowned chef, René Desjardins, as a principal consultant. Like many of GM's ideas, the facility at the time was adventurous and forward-thinking. It was, however, costly and eventually unsuccessful.

Stent's idea was to produce meals centrally which could then be served in all GM-contracted units by being heated at point of service. It was particularly aimed at hospitals but it was thought it would also be useful for smaller outlets in B&I and schools that did not have the space for extensive kitchen staff and dining rooms or have the skilled staff.

For three years, the research department evaluated raw materials and necessary skilled staff devised new processing methods, conducting experiments on blast freezing, recipe formulation and cooking practices. The unit experimented with different cook

chill dishes and, although not ahead of its time – Lyons, for example, for some time had had a central production unit in operation at Cadby Hall providing chilled and frozen food for its Corner Houses and other restaurants, and Forte had set up a frozen food production unit even earlier – it was an innovation for a contract catering company.

Forte's central production unit (CPU) was based in Spa Road, Bermondsey, supplying a range of items specifically for the many restaurants then in the company's ownership. The company was experiencing a severe shortage of skilled staff like every other caterer and it believed that rather than recruiting a chef for every restaurant, it would be more economic and efficient to open a central kitchen producing food which could be regenerated on site, on demand, for particular Forte restaurant brands such as its popular Quality Inns brand.

However, not only were the restaurants themselves very resistant to taking in the frozen food, there were also technical problems. Not all the menu items could be centrally produced so there was still a need for some production on site and Spa Road found it extremely difficult to match production to demand. The concept was abandoned almost as soon as it had begun though production of frozen meals and ice creams continued under the Puritan Maid brand, the vast majority being sold to airlines and to own-brand food wholesalers such as Ross Foods for onward sale to the retail and the catering sectors. As a result, frozen meals for restaurants represented a very small proportion of Forte's Spa Road considerable total output, This, perhaps, should have been a warning sign for Kew's experiments.

In 1970, after Trust Houses and Forte merged to form THF, the company was faced with owning two production units; it was decided to merge the two facilities and base them in one centre. Kew was much better equipped than Forte's Spa Road unit which by then needed considerable refurbishment, even though the latter employed some 50 staff and was also making money, which Kew never did. Spa Road was closed and all production was transferred to Kew. John Forte, a nephew of Sir Charles, who had been general manager at Spa Road, was appointed production manager of the two units and he soon took over as general manager.

The experimental kitchen into cook-chill which Gardner Merchant had launched was retained but it faced the same problem that Spa Road had encountered: it was almost impossible to synchronise the production of chilled meals with demands from the end-kitchens and it was eventually decided that Kew could only work as a cook-freeze producer and as a food factory rather than a CPU producing specific menu items almost to order. To try to make it viable, Kew had to become a frozen food production facility.

Much of the research at Kew was technical and was helped by major ingredient suppliers with food technologists playing a key role. Two brands were created: Silver Seal – a range of popular and relatively cheap dishes, such as stews, casseroles, roast meats in 10/12-portion foil dishes, which were aimed at staff restaurants, works and factory outlets, and Gold Seal, which was a range of à la carte menu items in boil-in-the-bag single portions. These were more of a classical nature such as duck à l'orange, beef stroganoff, coq au vin, beef bourguignonne. Findus was one company that took this range of products to add to its range of frozen foods.

The quality of these dishes was undeniable and so was their convenience, but operators at the sharp end continued to resist. The products tended to suffer from menu fatigue with criticism that 'everything tastes the same'. Unlike centrally produced food for the retail market, which demands no variation

between batches, dishes for the catering market need to have some variation in taste and appearance if they are to be offered regularly during the week. Kew lasted only two years as a chilled food production unit and only three more as a frozen food production unit before it was closed down in 1975. It could not be made profitable. However, another food production unit was then opened in Dunstable but this, too, eventually ran into difficulties and was closed in 1985.

* * *

For the contracting industry it had been pioneering work but it was not the end of the story. The introduction of chilled and frozen food items, often tasting better than fresh but poorly cooked items, became established and no catering company could, even now, survive without using them in one way or another though every contractor on its website currently extols its particular and especial emphasis on fresh local produce as a vital marketing tool. There is certainly a movement towards using local produce and extolling its provenance, but there remains little doubt that chilled and frozen foods will remain a key staple for many catering outlets, with CPUs now providing many commercial restaurant chains with basic menu items.

Cook-chill re-emerged when Gardner Merchant went on to acquire Tillery Valley Foods in 1996 based in South Wales, primarily to help it win contracts in hospital catering which was where 70 per cent of Tillery's output was destined to be used (the remaining 30 per cent was with local authorities). Prior to the sale for something in the region of £10m, Tillery had doubled its production capacity to support projected annual sales of some £20m.

Although eyebrows were raised at the time – Chris Bone, a former Gardner Merchant

director turned consultant said it was "a curious purchase and I'm puzzled as to why they are doing it" – Gardner Merchant correctly believed that the availability of cook-chilled meals would help it expand its presence in the NHS and private healthcare. The purchase was deemed a success and Tillery Valley continues under Sodexo ownership currently producing 600,000 meals a week for schools, hospitals and local authorities.

In 1999, Granada also set up a £2m chilled food production facility, Circadia, based in Wimbledon, which was initially introduced to produce first class meals for Eurostar when Granada won the train contract. It then began preparing meals for schools, hospitals and some leisure outlets, but a proposal to use the facility for producing cook-chill meals for some of the major hotel outlets which had been acquired in the Forte takeover came to nothing because of resistance on the part of the hotels.

Circadia became part of Compass and continued for some years but does not currently exist as a separate entity. Other companies set up their own CPUs. Frank Bell's CCG launched one for contracts in Scotland and Jim Cartwright's CPU, based in Nottingham, which used to provide chilled meals to all East Midlands branches of British Gas, was adapted to produce 20,000 school meals a week for Cygnet Catering. More recently, Compass established its own CPU based in Bournemouth for its school meals contract there.

Today, frozen and chilled foods remain essential to the wider catering industry but it is often forgotten that much of the original experimentation into their usage was undertaken on behalf of the contract catering sector. Contractors were certainly not afraid to experiment and were well ahead of the times even if their experiments did not always result in success.

CHAPTER EIGHT

Enter the Americans

Up to the 1970s, UK-based companies had contract catering all to themselves but in 1972 ARA emerged on the European scene.

Until 1972, Gardner Merchant, Sutcliffe, Bateman and Midland, with a clutch of other companies such as Taylorplan, Hamard and Stuart Cabeldu had only to compete against themselves. Then ARA arrived in the UK.

Based in Philadelphia, ARA (short for Automatic Restaurants of America) began life in the US as a vending company in 1936 when Davre Davidson (later joined by his brother Henry) founded what was to become one of the largest vending companies in California; in 1940, Bill Fishman, a budding entrepreneur who recognised the potential of vending, founded his own company with 200 candy and cigarette machines. Both companies prospered and in 1959 they merged to form ARA, becoming a public company a year later and changing the name to ARA Services in 1969 and to Aramark in 1994.

ARA quickly branched out into catering, winning the contract for the summer Olympic Games in Mexico City in 1968 – its first Olympic contract – as well as uniform and workwear rental, child care and book publishing (offloaded in 1998), followed by expansion into Japan and later into Europe, South Korea and China. It was the beginnings of what is now a US$15bn enterprise employing over 270,000 people worldwide.

Its first venture into the UK came in 1972 when it acquired three vending companies, including Cadbury Schweppes vending operations and a company called Eurovend which had been founded by a US entrepreneur, Bob Piker. For some time, Piker had been bringing over vending machines, some of them almost obsolete, from the US where they had become an accepted (and growing) part of the industrial catering scene. He was confident that they would be as successful in Europe and set about proving the point, tying up contracts with most of the European car companies.

So tight was Eurovend's contract at Ford's vast production site at Dagenham, where over 700 machines had been installed, that Stuart Hanson, Ford's outgoing food services manager, told his successor Philip Houldsworth, that one contract he could never change was Eurovend's vending contract. Part of the reason was reputed to be the one per cent commission going to Henry Ford in Detroit.

ARA's purchase of Eurovend was organised by Bill Fishman who had taken over as ARA's chief executive and clearly had ideas of world-wide expansion. The US market was so vast, and the opportunities so enormous, that it was said that the only reason why Fishman bought Eurovend was to provide tax free trips to Europe at a time when international travel was difficult and expensive.

Fishman put Dick Sterke (who had worked for him in the US for a number of years) in charge of the UK operation and Tricon, the consultancy run by Bob Payne and David Garner, was engaged to advise on the best way to expand the activities of the new acquisition. It was soon recognised that the quickest route was by further acquisition rather than waiting for organic growth and two regional catering companies came into view – West Riding Caterers and Lancashire Catering Services, both owned by Philip Thornton, a small-time caterer with big ambitions and some pretensions.

The purchase (for £195,000 – £2.3m today) included a holiday camp on the south coast.

In catering terms, Thornton's companies had been going nowhere and the majority of the 50 or so contracts he brought to ARA were small and insignificant, with negligible profits and earnings mainly from discounts. Nor was their quality anything to write home about. However, it was a start and Thornton, an operator with great communication skills, joined ARA on a full-time basis becoming chairman of the UK operations and then taking on a European role. He got on extremely well with Fishman and being the sole source of information on the UK operations to the US, Fishman came greatly to rely on Thornton's presence.

The expansion of the company in Europe was rocked by an ill-advised bid for the catering and vending contract at Ford's plants in Valencia, organised by Dick Sterke,

Philip Houldsworth: a canny choice for ARA but he ultimately paid the price for client defections.

which was expensively aborted and Sterke quickly disappeared from the scene leaving Thornton in charge of European operations.

Seeing that ARA needed some new talent to drive its expansion into the UK, he hired Philip Houldsworth as chief executive to replace his own role in the UK.

In every way Houldsworth was a canny choice. As employee services manager based at Ford Europe's head office in Warley in Essex, he had been liaising with the Americans for five years and had had plenty of experience dealing with his American bosses; he knew how to talk their language. He also knew about catering: one of his tasks had been to oversee Gardner Merchant's food service contract at all the UK plants and Eurovend's vending operation; his previous experience, overseeing the non-college catering at the University of Cambridge, was also highly relevant and he was a classmate of both Garry Hawkes and Stuart Hanson at Huddersfield Technical College.

On joining, he found ARA was a work in progress. "There was no company when I joined – there was just a way of working," he recalls.

He replaced a slew of managers, including Alastair Hopkins, Thornton's long-time associate, who was based in Leeds and in charge of the catering contracts; Tim Walton, the vending director, moved on to be replaced by Roger French who was a manager with Ryder Trucks. Offshore Catering, a company which specialised in the burgeoning North Sea oil market in BP's Forties field had already been acquired, but Houldsworth set about expanding and integrating a number of companies including J Lyons' contract catering company, Food Management, which brought in some high profile contracts including Barclaycard and all the London Courts. Principality, a profitable catering and vending company based in Wales, followed.

Then ARA entered another market sector when in 1977 at the behest of Bill Fishman, Arthur York known as Art, an assertive New Yorker, was sent over from America to oversee a new venture: a vending coffee system. He brought with him over 500 mainly redundant machines. It was a smart move and became a money-making operation for the next 30 years, creating ARA's lucrative Coffee Club. The catering division, however, operating out of Leeds was still barely profitable. Highly vulnerable to any downturn in the economy, many of the contracts were subsequently lost when factories and offices began to close in the 1980 recession which coincided with Margaret Thatcher's rise to power in 1979.

* * *

Nevertheless, ARA was never short of ambition. Again at the behest of the US, where the company majored in big event catering in such places as Pittsburgh and Dallas, Houldsworth looked at catering for football stadia in the UK and won Chelsea FC which was something of a coup as Stadia Catering had previously dominated the market. ARA showed how effectively it could produce and serve food and beverages to vast crowds.

The biggest coup came a few months later winning Wembley from Letheby & Christopher who had been operating the catering concession there for 53 years. For the presentation, Houldsworth brought over three people from the US including Larry Kilfoy, a marketing man, to help convince the Wembley board – which was then owned by BET – that ARA could deliver the goods.

All sorts of new facilities and amenities were scheduled into the offer including a CPU based at Wembley which would service 36 outlets and up to 50 trayboys (and girls) who went around the ground in specially

THE BIG MATCH
Yanks win at Wembley

THOSE HALLOWED SHRINES of British sporting life, meccas for devoted fans but wastelands of gastronomic delights, are being invaded by our American cousins.

And what has happened to Chelsea Football Club and now the massive Wembley Complex could herald the end of an era of British catering which for years has existed on the dubious fare of tasteless pork pies, stale crisps and little service.

The American giants of the catering business, ARA, made quiet inroads into British sporting catering with the hard-won contract for Chelsea Football Club. Now with the £50 million contract for the entire Wembley Complex, including the stadium, in their pocket, perhaps our British companies had better watch out!

Masterminding ARA's contract is David Osterhout, an American dynamo, with a track record of managing vast American stadiums behind him, who was whisked from the Houston Astroworld to head the British team's assault on Wembley.

All the foods dear to the English sporting man's heart remain, the pies, rolls, pints of warm beer and pickled onions. What is different is the choice of fare, the pizzas and hamburgers cooked on the spot, the upmarket menu in the conference centre, the aggressive marketing and above all that lovely, old fashioned word, "Service".

"You English", says David Osterhout, shaking his head in bewilderment, "seem to think working in the food service industry is some sort of apology. People out in the front line serving the customer are really important and however good your food, the people greeting a customer, giving him the service he requires—with a smile—can ensure that client comes back again. Yes, we have a captive audience who, because they are coming to Wembley, either to a conference, international horse show, craft exhibition or sporting event have to accept the catering we offer.

"But our approach is also to sell our catering facilities to say a group of tennis fans over for an international match before they reach Wembley.

"The people coming for a horse show will require a different sort of meal, than the men here for a boxing evening. The children who came for our first event, the Bugs Bunny Show, wanted Coke, hamburgers and ice cream, all served immediately!

"Perhaps our different approach from most British companies is our research and the marketing for enticing events to Wembley that will bring in catering.

"Coming here must be a total experience, people must want to come again, not just for the conference or sporting event they enjoyed, but for the friendly and efficient food service we believe we can give."

He might also have added the British souvenir collecting public will also go away with another reminder, in the form of their well designed disposable beer glass or coffee cup, carrying the discreetly linked symbols of ARA and Wembley.

But if the American conquest of Wembley has cut the chain of 53 years' unbroken catering management by a British company, so the story of how the contract was won must go down in the legends of catering history.

Allan Bailey, sales manager, heard the Wembley contract was up for tender last autumn—after the deadline date had expired.

"Who is ARA?" said a Wembley official, more at home with the British established catering giants.

That is when Philip Houldsworth, the company's chief British executive swung into action. Wembley agreed to extend the time limit for tender, albeit a tight one, and were obviously impressed when on the next plane from Philadelphia arrived ARA's vice-president and a team of analysts and marketing men.

They joined Philip and Allan who then spent the next weeks doing nothing but getting to know Wembley.

"You name any sporting event, exhibition or craft show, between us, we went to them all", recalled Allan. "We took photos, films and reams of notes about every aspect of the place and by the end of those weeks I don't think there was a square inch of the place untouched and unrecorded."

The presentation was made before the Wembley Complex management, the American team flew home and their British colleagues could do nothing else but sit back and wait.

One April day the telephone rang at 5 pm in Philip's Reading office. Fifteen minutes later he emerged from his office, sent down to the local off-licence for their best champagne and office girls, sales managers and executives joined in the celebrations—ARA had won the coveted Wembley contract.

Vic Laws was brought in from Grand Metropolitan Airport Services as new managing director for ARA catering, a division of ARA food services, and David Osterhout moved home from Houston to Chorleywood, Hertfordshire.

The contract runs for 10 years and represents a £750,000 investment programme—some of which has gone on the long shopping list for crockery, cutlery and the sets of Royal Doulton china for visiting Royalty and VIP's.

Vic and David, who look after the daily running of Wembley, interviewed all existing staff who wished to join the new contractors and hired the "Tray" boys and girls, rather like modern day cinema usherettes who at pop concerts and football games can speedily work their way along the aisles with hot snacks.

Most of the equipment is British, but certain items, like the rapid Coke dispensing machines, have been brought over from the States.

"This is not a McDonald's operation in the sense that the products and equipment are made to specification in the States", stresses Allan Bailey. "Yes we have American experience in knowing how to sell food and drink swiftly and efficiently, but they can learn a lot from us."

David Osterhout is also learning. How to translate the famous American Submarine sandwich into something like a ham ploughman, that the British public are not crazy about pretzels and savoury popcorn, and of course British beer must be warm!

STAFF AND WELFARE CATERER/OCTOBER 1981

Vic Laws, transferred from Grand Metropolitan Air Services to captain the ARA team.

Philip Houldsworth, the chief executive, celebrated with champagne in the office.

David Osterhout, experienced in managing vast American stadia, is bewildered by the English. "You seem to think working in the food service industry is some sort of apology".

STAFF AND WELFARE CATERER/OCTOBER 1981

How Staff and Welfare Caterer magazine reported the Wembley win.

arber, sales consultant

*chef, Martin Webb, trans-
merican favourites for British
lity*

7

A very public spat

In September 1980, *Catering Times* reported a gloomy picture. Under the headline 'Recession bites contractors', Philip Houldsworth was quoted: "The phone rings six times a day and it's all bad news. All contractors are bleeding and anybody who says he is not is either a liar or a knave... I don't believe there is any safe contract at present, except perhaps in the oil business." To add to the misery, the paper reported that John Twiselton, marketing director, and marketing manager Colin Boother had both been made redundant. "Any marketing needs we have for 1981 we will buy in," said Houldsworth.

Houldsworth's gloomy prognosis was not, however, shared by everyone. Garry Hawkes in a letter of response, said that Gardner Merchant was doing very nicely, thank you:

"The recession must and is having its effect, particularly in small sites, some of which are closing or drastically contracting. Sales, however, are running at record levels... and our profits will be 25 per cent higher this year."

And in a blistering sideswipe he added:

"For those contractors who actually deliver what they promise in their sales claim there is no need to fear the future. The demise of the unprofessional, the unprepared and the inefficient should not be of concern to anyone."

---

designed branded uniforms selling such upgraded items as hamburgers, pizzas, Cornish pasties, baked potatoes, doughnuts, popcorn and other goodies which are commonplace today but which then were revolutionary. The uniforms had a front pouch which acted as a cash till. Outside the stadium itself mobile vans sold fish and chips and other hot items. A major innovation was a special ARA-designed beer machine which drew 20 pints at a time and was part of the longest bar in England.

During the bidding process, Houldsworth sent Alan Bailey, a salesman, into Wembley insisting that he attended every event, taking photographs of the catering facilities as they were and how poorly they were organised. The photographs formed a major part of the presentation which was specifically designed to impress by bringing US-style catering pizzazz to what was England's premier football stadium.

The presentation to the Wembley board cost £20,000 to set up – a vast sum in those

David Osterhout: "I imported from the US, napkins in about 14 different colours – black, blues, greens, pinks and so on. Our corporate customers loved it because we offered something no one else had."

days – and Philip Thornton was initially opposed to tendering, warning Houldsworth and Don Green, a fellow director, of the consequences if they were unsuccessful; when help came from the States to develop the presentation he changed his mind and was quick to claim ownership. A factor in winning the contract was that one of the Wembley directors had known ARA in the United States and had been impressed by what he had seen – as well he might, as ARA was then catering in such vast US sports arenas as the Houston Astrodome. Indeed, David Osterhout, who had been in charge of the Astrodome, came over to run the Wembley contract for the first 12 months.

Houldsworth says that Wembley was knocked out by the presentation – indeed, so much was promised that a doubtful BET board member queried whether ARA could do what it was offering to do. ARA's deal was quite contrary to that of Letheby & Christopher's which was a split profit arrangement; ARA was proposing an airport-style concession agreement with ARA paying Wembley a percentage of turnover. An initial investment of £750,000 was required but the 10-year agreement was estimated to be worth £50m – even more if sales could be boosted through US-style merchandising. Though Houldsworth denies the story, Vic Laws, who was at the meeting and who had been brought in by Houldsworth because of his experience with concession catering at GrandMet, recalls:

"Larry Kilfoy pulled out a cheque book from his briefcase and wrote out a cheque for £1m for the first five years' concession rent, signed it and handed it over saying that was how confident we were. The BET board was mightily impressed and it almost certainly tipped the balance in our favour. Afterwards, when we were outside, I said to him that the gesture was incredible. What if they tried to cash it? He said not to worry. It only had one

signature on it and it needed two."

"We did some wonderful things at Wembley," says David Osterhout. "It was a wonderful experience for me. Some of the new units we built in the arena increased sales as much as 800 per cent. They looked as good as McDonald's on the high street, and our food specifications were full-on American standards.

"I had managed the concessions and catering at the Astrodome for many years prior to going to England. The stands at Wembley had bullet-proof glass with a slot the size of a beer cup to pass the food through after you collected the money in advance! I had never seen bullet-proof glass in a concession stand until I got to Wembley."

Osterhout imported 1,000 stainless steel tray stands from the US that were used for banquets and ARA installed a commercial on-site laundry for all concession uniforms, cooks' whites, and speciality linens such as napkins.

"At the convention center, we did a lot of high-end corporate events and product launches," says Osterhout. "You could only get napkins from laundry companies in red and white so I imported from the US napkins in about 14 different colours – black, blues, greens, pinks and so on. Our corporate customers loved it because we offered something no one else had."

The Wembley contract, though it entailed high up-front costs, was ultimately profitable and set ARA upon an acquisition trail.

In 1980, just before its Wembley success, ARA had acquired Sea Hotels from Bateman which boosted its offshore catering interests and which brought Shell contracts into Aramark.

"These were very different to those of BP and in my opinion were directly responsible for the lowering of standards in North Sea catering. I remember the food costs per day

in BP were £3.50 and in Shell at least £1 lower," says Houldsworth.

ARA then bought Thwaites and Matthews, the contract catering and vending business of Thomas Borthwick, the Australian meat producer with a chain of butchers' shops in the UK Thwaites and Matthews had about 100 contracts including some large clients in the site services sector. Its managing director was Richard Delderfield who didn't join ARA with the deal but who later worked briefly for Gardner Merchant.

Philip Houldsworth told *Catering Times* at the time:

"The acquisition of the Thwaites and Matthews business forms part of our planned expansion programme in the UK. An important factor is our need for additional experienced management and we feel that Thwaites and Matthews has a great deal to offer in this area."

The company's director of marketing, John Twiselton, added that ARA's catering division was now fifth in the market, after the 'big four' contractors. In the four years since he joined, Houldsworth had boosted ARA's annual turnover from £19m to £55m.

But a number of factors were adversely hitting the company, including the economic recession which was then sweeping the country and forcing numerous factory and office closures.

While the recession forced many existing ARA contract closures, not everything was going the right way anyway. ARA had tried to buy Frank Bell's business, CCG, later Castle View, but the talks came to nothing. The Thwaites and Matthews deal was also proving to be troublesome. ARA had underestimated the close relationship between many of the senior Thwaites and Matthews regional managers and their clients. With the recession hitting hard, clients were looking around for savings in the cost of their catering provision; this presented irresistible opportunities for executives who had long-standing client links and who were willing to defect from ARA and start up on their own. So many contracts were lost to Aramark employees starting up in business that within six months Philadelphia decided that heads must roll. Houldsworth took the hit and was fired in 1982 but given a generous

settlement. Roger French, who was head of ARA's vending division, succeeded but lasted only two years. Vic Laws left in 1983 when he refused to combine catering and vending: "I thought they were two different businesses and was later to be proved right when they sold off vending to Bunzle," he says. He went on to join Spinney's as managing director in the same year.

Houldsworth quit the UK and worked

in the Middle East for Inchcape organising and managing large site catering for four years, fortunately leaving Kuwait a couple of months before Iraq invaded. He came back to the UK taking up positions with Abela before setting up Ripon Consulting, which he operated for 25 years. He entered local politics in 2008 and at the time of writing (2015) was re-elected to Wokingham Borough Council for the second time.

Credit Action Plus

The FA Cup Final at Wembley Stadium, 1988. Catering for such vast crowds became an ARA speciality.

CHAPTER NINE

Spinneys – into the public sector

The privatisation of NHS catering and domestic services led to the arrival of Spinneys – and its early departure.

S pinneys was a company that burst briefly onto the UK catering scene in 1983 – only to be sold to Frank Bell's company, Commercial Catering Group, three years later. Its significance lies in the fact that it was among the first contractors to exploit the potential of public sector catering, just at the time when Margaret Thatcher was introducing compulsory competitive tendering.

Its genesis lay in the Middle East between the two world wars when Rawdon Spinney formed the company with a group of businessmen to provide catering and 'other household requirements' in 'certain liberated parts of the Ottoman empire.'

Within five years it was operating a chain of shops and cold store facilities throughout the region from which, among other services, it supplied the workers who were then building the pipeline from Iran to the Mediterranean.

Throughout the Second World War it was the main supplier to the allied forces in the

Until Spinney's arrival, with the government's competitive tendering policies, only a handful of NHS hospitals had contracted out their catering arrangements. More than 30 years later, the NHS still remains a difficult market and one that only the largest contractors can enter.

Middle East but in 1948 half of its shares were acquired by Steel Brothers, a UK engineering firm. It is not clear why Steel wanted to diversify into the service sector but it could probably see that profits could be made in the Middle East healthcare sector. Spinneys 1948 based in Beirut was thus formed.

The company quickly expanded to other parts of the region providing hotel services to a number of Middle East hospitals which encouraged it to look to the UK at the time when the UK government, under Margaret Thatcher, announced plans to introduce the privatisation of the NHS catering and domestic services.

As a result, in April 1983, Spinneys was launched in the UK to take advantage of this new opportunity with Vic Laws, who had just quit ARA, as managing director. He was joined by Philip Burton as marketing director from Spring Grove laundry and Christine Street from Grandmet Catering (soon to be Compass) as personnel director.

They set themselves a five year entry plan based on P&L contracts – an innovation when most other contractors were operating on cost-plus – aiming only at hospitals which were large enough to be self-accounting and had an annual turnover of between £1-£2m.

It took them two years and plenty of money to win the first contracts: Bethlem and Maudsley, a psychiatric hospital which Peter Merchant had won 20 years previously and which Gardner Merchant had since been running. It also won Orpington Hospital. Each tender cost well over £2,000 to prepare – a large sum in those days and a sign of the bureaucratic complexities contractors faced when trying to break into the public sector market.

Spinneys won despite having no other catering operation in the UK except

A subsidiary of Steel Brothers Holdings PLC

Spinneys was launched in the UK to take advantage of Margaret Thatcher's plans to bring competition to NHS catering and domestic services.

Gatwick Flight Catering, an in-flight kitchen operation which Spinneys 1948 had bought in 1979. Nevertheless, the parent company's experience in the Middle East was clearly an advantage.

Spinney's presentation argued for much stronger management input. The manager of each contract would not be a catering manager as such but a general manager able to control all the various disciplines and reporting directly to Laws as the managing director. It also offered to consider introducing a profit sharing scheme with staff and promised to bring in a computerisation programme which would greatly facilitate management practices.

The idea was, in fact, to offer hotel services such as catering, cleaning and

---

Hospital catering

Spinneys' win at Bethlem, which under Gardner Merchant had been one of only three NHS hospitals to employ a contractor, came at a time when the NHS was beginning to feel under siege. Mike Hawkes, chairman of the Hospital Caterers Association, admitted hospital caterers were under a lot of pressure – "not just from the threat of privatisation but from the tremendous amount of work involved in getting everything right before going out to tender" – something with which the contractors could only agree.

Only two other companies were then in the field: Allied Medical, set up jointly by Hamard Catering and Allied Medical Group which had just won the catering contract at Farnham Road Hospital, Guildford, while Catering by County had been running the catering for the Ellen Home and Brooklands School for 13 years.

---

laundry services to hospitals – an early form of an FM contract.

But it was not plain sailing. John Davies-Smith, managing director of Allied Medical, admitted gaining the Farnham Road contract had been a "long, hard slog". Catering by County's contract, valued at £41,000, was abruptly terminated when a successful in-house bid (against four contractors including Catering by County) prevailed. David Gravells, the contractor's managing director, learned of its loss through *Industrial Caterer* magazine, not from the Trust. Gravells, understandably, was "disappointed, to say the least" and said that "it was symptomatic and typical of the crass stupidity that is going on". He demanded (and received) a letter of apology from the Trust.

The bone of contention was the government's insistence on fixed price contracts for NHS business. This had forced Garry Hawkes, a few months earlier, to announce that Gardner Merchant was withdrawing, at least temporarily, from competing for NHS business, including the renegotiation of the Bethlem and Maudsley Hospitals contract which had left a clear field for Spinneys:

"The current situation for fixed price tendering, while including quotations from NHS caterers and always accepting the lowest quote, is obviously wrong and unfair," he told *Industrial Caterer*.

"It will result in the NHS system prevailing because they can always quote positively and optimistically. We have already seen proof of this in the fact that the first six catering contracts out to tender were all won in-house."

Although he received support from some – ARA's Max Harris, said: "We don't feel hospitals represent the most attractive areas to devote our sales and marketing efforts," while Graham Sheppard, at Taylorplan, was

also unenthusiastic – "We believe fixed-price tenders penalise the contractor and not the in-house caterer." Others were more favourably inclined.

Roy Munday of Commercial Catering Group said that he thought contractors could help the NHS without becoming involved in a complete takeover of the entire catering service within the hospital "which creates a lot of problems."

Sterling Gallacher at Sutcliffe said: "We are not turning down any tender opportunities," while Vic Laws pointed out that because the majority of tenders had price review clauses, some three monthly and others annually "and because our managers have local autonomy, they will

Vic Laws: Spinneys' win at Bethlem, which under Gardner Merchant had been one of only three NHS hospitals to employ a contractor, came at a time the NHS was beginning to feel under siege.

How does the trade view one company's stand on NHS tenders?

Some reservations, but bidding will continue

By Clare Walker

WHEN Gardner Merchant first revealed in *Industrial Caterer's* last issue (October/November) that the company was withdrawing – at least temporarily – from competing for National Health Service catering contracts, managing director Garry Hawkes believed he was embarking on a campaign which would receive the support of most of his fellow contractors.

Unfortunately, events conspired against him and his, now very public, stand against the Government's insistence on fixed price tenders as opposed to the more popular – and more customary – management fee system.

No sooner had Mr Hawkes – backed by Trusthouse Forte chief executive Rocco Forte – argued his case in the national press and the media at large, than it was learned that two contractors had finally broken the in-house monopoly on NHS contracts.

Spinneys won Orpington and Allied Medical took Farnham Road, Guildford.

Gardner Merchant's confident prediction that other contractors would follow suit in withdrawing from NHS tenders has not come true, as *Industrial Caterer* found when we asked a selection of contractors what they thought about NHS tenders and the fixed price system.

Wrong and unfair

Garry Hawkes, managing director, Gardner Merchant, reiterated his company's case in the staff journal *Communicator*.

"The only opportunity for success by contract caterers is by quoting unrealistically low with all the inherent risks to their income, or even worse, to the well-being of the patients.

"We believe the normal management contract is in the best interests of the NHS patients and the caterer.

"The current situation of fixed

● Garry Hawkes

"It will result in the NHS system prevailing, because they can always quote positively and optimistically. We have already seen proof of this in the fact that the first six catering contracts put out for tender were all won in-house.

"We believe we have something of value to offer and that

Outdated contracts method

Vic Laws, managing director, Spinneys

"We are quite happy to continue bidding for hospital contracts at a fixed-price, as long as the tender is correctly written by the authority, we are given the opportunity to examine the facilities available and have all the historical information regarding the number of patients and staff served.

"Remembering that the major-

Sitting on the fence

Graham Sheppard, sales and marketing manager, Taylorplan.

"As we see it, we will tender for hospitals on a selective basis, and the selection will be based on the type of hospital it is. We will tender on a fixed-cost or on a management-fee basis in a hospital where we think there is an opportunity to gain a contract.

"We are not fussy, even though we would prefer it if the system were switched to management fee. We believe fixed-price tenders penalise the contractor and

● Graham Sheppard

the privatisation of cleaning is much more advanced than catering.

"We have a little more optim-

The bone of contention was the government's insistence on fixed price contracts for NHS business: how Industrial Caterer reported the Gardner Merchant stand on NHS tenders.

be able to react to any changes without detracting from the quality of the food going to the patient".

Hawkes' well placed misgivings were the basis of Gardner Merchant's loss of the £2m Bethlem and Maudsley Hospitals contract. The hospitals were keen to improve productivity and introduce IT systems

but GM had withdrawn from the tender at the last minute when Hawkes realised that the only way to accede to a demand to reduce costs was by reducing the terms and conditions of its staff; otherwise GM would have sustained a financial loss.

Hawkes, who said that fixed price contracts meant that the quality part of the

service "is subordinate to the desire to cut costs," refused. "Neither option seemed worthwhile to us," he told *Industrial Caterer*. "It seemed unfair to pay our staff less and the other option was plainly wrong."

He continued to oppose fixed price contracts for NHS business (although GM operated these off-shore) but this did not prevent the company recruiting prominent figures in the following year to spearhead the company's expansion into three key public catering sectors, all of which were subject to government privatisation edicts: schools (Chris Bone, catering officer for Somerset), hospitals (Lee Seddon, district catering manager for Guy's Hospital), and the armed forces (Major Richard Atkinson, ex-Army Catering Corps).

Seddon's initial role was to boost GM's presence in the private hospital sector, though after the government later issued new guidelines for Local Authority tendering, Hawkes said he was content to compete for public contracts on the new terms.

As a result, more contractors began to make inroads into the NHS though, even by 2010 (latest available figures) the total share of the contracting market held by healthcare, which includes private hospitals and nursing homes where contracting is commonplace, is only just 15 per cent.

The NHS market remains difficult for contractors to successfully penetrate and contractors have some way to go before it matches their dominance of the B&I market. Continuing to this day, employment, pension and contractual challenges as well as severe cost issues hinder expansion into this market and this inhibition is unlikely to disappear as pressure mounts on NHS finances and more demands are made on its services.

In general, only major contractors offering a full range of FM services are able to consider entering the market. While efficiencies have been introduced into the system through better purchasing, stronger management and new methods of working (e.g. cook-chill), in many cases the NHS remains only marginally economic, though some caterers profitably specialise in it.

Margaret Thatcher's government opened up the NHS and other public sector markets to competition, thus offering caterers the opportunity to bid for contracts in large swathes of the economy.

The market remains time-consuming and expensive to penetrate and to maintain a sufficiently profitable foothold.

However, for the largest contractors, the introduction in 1992 by John Major's government, and later extended by the governments of Tony Blair and Gordon Brown, of 25- to 30-year PFI contracts opened up opportunities which attracted considerable investment into the NHS by Compass and Sodexo and their partners.

Over 90 per cent of all new NHS hospital construction has been through PFI contracts which has paid for 75 per cent of the cost of just over 100 new hospitals; they now owe £80bn in PFI loan unitary charges – the ongoing costs of maintaining PFI hospitals and paying back the loans which are indexed against inflation.

Unless these contracts can be renegotiated downwards, which is unlikely, they will remain highly profitable to their original investors.

By 1985, Spinneys was catering for six NHS hospitals, each with a minimum of 400 beds which, going forward, was ambitiously raised to 700 beds. Frenchay Hospital in Bristol was gained, then came Cane Hill in Coulsdon, Queen Elizabeth, Birmingham and three hospitals in Harrow. It also invested in a cook-chill bulk food production – Winterstar, a CPU at Luton – which was more for airline and retail business although it introduced long-life cook-chill to the UK hospital market.

The company was on something of a roll and claimed to be achieving savings of between five and 10 per cent in existing contracts. At the same time, other companies started to win contracts, including GM, Sutcliffe and Compass, through a purchase of Chris Pollard's Hamard Catering – a South Wales hotelier who had successfully branched out into contracting.

For Spinney's, however, the bright future did not materialise. It had to give up the Queen Elizabeth Hospital contract in Birmingham due to financial pressures and in 1986, much against Vic Laws' five-year plan, Steele Brothers decided to enter B&I, changing its philosophy and going head-to-head with the large contractors. Laws' disagreement with this policy was profound; he left the company, immediately starting up his consultancy AVL.

Spinney's incursion into B&I met with only limited success and with the partial demise of British and Commonwealth Shipping (which had by then acquired Steel) the company was sold to CCG.

Frank Bell saw the advantages of the computerised systems that Laws had developed and bought the company and the existing contracts for a small five-figure sum, always maintaining that he made an immediate return on his money by using the software in his own contracts. The remaining hospital contracts were offloaded.

Spinneys disappeared from the UK market though it remains a highly successful operation and active in the Middle East.

Over 90 per cent of all new NHS hospital construction has been through PFI contracts.

CHAPTER TEN

Bateman and Midland and the unexpected job swap

Bateman Catering and Midland Catering competed against each other for 10 years while part of GrandMet – and then came the merger.

In the 1970s, while other companies were entering the contract catering market – sometimes with only partial success – two of the bigger players were beginning to settle down under the same ownership. The purchase of Bateman Catering and Midland Catering by GrandMet brought some immediate advantages to the senior teams of each company. Each member was provided with a GrandMet card which allowed a 50 per cent discount on any of the company's hotels – "And boy, did we use it", says Tony Ward-Lewis cheerfully. But otherwise, GrandMet left the companies alone as was the fashion later when it acquired other companies such as Empire Catering, Berni Inns and Express Dairies. It was not Max Joseph's intention to interfere in the companies within the group unless there were serious problems, as was the case with his acquisition of Watney Mann.

GrandMet decided to maintain the separate identities of Bateman and Midland in the belief that competition between them

would make them more effective and more profitable; it was a situation that lasted for the next 10 years. By 1977, when Grandmet Bateman Holdings was formed to take into account all the company's various contract catering interests including extensive overseas and North Sea oil contracts, the company boasted 8,000 staff and 700 units,

while Midland had over 500 units and 3,250 staff. By 1981, the year of the merger, the two companies had grown to 16,000 staff in over 1,500 units.

Graham Lewis as chairman and Pat Lichtensteiger as chief executive ran Bateman while Tony Walford, as managing director of Midland, reported to Lewis.

Pat Lichtensteiger with staff, in happy times.

Pat Lichtensteiger: *"His departure was very emotional... he was very sad at having to move to Berni."*

Lichtensteiger had started with Bateman in 1950 as second deputy assistant manager at the Isle of Grain, when the refinery was being built. Despite his name (both his parents were Swiss) young Pat was born in Manchester and went to school there; if anything, he had a northern accent. At the time of his arrival, Bateman had about 40 contracts run from a back office in Ealing and Jack Bateman used to collect the takings in a biscuit tin on a Friday afternoon – shades of Mike Taylor's and Clive Gilpin's bike rides on Fridays for Midland Catering.

Lichtensteiger was a tall, commanding figure out of the Ken Graveney mould, being well over 6ft tall. He was also a shrewd and highly regarded manager who was quick on the uptake and – to quote one ex-colleague – "Very on the ball". Peter Aldrich, who joined Bateman in 1974 as a trainee manager and who later moved over to Sutcliffe to become managing director, says that he was in total awe of him. "He had an aura about him."

He also had a great sense of humour. By

The decline of cost-plus contracts and the growth of branding

In the early days, most contracts were cost-plus – the client paid for all costs and a management fee. Later, when clients wanted lower costs, fixed-price/performance guarantee contracts – where the client agrees a total subsidy and costs cannot rise above that figure – became more prevalent. Later, profit and loss and concession contracts were introduced in larger units to provide catering on a commercial basis with little or no financial input from the client – indeed, the caterer and the client share the profit (or the loss). In total risk contracts, the caterer invests in the facility and earns all the revenue.

In 1994, cost-plus contracts represented 53 per cent of the total number which, by 2010, had shrunk to under 25 per cent. Fixed-price contracts grew from 37 per cent to 64 per cent.

The decline of cost-plus contracts, 1994-2011

	1994	2000	2005	2011
Cost -plus	7,925	5,791	5,182	4,143
Fixed-price/ Performance Guarantee	6,147	10,752	11,212	10,556
Profit & Loss/ Concession/ Total Risk Contracts	842	1,287	575	1,887
TOTAL	14,914	17,830	16,969	16,583

BHA Food and Service Management Surveys

The decline of the cost-plus contract coincided with the introduction of branded outlets. Between 1994 and 2009 the number of branded outlets quickly expanded as caterers became aware of the benefits of more skillful merchandising and marketing. The significance of branding lies in its ability to boost sales, particularly when catering for the general public – high street brands are

Branded outlets in contract catering, 1994 - 2009

	1994	1998	2000	2005	2009
In house/own brand	147	1,636	4,352	8,621	8,609
High street / franchise	26	248	299	532	1,064

BHA Food and Service Management Surveys

particularly successful in encouraging meal take-up because of customer familiarity. Branding has thus become a critically important management tool. However, most companies have developed their own in-house brands as a more flexible (and less expensive) option than using high street brands with their high franchise fee structure. The growth of high street brands has primarily been restricted to major companies and locations where there is significant customer footfall.

1967 he had become chief executive with Lewis as chairman. A keen sailor and car rally enthusiast, Lichtensteiger could also be very grumpy – "You're the best of a poor bunch and not really what I want," he told one regional director on his appointment. He used a slide rule regularly which fazed most people, and was chary about increasing salaries – "He used every trick in the book not to," recalls one unfortunate. Few people were indifferent to him – "You either loved him or hated him," says Pam Evans.

Tony Ward-Lewis recalls that Lichtensteiger had his favourites – "of which I was not one".

"I didn't drink hard enough at play nor did I chain smoke." He also had had three car prangs which annoyed his boss.

"We were all driving around 2,000 miles a week in crap cars because Pat kept the car scale depressed by having an ordinary Rover himself. In fact, when he went to Berni Inns in 1981 he said to me: 'Just watch the car scale zoom upward now that I'm gone.' It did, much to my pleasure."

Lichtensteiger's style of management was effective and straightforward but sometimes quite distant.

"He had his moods and you had to catch him at the right time," recollects Nigel Anker.

On one occasion, he selected a senior manager out of 10 candidates on the written answers to a series of 20 questions. They were all reasonable and legitimate but as the managing director, Lichtensteiger's own knowledge of the candidates should probably have told him who to select.

At the time, Bateman was widely regarded as a very well run company – certainly by its middle and senior executives. The company was awash with cash and Cliff Green, the finance director, was reputedly making more money placing the cash takings on the overnight money market than the company made in profit. Clients were

being charged for everything possible – 'if it moves, charge it,' was a company maxim, though Gerry Robinson was later to take this even further. The company was earning so much money from discounts, which very few clients understood, that it would have been commercial suicide to abandon them though Jordan's Dataquest figures (see Chapter seven) do not entirely support this. But there was tight financial control. One area manager, gambling his area's takings on the horses, was quickly spotted and fired. Kevin Birmingham, a regional director, regarded as rather tight-fisted, used to go through expenses with a toothcomb and would readily query petrol purchases on a Friday and a Monday – "What work did you do over the weekend, then?"

* * *

In the 1980s and later, much to the aggravation of many contractors, consultants came into the picture. Against a background of an evermore competitive industry, fees were under pressure. As a result caterers' purchasing power was used to earn supplier discounts which then helped to ensure reasonable returns – at an average net margin of between two and six per cent the industry can hardly be accused of profiteering.

Consultants came into the picture, initially encouraged by public sector bodies looking for independent advice in awarding catering contracts. From the contractor's point of view, most consultants were regarded as a significant nuisance and were frequently labelled failed caterers who were now attempting to earn a living on the back of the very businesses which had previously employed them; there were accusations that any perceived savings for a client were taken up by the consultant's fee. Consultants, of course, believed (and still do) that

their advice is helpful to clients who have no intimate knowledge of catering and that their fees represent fair payment for their efforts.

Whichever side is taken, there is no doubt that the introduction of these middlemen began to muddy the waters in the relationship between client and caterer; accusations became commonplace that consultants tended to favour one contractor over others because of their financial arrangements with the favoured contractor. Were caterers being transparent? Were clients being told exactly how contractors made their money? But caterers replied that clients didn't need to be told if they were satisfied with the service they were getting. But how serious was the problem?

"In all my years in the industry I can recall only four or five instances where the client has raised the issue of inter-unit prices and I do not remember any of those resulting in a lost unit," says Jim Cartwright.

* * *

Bateman was certainly a happy ship. Howard Goodman, who had joined Bateman Grandmet Holdings as group management training officer in 1978 and then went on to become regional catering manager for Bateman Catering, remembers it as an excellent company to work for. "They ran a great company. Everyone I was in contact with generally enjoyed working for it. A fantastic camaraderie ran through the company for the seven years I was there. There was lots of autonomy – maybe at times a bit too much."

Peter Aldrich recalls that Bateman was highly focused, with a good marketing strategy and a very aggressive sales force which sold catering contracts, equipment, vending and other services. The commitment to training and developing

Tony Walford opens a new Midland Catering office: "My view is that good food, well cooked by well-trained staff and well presented will always be required in industrial catering."

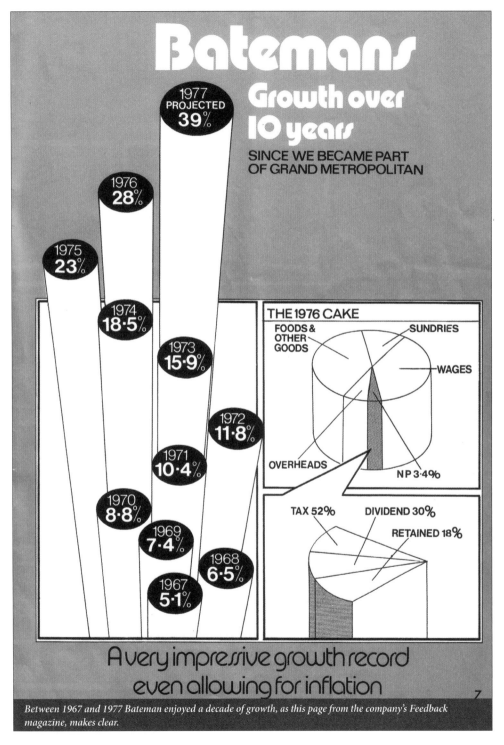

Batemans
Growth over 10 years
SINCE WE BECAME PART OF GRAND METROPOLITAN

1977 PROJECTED **39%**

1976 **28%**

1975 **23%**

1974 **18·5%**

1973 **15·9%**

1972 **11·8%**

1971 **10·4%**

1970 **8·8%**

1969 **7·4%**

1968 **6·5%**

1967 **5·1%**

THE 1976 CAKE

FOODS & OTHER GOODS

SUNDRIES

WAGES

OVERHEADS

NP 3·4%

TAX 52%   DIVIDEND 30%

RETAINED 18%

A very impressive growth record even allowing for inflation

Between 1967 and 1977 Bateman enjoyed a decade of growth, as this page from the company's Feedback magazine, makes clear.

the staff ran through the company like a lodestar. In 1978, Aldrich himself went on a six-month sales training programme when he was chef manager in the West Country and had expressed a wish to switch into sales, despite some opposition from his immediate boss.

"The company put me up in a flat in London for the duration of the course," he says. "It was quite a commitment."

The importance of Bateman and Midland to the parent company was emphasised at the time of GrandMet's purchase of Watney Mann, the brewers, an acquisition which almost brought the company down. Howard Goodman recalls:

"I remember being called to a general meeting which was conducted by Graham Lewis, who was a main board member, who said that the company needed all the cash it could get and that Bateman and Midland had a huge part to play as cash generators. Money had to be banked daily, revenues enhanced and costs cut back to the minimum to help GrandMet survive.

"Senior management didn't bury their heads in the sand – they explained the problem and asked for help, which worked."

* * *

At Midland Catering, Tony Walford's background was in hotels and catering. In late 1971, however, just after Grand Metropolitan had bought the company off the Webb family, Ernest Sharp, GrandMet's joint managing director, headhunted him to be managing director of Midland Catering.

Walford had charm in spades; he was also highly competent, far-seeing and a good motivator. Immaculately dressed – he typically wore a white shirt with a red handkerchief stuffed neatly in his breast pocket – he immediately set about reorganising Midland, creating four divisions with a director in charge of each and took Midland into the private hospital and schools market. Within a year of joining, in 1972, he had organised the company's first meeting of unit managers, warning them that clients were already moving towards insisting on some cost guarantees. In the long-term, he said, clients were not going to continue signing a management fee and a cost-plus contract which meant they did not know what their precise costs would be. He aimed to boost Midland's share of the market from 420 contracts to 600 in two years (by the end of 1974).

"We have all heard about the new ideas in catering. We can't rule out the developments that are taking place. I'm all for new products and new systems but we have got to make sure that that they are good products and good systems. We've got to get the catering right.

"My view is that good food, well cooked by well-trained staff and well presented will always be required in industrial catering."

Walford was keen to promote the traditional values of catering but he did not overlook how that could be achieved. Recognising that more emphasis had to be placed on training and development he also wanted to empower managers and staff, encouraging ideas to flow upwards from unit managers as well as down from board level. It was all based on putting into practice the management principles which he had been promulgating at the Training Board. To those in Midland it came as a breath of fresh air.

* * *

Meanwhile, at Bateman, since the acquisition by Grandmet in 1967, turnover had grown by an average of 13.5 per cent annually while Midland was equally buoyant – this in spite of the chaos of the three-day week in 1974

and other disruptions. This growth was partly the result of Ernest Sharp, who had decided to spread the company's industrial catering activities as widely as possible overseas in order to create a buffer for any downturn in the UK market. The emergence of GrandMet International Services (GIS – see Chapter 12) certainly brought huge benefits. But in 1981 came a raft of changes that set the contract catering industry on a new course entirely.

* * *

GrandMet finally decided to merge Bateman and Midland to form Grandmet Catering Services, with the appointment of Dick Turpin from Berni Inns as managing director and the removal of Pat Lichtensteiger from Bateman to Berni Inns – a job swop which neither of them wanted.

The reason behind these appointments, poorly received in the industry, was probably nothing more than the result of some new management thinking on the part of GrandMet rather than a reflection on the abilities of the two people concerned. Increasingly, the company was turning its attention towards the USA; its impending purchase of Liggett was just around the corner and, a little later, InterContinental Hotels were acquired.

At the time, one of GrandMet's main board directors had gone to the US on a high level management course which had explored how to revitalise languishing management structures; with two joint managing directors, this was a state of affairs that GrandMet was beginning to face. The lecturer cited a multi-product conglomerate which had simply shuffled its pack of senior executives, putting all of them in positions in which they had no previous experience or, indeed, interest – a move which, it was claimed, made them bring fresh ideas to the

business and to look at it in a new way.

This idea was adopted in GrandMet in the hope that a similar shake-up would yield beneficial results. The company's industrial catering division, including GIS, was lumped together with Berni Inns and the County Hotel operations under John Travers Clark, chief executive of GrandMet's Express Dairies division. In the words of one contemporary, Travers Clark may have known about milk but not much about catering (he went on to become chairman of the Hotel and Catering Industry Training Board).

He, in turn, shuffled his senior people: Graham Lewis, chairman of Bateman, who sat on the main board, was given the County Hotels division as well as industrial catering; Pat Lichtensteiger, who would have been the natural choice as managing director of the new industrial catering company, was put in charge of Berni Inns, and Dick Turpin, whose career had been spent entirely in the commercial restaurant world, latterly in charge of Berni Inns, was appointed to head up Grandmet Catering Services, the new name for the combined Bateman and Midland operation. In short, their jobs were swopped. Tony Walford left Midland to take over GrandMet's London and overseas hotels while David Unwin remained in charge of GIS. This did not last long, however. Lewis quit soon after as chairman and went on to act as consultant to Stakis hotels for a couple of years, even living in Glasgow for a while. He died in 2004 at the age of 85.

Turpin's appointment was queried by many because the contract catering sector in the 1980s was quite different to the restaurant sector though with the increased reliance on commercial catering offers by contract catering companies, there are far greater similarities today. The shake-up was very poorly received, particularly among the Bateman ranks where Lichtensteiger,

(Flotta oil terminal: Calum McRoberts)

The Flotta oil terminal – the contract that landed Pat Lichtensteiger in the Old Bailey (inset) on a charge of corruption – which was admitted and was probably a factor in his move to Berni Inns a couple of years later.

immensely popular, had spent his entire career, driving the company forward to become one of the industry's major players. He had no experience of high street catering and Turpin had no experience of industrial catering. Many in the company were mystified about the move and there was resentment at senior levels in Bateman that they were being used as pawns to prove some theoretical management concept.

Lichtensteiger took the move very badly. On his last day at Bateman he went around the office saying goodbye and then retired to his own office where 10 or so of his colleagues, including Philip Morley (then a director of GIS), Pam Evans (Bateman's IR director), Bill Stead (sales director), David Unwin and others gathered "and we drank the booze cupboard dry," says Pam Evans. "He was very distressed."

"Yes, Pat was very unhappy about it," says Philip Morley. "His departure was very emotional. I drove him home from his farewell party and he was very sad at having to move to Berni.

"He had always been as unflappable as a Swiss clock – strict, fair and totally dependable. Berni Inns was not where he wanted to be."

But professional to the last, Lichtensteiger stayed at Berni for five years until 1986 when, at the age of 57, he quit as a result of an internal reorganisation that didn't suit him. He died soon after of lung cancer; he had been a lifelong smoker.

Significantly, the reshuffle also had to do with the fact that Lichtensteiger had been the fall-guy in a court case only a year or so earlier.

In late 1979 he had pleaded guilty to authorising two corrupt gifts – £2,500 worth of furniture and £700 cash for a holiday – to two employees in the Turriff Taylor Tarmac Consortium which was building an oil terminal on the Isle of Flotta in the Orkneys

for which Bateman had successfully bid. It was commonly believed that Lichtensteiger had taken the rap only because he was the titular head of the company.

The case, which was heard at the Old Bailey, was the result of a whistle-blower who discovered that there was an accounting irregularity relating to the Flotta contract as far back as 1974, five years previously. The whistleblower, who worked in Bateman's finance department, had overheard a conversation about how the company was going to be able to cope with paying commissions and fees to middlemen and others when obtaining contracts overseas; backhanders, in those days, were endemic in the Middle East and especially so in the oil industry. He took it upon himself to go back through past accounts to check and found some anomalies in the Flotta accounts, which he reported. The subsequent case alleged that the gifts were made after Bateman had successfully tendered for the contract to cater to the consortium's workforce on Flotta.

The case became something of a *cause celèbre*. GrandMet hired Victor Mischon, then reputed to be one of the best defence lawyers in the land, to act on Lichtensteiger's behalf. Advised to plead guilty, Lichtensteiger was fined £7,000 admitting both cases of corruption. Both the employees denied receiving the gifts (in fact, the jury cleared the one employee of corruptly accepting £700). With the case gleefully reported in *Private Eye* and in most of the nationals, Mischon assured the judge that Lichtensteiger had since issued 'stringent memoranda' making it clear that the company was not prepared to tolerate the making of such payments again.

At a time when huge multi-million pound contracts were in the offing not just in the UK but abroad, it is difficult to believe that this was an isolated case – it

was (and remains) commonplace in the Middle East – but GrandMet had had its fingers burned and the government of the day threatened to prevent Bateman winning any new government contracts. GrandMet paid the fine and Mischon's hefty fee and Lichtensteiger remained in post, but when the merger between Bateman and Midland was created two years later in 1981, the case was almost certainly an additional factor in moving him out of the firing line of contract catering and into Berni Inns.

As an addendum to the story, the whistleblower retained his job but resigned when the company's finance department was moved from London to Birmingham.

The merger of Bateman and Midland created some havoc. With hindsight, it would probably have been better to have merged the two companies much earlier so preventing them from consolidating their individual identities; at the same time they would have been able to reap the undoubted rewards of amalgamation in terms of head office and regional office costs. Catering standards would have benefited, too.

The returns between the two companies were also noticeably different, though the analysis by Jordan's Dataquest (see Chapter seven) implies that Midland, not Bateman, was by far the more profitable of the two companies and raises the question as to why Graham Lewis had allowed the differential to be so marked during his tenure as chief executive and then chairman. In fact, there is evidence that Lewis did write a note to all Midland Catering directors criticising their performance – "except that of Mike Taylor" – but whether this was justified and how effectively it was followed up is not recorded. The truth probably is that both companies were generating ample cash flow which was helping GrandMet to provide funds for future acquisitions.

CHAPTER ELEVEN

GrandMet Catering – and the beginnings of Compass

In 1981, Dick Turpin faced the job of merging two disparate companies into one. It was not an easy task but it was the foundations of an empire.

At the time of their merger, both Midland Catering and Bateman Catering had a different ethos even though both were seen as paternalistic companies still operating to old-fashioned values of service. But it was as if two warring children had been told to live together and get on with it – "It was never going to happen," says Pam Evans, who had been appointed head of personnel under Hilary Charles, the personnel director. Charles, who describes the two companies as 'chalk and cheese', found herself in a particularly difficult position.

At Bateman, she had carved out a powerful position as a key member of the top triumvirate with Graham Lewis and Pat Lichtensteiger. Although director of personnel, not always such a position of power and influence, her length of tenure at the company, her undoubted ability and her relationship with both Lewis and Lichtensteiger which was long-standing

and close, had positioned her at the top. She had built up the Bateman staff ethos, had introduced new management ideas, and had travelled widely throughout the world on behalf of GIS. Bateman had been built up over a number of years largely by the efforts of the three and merging the two companies was seen by them as nothing short of a betrayal.

"We had spent the last 10 years totally ignoring Midland, even though it was a sister company. There was absolutely no doubt in our minds that Bateman was by far the superior company in terms of the quality of the staff and the contracts we had – indeed, in every sense," says Charles.

There was also the feeling that in combining the two companies inevitably something would be lost.

"I did not think it was a very happy ship. And, for me at least, the longer the merger went on, the more unhappy it became."

Little wonder that her relationship with Dick Turpin got off to a poor start and never recovered. Others – not just her close staff – were similarly antagonistic. With Lichtensteiger now at Berni and Graham Lewis out of the company altogether, she

was the sole survivor of the Bateman era and she didn't like it – nor, indeed, did she much hide her unhappiness. Others were also unhappy.

"One thing I have to say about Bateman in the old days is that if you did a good job, they always rewarded you for it," says Alan Robinson, who eventually became a director. "My reward for pulling Turriff around was to be given a deposit for a new car and expenses to go with it. It made me feel I had arrived." Unfortunately, only a few years later, Robinson's reward was rather less welcome: he was fired by Tony Coles in 1984.

There were similar examples of this at

Dick Turpin set up a working party to plan the merger and it was clear that some people on both sides were fiercely opposed. Neither side wanted to lose its identity.

Midland Catering. Both companies had grown in the 1970s and generated quite fierce loyalties among their respective staff. Turpin's style of consensus management was emollient but it was quite different to that of the forceful personalities who had previously led the companies.

Doubts and concerns at senior level were manifest. Turpin set up a working party to plan the merger and it was clear that some people on both sides were fiercely opposed. Neither side wanted to lose its identity although, lower down the line, most employees at unit level were unaware of the tensions at head office. On the Bateman side, there were particular concerns that some of Midland Catering's contracts were seen as 'canteen catering' and were regarded as too insignificant to be worthwhile. Even Midland's British Rail contract, a prestigious gain for the company in the 1970s, was not considered sufficiently profitable at the time of the merger; afterwards, over 10 per cent of the Midland contracts were allegedly surrendered, though this is difficult to verify. There was also rivalry and some ill-will towards Midland by Bateman people, and vice versa. Alan Robinson, who was appointed regional director for the South West of the merged company, had particularly strong views and believed that there were no benefits to the merger as far as Bateman was concerned. He says:

"We were never in competition with Midland because we really didn't want the kind of business they were in. After the merger, we were very reluctant to take on the Midland contracts because many of the returns were too low to be economic and the standard of catering was not good."

Howard Goodman, by then a regional manager, says that despite being a sister company, Midland was perceived as the poor relation.

"We didn't talk to or with them, which I suppose was snobby, but they catered in lots of chef manager low fee sites, which was only confirmed when we merged."

"At the time of the merger, Sutcliffe were regarded as good caterers and Bateman were regarded as good managers," says Nigel Anker. "Gardner Merchant was a bit of a closed shop and Midland was at the bottom of the pile, operating factory canteens."

However, Del Bampton, by then a regional operations manager for Bateman and a company man through and through, remembers Midland as "not a bad outfit. It had some good contracts and some good people." This is a view echoed by Jim Cartwright who tried desperately to share out the jobs of Midland and Bateman people in his region fairly between the two companies – unlike some of the other regions. "Midland had some very good contracts," he asserts. But the general consensus was that it also had some very bad contracts.

* * *

When Turpin took control of Bateman and Midland in 1980, no decision had been taken to merge the two companies even though it seemed obvious to most observers that this must be the logical next step. Even so, Turpin spent eight weeks setting up the working party, visiting regions and talking to staff and clients before deciding that, indeed, a merger was the best way forward. Despite the fact that the working party itself was divided on the merits of a merger – old loyalties died hard – the decision was taken and the reason was predictable – "It would harness the undoubted strengths of both companies into a single, powerful group committed to a common purpose," was how Turpin described it in the company's first staff newspaper – *Grandmet Catering World.*

He said: "We believe that a combined company, trading under a name strongly associated with one of the most successful international companies in the world, will provide the right framework for us to develop our activities."

He set about welding the two companies together with a board that included two Midland Catering directors (Tony Coles and Mike Taylor) and seven from Bateman (Alan Robinson, Hilary Charles, Tony Ward-Lewis, Cliff Green, Kevin Birmingham, David Carter and David Thompson). The two companies employed 16,000 people and had separate traditions, different pay structures, different fringe benefits and different styles of management. As Joe Hyam, then editor of *Caterer,* said in an article at the time, "no easy task".

Turpin and his team set about it in a methodical manner but there was much residual disquiet at his appointment. Many people in the company considered Berni

Tony Coles began to emerge as a centre of power and influence, which Turpin appeared happy to cede.

Inns to be a very formulaic business, with set menus and rigidly laid-down standards of operation and décor. All carpets had to be red; when a green one was mistakenly installed in one branch, it had to be immediately taken up and replaced. The menu offered no opportunity for any local initiatives. Those in contract catering considered the Berni Inns operation to be an easy ride compared to the challenges posed to contractors with their need for an ever-changing daily menu, five days a week or more, with the concomitant need to satisfy both client and customers on very tight margins.

So while Turpin was recognised as an experienced and skilled commercial caterer – cuttingly by Hilary Charles: "He used to run steak bars!" – there were residual doubts that his background in Berni was relevant to the far more complex job of merging the Bateman and Midland companies. Despite his best efforts, these doubts never really went away.

A road show visited every region in which he described to staff what was happening and why. Full colour brochures and other print material were introduced together with a £100,000 advertising campaign. Staff communications were improved and the message went out to clients and potential clients: this was a new company in the contract catering firmament. The front cover of *Caterer* helped promote the image.

The approach to the merger reflected Turpin's own collegiate approach to management: cautious, not given to hasty decisions and very consultative. He wanted to take the 16,000 people along with him; he did not want to drive them into agreement – he sought agreement and eschewed confrontation. He was also keen not to upset clients by any hasty decisions. His style of management meant he was widely liked

The Bateman/Midland merger merited a front cover of Caterer. Left to right around the table: Alan Robinson, Hilary Charles, Mike Taylor, Tony Ward-Lewis, Dick Turpin, Tony Coles, Cliff Green, David Carter and David Thompson.

in the company on a personal level. "He would do anything for anybody," says one ex-colleague – something that Mike Bailey was to experience later when Turpin put him in touch with Chris Bucknall after the Compass buy-out. "He was something of a sage," says another. "He was someone you could talk to." But to those who had been brought up in the hard school of contract catering the new managing director had to prove himself to a great many new people.

This might have happened had he taken a more determined approach to re-organising the merged company. He told Hyam in the same article that he was adamant that the merger had resulted in "scarcely any redundancies", yet the underlying justification of any merger is to purge jobs and activities, not to save them, in order to take advantage of both companies' strengths and eliminate their weaknesses. Many may consider this to be the wrong approach and it was, indeed, something that ran against the grain of Turpin's character which Gerry

Robinson was quick to exploit in 1985 when he was appointed chief executive of the Compass group by GrandMet; within weeks, he had culled the entire board, including Turpin himself, with only Jim Cartwright as a divisional director and John Kane as company secretary remaining. In trying to save everyone's job, Turpin had deliberately not taken the opportunity to wield the axe with abandon – an action that would have made it a more efficient organisation. Adverse client response was one reason put forward to explain why he took such a cautious approach.

Nevertheless, he was nothing if not realistic. He recognised that contract catering was on the cusp of change and in a remarkably hard-hitting and prescient speech to the Industrial Catering Association in 1982, only two years after he took over, he emphasised that contractors had to take a more commercial approach. The majority of clients, he told delegates, were already questioning the value of

the catering subsidy:

"Their questioning will lead them to one conclusion – that employee catering must move towards a more commercial approach.

"For too long, contract caterers have ignored changing consumer tastes and rising standards because of their own shortcomings or because of their own faint hearts.

"This attitude has been reflected in the menus that we offer – stodge and plodge – the quality of the food we serve, the standards of hygiene, the canteen image that we have created and the Dickensian changing rooms for our staff."

He could hardly have made a bolder criticism of the business in which he had been plunged but his reference to stodge and plodge won him few friends in the business:

"That was totally wrong," says Hilary Charles. "Our style of catering depended on the requirements of our clients. They were always referred to as staff restaurants, rarely

Badges were more or less obligatory in the early days and male dominance continued though with a little more female representation. Left to right front row: Jenny North, marketing executive, Pam Evans, head of personnel and Hilary Charles, HR director.

as canteens. We provided a bespoke service."

Nevertheless, his solution in many ways foreshadowed the changes that were around the corner for the industry.

"Why don't we inject excitement and fun into our staff restaurants? Why don't we operate our restaurants so that employees are anxious to spend their money with us? Why don't we need to survive on the same premise that the commercial restaurant survives – that the customer has to receive good value for money for the price he pays?"

Over 30 years later, Turpin's speech still resonates. The attitude towards staff feeding now is as commercial as Turpin envisaged it in 1982. He was a man well up-to-speed and who saw the direction in which contract catering was heading. He saw the need to offer other support services – cleaning and security in particular – which were, in fact, profitable new businesses.

He also recognised that new markets were opening up: leisure and retail catering, for example, as well as the more traditional ones of schools and hospitals. As early as 1981, at the time of the merger, the company was already lauding its success in winning the contract for staff and retail catering at Hamleys, the toy shop in Regent Street, Burton's the tailoring chain, and Owen Owen the department store, though these had largely been set in place earlier by the Bateman and Midland companies. With Turpin's retail experience, the move into his old sector was understandable, but Grandmet Catering and then Compass still had their roots in contracting, not in retail catering. When Peter Smale joined the company from Wimpy in 1983 as marketing and development director, he instantly recognised the difference in approach. In an in-house article, he questioned whether the company had the commercial nous to adopt a more commercial approach. "Have we got the necessary

services and resources to satisfy the market needs? If we have, how can we exploit our resources to the best advantage? If not, how best do we develop new services?" he asked.

On the premise of nothing ventured, nothing gained, Turpin persevered. He encouraged special days – commonplace today. He backed a new, inexpensive, fast food takeaway concept called Hillbillies that John Symonds at Bateman had led before the merger. This trialled at the Midland Bank and was aimed at units where space was very limited. Some dozen or so units were fitted out but the concept did not catch on as widely as had been hoped, partly because regional directors thought they were too small and insignificant and some sales staff (as well as regional managers) were not convinced that the concept was right, anyway.

New uniforms and training programmes were created, together with the appointment of a slew of new training officers to upskill staff to meet the new demands being made on them. Some big new contracts were won including British Leyland at Longbridge, CBI in Centrepoint in London, the RUC in Northern Ireland – 130 in the first year – at a time when the economy was in the doldrums and factories were closing.

There was a feeling that the company was on the move and, despite some residual internal strife and ill-concealed opposition, Turpin [unfortunately, in the preparation of this book we were unable to talk to him because of his ill-health] was able to look back at a successful first year and look ahead to an exciting future, recognising that contract catering was adopting a far more commercial approach to the provision of its services than it ever had before. At the time, he had pointed out that Bateman and Midland were each making about £1.5m profit – "but that should equal £4m now," he told a meeting of senior people.

Grandmet Catering Services

At the time of the merger in 1981 the company had won a number of contracts, including staff and retail catering at Hamley's, the toy shop on Regent Street.

Credit PA Photos/Topfoto

Grandmet won 130 contracts in its first year, including catering for the CBI in Centrepoint in London.

Credit TopFoto

The company continued to win new contracts – 360 by 1984 – reducing inevitable losses, but Turpin's laid-back style of management – "I can't remember him introducing anything new," says one ex-colleague perhaps unfairly - was not entirely successful. With 16,000 employees, it was a large organisation to control and with five divisions and 16 regions it had a complicated structure. He let others get on with their job yet he had a habit of leaving yellow Post-it notes on people's chairs with suggestions of things to do, which tended to greatly irritate. His enthusiasm for wearing name badges on every possible occasion was both legendary and infuriating. "It's as if we were at school and didn't know the new boys," remembers one ex-colleague. "We called him Mr Badgeman," says another.

More seriously, he allowed others to fill a management vacuum and Tony Coles began to emerge as a centre of power and influence, which Turpin appeared happy to cede.

"It became clearer and clearer that Tony was taking control and Dick seemed very happy to let him," says Pam Evans.

Tony Coles was ex-Hendon College and had spent the early years of his career in personnel and training at Midland Catering, gradually climbing up the ladder; he was appointed director of the Grandmet Catering eastern division in 1981 based at Dunstable at the time of the merger. His forceful personality and no-nonsense manner, his ambition and free-spending approach endeared him to his immediate staff even if some of his new-found Bateman colleagues were not so enamoured. Nor did his background in personnel enthuse many of those who had climbed up the ladder from the kitchen.

"Tony was extremely talented and had a great deal of ability," says one ex-colleague. "He understood the business well and he was a good leader and very loyal, if you were willing to be part of his gang. But his egotism got in the way of a great talent."

"He was a great showman," says another. "He was a shrewd operator and he gave you chances."

The original board had taken the company two years into the merger but things were about to change. In the summer of 1983, Coles emerged as director of UK operations and second in command to Turpin, with a new two-tier board structure.

"We now need to build on success by stronger divisions and regions," Turpin told his staff. "This will keep our decision-making process where it should be, nearer to the client, but it will also provide us with the time and resources to develop into other areas of catering."

In effect, the previous regional directors had been demoted and were now answerable to the new director of operations. The new five-man main board – Turpin, Coles, Tony Ward-Lewis (Compass Vending), Peter Smale (marketing and development) and Martin Clayton (a newcomer from Chloride Batteries) as finance director – emerged as the body "concentrating on realising our full potential not only in our traditional area of staff feeding but in commercial catering as well," said Turpin. An operating board, chaired by Coles, comprising the regional directors, took day-to-day control of the company. The number of divisions was reduced to four and regions to 14.

In management terms, it was a step in the right direction but it was certainly not a happy time. Of the original board, Cliff Green, the financial director, had already retired and a clear-out of senior staff had taken place: Hilary Charles and David Carter (purchasing director) had quit more or less at the same time. Pam Evans also left and so did David Thompson, northern division director, who was succeeded by

Jim Cartwright. Mike Taylor stayed on for a while but left to open a market garden near Broadway in Worcestershire, horticulture being an abiding interest. Redundancies reached lower down the line. Graham Stone, commercial general manager for the Midland Division, who had joined Bateman as a management trainee in 1966, was one also made redundant.

Hilary Charles, the longest serving of all the directors with 27 years in the company, latterly extremely unhappy and frustrated at the turn of events and always opposed to the merger and with little personal regard for Turpin even in public, more or less brought her own position to a head when she asked Turpin whether she was doing what he wanted her to do and was told everything was fine. She was devastated when, a week later, he told her that the chemistry wasn't right and gave her an extraordinarily generous payoff to compensate. Del Bampton describes her as 'heartbroken.'

Another Bateman old hand, Alan Robinson, moved from a 'comfortable' office in Harrow and found himself in Dunstable as director of the Central Division, where he was surrounded by people, largely from Midland Catering, who he did not know and who he did not entirely trust. Despite growing the business in his division by 10 per cent per year since the merger against a target of seven per cent, he gradually realised that his face did not fit in the new regime; he was fired by Coles early in 1985 with a severance package (after the threat of an Industrial Tribunal hearing) that was so generous that it appeared to acknowledge the company's culpability.

Indeed, it was a far more favourable package than other Compass directors later received when Gerry Robinson culled most of them on his arrival as managing director.

* * *

The creation of the new board coincided with a change of name. At the time of the merger, it was thought that the powerful GrandMet name would be a benefit to the new company in selling its catering services to major new clients. However, the GrandMet association was never wholeheartedly accepted and the merged company was the only subsidiary within the GrandMet organisation, apart from Grandmet International Services (GIS) to use the parent name. Within two years, came the change.

A note in *Grandmet Catering World* told its readers:

"Our parent company, as you know, has always been shy about the use of the Grandmet name which is confusing in the marketplace due the different business activities. The inevitable outcome is that Grand Metropolitan has decided that all its companies using derivatives of the name must change."

The cost of revising all the corporate literature and marketing material was never revealed but it was at least as

Compass Services

NEARER YOUR NEEDS...BY FAR

The logos changed from Grandmet Catering Services to Compass: the new name was actually the name of a major conference the company had previously held at the Chateau Impney in Droitwich.

large as the £100,000 cost of introducing the Grandmet Catering Services name two years earlier in 1981. But why the use of the Grandmet name would be confusing in the marketplace is something of a mystery and the real reason, almost certainly, is that thoughts of hiving off the company, either by an outright sale, a flotation or a buy-out, were already being considered. There was also the consideration that any bad publicity from a unit that suffered a food poisoning outbreak, for example, would reflect badly on the parent company. So, in 1984, the Compass name emerged.

A high-powered committee was set up to suggest a possible name and Jim Cartwright remembers a meeting on a hot summer's day at the Britannia Hotel in Grosvenor Square, London when a vast number of names were put forward – Britannia being one – until Compass was suggested.

In fact, Compass was actually the name of a major conference that the company had previously held at the Chateau Impney in Droitwich which cost a reputed £800,000 – an eye-watering sum today but even more in 1984 when the profits were not much more than £3m. But Tony Coles remembers a meeting he held with John Symonds, regional general manager for the City of London, and Jenny North, the company's marketing executive, to discuss the new name.

"We were in the meeting and John suddenly said: 'Why don't we call it Compass?' And Compass it was. It was the name of the conference we had just had."

Whatever the derivation, the company was now looking forward to an even brighter future with a new main board, a new operations board, and a new name.

"Gaining contracts to provide catering services in places like department store restaurants, night clubs, leisure centres, sports grounds and museums have all shown that our catering knowledge and experience and management expertise have a very wide application," Dick Turpin told his staff (now 18,000 strong) in the first edition of *Compass World* in Autumn 1984.

"Our big step into other areas of contracting has been highly successful, too, winning us many new cleaning and security contracts... We can look to the future with enormous confidence."

In truth, the venture into night clubs had been a disaster and progress into leisure centres was only intermittently successful to say the least, while in-store restaurants depended as much on the store's retail success as on Compass' catering expertise. But moving into other support services acknowledged the expanding facilities management market and Compass was clearly keeping up with, if not leading the competition in recognising its potential.

Unfortunately, all but one of the senior people who had helped see the merger through were about to realise that the future of Compass would not involve them. Gerry Robinson appeared on the scene and nothing would ever be like it was.

*All badged up and ready to go – into an all-male world. A later group of **Grandmet Catering managers** with only one woman – Gillian Medcalf – who was regional general manager, Western Home Counties.*

CHAPTER TWELVE

Pioneering in the oil fields

In the 1970s UK catering companies looked to take advantage of the opportunities presented by the boom in worldwide oil exploration.

In the beginning, Britain's catering companies concentrated on the North Sea where the first well was drilled in 1967; the first major find, Amoco's Montrose field, was drilled two years later. In 1970, BP successfully opened up the Forties field and in 1971 Shell's Brent field off Shetland opened up. Even so, oil did not come ashore until the Cruden Bay terminal in Aberdeen was completed in 1975.

From the start, these rigs demanded full-on catering and support services and the opportunities were immense. Among the first to recognise this was Scottish-based Kelvin Catering. Kelvin, a small-time catering outfit run by two brothers, had been in business since 1954 and had established itself as a reliable contractor in the north of Scotland. In the mid-1960s it saw the potential in servicing the many platforms that would eventually be needed to bring the oil ashore, as well as the on-shore rig construction sites in Aberdeen and further down the east

Oil rigs in the North Sea – and elsewhere in the world – offered profitable new business for caterers.

Credit Topfoto.co.uk

Kelvin Catering was active in the North Sea and elsewhere, including providing the catering and accommodation facilities for the Channel Tunnel, at the time the biggest construction project n Europe. But the Piper Alpha oil rig disaster in 1988 claimed the lives of 23 Kelvin workers.

coast. Another company, Chalk Drillcater, founded in 1965, saw similar, almost limitless opportunities as did Frank Bell's Commercial Catering Group. By 1970 they were all winning business both in the UK and overseas, mainly in the Middle East. ARA (later Aramark) also took a keen interest, tempted by the opportunities that could yield a £1m a year turnover on a single rig. Although competition was fierce and the environment extremely tough and potentially dangerous, the profits were good enough to encourage Gardner Merchant to dip its toe into the North Sea water in 1983 by acquiring Kelvin for some £4m. It was an excellent purchase with plenty of promise, but three years later a disaster rocked the company.

In 1986, Chevron's Piper Alpha rig sank with the loss of 167 lives including the entire Kelvin workforce on the rig, 23 workers in all. It was a shattering event that sent the Kelvin head office staff into meltdown. Gardner Merchant was then

still part of THF and Lord Forte made an emergency donation to each of the stricken families; by the time the final compensations was settled by the insurers all kinds of domestic irregularities had been revealed including the appearance of six previously unacknowledged children; people work on rigs for all sorts of reasons.

The horror of the accident did not, however, deter Kelvin and other operators. Kelvin had already expanded from its North Sea operations to win business overseas, which it continued to do with major oil field projects in Abu Dhabi, Kuwait and Kazakhstan; in Hong Kong it was involved in servicing the construction of the new airport. It was a time of huge expansion for companies that could offer full site services. Back home, it was contracted to feed and accommodate the hundreds of construction workers building the Channel Tunnel – Europe's biggest construction project at the time – but its largest (and reputedly most profitable) was a huge contract providing

the catering and accommodation facilities for 2,000 workers building the airport and a new hospital in the Falkland Islands.

Competition was cut-throat but there was plenty of work to go around. By 1995 Aramark was feeding staff on 17 platforms; a couple of years later Kelvin won a £10m a year contract to produce 6,000 meals a day to 2,000 staff on 15 platforms, some taken from Aramark and CCG.

* * *

It was a time of almost limitless opportunities which had not gone unnoticed at Bateman. Bateman was no stranger to site services. It had already been active in the UK when it had won the contract to provide catering and accommodation with Occidental Oil in Flotta in the Orkneys and BP in Shetland – contracts which had been obtained by Philip Morley, then Bateman's regional sales manager for London and the South West.

Philip Morley: he embarked on a globetrotting exercise that resulted in seven contracts being won in the space of two years. In one eight-day period his airline tickets read London, New York, Anchorage, Tokyo, Singapore, Bahrain, London (including two trips on Concorde).

David Unwin and Philip Morley outside the The Shetland Hotel, which GIS planned, built and operated for some years.

Calculating profit

There were some unusual management practices that had to be updated. In Libya, the authorities insisted on local participation which gave rise to GISS having to find a local food supplier in Tripoli who agreed to supply food to the oil well camps, deep in the desert, run by GISS as a joint venture.

The owner of the company had a novel approach to the meaning of 'profit'. He would place all the money received in a month in the right hand drawer of his desk and all the bills he received in the left hand drawer. At the end of the month he took the bills and paid them and whatever was left in the right hand drawer was profit, which he took.

Fortunately, he subsequently agreed to adopt the more Western approach to accounting.

Morley, who became a director in 1978, had joined Bateman in 1969 and had recognised the growing number of opportunities that high value oil industry contracts presented to caterers. But the Bateman name, though familiar in the UK, was unknown outside. For this reason, it was decided that the GrandMet name, which had a much higher international profile, would be more commercially useful in the United States, Europe and the Middle East. So Bateman Grandmet Holdings, with Pat Lichtensteiger as chief executive and David Unwin, another old Bateman hand, as managing director, was formed.

The new group included Grandmet International Services (GIS), Grandmet International Site Services (GISS), a subsidiary, specialising in construction site operations, Grandmet Technical Services, Sea Hotels, Commercial Catering Equipment and JMS Leroy Services (a cleaning company) – all aiming principally at the overseas market.

The move initially proved extremely successful. The creation of GIS coincided with its first site project outside the UK; this was for Technip Procon-France providing catering services for 5,000 workers and housekeeping services for 850 at a site in Sines in Portugal.

GIS went on to gain some staggeringly large contracts. In 1976, it won a contract, worth over £40m a year to house and feed 27,000 workers at Shedgum on the east coast of Saudi Arabia. The workforce housing and feeding contract was controlled by The Bechtel Corp of the USA and so big was the project that the tender documents filled three airline pallets when sent to the USA for evaluation. But it was worth the effort – it projected the company onto the world stage.

From then on, GIS grew to such an extent that it was providing catering and accommodation both on land and on sea, for oil workers in Europe, the Middle East and the Far East. Two contracts in particular, both with ARAMCO in Saudi Arabia, were worth £54m (£339m today) and were then believed to be the largest of their kind ever awarded.

In 1977, perhaps the boom year, there was a big push to capitalise on the oil and gas exploration in North Africa with Libya and Algeria being the most prominent. Morley recalls it as being the most "frenetic period of my business life". He embarked on a globe trotting exercise that resulted in seven contracts being won in the space of two years. In one eight day period his airline tickets read London, New York, Anchorage, Tokyo, Singapore, Bahrain, London (including two sectors on Concorde).

The following 10 years was a decade of travel: Morley took 115 flights covering 744,000 miles. Business was so good that his expenses were never queried: a return trip to Singapore to sign a £41m (£185m today) deal to build a large construction camp in Algeria by Concorde cost £2,253 or £11,500 in today's money.

Some years later the operation in Libya came to an abrupt end when the site manager, Peter London, who had worked on many of GISS' most challenging projects, was put under house arrest pending the payment of a massive 'deemed' tax, unexpectedly imposed on the company by the government. The amount was never disclosed but it was thought to be greater than the entire turnover of the company since commencing business in Libya. Maxwell Joseph, chairman of Grand Metropolitan, was reported to have authorised whatever amount was necessary to free the manager; happily, after a few months, London was smuggled out of the country and arrangements were eventually made to reach an accord with the local tax authorities.

In 1977, GISS won the contract with McAlpine to house and feed an enormous workforce creating the world's largest sugar plantation on a 169,000 acre tract of land on the White Nile at Rabak in southern Sudan. It imposed considerable logistical challenges. The first job was to cater for the men moving a huge convoy of plant and machinery from Port Sudan, a journey of over 1,100 miles. Chris Shillinglaw, one of the GISS men on the ground, took charge of the operation but unfortunately the convoy lost its way and ran out of provisions.

Shillinglaw had to scour the local villages for supplies and was so successful that his reputation as 'The Scavenger' remained for many years. Appropriately, he went on to run the GISS procurement department in London.

In a note to Morley in September of 1978, congratulating him on his efforts, Pat Lichtensteiger referred to the North African campaign as "assisting enormously in counterbalancing the Middle East 'tilt' of the company", adding an instruction to Morley to take his wife out to dinner – "and charge it to the company". In view of the multi-million pound value of the contracts, it was probably not the most generous of offers.

* * *

By 1979, the division was producing record annual profits of some £25m which led Max Joseph, in his 1977 annual report, to remark on GIS' "explosive increase in profits". A year later offices were set up in Houston, Texas in order to take even greater advantage of the oil boom, which led to it obtaining contracts in Alaska, catering on the trans-Alaska railway line and for BP at Prudo Bay.

Such are the exigencies of working in trouble spots, not everything went entirely to plan. An enormous project in Argentina to re-house 150,000 people in the northern part of the country, at Yasi-Rita, to make way for a 54 kilometre cofferdam and hydroelectric scheme on the Parana River,

Camps weren't always static. In this one, as the pipeline was being built, the camp had to move every month or so.

was thwarted by Mrs Thatcher's decision to go to war over the Falklands. With only hours of warning, the two British members of the local bidding team had to flee the country, leaving all their possessions behind. Ironically, after the war, GIS won a contract in the Falklands, providing accommodation, all housekeeping and catering for 800 construction workers rebuilding the island's infrastructure. It was as demanding as most. With supplies having to be shipped 8,000 miles, in a year the camp consumed 500,000 eggs, 70 miles of chipolata sausages, 450,00 butter portions, 200,000 lbs of potatoes, 250,000 lbs potato chips, 190,000 lbs frozen vegetables, 60,000 lbs bacon, 12,000 lbs lamb chops, 70,000 pints longlife milk and 340,000 individual pies. Kelvin's contract to build the airport and hospital was just as large.

There were tragedies, too. The Piper Alpha disaster had shown how vulnerable workers could be working in a hostile environment. In the Far East, a base was established in Singapore led by Mike Hobson, who had joined GIS some years earlier. He had helped Philip Morley win contracts to manage the famous Singapore Polo Club and the Royal Selangor Cricket

A threat concludes the negotiations

By 1980 GIS was working in 14 different countries, most notable at the time was a contract to house and feed 3,500 Japanese workers at Kaduna in northern Nigeria. The project to build a petrochemical plant lasted four years and it was the first contract let to a Western company to look after Japanese workers.

Negotiating the contract, however, proved difficult and illustrated the problem of tendering in faraway countries. The tender document was split into 15 sections requiring evaluation by 15 different teams within the company, usually without cross-referencing their findings. This made for slow negotiations, requiring many visits to Japan at short notice. The cost of these negotiations began to spiral out of control and Pat Lichtensteiger decided that he would allow only one more trip to complete them before withdrawing, which resulted in a surprisingly quick decision to award the contract the next day.

The success of this led to more Japanese oil companies contracting GIS to look after their workforces in Algeria, Libya and West Africa.

Senior Compass personalities at an industry dinner: around the table, left to right: Terry Brannigan (facing the camera), Sandy Ross, David Unwin, Gary Green, Peter Mills, Clive Grundy, Trevor Briggs, Philip Morley, Richard Dickson, Howard Potter, Chris Gray and Charles Allen.

Club in Kuala Lumpur and in Indonesia a large contract had been won with Bechtel in the jungle of North Sumatra near the city of Medan. Colin Harris, a long-serving Bateman and GIS executive, managed this very remote operation until his light aircraft went down near the site on his way home to the UK. His wife, Irene, five months pregnant, survived the accident but Harris was unfortunately killed.

* * *

In the meantime, GIS had been divided into three operating companies, allowing for greater sales penetration and operational supervision. The three companies were responsible for Saudi Arabia, the Gulf States and the rest of the world.

Nevertheless, by then, GIS was beginning to run out of steam. In an editorial in the Bateman staff newspaper, *Feedback*, in 1980, there were hints that not everything was as it should be:

"The past success of the company is highly commendable but to maintain the growth calls for constant awareness of what is happening in the construction and petro carbon industries and the ability to get up and go anywhere at any time. GIS is geared up to react to such demands and although political unrest in some parts of the world limits operating in certain countries, the future for GIS is one of confidence."

The caution was obvious. GIS had been able to charge up to $100 a day per person for services provided in many of the camps which racked up the profits but eventually budgets began to be cut and payments withheld. The oil boom was over. By the early 1980s the global recession had already affected much of the developed world and GIS was finding trading tough. A few years later, in Grand Metropolitan's annual report for 1984, Maxwell Joseph wrote:

"GIS had a difficult year. On the one hand, increased competition for contract renewals in the Middle East brought down margins to levels that are barely economic. On the other, opportunities to develop profitable business in other parts of the world were affected by a general cut-back in spending on large capital projects. We responded to the changed conditions by reducing central overheads and closing down several overseas offices, but failed to avoid incurring a small loss for the year."

The business, which had been hugely profitable in the mid-1970s after the 1973 oil price hike, had become a victim of its own success. It had expanded out of the Middle East but oil brought wealth to the countries that Bateman had pioneered and with it came the ability to provide such services on a local basis at a much cheaper price.

In Gerry Robinson's later words, the Arab countries 'had wised up' and toughened their negotiating stance.

With contracts more difficult to get, GIS Hotel and Leisure Management was born in an attempt to widen its market base and Philip Morley was put in charge. The new company aimed to develop contracts, mainly hotel and restaurant operations, into China and the Far East. (Coincidentally, at the same time, GrandMet had acquired InterContinental Hotels which it had purchased from Pan Am – a purchase that caused the president of Pan Am to say that they should have kept the hotel group and sold the airline to GrandMet. Pan Am went bust two months later.)

In a note in *Feedback,* Gerry Robinson (see Chapter 14), who had by then moved within GrandMet to take control of Compass, warned:

"We have experimented in many fields away from our mainstream business with the almost inevitable result that we took our eye off the ball. That ball is the provision of high quality life support services for large projects... Only by growth can GIS become a major company in its own right."

* * *

But the going only got tougher. When, in 1987, Robinson led the Compass buy-out, GIS was not going to escape his critical eye, though initially it was heralded as a key part of the new Compass. GIS' overseas activities gave the sale prospectus some 'international sizzle' even though it was likely that Robinson had already made up his mind to focus almost entirely on the industrial catering business in the UK which was far more consistently cash generative. Many of those on the inside rightly believed that as soon as the share price of Compass had settled down all the businesses, except the core Compass Services, would eventually be sold off. They were proved correct.

GIS continued for a few more years after the buy-out but with little prospect of the kind of profits that Robinson wanted or, indeed, expected. This was mainly because of the losses being sustained in the Middle East where GIS had not recognised the need to restructure its now much-reduced activities, thus predicting a £2m loss in the 1984 budget.

In his biography of Gerry Robinson, *Lord of the Dance,* by William Kay, Robinson says:

"We had people having a wonderful lifestyle in Bahrain when it could have been run by one manager. It was plainly a business that was going to die in due course. It had already sunk into losses."

On his first day as managing director of GIS, Robinson called John Greengrass, a GIS director, into his office to discuss the budget. Greengrass, another long-serving Bateman hand (he joined the company in 1974) had just returned from the UAE with no specific job in mind. Robinson sent him to Saudi as managing director, replacing Robert Pawsey who went to work in Hong Kong on a housing project on a remote island (now Hong Kong airport).

Greengrass was given a mandate by Robinson to reduce the overheads generally. He achieved this, even producing a small profit in the year. At the time Charles Allen was based in Saudi as an internal auditor. With his task complete Greengrass returned to be operations director working for David Unwin, still the managing director.

However, the company was quickly reorganised with five new divisional directors: Philip Morley in the Far East, newly recruited Bruce Allen in Saudi together with Ted Daniels (who joined the company in 1973) in USA and Chris Barr (who had joined Batemans in 1972 as a national accounts executive and went on to be national sales manager) in the Gulf States. John Greengrass took charge of Europe and Africa. Bruce Allen promoted Charles Allen (no relation) to finance director of the Saudi joint venture but a year later Gerry Robinson brought Charles Allen back to the UK as managing director of Grandmet Vending, reputedly with a specific charge to sell it off. It was the beginning of a long association that brought the two of them together to Granada and the Forte takeover.

* * *

Morley, who had been developing the Far East opportunities from London convinced the board of the merit of establishing a Hong Kong base with the help of a powerful local trading company. Good headway was made and after just 18 months the business had a £25m annual turnover. But after the buy-out the signals from London were not helpful. It became clear that everything was going to get closed down or sold off. With great regret Morley made the decision – "in the time it took to drink a large whisky after a call from Gerry" – to return to the UK.

With hindsight, closing down the Far East enterprise was perhaps a decision taken in haste though Robinson had already made his mind up, believing that there was no critical mass to the business. Nevertheless, GIS had made a first foothold in China by establishing GFIS, a joint venture with the highly successful Fung Ping Fan family (the 'F' in GFIS) who were also partners with International Distillers and Vintners (IDV), a Grand Metropolitan subsidiary. This was at a time when the whole region was just opening up.

GFIS had become established as the manager of some of Hong Kong's most exclusive business dining clubs; it had also won six contracts in as many months. In addition, it had signed an agreement with the Chinese government that gave GFIS exclusive catering rights on the oil rigs in the Pearl River estuary, now almost as big as the North Sea operation. At one stage, no bank in Hong Kong would have looked at funding a hotel in southern China without GFIS undertaking a feasibility study. A clairvoyant might have foreseen the enormous opportunities that lay ahead. Had GFIS stayed in business it could well have been a major player in the explosive growth of the hotel and catering market of the entire region. The opportunity was lost however when, in 1989, the decision to sell or close down what remained of GIS in the Middle East and Hong Kong was taken. By then, Robinson and Allen had departed to Granada.

Philip Morley and John Greengrass

approached Francis Mackay, who had become chairman of the Compass Group, with an offer to buy the company. It took them a year to raise the finance, at which time the GIS name returned to the two people who had done much to create it back in the 1970s.

GIS had been brought low by the completion of the massive infrastructure projects and by over-expansion, but this cannot deny that the UK company was a world pioneer. Like many pioneers it had been overtaken by events. Nor did Gerry Robinson's vision of the Compass Group include such high-risk ventures as GIS, which he later described as a 'shambles'. His reputation for reshaping and focusing companies on their core activities, thereby maximising shareholder value, was not about to be damaged by this failing giant.

The sale brought to an end one of the UK contracting industry's most colourful companies. Now part of the Levellight Group formed by Morley and Greengrass to acquire the remaining GIS leisure management activities, mainly in Spain and Portugal, it trades under the name of Vacation Care International Ltd. This successfully contracts the management and administration of timeshare resorts in Europe, with Morley and Greengrass as co-owners of the company.

Compass later re-entered the off-shore and remote site services market with ESS Site Services, while Aramark remains a key provider. Sodexo, after acquiring US-based Universal Ogden to form Universal Services, absorbed Kelvin to form what is now Sodexo Site Services, which currently (2015) employs over 1,600 people on 70 on-shore and off-shore North Sea sites.

The pace of developments for remote site services in the North Sea may not now be as frenetic as it was in the 1980s but the opportunities remain.

CHAPTER THIRTEEN

Gardner Merchant:
Garry Hawkes takes control

Garry Hawkes remained with Gardner Merchant for 38 years, in which time he had built the company up, foiled a takeover attempt by Compass, overseen its buy-out from Forte and organised its sale to Sodexo.

Sheffield born and bred, Garry Hawkes left school at the age of 16 – "the happiest day was the day I left" – with five O levels and a determination to become a chef. All the glamorous Hollywood films at the time had initially given him the idea of becoming an actor but somehow these translated into a wish to take up cookery, partly encouraged by the careers teacher at his school who confessed he himself had wanted to become a chef in his youth. The idea did not find favour with young Garry's father, however, who was a civil servant and who considered job security more important than job creativity and career excitement – not the response that his son wanted to hear and which he ignored.

He spent three years at Huddersfield Technical College, taking the national diploma which led to membership of the (then) Hotel and Catering Institute before

Garry Hawkes: despite blandishments from almost every other catering company, Hawkes, pictured here in 1986, remained with Gardner Merchant for 38 years.

being called up by the RAF for his National Service. Two years later, he worked for a Leeds-based contractor for a couple of years before joining Peter Merchant in 1963 as an area supervisor in South Yorkshire. Despite blandishments from every other major competitor in the business, he was to remain a one-company man, staying with it in its various forms for the next 38 years until, as chief executive and chairman, after organising the management buy-out of Gardner Merchant from Forte and then its sale to Sodexo, he decided to call it a day in a blaze of publicity that he had neither planned nor desired.

"I'd given my life to Gardner Merchant. It was time to walk off the stage and do something else," he says.

* * *

Few other personalities have played such a major part in the development of the contract catering industry. John Gardner, Jack Bateman, Roland Webb and John Sutcliffe all started their own companies and had sold out in earlier, more relaxed times. Most of them had been able to take advantage of favourable wartime legislation which practically forced contracts into their lap. True, there were difficulties imposed by rationing and skill shortages but none of the companies had to fight for business. In the wartime years at least, growing the business was more a case of turning it down because there was too much of it, rather than having to win it. But Hawkes' career blossomed in the 1970s and 1980s by building up Gardner Merchant in more competitive times. And unlike the earlier pioneers he was a caterer to his fingertips.

Like many of his contemporaries who went on to senior management positions and success – Don Davenport, Stirling Gallacher, Mike Bailey, Geoffrey Harrison, Bill Toner and others – he had been to catering college and knew his way around the kitchen. He loved the business and unashamedly loved the company. At GM, an outpost of Trust Houses and later of Lord Forte's empire, and part of a much larger and largely family-run business, he inevitably had to deal with the kind of company politics that none of the entrepreneurs who had gone before him had had to tackle. His position on the main Forte board didn't mean a great deal to a company which was far more concerned with its hotel and restaurant interests and with its overriding, never-ending and ultimately unsuccessful struggle to take over the Savoy Hotel group. It was this feud with Sir Hugh Wontner, chairman of the Savoy Group, which occupied so much of Lord Forte's later time and effort when at the helm of his empire. GM was never high on the list of Forte's priorities. As long as it could meet budget, its existence was accepted rather than glorified despite the many Royal Warrants that GM had picked up along the way.

* * *

A handsome man of undoubted conviction and presence, highly articulate with forceful views on most subjects, (not all of them, he admits, charitable) and rarely reluctant to give his opinion, a powerful motivator and an extremely effective leader, Hawkes' rise to the top was largely the result of these innate qualities. His ability to lead a team is legendary. Don Davenport, who worked with him at GM for many years before defecting to Sutcliffe, but who has remained a great friend, rates Hawkes as a hero:

"I would have walked off a cliff if Ken Graveney had told me to, and the same with Garry. He came to Ford's once when I was there and meeting him had an extraordinary effect on me. I felt I could conquer the world.

They were both extraordinary motivators, extraordinary leaders."

"He was such a charismatic leader," says Phil Hooper, who joined the company in 1975 with an HND from Hendon College and who is still with Sodexo at the time of writing. "His commitment to sales and training was legendary. He made Gardner Merchant what it was."

"Garry's strength," says Bob Cotton, who worked closely with him for over 20 years, "is that he is such an inspiring people person. He's a superb motivator. He understands that any business has to depend on good team work and creating good teams must be the prime aim of every business. And every manager has to be a great motivator. That's Garry's strength. But he's not an entrepreneur." Hawkes would not disagree.

"I'm a manager, not an entrepreneur," he says. "I like running companies – getting the best out of people and driving the business forward. It's people who are at the core of any organisation's success. Buying and selling companies is not my style though we did it with Gardner Merchant. I don't like the politics though, God knows, there were plenty in my time."

* * *

Hawkes' career blossomed. In 1967, at the age of 32, he found himself in charge of GM's northern region (which spread as far south as Birmingham), succeeding Stirling Gallacher. He had very nearly been head-hunted by Midland Catering and his 10-week notice period had almost expired when Leslie Bond, who had joined Trust Houses as head of personnel in the early 1960s, but who had moved over to take responsibility for Little Chef and popular catering including Gardner Merchant in 1969, appointed Gallacher as GM's director of sales and operations; this allowed Hawkes to take over Gallacher's job in Manchester. Based in the north for the next seven years, Hawkes built up GM's business in the region to 300 contracts.

Meanwhile, there had been changes in the industry. In 1970, Trust Houses merged with Forte (Holdings) to form Trust Houses Forte (later Trusthouse Forte and, in 1991, Forte plc). Rather than an amicable alliance between two companies, which it was optimistically billed to be, the merger became an unseemly battle ground between the Trust Houses and Forte interests, presaging months of infighting between the rival factions. The sudden death at Heathrow Airport of Lord Crowther, the former Trust Houses chairman who had been appointed chairman of the combined company, closely followed by the departure of Michael Pickard, the company's chief executive (the

Father and son, Lord Forte and Rocco: as with so many family-dominated companies, Lord Forte's control was absolute. Though he passed control over to his son, Rocco, in 1983, he remained chairman until 1992 when he was elected life president.

former Trust Houses chief executive), saw the controlling emergence of Lord Forte and the family's associated long-term directors. Within two years, only one ex-Trust Houses director remained – Donald Durban, the company secretary.

Rather than a merger, it had been a complete, if very messy, takeover. Lord Thorneycroft, a Tory grandee, was appointed chairman and Sir Charles Forte (as he then was) became deputy chairman and chief executive. Two vice chairman (Sir Leslie Joseph and Eric Hartwell) and three deputy chief executives (Eric Hartwell, Denis Hearn and George Hendrie) – all Forte *confrères* – were the key appointments. The board also included Len Rosso, Jack Bottell and Jack Hollingshead, long-time Forte directors, and some independent appointees including Lord Robens, the former chairman of the National Coal Board, and Sir Charles Hardie, an accountant and a former chairman of BOAC. Lord Forte's children, Rocco Forte and Olga Polizzi, joined the board later.

As with so many family-dominated companies, Lord Forte's control was absolute. Though he passed control over to his son, Rocco, in 1983 remaining chairman until 1992 when he was elected life president, the company was run almost as a personal family fiefdom. The Forte family owned only eight per cent of the shares but it was a company where family and friends mattered. In the biography of Lord Forte in the Oxford Dictionary of National Biography, it is claimed that "institutional shareholders grew restive at his baronial style of management and complained that the Forte's board was a gerontocracy". It is fair comment on a company where it was difficult to get a hearing if you were outside the ruling regime.

In this environment Garry Hawkes, being a northerner and still with a trace of his Sheffield accent, was not appointed to

the main board until four years after taking control of GM; he was palpably not part of the family and he felt he was not considered to be part of the close internal network of Lord Forte's long-serving directors in spite of the fact that he was running a business worth some £500m. Hawkes believed that GM was regarded by the Forte clan as being below the salt. Canteens didn't loom large in their field of vision. "I always felt that we were socially *declassé*," he says. The company's hotels, restaurants and the all-consuming siege on the Savoy Hotel Group were preoccupying issues at most board meetings; little wonder that all the arguments over these concerns passed over the head of the company's contract catering arm.

* * *

After the merger, GM absorbed Forte's own small contract catering division, Forte Catering, and it later became responsible for the significant airline catering business on the retirement of Jack Hollingshead, its managing director, though this didn't last long, much to Hawkes' relief. On the positive side, the merger brought some benefits in terms of cost savings and better leverage on suppliers, as well as offering more opportunities for employees. Under Leslie Bond, GM was also encouraged to expand overseas. In 1971 came the first move abroad with the purchase of two South African companies catering for mine and industrial workers. The two were successfully merged to form Fedics which traded well for many years latterly under John Taylorson (who later joined BA as catering director) but it was sold in 1979.

In 1973, in the same year that GM made its first £1m profit (£10.8m today), it established a joint venture in Europe with Unilever, providing a management, consultancy and supply service for clients on the continent, combining Unilever's food production facilities with GM's catering management experience; it was a partnership which lasted 10 years. The company also acquired Van Hecke MCA, a catering contractor, as a foothold in Holland and set up Interserve SA in Belgium in June 1974 following the establishment of a German arm, Interserve Gmbh, a year earlier. At home, Gardner Merchant acquired Smallmans, the Manchester-based contractor, and Four Square Vending, a subsidiary of Mars, which added a significant vending operation to the company's catering offer.

In 1975, because of the growing importance of the overseas business, Hawkes was plucked out of Manchester to take charge of GM's European expansion – a big move for someone who had largely based his career in the north. Moving to Rotterdam with his wife and children, he found Holland was a country offering new challenges; within reason he was his own boss. He settled in, arranged school for his daughter and looked to the future in Europe. But not for long. Within two years, he was back in Britain as GM's managing director.

In 1977, Stirling Gallacher was head-hunted to take control of Sutcliffe Catering after the departure of Marc Verstringhe and others to form their own company, Catering & Allied. Gallacher's move had opened the way for Hawkes to take the top job at GM. He was appointed by Rocco Forte, then director of group personnel who also became GM's chairman, succeeding Leslie Bond. Hawkes was then appointed to the main THF board and the parent company's Executive Committee, chaired by Rocco.

* * *

He came back with plenty of new ideas but at a time of impending economic uncertainty. A recession had forced many business closures and clients were looking ever more closely at catering subsidies; between 1980 and 1984, according to the Industrial Society, subsidies fell by 13 per cent. All contractors were suffering and GM was no exception; it was losing more contracts than it was gaining and it took another five years to turn the company around, at which time it was gaining three contracts to every one lost. Attitudes towards staff were exemplified by staff uniforms.

"In the UK, our uniforms cost £1.50; in Holland they cost £14. That was the difference between the two companies. I could see we needed a complete reassessment of our values and structure," he says.

There had to be a greater commitment to training, promotion from within and empowerment; his more inclusive management style was based on a people-centred philosophy. The company's standards needed to be enhanced and a greater effort had to be made to sell its services. He decentralised, split up the five divisions into 15 regions (later 17), making each region responsible for no more than 150 contracts. Weekly divisional meetings were introduced. Just as important, he made each region responsible for selling new contracts.

"Without a successful sales effort, you don't have a business," he says. "Contracting is never static. You have to win new business all the time."

But he believed that it was always better to sell through the operational teams than through salesmen: that way they could always talk to the potential client with knowledge and experience. As a result, every area manager went on a sales course. "It was a key part of the Gardner Merchant training programme," says Ian Hall, who was HR director at the company for many years.

"Even Garry went on one. We were totally sales driven and everybody was trained to sell. It was part of our strategy to take operational guys and put them in a sales position for a couple of years – Bill Toner was a highly successful example."

Phil Hooper was an early candidate on a pilot sales course (he eventually became director of sales and helped to organise them) and was impressed by the effort put into them. "They covered everything – even as far as how you looked," he says. "But they produced a bunch of people who were very sales-orientated at a time when the market was absolutely ripe for exploitation."

The courses were also highly motivational. Staff turnover dropped to 20 per cent overall and to just over two per cent for managers and other executives.

Hawkes was also concerned about communications within the company which had now grown to 30,000 employees. How best to keep in touch with them? With so many staff working in so many far flung outlets (the company was operating over 2,000 contracts by then) he recognised that keeping them informed of the company's aims and activities, and making them feel motivated as part of a very large organisation, was a significant challenge. One answer was a company newspaper.

"We went tabloid," says Bob Cotton, who was responsible for the publication which was actually produced by Johnny Johnston, an HR veteran. "We called it Communicater, and it was what it said on the title. It was a newspaper that kept catering people in touch."

In fact, employee newspapers became a common feature of all companies. Bateman's Feedback was an early example, as was Sutcliffe News; later, Dick Turpin launched Grandmet Catering World which became Compass News. Although some were relatively amateurish home-grown affairs,

Raising the catering standards

The standard of public catering in the late 1970s was only just beginning to improve and Peter Roberts, who became Gardner Merchant's research director, remembers complaints from the café downstairs at the Eastbourne Training College, which GM ran as part of the training programme.

"We began to get complaints that the quality of the coffee and the croissants had got poorer since we had taken over the café. What they didn't realise was that the croissants came daily from France and the coffee was freshly brewed – it was all of a much higher quality but people had got so accustomed to British standards!"

Peter Roberts

both *Communicater* and the Compass publications were produced by practising journalists and their design and layout rivalled those of national tabloids. At Gardner Merchant, a monthly tape – Radio Reigate – was issued so that staff could listen to company developments in their car or at home; internal meetings were beefed up to boost communications.

Soon after his return from Holland Hawkes set up a national training college above a Zetland café in Eastbourne, believing that the company needed a residential training centre; it eventually provided 25-30 rooms, a training kitchen and dining room. The primary object was to teach managers control systems. Hawkes believed in investing in people and the school was merely a reflection of this

COMMUNI*cater*

July 1993   *Europe's largest caterer*   Issue No. 83

SOARAWAY SALES SUCCESS

SALES ROCKET TO £1 MILLION IN SIX WEEKS

Target-breaking feats set course to obliterate all records

The front page from the last edition of *Communicater*

Communicater was the Gardner Merchant staff newspaper. Professionally designed and laid out, it was an effective means of keeping the thousands of staff in touch with developments in the company – and with each other. Radio Reigate was another regular means of communication.

belief; he was also looking forward. After the recession experience and skills would be of even greater importance. The centre was deemed a success and almost everyone with any management responsibility in the company went there.

At the same time, through Peter Howell and Peter Hazzard, GM's training team, the company produced recipe cards with the idea of setting down a uniform standard recipe and its cost for each dish produced – how can you control client costs if you can't control production costs? was Hawkes'

refrain. Inevitably, not all of them (or their managers) followed the cards but they set the right approach to the business.

Then came Kenley. Kenley was originally a large gentleman's residence in Surrey that had been built in the 1870s and set in acres of grounds but had latterly been used as offices by a company that had since moved out. When Rocco Forte had visited Eastbourne and saw what was going on there he suggested to Hawkes that GM should buy larger premises and use them as a training centre, cum laboratory and

research centre. Hawkes jumped at the chance. A site near Gatwick Airport was considered and subsequently abandoned before Kenley came on the market, sufficiently large for his purposes and with ample space for car parking. It was bought for £1.8m but converting it cost more than the same again. Though others thought the building too grandiose, Hawkes says it was perfect.

"We had training kitchens there, seminar rooms, a food laboratory and offices for the headquarters team. It became one of our most powerful sales tools and set the standards for management and staff."

Potential clients were driven down to an imposing house that oozed confidence and success. Royal Warrants on the door faced them as they entered (Gardner Merchant had won them for catering at Buckingham Palace garden parties); they were shown around the training rooms, saw classes in action, went into the training kitchens, talked to the laboratory technicians before being provided with a meal that rivalled a five-star restaurant. This was the Gardner Merchant standard; isn't this what you want for your employees? was the implied question.

The answer was yes, though some might have wondered what the facility would be costing them in management fees. However, the sales team converted almost every prospect who came down to Kenley into a contract gain. Clients were invited from all over the country, some even flown down from Scotland for a party, a dinner or some other event. It was a time of much corporate hospitality, something which does not now exist on the same scale. Hawkes was in his element. "It was phenomenally successful," he says.

Phil Hooper agrees. "Kenley was incredibly successful. It was the heart of the company. Because it was residential,

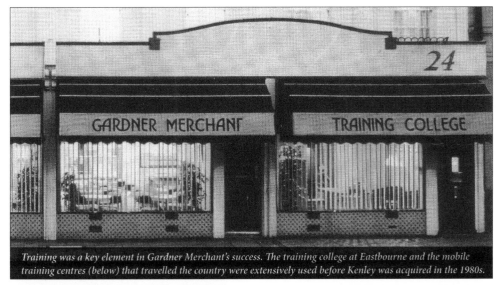

Training was a key element in Gardner Merchant's success. The training college at Eastbourne and the mobile training centres (below) that travelled the country were extensively used before Kenley was acquired in the 1980s.

and so many executives had their offices there, it meant they met the trainees every week which generated a terrific team spirit. It was GM's Centre of Excellence where we could prove how good our offer was. It was the absolute manifestation of Garry's commitment to training."

In view of its success Hawkes was not the only one to be mystified when, after the alliance with Sodexo and the name change, Kenley was closed down and sold off. Some believe it was because of the cost of the operation, others because it was based deep in the countryside and too far from the centre of things to be an effective headquarters. There may also have been a feeling that it was too redolent of GM at its prime.

Between 1980 and 1989, GM acquired two small vending companies but these were overshadowed by the purchase of Kelvin Catering operating the oil rigs in the North Sea and elsewhere. There was expansion in Europe, too. The Dutch company, Van Hecke, had grown from 35 contracts to 500 and Interserve in Belgium also showed significant growth, though the German Interserve company was much slower to develop and become profitable.

The company was on a roll in the US, too. As far back as 1979, THF had acquired the Westbury Hotel in New York and with it, its sister hotel in London's Conduit Street and a contract catering business which had 15 or so contracts including catering for some New York banks and the UN building. THF offloaded the contracting business to Gardner Merchant, which thus became GM's first foray into America, followed in the next couple of years by the purchase of Eastern Food Services in Connecticut in 1984 and, in 1986, another contractor Blakie Miller and Hines, along with Superior Restaurant Equipment, an equipment business similar to Lockhart in the UK

It was a period of heady growth and strong profits driven by Garry Hawkes who was left to run the company by the Forte board largely on his own. Relations were thankfully distant – "We took care not be seen much at THF's head office," says one. Kenley also had the added advantage of being well away from THF's headquarters in High Holborn and Hawkes and his team were determined to keep it that way. Bob Cotton remembers that every year there was a very rigid budget process:

"For three months we prepared the budget in every key respect – expenditure, revenues, staffing, turnover etc. The THF directors would review it amazingly closely – every new headcount position was queried – but once it was accepted, provided the budget figures were achieved, we were left in peace. Garry and I spent a week before each presentation prepping every potential question."

Gardner Merchant continued to make good profits out of rising turnover and it consolidated its reputation as a high class, extremely well organised operation employing some of the best talent in the business and catering for some of the country's most prestigious contracts. But success brings more than rewards. It also attracts the attention of competitors.

By 1991 Francis Mackay had reorganised Compass to such an extent that it was hungry to expand. He reckoned that GM would be a perfect addition to the Compass stable. It was a move that Hawkes and his team, unsurprisingly, most strongly opposed. It helped that, while Hawkes' relationship with the main THF board was distant, his relationship with Rocco Forte, GM's chairman, though far from close was at least amicable. Hawkes' relationship with Rocco might well have had a positive bearing on Compass' failure to wrest the company out of Forte's hands.

It was not all work and play. Gardner Merchant fielded a number of regional football teams and inter-company rivalry was rife for a number of years. In this match, the South West regional team beat the South East team against all the odds. Among the players were, back row: Martin Waller (second from left), Frank Whittaker (third from left), Bill Dickie (second from right); front row: Don Davenport (fourth from left) and Grant Butcher (second from right).

CHAPTER FOURTEEN

The big Compass buy-out

Gerry Robinson led the buy-out of Compass from GrandMet, and showed how to make money in contract catering.

Gerry (Gerard) Robinson, knighted in 2003 for services to the Arts (he subsequently became chairman of the Arts Council), the ninth of 10 children of an Irish father and a Scottish mother, was born in Donegal but moved with his family to England in his early teens. A brief spell in a seminary in Lancashire persuaded him that the religious life was not for him; instead he went into accounting. He joined Matchbox Toys as a clerk, took the Chartered Management Accountant qualification and eventually became chief accountant for Lesney Toys in London.

In 1974 he joined Lex Vehicle Leasing as a management accountant, becoming finance director before leaving in 1980 to join the UK franchise of Coca-Cola, first as finance director, then sales and marketing, and finally as managing director. The franchise was owned by Grand Metropolitan and Robinson describes it as a wonderful job. Indeed, so successful was he that GrandMet

sold the business back to Coca-Cola over his head in 1983, reaping a £36m reward. Bitterly disappointed, but acknowledging that the decision to sell was correct, in 1984 Robinson was moved by Anthony Tennant, GrandMet's chairman, to the company's contract services division as managing director. For the first time he was brought into contact with the recently named Compass Services – formerly Grandmet Catering Services.

The division consisted of the company's UK catering interests (Compass Services), its overseas interests (GrandMet International Services – GIS), GM Healthcare (a new venture in building and operating private hospitals), Compass Vending and Rosser and Russell, a long-established mechanical and electrical engineering (M&EE) company. Not all of them were in good shape.

Compass Services was doing well but not making the profit that it could make. GIS had expanded from catering and providing FM services in North Sea oil platforms to sites in the Middle East. However, by 1983 it was losing money. Rosser and Russell was acquired by GrandMet in 1983 for £1m; the purchase was made with a view to broadening the range of contract services

that GIS could offer to clients worldwide. Unfortunately, the company was not quite the bargain that it appeared to be and Max Joseph was forced to admit that its UK contracting business had to be completely re-organised – "And this has ruled out any possibility of developing international

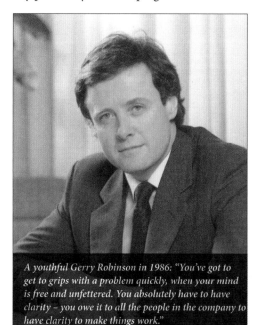

A youthful Gerry Robinson in 1986: "You've got to get to grips with a problem quickly, when your mind is free and unfettered. You absolutely have to have clarity – you owe it to all the people in the company to have clarity to make things work."

business for the time being," he declared. In fact, losses continued to pile up before they were brought under control; in 1987/8 it turned in a £2.5m trading profit but the company was sold in 1990 to Norwest Holst.

Compass Vending, the last and smallest of the companies in the division, was the rump of the vending interests of Compass. With sales of just over £7m it was here that Charles Allen first appeared to play a part in the development of Compass; in 1988, he sold the company to GKN Vending.

GrandMet's move into private healthcare by building and operating private hospitals was the fifth arm of the company and was showing promise. By the time of the buy-out, it had opened seven hospitals with an investment of over £21m and had annual sales of £12.5m. Nevertheless, the division was soon sold off as Robinson increasingly concentrated on the provision of catering facilities that did not need capital investment.

In his biography, Robinson says that turning the contract services division around in the short period after his arrival and before the buy-out was not easy.

"It was an astonishingly difficult business to get right. The UK catering was all right. M&EE was losing money hand over fist and the private hospital business was beginning to look interesting."

Robinson first turned his attention to the contract catering company which was, at the time, making some £3m a year profit on a turnover of some £100m. His reputation as a cost cutter had hardly yet been established but his immediate actions certainly set it in train.

Within weeks, Dick Turpin had left, with the remainder of those directors who appeared on the original cover of *Caterer* – Tony Coles, Mike Taylor, Kevin Birmingham, Tony Ward-Lewis – only three years previously. All were given pay-offs which were, reputedly less generous than those

that Alan Robinson and Hilary Charles had earlier negotiated.

In fact, the entire top floor at the company's headquarters, Cambridge Grove, which housed many of the regional general managers, was also culled, reducing the number of regions from 13 to seven.

Nigel Anker, one of the regional general managers made redundant in Robinson's clear-out, believed that the redundancies were understandable.

"Gerry was a professional businessman. He could see we had all had it a bit too easy. We were deep in our comfort zones and as long as you met budgets and didn't lose clients, you had a very comfortable job. We were totally autonomous, except for purchasing and accounts, which were functions undertaken centrally, so we were really our own boss. We were used to returns within seven to 10 years. Gerry needed them within one to three years. He understood that the business needed shaking up and it needed new people to give it new drive."

Anker describes his redundancy as a piece of good fortune. Within a couple of months he had joined Marc Verstringhe at Catering & Allied, happily running a business but one that was smaller than the one he had been running at Compass.

"I got back into catering proper and even had to open a unit, which I hadn't done for years. With Marc I got a taste of running my own business."

Peter Smale, newly installed by Dick Turpin as marketing director, recalls that he and others had already prepared a new business plan which, they believed, would have taken Compass forward but Robinson wasn't interested. His management philosophy was simple and his approach to Compass was uncompromising.

"You've got to get to grips with a problem quickly, when your mind is free and unfettered. What's the right thing to do for

Nigel Anker: being made redundant was fortuitous: "I got back into catering proper and even had to open a unit, which I hadn't done for years."

the company? What can you do about it? You absolutely have to have clarity – you owe it to all the people in the company to have clarity to make things work."

And he adds: "You have to cut deep. The very worst thing you can ever do is to have to come back for a second or third bite of the cherry."

The removal of Compass' established directors left the remainder of the company's senior team shell-shocked, though little of this filtered down to the units. Two divisions, north and south, were established with Jim Cartwright promoted from regional director to northern divisional director and a newcomer, Ted Daines, ex-Royal Navy and from Avis, in charge of the south. The new board of Compass Services consisted of Richard Dickson as managing director; Mike Donnelly as finance director; Jim Cartwright and Ted Daines; Terry Brannigan, an internal appointment, as marketing and sales director; and Clive Grundy, a recruit from outside the company, as personnel director.

Charles Allen (later Lord Allen of Knightsbridge) was appointed managing director of Compass when Richard Dickson left.

A reputation won on wringing cost out of a business

Gerry Robinson's reputation was forged on his ability to increase profits but, at the same time, he was committed to raising and maintaining quality standards.

"We must become almost paranoid about customer care," he told staff in *Compass World*.

It was a message for the troops but it hadn't stopped him reducing the number of divisions from five to two. The number of area managers was also cut down on the premise that, if they were doing their job properly, unit managers should be able to ensure good client relations without extensive area manager cover. This was not a policy that other companies would have agreed with.

But he introduced a new appraisal process which sharpened up the company's focus on management skills and revenue generation which, in turn, led to new training schemes for management and operators; two environmental health officers were appointed among other new engagements.

Even more significant, he tightened central purchasing in order to squeeze much better discounts from suppliers and reviewed what was chargeable to clients and what was not, with the result that many overheads were charged out; charging out the cost of uniforms, for example, yielded huge savings.

It was a classic case study of how to wring more and more revenue out of a business.

David Unwin, managing director of GIS, was appointed development director.

The shake up illustrated Robinson's ruthlessness as well as his philosophy of management clarity – stick to what you're good at. It pointed the way ahead. Looking at the business, he was cautious about commercial catering. In an article in *Compass World* of March 1987, he is quoted as saying: "The skills required are quite different to those of our mainstream operations" – a conclusion that Peter Smale and others had reached back in 1983 when the company under Dick Turpin was flirting with commercial restaurant contracts. He also claimed that Compass would continue to offer clients a cleaning service and he called security "a great success story" – both were services which Turpin had enthusiastically pioneered. However, Jim Cartwright remembers differently:

"Gerry took both cleaning and security out of the sellers' kit bag. He wanted to focus on the catering operations. He was never interested in cleaning – in fact, he refused to sanction the purchase of a security company in Glasgow which I eventually bought with a couple of others and this precipitated my move from Compass," (Chapter 29). It didn't take long for Cartwright to be proved right. Compass Security was sold in 1990 as well as Rosser and Russell.

While Robinson was in his element as chairman, Richard Dickson had a less than happy time as managing director. His personnel background and his experience in such companies as Hoover, Lex Group (where he met Gerry Robinson) and Revlon, was not an ideal training ground for such a large, service-orientated company as Compass Services. Robinson, ever the man to see through a problem, acted decisively and Charles Allen was appointed managing director within a year or so. For Allen, who had been looking for a bigger role, it was a fateful first step up a ladder which led to

Compass' biggest early gain was the BT contract which added nearly 600 locations worth £60m.

much greater things.

Charles Allen (later Lord Allen of Kensington and currently chairman of Global Radio and ISS, the Danish-based catering and FM contractor) started as an accountant in the steel industry in Scotland and was recruited to GIS as commercial manager in 1981 at the age of 24. He stayed in the Middle East for nearly four years, recruiting huge numbers of people to work on oilfield sites, some housing as many as 40,000 people. Gerry Robinson brought him back to take over Grandmet Vending which he sold within a year. The company had introduced the Daisy fresh milk machine which, rumour had it, led to clients complaining that their machines were leaking sour milk over the carpet and demanding that they be taken out and the carpet replaced. Tony Ward-Lewis denies this but says that operators might have spilt milk during the twice daily piping change 'but I never had it reported to me.' At the same time, the value of the machines kept on being written up. The sale to GKN was hardly before time.

With GIS facing ever more acute

Francis Mackay: Gerry Robinson and Francis Mackay got on well together, but they felt there wasn't room in the company for both of them.

The first Compass board in 1988: seated, Gerry Robinson, Dr A I Lenton (chairman), Chris Bucknall; standing, Charles Allen, Francis Mackay, L N Olsen (non executive director), Richard Dickson, Fritz Ternofsky (non executive director) and David Harris.

GRAND METROPOLITAN
CONTRACT SERVICES LIMITED

8 June 1987

Dear Phil,

Following his appointment as Chief Executive of Grand Metropolitan Allen Sheppard began a major review of long term business strategy. In essence this has resulted in a decision to concentrate on a limited number of core businesses, rather than risking a dilution of focus by attempting to manage too wide a range of businesses.

In Contract Services we have produced excellent results over the last two years but it has always been clear that the real way forward within Grand Met would involve growth by acquisition. With the purchase of Heublein, a sizeable acquisition by Contract Services was ruled out and the Board of GM decided that Contract Services was not to be one of its core businesses. Accordingly I was advised by Allen earlier in the year that the decision had been taken to dispose of this group of companies. Despite our significantly improved profitability and potential, this is both logical and understandable.

Against this background I and my senior colleagues who have been closely involved in the building of the Contract Services Division and who have great confidence in its future, decided that there was a real opportunity to develop these companies further. I therefore asked if Grand Metropolitan would consider selling these businesses to that senior management team and was told that we would be treated on equal terms with any other potential external purchaser.

Accordingly, we set to work to prepare a management buy out proposal which in brief has meant that the management team has worked with a leading finance house, Investors in Industry (3i), to raise the capital needed to finance the purchase. This has entailed convincing potential investors of the realism of our business projections and forecasts and therefore of their opportunity to make attractive long term returns by investing in the Contract Services Division.

A three-page letter from Gerry Robinson was sent to all senior executives at Compass advising them of the impending buy-out.

problems, Allen went back to the Middle East for 18 months with the intention of selling it off to co-partners before returning to take over a company called Grandmet Developments – another job which didn't last long – "They spent more on producing a brochure than they made in profit." He soon closed it down at which time Robinson moved him to Compass to take over from Richard Dickson.

He found the company struggling. It had stripped out its costs but it wasn't growing organically. In Allen's words, "The cash flows were dreadful." He centralised procurement – an obvious area – and introduced three levels of discounts which varied according to the size of the client's purchasing bill. He also took a sharp eye to pricing.

The company's fortunes turned the corner in 1991 when it won the huge £60m BT contract, with 596 new locations bringing the Compass total to 3,300. A special team was set up to oversee the new business which involved training 450 BT managers in Compass systems and which added £30m purchasing power to Compass' armoury.

Allen introduced an addition to the Compass 'We Care More' mantra: 'Getting it, Keeping it, Growing it, Getting paid', which bluntly summed up the company's new focus. Retention levels began to improve and within two years under his leadership, Compass was making £36m profit. His three years at

Robinson's impact on profit

In the three years between the Compass buy-out and Gerry Robinson's departure in 1991, there had been a measurable impact on profits; within a year, they had risen from £4.4m to £9.2m; by 1990 they had risen to £29.5 on sales of £353m.

This announcement appears as a matter of record only. August 1987.

Chiefrule Limited shortly to be renamed

COMPASS GROUP LIMITED

A NEW COMPANY FORMED BY MEMBERS OF MANAGEMENT AND BY A SYNDICATE OF INVESTORS TO ACQUIRE THE CONTRACT SERVICES DIVISION OF GRAND METROPOLITAN PLC FOR £160,000,000.

The following syndicate subscribed a total of £60,000,000 for shares in the company.

Underwriters and Investors

Prudential Venture Managers Limited Investors in Industry plc CIN Industrial Investments Limited

Investors

Barclays Development Capital Limited	Mercury Warburg Investment Management Limited
Charterhouse Development Capital Limited	Phillips & Drew Development Capital
Citicorp Venture Capital Limited	Schroder UK Venture Fund
Close Investment Management Limited	Scottish Amicable Life Assurance Society
Commercial Union Assurance Company plc	Security Pacific Hoare Govett Equity Ventures Limited
County NatWest Ventures Limited	Standard Chartered Bank
F&C Ventures Limited	The Standard Life Assurance Company
Globe Investment Trust plc	

Syndicate Leader

Investors in Industry plc

who in addition provided a mezzanine loan of £30,000,000

INVESTORS IN INDUSTRY

The official Compass buy-out advertisement.

Compass saw it consolidate its position as one of the country's leading contract caterers.

* * *

Soon after arriving at Compass, Robinson had the thought of buying out the division. He had already approached Anthony Tennant (later knighted) to suggest that Compass was costing too much in management time and should be sold to a management buy-out. Tennant didn't buy the argument – "Bad luck," he said, as told in Robinson's biography. "It's not for sale because it's a good business and you go on and run it." Robinson tried again later and got the same dusty answer. It was not until 1987 when Tennant moved to Guinness as chairman that there was any movement. His successor was Allen Sheppard (later Lord Sheppard).

With growing rumblings that GrandMet needed to streamline its business activities, a decision was made to concentrate on brewing, retail food and wines and spirits, which sidelined both hotels and contract services. Sheppard was thus more amenable to selling the division than his predecessor.

By this time, Robinson had joined forces with Francis Mackay, a genial newcomer to Compass, an accountant by training, who had joined the company as finance director only a year earlier from GUS, previously Great Universal Stores; he also had experience of contracting with Sutcliffe Catering, where he had been group finance director from 1979 to 1983. Mackay had seen the potential in a buy-out. In his biography, Robinson admits: "He got me from thinking about it, like many managers, to actually doing it. He didn't see any barriers and I am very grateful to him for that."

Mackay and Robinson were unquestionably the two key players in the buy-out but three others also came aboard:

David Harris, who was managing director of GIS and Richard Dickson, both personnel men by training. The fifth man was Chris Bucknell who Robinson knew from his Coca-Cola days where Bucknall was production controller; Bucknall took over as managing director of Rosser and Russell in 1986.

It was this collection of businesses which Robinson had turned around in the three years before the buy-out. Indeed, thanks to his efforts, the division had moved from a thumping loss to a profit of £10.2m in 1987.

In his biography, Robinson laments the timing of the buy-out and the fact that they had had to put up the value of the company beforehand; he admits, however, that without the profile that the profit gave them, it would have been very difficult to raise the money. In fact, raising the money – £163m (nearly £400m today) – was not as difficult as it might have been. Organised by 3i, the venture capital house, with Rodney Hall and Rupert Wiles leading the negotiations, together with CIN Industrial Investments (the pension fund for the Coal Board – later CinVen – destined to play a part in the Gardner Merchant buy-out) and the Prudential, the timing was fortuitous. Compass, with all its divisions now performing well, was considered a good prospect with little downside. Gerry Robinson's turnaround measures had been proven to work, laying the foundations of the buy-out on solid ground.

What was more difficult was persuading GrandMet to sell to the management; it was, at the time, the largest buy-out in corporate history though much bigger ones (including Gardner Merchant's in 1993) were around the corner. As Robinson knew only too well, companies selling in these circumstances are inevitably aware that the people buying are destined to make a lot of money out of the deal. This was certainly the case here and GrandMet took some persuading,

particularly as there was plenty of interest from other companies looking for a quick purchase. In the end, it succeeded on grounds of 'cost, speed and simplicity' as a special edition of *Compass News* phrased it, but it was probably Robinson's and Mackay's own powers of persuasion that finally tipped the scales.

In his biography, Robinson recalls that it was a very intense time:

"The whole legalese thing, and getting advice from merchant banks and stock brokers and accountants was difficult to get used to because previously it had been done by other people in the company. It was a very intense time. It's very messy and you are up all hours."

* * *

The buy-out was successful. The intention was always to cash in on it with a flotation on the Stock Exchange within a year. This it did. The float was for £178m through Lazard Brothers, the City merchant bank. Initially, the shares were undersubscribed – the stock market was going through a difficult time at the end of 1988 – but they recovered opening up at a slight premium. Within seven weeks, they had risen by 25 per cent. Compass was on the long journey to success, but not without a few hiccups on the way.

"The combination of our caring philosophy and public company status has resulted in a strengthening of Compass' image. We are now the only independent publicly quoted catering company, since our two main competitors are both part of much bigger and more diversified groups," said *Compass News* in a celebratory issue in March 1989. At the time, Gardner Merchant was part of Trusthouse Forte and Sutcliffe was owned by Sterling Guarantee Trust.

The flotation made millionaires of all five of the launch directors but, unlike the

John Symonds, another Compass refugee, became managing director of Breakmate's 30-strong contract catering arm, Breakmate Executive Catering. He later set up his own company, Hallmark Catering, later sold to Elior.

GM buy-out and sale to Sodexo four years later, no other staff benefited from the deal. Robinson admits it was a scary time. It was the first time he had taken control of an independent company which he describes as "quite frightening, quite unnerving". He had become the boss and there was no-one to whom he had to refer except, now, his newfound shareholders.

But already he was getting restless. With Allen in day-to-day control and Francis Mackay a powerful force in the background as finance director, there was little more for Robinson to do at Compass. It also came at a difficult time, as John Nelson, then with Lazard Brothers, explains in Robinson's biography:

"He and Francis Mackay, while they got on well, felt that there wasn't room in the company for both of them. Francis is a pretty forceful character... They thought about selling Compass, about one of them leaving and about carrying on as they were. So, one reason for Gerry spending more time with his family was partly to give more space to Francis."

In fact, particularly given Mackay's subsequent record, Robinson admits that walking away from Compass in 1991 was "quite a sensible thing to do".

"I think Francis was quite keen to get the opportunity to run Compass and, as it turned out, he had more aggressive ideas for the business than I did."

In 1988, it had begun what was to become a string of acquisitions, though an ill-advised £100m bid for Sketchley, the dry cleaning group, rocked the boat.

Sketchley had bought Breakmate, a vending and catering company for £8m in 1986 in an effort to expand into the contract catering sector. Tony Coles had joined the company from Compass in 1986, as chief executive of the services division and he had recruited John Symonds, another Compass refugee, to take over as managing director of Breakmate's 30-strong contract catering arm, Breakmate Executive Catering, succeeding Michael Thwaites. Breakmate was making good money, particularly on the vending side, which encouraged a boardroom decision to expand the company's vending activities by purchasing Roboserve for £20m – a handsome sum in those days.

The Roboserve and Breakmate catering contracts were absorbed into a new company, Sketchley Executive Catering, with Stuart Hanson as managing director under John Symonds, who was managing director for the whole catering and vending operations. However, the Roboserve purchase was a disastrous mistake. Subsequent investigations revealed that the new acquisition was actually losing money. Nor had it written down the value of its vending machines so it had a pile of unusable and overvalued vending machines on its balance sheet. Its book asset value was much overstated. Sketchley had already seen off a bid for

£126m by the Godfrey Davis group and Compass, sensing that Sketchley was now vulnerable, put in a near £100m hostile bid after it had been brought in as a white knight to save it. With over 600 shops, Sketchley had a big retail division with some hefty commercial cleaning contracts for uniforms. Robinson thought that "all we had to do was to take it over and make money out of it", but Sketchley's shareholders, led by the likes of M&G and Britannic Assurance, were unhappy about the reduced offer and they put in new management. Meanwhile, Compass' shareholders were also far from happy.

In his biography, Robinson says that a presentation to Standard Life, one of Compass' shareholders, went very badly, "The senior manager just turned around when I'd finished and said: 'What the hell do you think you're doing making this bid at all?'"

Compass' share price fell from 400p to 290p. Without any support Robinson abandoned the bid and they saw the share price take off again. It was a fortunate escape for Compass ("Weren't we lucky!" smiles Francis Mackay) though Robinson would probably argue that he would have made a success of the acquisition. Sketchley sold off its catering operations to both Jim Cartwright's Shaw Catering and Gardner Merchant and its name disappeared from the high street in 1998 when the Minit Group bought it for just £1.23m – a far cry from Compass' bid some eight years previously.

But some purchases were successful. The small Brighton-based Red Ball Group brought in 40 contracts, the first to be organised by Roger Matthews, the newly-appointed commercial director, tasked with spotting likely acquisitions.

* * *

Gerry Robinson's subsequent arrival at

Granada was not foreordained. Truth to tell, the scuppered Sketchley bid had burned his fingers and he reckoned that any similar bid would fail in the same way. Without much possible expansion in the immediate future, his work at Compass was largely completed and for 18 months he coasted along, spending a couple of days a week at Compass while spending more time with his daughter, Samantha, and Heather, his second wife, who was pregnant.

With time on his hands, word got around and he was head-hunted for BET, which had changed its name from British Electric Traction, to take over from Nicholas Wills, the chief executive. He didn't get the job but the exercise certainly made him realise that, in his own words, he wasn't totally happy at Compass, and that his days at the company were probably over. He was head-hunted again, this time for the top job at Granada where Derek Lewis (who went on to become head of the prison service and was the subject of Jeremy Paxman's famous grilling of the home secretary, Michael Howard on *Newsnight*) was under pressure as chief executive. Granada was suffering from a slide in profits as a result of some risky acquisitions causing its share price to fall from 357p to 161p; in 1991, it posted a £110m loss on a turnover of £1.4bn. The chairman, Alex Bernstein, interviewed Robinson three times before making up his mind but it was a combination of able talents from the start. Bernstein – "one of life's gentlemen" in Robinson's words – recognised that Robinson was the man to get Granada off the hook. Robinson knew he could turn Granada round.

"The only thing that occurred to me was that it had had a pretty bad run and I could do quite a lot with it quite quickly... that I could sort it out," says Robinson in his biography.

The appointment made, Robinson quit

Compass, though with some reluctance, little realising his old company would re-emerge in his life a few years later in a merger that shook the industry.

Robinson agreed with Francis Mackay, by now Compass' chief executive, not to head-hunt any Compass senior personnel and had agreed that Chris Bucknall, who had sorted out Rosser and Russell for Compass, would join him at Granada. Technically not being a Compass employee, Bucknall's departure meant that the agreement would not be breached. But Charles Allen was not hitting it off with Francis Mackay in the way he wanted and was keen to leave. In Robinson's biography, Allen makes it plain that he wasn't comfortable with Mackay's style which was to get involved in the details.

"The cultural values at Compass changed. Francis is a very good negotiator and good at dealing with people. But he's not as good a communicator as Gerry and the Granada canvas was much bigger."

This did not stop Allen being made Industrial Caterer of the Year in the 1990 Catey awards, which he accepted wearing his tartan kilt. Robinson had written a citation for the ceremony:

"He is an extremely unusual combination of someone with a financial background who also has an exceptionally good feel for people. In the catering industry, that seems to be unique."

In a remarkable show of amity, Bucknall and Allen swopped jobs. Allen moved to Granada as chief executive of Granada Television and Bucknall stayed put with Compass, becoming managing director in Charles Allen's place, only later joining Granada as chief executive of Granada Purchasing.

Robinson now had his new team in place to replace the departure of David Plowright, Granada Television's managing director, which caused a national outcry. When the news was announced, John Cleese's comment "Why don't you f*** off, you upstart caterer?" reverberated throughout the media and shook Robinson in its ferocity. It was a comical charge – one thing that Robinson had never considered himself to be was a caterer – and his reaction showed some grace – "I obviously admire him more than he admires me." But it was a painful and highly publicised time. Emotions cooled, Robinson and Cleese have since dined together on a number of occasions: "Cleese is a very complicated man," says Robinson.

* * *

In 1991, with both Robinson and Allen off the Compass scene, Mackay, as chief executive, was able to get on with developing Compass in the way he wanted. Chris Bucknall reshuffled the management team, moving Clive Grundy to deputy managing director, Trevor Briggs to managing director for the north and Gary Green in charge of the south; Fatima Chogley, a recruit from Rosser and Russell, joined as commercial director in charge of finance and information systems. Clive Gilpin, who had announced his intention to retire in 1992, stayed on the board "to support it and offer much valued advice" as Bucknall explained.

Bucknall, though stressing that quality remained the key priority and that staff were the company's key asset, nevertheless, displayed a slight paranoia about the catering industry which had been a recurring theme of Allen's messages in the Compass staff newspaper. Both appeared preoccupied about the industry's image:

"The industry as a whole does need to improve its image and has to decide how it wants to position itself. Compass has an important role to play in this process" adding quickly, "Compass already has an excellent image but I want to build on that."

Building is what both he and Mackay did. In the following years Compass grew by both internal growth and acquisition. In 1992, it bought Travellers Fare and Letheby and Christopher, giving the company a foothold in the travel and transport market as well as sports and events; both were well known brands. Travellers Fare, itself the subject of a management buy-out in 1988, had an annual turnover of £77m and brought Compass into popular catering mainly at railway stations. It was a venture into the commercial catering world that Robinson had been so cautious about a few years earlier. Letheby and Christopher brought Compass into sport and event catering, including race courses like Ascot and Cheltenham.

At the same time, Chartwells, led by Mike Bond, was created to oversee Compass' expansion into education catering while the name of Bateman Catering, led by John Greenwood, was resurrected to organise the company's push into the NHS. In 1992, Compass also bought Eaton Exclusive Catering, a small City of London company specialising in catering at Livery Halls, and won some major new contracts: House of Fraser brought in 31 public restaurants and 22 staff restaurants while Roedean was a scoop for the newly formed Chartwells division. There was no doubt that Compass was becoming a force to be reckoned with.

The moves highlighted Mackay's conviction that branding was the way forward and would become ever more significant in its success.

The acquisitions presaged Compass' much bigger purchases in the UK, Europe and America within the next few years and set down a marker for the company's ambitions. Mackay's aggressive ideas, which Gerry Robinson had noticed in 1991, were beginning to bear fruit.

One of these ideas was a bold expansion in the UK. There were plenty of smaller

By 1990, Del Bampton had spent 25 years with Bateman and then with Compass. He was presented with a set of golf clubs. Left to right: Clive Gilpin (operations director, North), Roger Matthews (finance director who later moved to Sainsbury's and is currently chairman of Mitie), Charles Allen, Del Bampton and Clive Grundy (HR director and operations, South).

companies to be acquired at the right price but the prize was Gardner Merchant.

With its success in America and Europe, GM was the biggest contractor in the UK and had become a major world player. Francis Mackay, ever keen to expand the Compass business, recognised that if the kind of margins and additional profit that had already been achieved with Compass could be squeezed out of GM, it would be a very worthwhile acquisition indeed. He decided to move. Joining forces with Aramark he approached Rocco Forte and set in train several months of argument and recrimination.

Letheby and Christopher brought Compass into sport and event catering, including Ascot Racecourse.

CHAPTER FIFTEEN

*Gardner Merchant rebuffs the
Compass siege*

*A bid for Gardner Merchant by Compass, its
greatest rival, set the scene for a bitter clash
between the two companies.*

In 1992 it became clear that Rocco
Forte was considering his options
with regard to the future of Gardner
Merchant. The board at Forte plc, of
which Garry Hawkes, GM's chief executive,
was now a member, had already decided
that Forte plc should focus on hotels and
restaurants in order to bring some structure
into its sprawling empire. Highly profitable,
and largely left to its own devices under
Hawkes' dominating presence, GM was a
self-contained entity which could be sold
off without damaging any of Forte's core
hotel and restaurant interests. Forte's airport
business, including in-flight catering, airport
shops and aircraft cleaning, came into the
same category – profitable but peripheral to
what was now deemed to be the company's
main focus. In a similar manner, Forte's
specialist outside catering division, Ring &
Brymer (caterers at Royal Ascot and other
racecourses, Chelsea Flower Show, sports
stadia, The Open golf and a number of
other prestigious locations) didn't fit with its

hotels and public catering activities and its
profitability was volatile. It was decided to
dispose of the three businesses.

The decision came at a time when
the company had hit rough times. It had
just reported a drop in profits and City
pressure was on it to reduce its hefty £1.3bn
borrowings. But if the company needed
money, the depressed property market was
not the answer. There was little prospect of a
good sale of any of its hotels, something that
Forte would have been reluctant to consider
anyway; its hotels were its crown jewels.
The company had grown largely through
acquisition rather than through organic
growth; even selling GM, while it had its
attractions, must still have been a wrench for
Forte to have to consider.

Even so, GM's profits, though significant
at some £30m, were less than those of
Grosvenor House, the Forte hotel and
apartment flagship in Park Lane which, at
the height of its success, was turning over
£90m a year with £35m going straight to
the bottom line; the loss of GM to the Forte
profits had to be put into perspective. Any
interest in the contractor was thus welcome
news providing the price was right. And for

COMMENT
Time to take off the gloves

One of my biggest personal regrets about the collapse of our negotiations to buy Gardner Merchant is that, had we done so, we would have made it a far more efficient organisation than it is. Despite the crippling recession which has bitten deep into the country's economy for the past couple of years, we have fared very well — far better than many others in fact. The reason for that is not only our efficiency, but also our investment and financial stability and our independence.

I sincerely believe that we are better than any of our competitors and I am proud of that. Our professionalism is second to none, particularly when it comes to offering quality and service. This cannot be said for our competitors, both large and small, who have attacked us in a most unprofessional way via the press and even directly to our clients.

As has been our way, we ignored them. But for too long Compass has played the gentleman and meekly sat back and taken such knocks. Not any more though!

I am no longer prepared to accept unfair, or worse still, untrue claims which are made about our company concerning our costs and profit margins.

The fact that Compass has a greater profitability than our main rivals is because *we are more efficient*, with *considerably lower overheads*.

There is nothing wrong with profit. It's what keeps people in jobs. But we will continue to concentrate on quality and efficiency which benefits both Compass and our clients. And we have many new initiatives in the pipeline which will offer an even better service.

*The backlash from the failed GM bid led to
Chris Bucknall's comment in Compass News.*

Rocco, newly installed as both executive chairman and chief executive and with his father, now president but out of play (though undoubtedly still influential), it was an early test of his negotiating skills. The word went out that GM was in play to be sold.

As a main Forte board member, Hawkes had been fully consulted about the sale of GM and agreed to the proposal but he was dubious about the price being proposed – in excess of £500m – which he considered was too high. It took weeks of internal wrangling before his objections were overruled and the decision was made to sell all the businesses in the same package at the original mooted price.

Interest came from a variety of sources. The flotation idea had a number of drawbacks but Ken Costa, a senior partner in SG Warburg, one of Forte's merchant bankers and a friend of Rocco, introduced Kohlberg Kravis Roberts (KKR), the US-based leveraged buy-out specialists who, at the time were seeking to establish a London base and believed the GM deal would be a big step along the way. The deal, which Hawkes supported and was worth £425m, would have replicated the Compass buy-out from GrandMet and would have set GM on a similar independent course with an eventual listing on the Stock Market in the same way that Compass emerged as a force to be reckoned with in 1986. Intense negotiations followed and a deal was agreed but the KKR bid fell apart two days before the deal was due to be signed. Then Compass entered the fray with a £550m offer, calculating GM at £440m and the inflight and airport business at £110m.

For Forte, the new offer was hugely tempting. For GM it was the very worst news. A merger with Compass was the last thing that anyone at GM wanted. Rivalry between the two companies was already intense and growing and the manner in which Gerry

Robinson and Francis Mackay had swept through Grandmet Catering a few years earlier was still reverberating around the industry. There was little doubt in the mind of senior people that the same fate would befall them if GM fell to Compass.

For Compass, however, the deal was just too good to miss. Full of ambition, highly regarded in the City, profitable and eager to expand in both the UK and overseas, the company was like a tiger ready to pounce. Acquiring GM, then the UK's biggest contractor, would let that tiger loose. It would create a company which would be by far the dominating influence in the UK contracting industry with some 60 per cent of the market and with extensive overseas interests. But that was itself a problem. Its share of the market would certainly have attracted the attention of the Mergers and Monopolies Commission (M&M).

It was the thought of an M&M Commission investigation that encouraged Compass to team up with ARA to prepare a joint bid. Mackay was convinced that any argument with the M&M Commission was winnable because the competition, particularly considering the multiplicity of self-operators, was strong and extensive; the fact that the later Granada Compass merger got by without any trouble backs this up. But the transaction was too big for Compass to get it wrong.

Compass was, in fact, quite a small company when it bid, with an annual turnover of £263m, so teaming up with US-based ARA, an even smaller-time operator in the UK with an £83m turnover, for an asset which Francis Mackay, Compass's chief executive, had already described as 'a very good business' gave it more clout. For two rival companies to bid for a third was certainly unusual and made the process more complicated than it might have been. Undoubtedly, Compass would have

preferred to bid for it alone but the threat of a monopoly investigation was too high; it reckoned that a successful bid by the two companies, with the spoils shared, would escape an investigation. Dick Vent, who was responsible for ARA's overseas businesses, came over from the US to head up the ARA team in London. Compass put in about £450m and ARA put in the balance.

The bid generated huge speculation with commentators having a field day in the trade and national press. *Caterer* speculated that the new company would split all of GM's 3,400 outlets down the middle; another proposal was that the new company would be called Gardner Merchant Compass and would drop the Compass name after two years – even at the time a highly unlikely outcome. It was speculation that Mackay firmly brushed aside, saying that Compass, not ARA, would gain the sole rights to the Gardner Merchant, Ring & Brymer and Town and County names – "which obviously holds a lot of attraction".

"We're looking at a beauty parade of brand images," he claimed.

Behind the speculation, however, Compass had got as far as carrying out research into the new company name and logo, with client recognition as a key factor in selecting the new identity.

The initial agreed division of the spoils was that Compass would take over Forte's airport services, some GM contracts (the balance and those in the US going to ARA), Ring & Brymer, Town and County, Kelvin (GM's off-shore catering business), and all GM's other overseas businesses. According to Mackay, the split was actually education and off-shore going to ARA and B&I and healthcare going to Compass – "thus making a complicated transaction as simple and efficient as we could".

In high spirits, Chris Bucknall, newly appointed as managing director under

Mackay, claimed, rather prematurely:

"We will be the largest contract caterer in Europe but we will have to be the best, so all our management attention will be going into getting the right people on board to push that quality issue forward.

"It was an opportunity that we quite honestly didn't expect to happen," he told *Caterer*.

Negotiations, however, which went on for weeks longer than planned, unsettled both shareholders and employees. Compass attempted to interview GM's senior personnel with a view to weeding out the strongest and the weakest, some of whom tried to encourage either one or other of the companies to vie for their services with very divisive results. Compass' shares were suspended during the eight-week bidding process and GM couldn't make sales while its future was in doubt.

The negotiation reached a "pretty final stage" in Mackay's words "when, at the last knockings, we discovered an error in the information memorandum produced by the accountants, which affected the expected level of profitability which meant that the value – and the price – of the company was reduced."

In fact, there had been an accidental double counting and Compass wanted to reduce the bid from £550m to £535m (£425m for GM and £110m for the airport catering services). Due diligence also revealed that the contracts of some of GM's key clients, including Midland Bank, British Aerospace and Eagle Star contained clauses that, in the event of a change of ownership, gave them the right to terminate the contract. These clauses would have meant the companies would have to agree to Compass taking over their catering provision – an unlikely outcome as all three had already written to Forte (at the instigation of GM) objecting to the bid, while two of them had pointed out

The letter that set the bid alight

It was in the middle of the bid process that Bob Cotton wrote his notorious letter which *Caterer* published. At the time, Cotton was director of public affairs for Gardner Merchant and personal assistant to Garry Hawkes. Although he wrote it in a private capacity, those who knew (who were most people in the industry) recognised the name; many were even sympathetic to the sentiments expressed. In writing it, he had nothing to lose. It was clear, if the takeover had gone ahead, he and a large clutch of other top GM people would not be joining Compass.

Ostensibly, he was replying to a letter in the previous week from Bob Payne of the consultancy Tricon, which, said Cotton, "reads like a calculated attempt to win the approval of those trying to acquire Gardner Merchant without alienating those opposed to the bid". In fact, Payne's letter had been deliberately planted and Cotton's reply was a full-on attack on the proposed merger.

"How does the declared intention of Compass to increase Gardner Merchant's margins from four per cent to at least nine per cent equate with the view that customers will still benefit from this deal? To what extent will the high price paid for Gardner Merchant necessitate a ruthless pruning of the quality back-up services which made Gardner Merchant a market leader, like dietetics, hygiene services and training?

"How can anyone believe that withdrawing from the American market would enhance the new company's ability to attract the best staff and to balance any setback in the UK economy with success overseas?

"A less commercially driven consultant could have argued that the bid from ARA and Compass is bad for customers, bad for Gardner Merchant employees and bad for Britain.

"Maybe that consultant could have gone on to argue that if a significant number of Gardner Merchant clients deserted it for fear of lower standards, the deal would be bad news for Compass shareholders and company employees, too."

The broadside, seen as a gross impertinence by Rocco Forte, summed up the growing feeling of frustration on the Gardner Merchant side. One of the industry's longest-established companies was being sold off to the highest bidder who was also a hated rival. Rocco, however, is reported to have said: "We are just selling something that we own."

Bob Cotton's letter crystalised the opposition to the Compass bid – he survived Rocco's call for his dismissal and in 2000 was appointed chief executive of the British Hospitality Association.

The catering contract with BA was worth some £90m a year in turnover and was one of the bargaining chips used by Gardner Merchant in the sale negotiations.

would accept. This was despite being told by his two leading advisers, Warburg and Phillips and Drew, that the offer was realistic. Forte remained adamant. He would not accept less than £537m. The negotiations hit a brick wall.

Compass had stated that jobs would be safeguarded after the merger and Chris Bucknall's earlier statement (and subsequent senior employee interviews) certainly implied that Compass wanted to keep the best people. But did the best people want to work for Compass? People also recognised that this did not necessarily apply to all senior positions and one of the purposes of the merger, as stated by Compass was increased purchasing power and administrative synergies, i.e. job losses and office closures. There was no doubt that Compass, like any other would-be purchaser, saw huge savings in cutting out senior positions, regional offices and merging back-room support services. It was also true that Francis Mackay had offered Garry Hawkes

that they had shortlisted neither Compass nor ARA when their contracts had last came up for tender.

Clients with multi-site contracts also had concerns that the new company would carve up their sites between them when one of the advantages of engaging one contractor, such as GM, was that they had only one catering provider to deal with. This was a serious complication and one which GM did not hesitate to exploit behind the scenes.

With assets of only £131m, GM's value lay in the strength (and length) of its contracts which yielded £350m in turnover in 1991. A purchaser would want to be sure that all of them would continue under the new ownership; on the other hand, Forte did not want any claim for compensation if important contracts were immediately set aside. In fact, this was just what Compass and ARA were seeking – warranties from Forte for compensation if any projected

revenue failed to materialise. It was a stumbling block which led to significant delays in the negotiations.

Compass' profit record had also preceded it, somewhat to its disadvantage. Some clients were concerned that Compass' more aggressive approach to business (its margins were then 9.8 per cent compared with four per cent of GM and rival Sutcliffe) would lead to a reduction in the quality of GM food and service and an increase in costs.

The more serious objection came from BA for whom Forte's airport catering business was providing meals for the airline's shuttle services, then worth some £90m a year in turnover yielding £10m profit annually on a 10-year rolling contract. Colin Marshall, BA's chief executive, told Rocco that if the ownership of the business changed, BA would replace it with a 90-day contract.

Rocco Forte refused the revised offer, saying that £537m was the minimum he

Rumour had it that Garry Hawkes (seen here with Francis Mackay at a later industry event) had been offered a top job in the proposed merged company but few could believe that they would ever have been able to forge a creative and long-lasting partnership.

Press release...Press release...Press release...Press release...

For Immediate Release   Friday 3rd July 1992

Forte Plc announced today, 3rd July, that it had ended negotiations with Compass Plc and ARA Services Inc. concerning its contract catering operations.

Mr Rocco Forte, Chief Executive of Forte Plc, said:

"After protracted negotiations arising from the approach from Compass and ARA it has become clear that the parties are unable to reach agreement on terms and conditions, including price.

Our long-term strategy is to dispose of the contract catering businesses and concentrate on the international expansion of our hotels and restaurants. We have recently announced a joint venture to operate hotels in Italy and have several other prospects under discussion at present. None of these is dependent upon us selling the contract catering operations.

Gardner Merchant and Forte Airport Services are excellent businesses which are continuing to grow their customer base and profits. Such premium businesses deserve a premium price.

We have a number of options which avoid the need to split Gardner Merchant, including other approaches which we have received, and we are considering these at present."

- E N D S -

For further information, please contact:-

Rocco Forte	Chief Executive Forte Plc	071-836 7744
Richard Power	Director of Corporate Communications Forte Plc	071-836 7744
Alan Parker	Brunswick Public Relations	071-404 5959

The sale is off: how Forte told the world that the Compass/ARA bid had finally been refused – but only a few million pounds separated the two parties.

a high position in a merged company but cooler heads recognised it was completely unrealistic to believe that the two men would ever have been able to forge a creative and long-lasting partnership. Both had charm in spades but they also had strong personalities, strong opinions and were accustomed to getting their own way in their own organisation. Mackay was a Compass man and Hawkes was a lifelong Gardner Merchant man. It was an unlikely combination.

Bob Cotton's letter to *Caterer* was sent without the knowledge of Hawkes or anyone else in the company but the reaction was immediate. Rocco Forte demanded that Cotton should be fired and queried with George Proctor, Forte's legal counsel, whether the letter had broken the law. The answer came back that it had not. Hawkes, believing that the letter was merely 'foolish' (but no doubt privately agreeing with its contents) demurred and sent Cotton to purdah for a month in the company's City office, run by Rodney Widdowson.

It took some weeks before the storm had died down but the letter crystalised the issues between the companies – the choice between a highly successful company with a long tradition in the business and an ambitious new organisation with plans for worldwide expansion.

The intervention was unwelcome for Compass, too – "but we brushed it off as of no consequence," says Mackay.

Negotiations dragged on for two more months which included a difference of opinion over the valuation of the pension fund. Mackay, offering £535m, recalls one particularly lengthy meeting trying to come to an agreement with Forte but whatever Compass suggested was rejected, with Iain Carslaw, GM's finance director, playing a particularly strong hand.

"We were willing to go more than half way to clinch the deal, but the other side was obdurate," says Mackay. "It was not a meeting of minds."

"We are not a forced seller so why should we sell if we are not completely happy with the terms of the deal?" Rocco Forte asked *Caterer*. Rocco was insisting on £537m.

In the event, much to the relief of Hawkes and other senior GM people, Compass walked away but only as a result of a few million pounds difference in the purchase price and the lack of any warranties that they were seeking in order to protect their purchase which Forte was unwilling to undertake. ARA had significant return on capital hurdles built into their finance arrangements and Mackay had already pushed the Compass boat as far as he thought sensible. "It was a step too far," says Mackay. Rocco Forte, who had put GM into the jaws of the Compass tiger, had pulled it out just in time.

The experience, however, further soured relations between GM and Compass and did little to help their on-going relationship. For a while, competition between the two became even more intense with each bad-mouthing the other.

However, GM was still in play for a sale. It was clear that pressure on Forte to dispose of the company in one way or another remained despite Rocco's denial that it was a forced sale. Other offers came but were seen off as inadequate. Then Granada, the media group, which was now under the control of Gerry Robinson and Charles Allen, showed interest but this, too, was swiftly rejected by Rocco – a fateful decision that probably set the seeds for Granada's later hostile bid for the whole of the Forte empire which subsequently generated so much ill-will. BET, which was trying to develop its contract catering interests, was also reputed to be interested, as was P&O, Sutcliffe's holding company. Even Sodexo put in a bid, offering £400m for GM alone without the airport business.

Forte Plc
Registered Office:
166 High Holborn
London WC1V 6TT

Registered in England
No. 76230

7 December 1992

To the shareholders of the Company (and for information only to the holders of the secured and unsecured loan stock of the Company).

Dear Shareholder,

Disposal of Gardner Merchant

Your Board announced today that it has reached agreement for the disposal of Gardner Merchant to GMSG, a company specially formed for the purposes of this transaction by CINVen. In view of the size of the proposed transaction, the Disposal is conditional upon the approval of the shareholders of Forte. I am writing to you to set out full details of the Disposal and to explain why your Directors are recommending that shareholders should approve it. Notice of an Extraordinary General Meeting to consider the Disposal is set out at the end of this document.

Details of the Disposal

Forte has entered into a conditional agreement with GMSG for the sale of Gardner Merchant. The consideration comprises:

(i) £342 million in cash, inclusive of repayment of inter-company loans owing to Forte;

(ii) £29.6 million in deep discount bonds with a yield to redemption of 21 per cent. per annum;

(iii) £28.6 million in redeemable preference shares carrying a net dividend of 6 per cent. per annum; and

(iv) £1.9 million in ordinary and convertible redeemable preferred ordinary shares, which it is expected would represent, on a diluted basis, a 24.8 per cent. interest in the equity of GMSG.

The New Shares and the Bonds will be held by the Group on substantially the same terms as other institutional investors in GMSG.

Mr. Garry Hawkes, managing director of the Gardner Merchant Group, and his senior management team will continue to manage the business following completion of the Disposal and he, together with certain members of the Gardner Merchant senior management, will be subscribing for 8 per cent. of the ordinary share capital of GMSG. Management's percentage interest in the equity of GMSG may be increased if certain performance criteria are met. On completion of the Disposal, Mr. Hawkes will resign from the Board of Forte and a representative of Forte will be appointed to the Board of GMSG.

The principal terms of the Disposal Agreement, the Shareholders Agreement and the Bond Instrument and summary information on GMSG are set out in Appendix 3.

4

Rocco Forte's letter to shareholders revealing the impending sale of Gardner Merchant to the management team.

Pierre Bellon, Sodexo's chairman, was keen but couldn't sell the deal to his board. Ironically he paid £730m only two years later.

If there couldn't be a trade sale, went the reasoning, how about a management buy-out? In fact, the idea of a management buy-out for GM was not new. The Compass buy-out a few years earlier had set the trend and they were fast becoming a popular route for conglomerates that wanted to divest themselves of unwanted subsidiaries. But for any buy-out to succeed GM had to have a willing buyer and a willing seller and the company had to be seen as a separate viable business on its own and not part of the parent company.

Hawkes and the GM team began to press all the PR buttons, producing an annual report of its own to make it identifiably different from Forte plc. It began to get coverage in the media, taking advantage of national events like Ascot and Henley to place artful pictures in the nationals, and generally raising its profile. Hawkes, never one to hide his light under a bushel, became ever more identified with the company while the Forte ownership was studiously kept in the background of every story planted.

The strategy worked. GM's profile became established almost as an independent company in its own right. But it took another five months before the main imperative was reached – having a willing buyer and a willing seller.

By the autumn of 1992, conditions in the industry had changed for the worse. Forte plc was under increasing financial pressure and Rocco had finally taken the decision to offload GM in order to reduce the company's debt. In the Forte circular to shareholders on the management buy-out he admitted that the Forte board had been considering the disposal of GM for some time:

"The board has examined a number of disposal options and concluded that the proposal received from CINVen offered both an attractive cash price and the opportunity to obtain a significant investment in GMSG [Gardner Merchant Services Group]."

Apart from retaining an investment in the new GM (which was repaid handsomely two years later through the purchase by Sodexo), Forte was also keen to use the cash proceeds to reduce net debt and to expand the company's hotel and restaurant interests internationally.

Seeing the opportunity, Hawkes and his senior team, principally Iain Carslaw the financial director and Ian Hall, his trusted HR director, had responded quickly to grab the opportunity of a buy-out. Hawkes had been at GM, man and boy, for nearly 30 years:

"I had been with the company since 1963 and the company was in my blood. I had helped build it up through my own efforts and latterly leading a very strong and greatly admired team whose efforts also needed rewarding. The last thing we wanted was to be taken over by a competitor who would not want to keep most of the senior people. We had been making impressive profits and were catering in some of the greatest places in the world. Why shouldn't we reap the rewards of all our efforts?"

Hawkes had already explored a number of possible organisations but no substantial negotiations took place until Rocco and Donald Main, the Forte company secretary, approached CINVen, the venture capital company linked to the pension funds of the coal and rail industries. CINVen had already helped Forte with an expansion of the Post House programme and Rocco suggested that GM could be off-loaded through a management buy-out that CINVen could organise. The airport catering business was not included and was spun off two years later by Forte as Alpha Airports Group in a successful IPO worth £211m.

The list of contracts that GM then had was impressive indeed and its profitability was rising steadily, as the disposal document revealed.

P&L account for Gardner Merchant for three years ending 31st January			
	1990 £m	1991 £m	1992 £m
Sales	700	751	824
Operating costs	667	716	784
Gross trading profit	33	35	40
Profit before interest and taxation	25	27	33

For a company with only £162m of fixed assets, of which £131m were debtors, GM was doing well. It catered for 74 of the UK top 100 companies and it was little wonder Compass had been so anxious to acquire it.

GM's management buy-out offer was £402m, lower than many in the City had expected and certainly lower than the Compass bid, even without the airport business, but it created very high debt using deep discount bonds that generated very high premiums of some 30 per cent. Rocco received some stick for agreeing the deal with City investors querying his decision for not getting a better price. He accepted it on the grounds of expediency. All other attempts to sell had failed, though partly through his own obduracy, and the GM buy-out was now temptingly the last bid on the table. Robin Hall, at CINVen, is alleged to have rung Rocco and told him to accept the buy-out bid – "Because they are such a bloody stroppy lot!" As a part consolation, Rocco was selling it to people he knew and Forte plc would retain a 25 per cent stake in the company and so would enjoy some of its future success.

This did not mean that negotiations were easy. £400m was needed for acquisition finance and a further £20m for working capital. A fruitless trail around the major British banks and some leading insurance companies revealed that no British funder was interested in backing the deal. The bank finance eventually came from a consortium of foreign banks led by the Bankers Trust of the USA and including others from the US and from as far afield as Japan. It was a time of huge economic difficulties and plunging stock markets with the deal actually being signed just three months after Black Wednesday, the day the UK came out of the Exchange Rate Mechanism and when interest rates had shot up to 15 per cent. Looking back now, Hawkes and his team were brave to complete the deal and in true dramatic fashion, it went to the wire.

"We were based in Clifford Chance's offices for the signing with 100-plus people in the negotiations, taking over the whole ground floor suite of offices – and corridors," recalls Bob Cotton. "There were bankers and lawyers and our own people and the Forte people and there was so much to-ing and fro-ing between the various parties and between Rocco and his advisers that you could hardly believe this was a serious negotiation."

The talks started on Friday morning and went on all day, with redrafting overnight; the negotiations continued over Saturday and Sunday until the deal was signed off on the following Monday morning. Cynics reckoned the negotiations were happily strung out to enhance the lawyers' fees.

In the end, the headline value of the buy-out remained at £402m; Forte held 25 per cent of the equity, CINVen had 25 per cent, Charterhouse, Candover, Prudential, Legal & General and others had substantial percentages and the management subscribed eight per cent. The rewards were considerable and widely spread. Over 1,000 GM staff, from directors to unit managers, bought direct stakes in the business ranging between £1,000 and £40,000, according to status and length of service, with the 12 key directors receiving substantially more and making millionaires of them all (a term that meant significantly more then than it does today).

Initially, this gave them eight per cent of the business but, aided by a clever ratchet arrangement thrashed out with CINVen by Iain Carslaw and Ian Hall, the management percentage doubled its share to 16 per cent and, eventually, to 20 per cent on the back of improved profits, spurred on by the efforts of 1,000 new entrepreneur management/owners. Because of this wide dispersal Hawkes' own share was significant – allegedly some £15m but thought by some to be much less. He admits that he still rankles at the even higher financial returns that other company founders later received from the sale of their much smaller business to Granada and others – and after a much shorter period of time building it up.

But the buy-out, benefiting so many people, became a distraction in the eyes of some. "The whole atmosphere in the company became poisoned because people were calculating how much they would each get, how much they would be worth. There was an atmosphere of greed in the company which was very distracting," says one.

Nor was the buy-out the end of the story, but it set GM off on an independent route – Hawkes' desired objective.

"Ownership is motivation," he says. At the time, it was the biggest corporate buyout by far with the widest distribution of the spoils.

But if it wasn't the end of the beginning it was the beginning of the end. Two years later Sodexo re-emerged as a suitor with an offer that the GM buy-out team and the other shareholders could not refuse.

A Fellowship of the BHA for Rocco Forte – presented by Garry Hawkes, then BHA president, in 1999.

CHAPTER SIXTEEN

The Americans consolidate

ARA survived a management putsch and acquired Stuart Cabeldu – but it was not all plain sailing.

Since launching in the UK in 1972, ARA had created five divisions. All with the exception of leisure, started through acquisition. Off-shore, servicing the oil platforms, was by far the most profitable; Coffee Club, which provided ingredients for pour-and-serve services to small offices and businesses, was also very successful. The newly formed leisure division included Wembley. Vending was barely profitable while catering was just about breaking even. Vending and catering were the most troublesome divisions and were eventually combined but with the recession upon it and losing contracts, catering was making heavy weather of its expansion plans in the UK and lacked any real identity or image. Arthur Meakin, who was a Bateman's regional catering manager and was head-hunted to join ARA as the catering division's southern regional director in 1981, remembers a company that was strong on US methods of operation that did not suit the UK market, with poor levels of service and indifferent client liaison.

"All ARA's systems were designed for big locations with layers of senior management and a full accounting staff. The UK is quite different, with much smaller contracts. The bookkeeping was far too complicated for the UK's needs.

"Beheadings were taking place every week and there was no-one in the company with more than five years' service," he says.

The business was also hidebound by operational manuals – there was one for every part of the business – and strict cost controls were introduced with flash reports every month forecasting revenues and costs which had to be reconciled with actuals at the end of the month. Operating the flash reports became a major part of the management job.

When he joined, Meakin found a region that was losing jobs together with a demotivated staff. Philip Houldsworth believes that ARA at the time was never willing to make the investment necessary to put the right people in the right slots, a judgement with which Meakin agrees. Nevertheless, he set about recruiting (many from Bateman and Midland, which only

in the previous year had been merged into Grandmet Catering), and gradually the region was turned around. Within a 14-month period, it didn't lose a contract.

In 1985, Philip Thornton, who had been appointed chairman of a new board of

In 1985, Arthur Meakin was promoted from director of ARA's southern region to be managing director of ARA's catering and vending operations.

Barclays Bank was a major contract gain by ARA.

directors after a management buy-out in the US, reported that William McCall had been appointed CEO of ARA Services to succeed Roger French and Meakin was appointed managing director of the company's catering and vending operations. McCall, a chartered accountant by profession, had joined Aramark in 1977 and had been appointed finance director in 1981.

"ARA Services is now a much stronger, more competitive company than it was at the beginning of 1985," he told readers of the company's staff newspaper.

Indeed, business did prosper. In 1986, turnover exceeded £50m and in 1987, McCall was able to tell his staff that the year had been 'record-breaking'. In the 1987 Christmas edition of the staff newspaper, he said:

"All business sectors have made a leap forward, doing superb work at all levels, thinking bigger, achieving bigger goals and going from strength to strength."

During this time Meakin set about upgrading ARA's image winning a number of new and important accounts such as Arthur Andersen, Barclays Bank, Xerox, City Bank, Philips, Ministry of Defence and the Home Office (Police and Emergency Services Colleges). He went over to the US on a number of trips to check out the American operations of ARA and came back with a few ideas, one being introduced called weigh and pay: customers selected what that they wanted to eat and then had it weighed before they paid. Although the idea was subsequently introduced in the UK and helped ARA to win some prestige accounts, it caused more problems than it solved and it never caught on, relying as it did on the use of disposable plates. China plates, which the UK customers preferred, varied in weight and it proved impossible to set the scale 'tare' weight to accurately reflect the weight of the food on the plate.

ARA's image in the UK improved and

business expanded to take in the now burgeoning Ministry of Defence contracts sector, becoming a major provider; it was also successful in becoming the number one supplier to the Home Office – both sectors being very profitable. Meakin, swamped with the many small accounts that previously predominated, took the conscious decision not to grow by acquisition; he preferred to grow the business organically by targeting larger, quality accounts. The strategy worked and turnover rose to some £200m, making ARA the fourth largest contractor in the UK.

But not everything was working well. William McCall's strength lay in accounting – "he wrung every penny out of the business," says one contemporary; another comments that "managing and leading a business are two different things and William was strong on managing. I don't think the business created anything under his regime – nor has it since."

In 1990 Meakin and a clutch of other

OSCARS GREENHOUSE MENU

Today's Specials

Seafood Cocktail
Lasagne Verdi
Home Made Cornish Pastie
Jacket Potatoes, French Fries
Rhubarb Crumble & Freshly Whipped Cream

Soup of the day served from the soup kettle.

"Pay as you Weigh" Sandwiches

Choice of Breads
Cracked Wheat Roll, Petite Baguette, Croissants, Mini Hovis,
Wholemeal Pitta, Granary, Cottage Cob, Sesame Seed Bun.

Selection of Fillings
Honey Roast Gammon, Salt Beef, Liver Sausage, Ox Tongue,
Flaked Tuna, Assorted Cheeses, Roast Turkey, Assorted Salad.

"Pick n' Mix" Salads

"Pick" from these assorted items
Roast Rib of Beef, Chicken Quarter, Cottage Cheese & Pineapple,
Smoked Mackerel, Pressed Ox Tongue, Egg Mayonnaise with Anchovy.

"Mix" with these freshly made salads
Crispy Lettuce, Sliced Tomato, Potato & Chive Salad, Diced Beetroot,
Sliced Cucumber, Fresh Coleslaw, Russian Salad, Sliced Green Peppers.

Selection of Desserts

Choice of Milk Shakes, Tea, Coffee, Minerals.

Some items in Oscar's were sold on a weigh and pay basis – but china plates, which UK customers preferred, varied in weight and it proved impossible to set the scale 'tare' weight to accurately reflect the weight of food on the plate.

managing directors became increasingly unhappy at the impersonal style of the UK management. After a number of conversations with McCall as a last resort Meakin and his fellow managing directors raised their concerns with the international president, Dick Vent. The move backfired. They received little sympathy from him. Realising it had been a putsch that had failed, McCall was taken aback by the action and all but one of the directors left the company.

Meakin was succeeded by Ted Monk, an area director, and went to Sutcliffe working with Mike Oldfield as director, eventually becoming divisional managing director, before setting up his own business, Catering Business Solutions. As poacher turned gamekeeper he now advises clients on appointing contracted services.

Two years later came the Stuart Cabeldu purchase and it was clear that few lessons had been learned.

Stuart Cabeldu had spent the war in the Army Pay Corps. A short, stout man, he knew his own mind and was autocratic, like many an entrepreneur before and after him – 'I want it done this way,' was his demand. He was a difficult man to work for; if he didn't like you, you probably didn't last long. On demob, like John Sutcliffe and others, he thought that the catering industry offered him a profitable way back into civvy street, even though, again like Sutcliffe, he knew nothing about catering. What he did have, however, was a good handle on administration which he probably learnt in the army; he was also a born salesman. It was a strength that held him in good stead as he built up the business.

In 1947, he launched Management Catering Limited and started, like many others, pounding the streets looking for business opportunities. He was helped in this by his ability to network – he was a good golfer which introduced him to clients and he employed skilled sales people though, according to one observer, they seemed to pass through the company quite quickly. His territory was London-based, especially in the Wandsworth, Raynes Park and Wimbledon areas, and he won some decent contracts such as Kango Hammers, Crown Merton and Bowater's, all well known names.

The catering operations he offered were typically fairly basic but this was not a time of sophisticated demand: at least one hot meal option and usually a full tea trolley service twice per day. He also had an unusual way of winning business, recalls David Greenwood, who joined the company in 1973 after a three year catering management training course with Philips Electrical Group. He was appointed director in 1984 and managing director in 1989.

"Frequently, he would arrange for a member of his staff to go to work undercover for a couple of weeks in order to establish what was going on in the target company. At the end of the fortnight, the member of staff would resign and, a week later, Stuart would ring the MD to highlight how costs could be reduced. The two week 'survey' often

The BCCI collapse

Cabeldu gained several high profile contracts, the largest of these being Price Waterhouse in the City, which was won as a result of first meeting the client on the golf course. Deloitte was another win. Another notable gain was the contract with the Bank of Credit and Commerce International, but this nearly sank the company. Despite a system of fortnightly standing orders, the collapse of the Bank was catastrophic; in the space of six weeks the debt rose to over £330,000. Cabeldu survived but lost £120,000.

identified whether the catering manager or chef was on the fiddle – sadly not an unusual occurrence in those days."

The company grew steadily, gaining several large contracts including four power station construction sites for the Central Electricity Generating Board as well as a good portfolio of quality business in the City. On the way, it had acquired a number of companies in other areas including a contract cleaning company (Claremont). In addition, Cabeldu had started an equipment and kitchen design company as well as launching a vending ingredient supply business, Convena. But by the early 1970s competition was hotting up and in 1971 he decided that the company needed to change to meet the challenge.

Dennis Coates, a well known consultant and author of *Industrial Catering Management*, which was published in 1971, joined on a short-term consultancy contract. Cabeldu was savvy enough to know that the business was changing and Coates, who had extensive experience in the catering industry, was able to advise. One result was that the company's name changed from Management Catering Limited to Stuart Cabeldu Ltd. The aim was to project a more individual approach and a more tailored catering service, which it largely achieved.

Announcing the name change, he said that the company had existed in a variety of forms "with hardly any relationship to each other". Now, all the various companies would trade under the Stuart Cabeldu name, thus promoting one brand.

In 1972, Cabeldu recruited two people from Gardner Merchant to spearhead the change – Ronnie Ward as managing director of catering operations and Peter Holden as the finance chief. The hiring of the two was not entirely successful, however. Holden was a highly competent executive but relations between him and Pat Bowden, the company

secretary, were uneasy to say the least. Ronnie Ward also did not feel at home. He had great difficulty in transferring from a very large company, like GM with its huge resources, to a relatively small company with a resolute chairman who knew what he wanted. Ward's demise was relatively swift. One of Cabeldu's larger contracts, the Metropolitan Water Company with four sites, decided to retender. Ward led the sales effort and, as part of the deal, offered an investment of £100,000. Unfortunately, he didn't clear this with Cabeldu himself.

Investment in client's premises, now fairly commonplace, was just emerging as an incentive in exchange for longer term contracts and Ward's efforts won the contract only to find that Cabeldu refused the funding. As a result, the company lost the contract with its four sites and Ward lost his job to be replaced by a succession of people.

Although respected by most people in the organisation, this highlighted one of Cabeldu's idiosyncrasies – he tended to give responsibility but not the associated authority. He was very reluctant to slacken the reins of control and this was something

David Grenwood: cash flow was king.

which became a constraint on the business. Only in his latter years did he allow the directors, now including David Greenwood (who stayed with the company into the ARA purchase and later joined Granada), Roy Munday, Graham Sibthorpe (who went on to found Brookwood Partnership with a colleague Kate Martin – and who died in 2013), Rosemary Walsh and Ron Lord (a non-executive director), the scope they needed.

In spite of the Ronnie Ward hiccup, the company experienced significant organic growth throughout the late 1980s with Greenwood, Munday and Sibthorpe in the forefront of the expansion.

The company's secret of success lay in the fact that it operated in a tight geographical area, within central London and the M25 circle. It also employed high quality people in the units. As far back as the early 1970s, it used the services of an Australian consultant, Bruce Ward, to conduct psychological tests on new employees before they were appointed. This was considered a giant leap forward in employee selection at the time though how successful it was is open to some doubt; however, it acknowledged a certain forward-thinking mindset in Cabeldu's approach to management. Area managers had 12 but never more than 14 contracts to look after and clients were able to have their accounts presented in their preferred format and on their own timescale. The company offered entirely flexible arrangements to all its clients.

Cabeldu derived income from the management fee charged, discounts and 'other charges' which included the levy then imposed by the Hotel and Catering Industry Training Board which was one per cent (but frequently charged out to clients at four per cent), stationery, marketing and other one-off charges. At one time over 15 per cent of the company's income was derived from the

interest gained in overnight investment on the money market. Although it boasted an open book policy with regard to all cost-plus contracts – then an attractive sales pitch in gaining contracts – few clients ever took up this option because of the cost involved in carrying out an audit.

In the 1980s and into the 1990s, many of the smaller contractors were being eyed by one or more of the majors; in turn, they attempted to merge with each other. Cabeldu was involved in discussions with both Red Ball, a Brighton-based company, and Hamard Catering (both later acquired by Compass). At one stage, an alliance looked likely with High Table, which had been created by Julian Rowe and Chris Ballendon and which was gaining a solid reputation as a quality City-based company, but the talks broke down and High Table was later acquired by Elior (see Chapter 23).

In 1989, however, serious talks did get underway. Stuart Cabeldu, then aged 63, decided to retire and sell but wanted the company to remain independent. A sale, for a reputed £1m with some 94 contracts – the company was probably worth much more than that – was eventually concluded in 1990 to Pat Bowden who, with his family, became the sole owner. Bowden raised the money by re-mortgaging his house and getting in some venture capital; within 18 months the money had been repaid. Stuart Cabeldu died in Worthing, soon after the sale.

Bowden had no formal qualifications but as a lifelong colleague of Cabeldu (he joined the company as an accounts clerk in the early 1950s) he had had great influence on him so the purchase did not come as a great surprise. Like Cabeldu, he was strong on administration and, although not an accountant, he controlled the money and was risk-averse. He opened the post every morning and it was only in the last couple of years that letters were allowed out of the

company without him personally vetting each one, such close attention to detail eventually becoming stifling. However, in the couple of years after the purchase, the company continued to prosper but Cabeldu's wish for the company to remain independent did not come to pass.

In early 1992 discussions with Sutcliffe Catering were drawing to a close when a whistle-blower, concerned with what was perceived to be reluctance on the part of Bowden to sell, decided to brief *Caterer* that Sutcliffe was about to buy the company. This unexpected announcement sent ripples throughout the 1,500 staff and also caused many clients to voice their concern. Bowden decided to pull the plug on the discussions; even so, a few months later he announced that he had sold the company to ARA for a reputed £5m – not a bad turnaround on his £1m investment two years earlier. At that point Cabeldu had 108 contracts, it employed 1,500 staff and had a turnover of £14m. A proposal to give the four key directors one to two per cent each of the company's shares did not materialise.

This was not, however, a purchase made in heaven. Some 18 months earlier, ARA had acquired Northern Catering with about 70 contracts, mainly in the north of England, only to lose almost all of them later.

This was repeated with the purchase of Stuart Cabeldu Ltd and for largely the same reason. Cabeldu had a strong portfolio in high-end, quality City business but the contracts had all been gained because the clients had made a conscious decision not to appoint a big player. They had deliberately chosen a small company because they considered a small company was best able to meet their needs.

ARA, perhaps not recognising this sensitivity, was proud of its name and re-branded Cabeldu as ARA within a few months of the takeover. This led to much

William McCall: a putsch against him failed.

client (and in-company) resistance.

At the same time, ARA wanted to impose its accounting methods on clients which also went down badly. The approach was heavier-handed than it needed to have been and proved to be a mistake. Over the course of the next two years more than 80 per cent of what ARA had purchased was lost.

David Greenwood, who stayed with Stuart Cabeldu Ltd as managing director for 15 months, remembers that cash flow was king:

"At the end of every day, the ARA managing director had to ring through to the US giving full details of all moneys banked that day. Every unit, whatever its size, was required to bank every day regardless of whether they were banking £1 or £1,000. Of course, this didn't improve the business performance one iota but it did instil a certain discipline in the business."

Nevertheless, the company did bring some positive American techniques to the UK, though not always properly applied. It was strong on in-house sales and marketing and good at boosting food sales but its strong US bias was not always helpful. It insisted that signage declaring that customers would get 'More food for your $' was to be displayed in all contracts but it would not allow the signage to be reworded to the use of 'your £'.

In early 1994, the Stuart Cabeldu name re-emerged when ARA introduced a series of 14 concepts under the general branding of Café Connections, an idea which had proved successful in the US and was designed to offer small outlets a choice of which brand or combination of brands they wanted. They replicated similar introductions of branded outlets by Sutcliffe and Compass. None of the brands has survived in the same form but their introduction confirmed the way contract catering was moving: away from mass catering to more focused, high street-style offers.

CHAPTER SEVENTEEN

Catering in a war zone

While the contracting industry was developing quietly in most parts of the UK, in Northern Ireland it faced unique challenges.

From the late 1960s onwards, Northern Ireland faced some seemingly intractable challenges with high levels of unemployment, low pay, social deprivation, sectarian issues, a unionist-controlled government since the Irish state was formed, underlying republican activity and a reliance on the UK government to pump millions into the economy each year. It was not a recipe for calm peacefulness. The province had been a world leader in many industries including rope making, linen mills, textiles, tobacco manufacturing, aircraft building and (at the time) had the largest shipbuilding company in the world – Harland & Wolff (H&W), where Titanic was built. All the while, the overriding preoccupation had been sectarian strife.

Before the 'Troubles' erupted in 1968, the province was a catering backwater dominated by three companies: Bateman, Gardner Merchant and Smallmans. The latter was actually based in Manchester but was run locally by a Lancastrian, John

Belfast in 1969 – at the start of the Troubles.

Credit TopFoto

Trevor Annon: always had a gun in his car as he travelled around the province.

Duckworth, a baker by trade. He had been in the contracting industry for many years and moved over to Belfast to manage the business until it was acquired by GM in the 1960s.

Smallmans had a number of army contracts on the mainland as well as running Redford Hall, then Barclays Bank's principal training centre but now a hotel, and the contract for running the public restaurants for Great Universal Stores. It also catered for outside events 'and for a lot of rubbish,' in the words of Chris Hind, who had joined GM at the time of Smallmans' takeover.

In Northern Ireland, its operating model was unique in that it had a small warehouse in east Belfast from where it distributed supplies to its units, its largest contract being the H&W shipyard where, at its height, it provided nine separate dining rooms for H&W's 30,000 employees. Smallmans had the contract to provide catering services when newly launched ships went out on sea trials for 10-15 days, often with up to 500 technical staff on board; they had to be catered for over a 24-hour period in galleys designed for 100 crew members. Smallmans also had the contract to provide catering services to a number of police stations in Belfast although, at that time, the facilities were basic.

When GM bought out Smallman's it became the largest catering company in Northern Ireland, then owned by Trusthouse Forte. The THF regional director for Ireland was a Co Down man John (Jack) Swinson, who had an overseeing brief on the total THF operation in Ireland from a set of offices in York Street, Belfast. Jack (later knighted) was an old style entrepreneur who, in addition to managing the THF business, also ran a high quality restaurant on the shores of Belfast Lough.

At this time another son of Northern Ireland emerged. Trevor Annon, born in Belfast in 1946, started his business career in 1964 in the brewing industry as a production supervisor in the province's only brewery which was owned by various groups including Bass, Bass Charrington and Interbrew until it eventually closed in 1998 when Annon moved to a bottling plant owned by Scottish & Newcastle Breweries as assistant production manager. He joined Guinness in 1971 as factory manager in Ireland's largest bottling plant in Ballymena, Co Antrim.

Two years later he decided on a career change, joining GM as a district manager. "I knew a helluva lot about brewing, but nothing about catering," he says. Annon managed a number of high profile sites including the multi-unit contract for the

The Drumcree march caused a supply crisis for the Mahon Street RUC/Army base.

A problem of supply during the Troubles

People from the Protestant/Loyalist community in Northern Ireland have always regarded the right to hold marches along any road in Northern Ireland as sacrosanct – but this frequently led to problems for Trevor Annon and his Mount Charles team.

Mahon Road, a joint RUC/Army base was located in Portadown in the middle of what was a loyalist area which relied on daily deliveries of food and other catering supplies. However, in 1995, a stand-off occurred in the marching season when the police prevented the Orangemen from completing their march from Drumcree church to Portadown centre along Garvaghy Road, a staunchly Catholic republican area; neither side conceded ground, effectively blocking the road to the station for re-supplies. The stand-off continued with the Orangemen setting up a base in the grounds of Drumcree Church and in the surrounding fields.

During the following few days, with the base fast running out of food, Trevor Annon and his staff were verbally abused as they attempted to make their way to the station which was feeding increasing numbers of police 24 hours a day as the stand-off escalated. Delivery vehicles were being targeted and damaged by the locals and it soon became clear that a way had to be found to ensure that staff could reach their work safely and deliveries made so that a catering service could be maintained. Some members of staff from the locality, now regarded with hostility by the locals, were uplifted from their home by police under cover of darkness and forced to live in the barracks on a full-time basis. Logistical difficulties

prevented army helicopters air-lifting food into Mahon Road but suppliers would not risk travelling to the station for fear that their vehicles were attacked and burnt out – yet police numbers were increasing day by day as the supply situation deteriorated.

To overcome this impasse, and in total secrecy, suppliers were asked to build up supplies which would last at least one week and were tasked to have their vehicles ready within four hours' notice for delivery to an undisclosed location (which was Mahon Road) during the cover of darkness. It was agreed that drivers and vehicles would receive protection from the police. They were instructed to be at a pre-determined location in Belfast by 1.30 am, where covert police protection would be waiting. Eventually, a convoy of 10 vehicles (mostly in unmarked lorries) congregated. Other vehicles came from different directions.

With a police escort leading and an armoured police vehicle taking up the rear, the convoy headed west along the M1 towards the Moira roundabout, a 30-minute journey. As it reached its destination, the lead police vehicle radioed ahead to the Roads Service who had closed off the roundabout to maintain secrecy, to open the slip road briefly to let the vehicles through.

Once all vehicles were in place (with an army helicopter hovering above) the convoy headed off and nerves were beginning to show as it approached the Mahon Road station, because it was at this point that the vehicles were travelling through a loyalist estate. On arrival at the station, normally all vehicles are stopped and checked, but the gates were immediately opened and the convoy sped through to the safety of the heavily protected complex. The supplies were quickly off-loaded and the vehicles left one at a time before daybreak.

province's electricity supplier, Northern Ireland Electricity, and also the Parliament Buildings, which was GM's flagship site. After a couple of years he moved into sales and had some notable successes both in Northern Ireland and the Republic of Ireland. At the time, Northern Ireland was managed by Bob Morris, a West Country exile who was transferred from the mainland along with his wife and dog; unfortunately, he decided the company did not require a sales presence in Ireland and Annon was made redundant.

The redundancy opened up new opportunities. Annon opened two restaurants, one in Belfast and the other in Banbridge, Co Down, but it was not long before he was approached by Carson Rea, regional manager for Bateman Catering in Northern Ireland, to head up its sales effort in the province. With two restaurants trading well, eventually a deal was done whereby Annon agreed to work 20 hours a week for Bateman so that

he could continue managing his private restaurant business.

The formula worked out well. Less than 18 months later Rea announced his retirement and Annon was appointed regional manager. As part of the deal he was permitted to retain his two restaurants although two years later he decided to sell up and focus on growing the Bateman business, acting as both regional manager and sales manager in the next couple of years and bringing in contracts, some of which were ex-GM units. In 1980, he decided to employ a salesman, Terry Brannigan, who proved so successful that he was head-hunted by Bateman's divisional director for the North West, David Thompson, a Scot operating out of Manchester. With Bateman Catering now absorbed into Grandmet Catering Services, Thompson was succeeded by a number of other directors: Alan Robinson hadn't been to Northern Ireland before and didn't feel comfortable in it, though he and

his wife spent a weekend there; Tony Ward-Lewis, as ever, presented himself as the suave Englishman who stood out in a crowd. Annon felt most comfortable with Jim Cartwright who, he felt, genuinely cared about Northern Ireland and the team working there.

It was during this time that the troubles in Northern Ireland were at their worst. Murder was not uncommon and there were frequent bomb explosions in the centre of Belfast and elsewhere. Annon found himself in the middle of the mayhem.

When the troubles had started in the late 1960s Bateman Catering managed the few (less than 10) RUC police stations which had catering facilities but, as the dissent developed into almost full scale war, the number of sites developed to the point in the mid-1980s when there were 80 full catering sites and over 40 sites with vending services. At its height, the RUC contracts annually generated revenues in excess of £5m, employed 360 staff and

Dick Turpin, seated, on one of his tours of the country, visited the RUC Training Centre in Northern Ireland when the contract was part of GrandMet Catering. Left to right, standing: Bernie McGrath, Trevor Annon, Alan Robinson, and Clem Hanna (catering manager at the centre).

Most Bateman quarterly divisional meetings were held on the mainland but this one was held in Northern Ireland. The team was picked up from the airport in an armoured Land Rover and was driven by a specialist high speed Land Rover instructor, who was asked to make sure 'he scared the team witless.' In the picture, taken at the entrance to the RUC Training College where the meeting was held, are: front, Trevor Briggs, Clive Gilpin, Tim Baker and Jim Cartwright; at the rear, Trevor Annon and Andrew Moon. No record exists of whether the driver succeeded!

was regarded as being in the top five catering contracts in the UK.

Annon had two experienced caterers as regional general managers to handle the contract - Bernie Mc Grath and Alex Graham - who had to cope with operational issues which would be regarded as unprecedented on the mainland. The team, catering as it was for the RUC, was regarded as legitimate targets by the IRA so they were issued with personal protection weapons and given training in handling guns. They always had a gun in their car as they travelled around the province.

In 1995, a murder took place which stunned the company and individuals working for it. In November, German born Kurt Konig, an area manager with Compass working exclusively on the RUC contract in Londonderry, was murdered by the IRA at his home, in front of his wife and children. The murder shook the company. At Compass head office Jim Cartwright, who was then regional director, and Gerry Robinson spoke to Annon offering to withdraw from the contract (and the province). But Annon was insistent. An Ulsterman born and bred, he wanted to stay. The show had to be kept on the road, he told them.

Both he and his deputies, Bernie McGrath and Alex Graham, always took it as their personal responsibility to ensure the safety of the senior company men on their visit from the mainland – 'the good and great' as they termed them. Picked up at the airport, they would be transported everywhere in their itinerary, not left alone at any time when they were in a public place, nor taken anywhere where their safety could have been in doubt. They were taken back to the airport at the end of each visit. It was a bizarre situation in which the visitors were effectively under the personal protection of the three of them. Annon says he never really knew how his various bosses thought about being

A member of the RUC is accompanied by a military policeman on patrol in the Bogside area of Londonderry, in 1969.

Credit: Topfoto

Feeding the prisoners

Once, when the prison officers at Magilligan Prison on the north coast went on strike, Annon and his team was required to feed 1,400 convicted loyalists and republicans but were not allowed to use the prison kitchen nor meet the prisoners face-to-face. Large screens were erected at each servery station and meals were then passed through a slot at the bottom of each screen.

On another occasion, when officers went on strike at the Maze Prison (Long Kesh) outside Belfast, the caterers were required to feed the police who had taken over control at the prison. At the main entrance the 40ft mobile kitchen was jammed in the entrance gate for four hours.

"We had a situation in which a police

convoy could not enter the prison to guard the prisoners because a catering unit had blocked it," says Annon.

Earlier, in his Compass days, the local police station in Newry, Co Down was hit by a 900lb mortar bomb, killing nine police personnel. A mobile building unit was being used as a canteen at the time and part of the mortar bomb hit the dining room of the unit but fortunately no member of the catering staff was on duty at the time.

Annon was on site less than two hours after the incident. Nine police officers had been killed but the plates stacked in the pass-through counter were untouched by the blast.

"It was such a sobering moment. It brought home to me how fickle life can be."

responsible for Northern Ireland "but I reckon they often dined out on the fact!"

By 1988, Annon decided it was time to move on. The siren voices of independence were ringing in his ears and he quit to set up his own company – to be called Mount Charles Catering – eventually developing it as one of the top three catering companies in Northern Ireland alongside GM and Compass.

At the time he did not have a name, an office, money or any business, but the budding entrepreneur had worked out that there was a gap in the market for a 'local' company which could compete against the big two.

As in many a start-up, he acted as managing director, operations director and sales director. The first contract was a small Social Security office in central Belfast, ironically opposite Mount Charles' current head office. At the time, he recognised that it was crucial to secure some of the many large government contracts which were available. He bid for the Social Security office at a price to win it – "then I could genuinely write on my sales proposals that I was an appointed contractor to government departments. It worked!" But the contract lost money. Even so, during the next few years the company grew, though the competition was tough and sometimes rough. Appointed by a large public school, one competitor complained to the school's Board of Governors. Annon took them to court, winning the case; it was a tactic never tried again, and 20 years later, Mount Charles still operates the same contract.

He gained the contract for the Northern Ireland Housing Executive from GM, this being the period when the TUPE legislation was becoming a reality (even though most contractors ignored it in the beginning). The contract involved 14 staff and GM decided to invoke the TUPE regulations for the first time in Northern Ireland. For a brief period Mount

Credit PA Photos / TopFoto

Ulster Unionist MP David Trimble squeezes through the RUC line, 1996.

Charles was the guinea pig in terms of TUPE matters throughout the UK, with all eyes being on the Industrial Tribunal in Belfast where the case was heard. Annon lost the case but gained tremendous publicity.

His first big break came in 1991 when Mount Charles was awarded the contract to provide catering services for a new government building which was opening in central Belfast. Ironically, it was for the Social Security Agency but this time it was for the government's largest office building in Northern Ireland, providing services for 1,300 civil servants.

It was a huge gain but two years later he was awarded an ever bigger one – the RUC contract, a gain from his old employer, Compass, learning of it as he was driving along the A55 dual carriageway in Belfast. He hardly needed to be reminded of the dangers involved. For two weeks he had to keep the news to himself – he didn't even have the nerve to tell his wife, Kate, either, bearing in

mind she had lived through his time with Compass when his life was under constant threat. At the time, he had promised not to become involved in the RUC contract again. Kate was not happy.

The RUC bid involved some restructuring with a number of redundancies and changes to rates of pay, but an understanding from the Police Authority for Northern Ireland that it would pick up any costs involved in a restructuring exercise could not be supported by a written undertaking. It was a sticking point: Annon's insistence on some financial comfort against staff taking tribunal action was wise. It was only at 11.30pm, the night before the contract was due to start, that he received sufficient comfort to proceed.

His judgement was sound. Less than three weeks into the contract some 300 Industrial Tribunal claims were lodged by the supporting trade union. At the time Mount Charles made history by being involved in the largest claim in the UK. It could have had him bankrupted overnight.

The contract was governed by huge strife and danger. Civil unrest was everywhere and it was almost impossible to recruit staff (mostly on minimum wage) because of the threat of reprisals. In many instances they had to be escorted to their place of work by armed police or army vehicles; on occasions, they were airlifted by helicopter to one of the heavily bomb-proofed police stations.

The threat to suppliers became so serious that Mount Charles had to create its own delivery system from a secret warehouse in a remote part of Ballymena, Co Antrim. This involved procuring a fleet of unmarked vans and lorries which were changed every six months, employing a team of drivers and helpers, using authorised 'false' number plates (issued by the RUC) and with all the drivers being issued with a personal protection firearm.

They also changed the name of the company to Corporate Catering Management (CCM) to try to distance itself from Mount Charles Catering (MCC) – although not noticed at the time, the initials CCM were MCC in reverse. "That has to be Irish," says Annon.

The number of occasions when large numbers of police were required to cover major events in often remote areas, frequently involving over 1,000 police personnel, resulted in the RUC providing Mount Charles with three 40ft mobile kitchen units, each capable of producing in excess of 2,000 meals a day.

Why did he and his team stick it out? Over the years, looking after their personal security had become a way of life. He says there was also the aspect of 'doing their bit' to support the country against the threat from the IRA. "We just thought it right to carry on," he says. "It was a job to be done."

Without this commitment, it is difficult to understand how the RUC contract could have functioned.

Stormont – home of Northern Ireland's assembly. Compass won the catering contract at Stormont in the 1980s under Trevor Annon and retains it to this day through Eurest.

CHAPTER EIGHTEEN

Sutcliffe –
long on laughs, short on profit

In its early days, Sutcliffe was a company dedicated to service and plenty of laughs – profit was almost secondary.

Marc Verstringhe joined Sutcliffe in 1960. Born in Belgium before the Second World War, Verstringhe and his family survived a grim German occupation. Since he was a boy, he had worked in his father's hotel in Knokke-Heiste folding napkins and welcoming guests – "Catering was in my blood" – before gaining more experience in the Villa Royale in Knokke-Le-Zoute, a former summer residence of the King of Belgium set in extensive grounds that had been turned into a hotel. Five years later, in 1957, he arrived in England to gain more experience and to practise the language. Through family connections, he joined the Lygon Arms in Broadway where he stayed until 1960 when he joined Sutcliffe.

If Verstringhe was an accomplished caterer by this time, Mickie O'Brien, Sutcliffe's managing director, was an accomplished organisation man. He knew how to motivate people and how to set an example of the standards he expected his staff to reach. Verstringhe recalls:

"Once, Mickie asked me to join in a business call to the Esso research centre at Abingdon. He threw me the keys of his Jaguar and said, 'You drive'. We motored down to Henley for a light lunch then onto Abingdon. Just a few miles before our destination, Mickie asked me to stop. He opened the boot, took out some freshly pressed trousers and a pair of sparkling black shoes and off we went. It was just one of his ways to demonstrate the Sutcliffe/Royal Marine standards."

Verstringhe remembers him as eager to help people in their work.

"Mickie was really my mentor. My English at that stage left something to be desired so he suggested that I should work with him on any major proposal on a one-to-one basis to get the English right. It was pretty tough going at times. He told me that I should read the sports pages of the *Daily Telegraph* every day, because the sports reporters' command of language was more descriptive and colourful, which was very good advice. And he told me to read the editorial so I would have something to talk about with the clients. Not that the clients wanted to talk much about politics."

By the early 1970s, both John Sutcliffe and O'Brien were keen to develop the business and with talk of Britain entering the Common Market (eventually succeeding in 1973) they asked Verstringhe whether there was any opportunity for the company in Europe.

"Yes," came the reply.

"So you think they will like English food?"

"No," said Verstringhe. "But they will like the Sutcliffe Commando team culture and the professional management approach."

"You'd better get started right away then," said O'Brien.

Verstringhe argued that he already had the London company to run.

"If you want to succeed, you need to be able to manage more than one company," replied O'Brien tartly.

It was the start of Sutcliffe's overseas ventures – first in Holland (where Belgian-born Verstringhe spoke the language), then Belgium and later in Germany with a company led by Frank Schmidt.

The new Sutcliffe Catering Netherlands BV was launched in 1969 with Gist Bocades in Delft the first contract and it went on to gain six more contracts in the next few years. Sutcliffe was the first British caterer to operate in Europe and it reflected Sutcliffe's and O'Brien's vision to develop on an international scale, though this did not really gain much momentum.

With Ken Graveney, who was then managing director for the West Country company, Sutcliffe was also keen to expand into Australia, the country which John Sutcliffe had pencilled in as a new target market as far back as 1954 when he sent John Smith to open an office in London. In 1972, the two of them had gone down to Australia, allegedly to investigate the potential of opening up there but more likely to watch the cricket. A five-page report was compiled in which were outlined the 'golden opportunities' that lay in store for the company there, if only it would take the plunge. The report no doubt avoided mentioning the fact that both of them probably saw the Australian venture as a good excuse to visit when the Test Matches were being played.

O'Brien first asked Gordon Wishart, then in charge of the Scottish region, to go down under and start the new company but Wishart's asthma was serious and he was advised against it on medical grounds, so Eddie Crutch, a longstanding Sutcliffe manager and latterly a director of the Midlands company, was asked to launch the new enterprise. Crutch was certainly a go-getter and an entrepreneur by nature. He saw the opportunities and was glad to go, taking his wife and five children with him, successfully launching the venture. However, questions about its profitability were soon asked after Sutcliffe was acquired by Jeffrey Sterling's Sterling Guarantee Trust. Christopher Stuart-Smith, appointed Sutcliffe's chairman by Sterling, was particularly dismissive. He demanded to know what the company was doing so far afield when it could only be contacted in a narrow time frame outside UK office hours because of the time difference (this was before the days of the internet).

In 1976 the decision was taken to sell it off or close it down. Crutch stepped in and offered to buy the company out. The deal was accepted and Crutch denies that he failed to mention at the time that he had just won the contract for the catering at Sydney Opera House, but the story lives on in company legend. He went on to build up a company with 120 sites before he sold it for Aus$10m (£4.5m) to the Spotless Group in 1987.

Gordon Wishart (inset) was first asked to open up Sutcliffe's Australian venture but his poor health kept him in the UK; Eddie Crutch then agreed, buying out the company in 1976 and ultimately selling it for £4.5m in 1987.

Christopher Stuart-Smith: demanded to know what Sutcliffe was doing so far afield in Australia when it could only be contacted in a narrow time frame outside UK office hours because of the time difference (this was before the days of the internet).

* * *

Sutcliffe's management philosophy was summed up in a book, *Managing to Serve*, written by Sally Heavens and published in 2002, which outlined the management approach of Catering & Allied. On Sutcliffe, she writes:

"There was never any question that the service was customer-led yet success in its provision would always be predicated on staff fulfilment and team spirit that derived in particular from the Royal Marines and was realised in highly skilled small groups combining leadership and camaraderie with the restaurateur's approach to hospitality."

The old guiding Sutcliffe principles were simple: total commitment to client satisfaction; people working with, not for the company; creating a mentor/protégé formula of support; wanting to be among the best in the marketplace rather than the biggest; giving attention to detail until it drives the bigger companies insane; being close to the customer and team; aiming at meeting a desire rather than a need – and having fun. The last was not insignificant.

Mickie O'Brien, not one to hold back on having fun himself, laid great emphasis on client contact and using it as a sales tool.

"Once your selling office has established a customer unit in virgin territory, that unit becomes your selling point," he said.

In fact, until Simon Davis arrived in 1978, marketing and sales had not been a function which Sutcliffe as a company had ever thought much about. It had adopted the unusual practice of publishing an annual list of clients, apparently confident in the knowledge that none of them would be enticed overboard to a rival contractor.

If any potential client was thinking of engaging Sutcliffe, they had only to ring a company on the list (even the phone number was helpfully provided) and they could discuss how Sutcliffe went about providing a catering service. Such a roll call of clients would be considered commercially unacceptable today – complete client lists are among the most sensitive company secrets – but the practice continued until 1988. In the 1954 brochure, it claimed that between 1946 and 1954 Sutcliffe had increased the number of its contracts to 94, employing over 900 people. So confident was it that clients would beat a path to its door that it made a virtue of the fact that Sutcliffe did not actively sell its services.

"Salesmen are not employed and for new contracts the Group relies on the recommendations given by one firm to another. No contract has ever been lost to a competitor," it claimed.

This extraordinarily self-confident statement was, however, omitted in the next and all subsequent editions but it set the tone. Sutcliffe was seen as a rather gentlemanly company, happy to be asked to provide a catering service but not aggressively seeking new business. In the case of its approach to selling, it was one that lasted until Simon Davis joined as marketing and sales director.

* * *

By 1971, John Sutcliffe was nearing retirement and ever-anxious to spend more time with his horses. His Grand National success with Specify had been achieved that year. At midday one morning, O'Brien invited Verstringhe, his deputy, for lunch and on the way to the Goldsmith's Arms in Acton, not in the customary Jaguar but in a new Mercedes, his first observation was unpromising:

"If you can accept a luncheon invitation at the drop of a hat, you can't be very busy."

"It was typical Mickie, designed to keep you on your toes," says Verstringhe.

But O'Brien had other things on his mind. In 1965 John Sutcliffe had decided to lay aside all day-to-day responsibilities to become chairman with O'Brien as managing director. But in 1972, Sutcliffe decided to retire and O'Brien was appointed chairman.

Throughout his career John Sutcliffe had been a very low-profile owner and a very private man.

After her appointment as PR manager, Jane Baker had tried to get John Sutcliffe some editorial publicity but he had always refused – indeed, he never thought it appropriate for the company either. "No – I don't want any publicity – nor does Sutcliffe," he always replied. It was a difficult response for a PR manager. O'Brien held similar views though presumably he had agreed to the new PR appointment and it was only when Graveney took control that the company began to move with the times.

When O'Brien became chairman in 1972, Verstringhe, who was in charge of the London company, was appointed in O'Brien's

Managing to Serve: Sutcliffe's management philosophy was summed up in a book, Managing to Serve, written by Sally Heavens and published in 2002, which outlined the management approach of Catering & Allied.

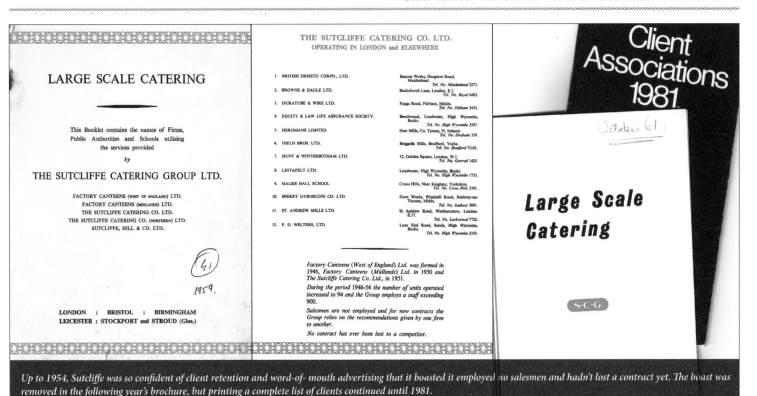

Up to 1954, Sutcliffe was so confident of client retention and word-of-mouth advertising that it boasted it employed no salesmen and hadn't lost a contract yet. The boast was removed in the following year's brochure, but printing a complete list of clients continued until 1981.

place as managing director with Brian Appleton taking over as managing director of the London company. It was a huge vote of confidence in Verstringhe but it was received in stunned silence by the other directors when it was announced by O'Brien at a board meeting; Verstringhe was not thought to be in the running and, in truth, he hadn't really wanted the job. When O'Brien had told him earlier of the decision to promote him he had said he was happy just being responsible for the London company and the continental operations.

"I'm not asking you, I'm telling you," O'Brien had replied sharply. The matter had already been settled.

Verstringhe and Gordon Wishart were sent on a three-month Advanced Management Programme run by Harvard Business School Faculty at the University of Wales – "to learn real business finance, marketing and all that," as O'Brien put it. It was the start of Verstringhe's lifelong interest in management education which formed such a key element in running his own company some three years later.

"The programme had an extraordinary impact on me which is with me to this day," he says. "It gave me the confidence to start my own business and the knowledge to talk to bankers and backers. On a personal note, it introduced me to people in other professions, bankers in particular, who have subsequently been immensely helpful to the business. And in one case, a potential client, knowing that we had been on the Harvard course, was so impressed that it influenced his decision to award us a major contract."

On his retirement from active duty, John Sutcliffe did not entirely lose all interest in the business. He had a habit of phoning up O'Brien to find out the price of apples, carrots and pears which he fed to his horses. O'Brien rang Verstringhe who, on the first occasion, confessed he didn't know.

"Shouldn't you have that information at your fingertips?" demanded O'Brien. Just as he believes that O'Brien is Major Jock Sinclair in *Tunes of Glory*, Peter Davies, Sutcliffe's HR director, likens John Sutcliffe and his fellow directors at the time to the Jack Hawkins film, *The League of Gentlemen*.

"They were really a bunch of army officers having a great time. They were full of life. The company employed over 6,000 people then but the whole concept of personnel management was anathema to them – you survived or didn't survive. The company was basically a licence to print money. The cash flow was tremendous, there was no risk

Chris Page: "I had a wonderful time at the company. I would do it all over again if I had the chance."

and no capital investment was required. You couldn't ask for more."

Long on laughs, short on profits. This was the philosophy that was ascribed to Squid Horton, when chairman of the West of England company, and it stuck, though Horton was certainly no pussy cat. A *bon viveur* more than most, he nevertheless generated a fearsome reputation at the Hotel and Catering Industry Training Board when negotiating training grants for the company. "With Major Horton on the line demanding something, the office almost literally trembled," says one contemporary.

Peter Davies describes Sutcliffe as "like a club and one which I never wanted to join so much in all my life. I loved it", he says.

Chris Page, who spent almost his entire career in the company, and latterly was managing director in the West Country, echoes the sentiment: "I had a wonderful time at the company. I would do it all over again if I had the chance."

Geoffrey Harrison, who joined Sutcliffe in 1980 from GM, says it was "a really lovely

David Barnes tackles the bugs

In January 1974, Sutcliffe West of England held its annual function at the Mecca Rooms in Bristol with company staff happily tucking into chicken in a basket. The results were disastrous. Ken Graveney, then the region's chairman, said he had never closed down so many operations in such a short time – albeit temporarily – so ill were so many of the Sutcliffe staff the following morning. The event alarmed him. The consequences of a major food poisoning outbreak in a Sutcliffe unit were all too obvious. Casting an eye over the company's food safety policies, he saw they were sadly lacking. The company had produced a hygiene and safety manual with general advice to chefs and general assistants but it had been written by the West of England's training department and was not comprehensive. With new legislation pending (the Health and Safety at Work Act was introduced in 1974) Graveney recognised the dangers and decided to act. He engaged David Barnes, a qualified environmental health professional, who had previously been responsible for food safety at the Walls ice cream factory in Gloucester, as the region's hygiene, health and safety manager. It was the beginning of 'Bugsy' Barnes's 25-year tenure with the company.

In the early days, he was not widely accepted. The company's chefs and caterers tended to resent his input and he was frequently accused of interfering with the way they had always worked. "No-one likes change," he says "but change was certainly needed in so many of the cooking practices at the time."

His work in the West of England spread to the company's other regions and eventually he became group health and safety manager and subsequently director of environmental services. It was a timely appointment.

It was the quite basic (but dangerous) food handling skills of Sutcliffe's kitchen staff that so alarmed the new recruit at the outset. This was the time before colour-coded chopping boards and a startling lack of knowledge of food temperatures which, in Barnes' eyes, posed the greatest danger of food poisoning to caterers. He made the introduction of the chopping board compulsory. A series of 200 audits across every Sutcliffe contract in the West of England threw up other problems: refrigerators too close to kitchen ranges, poor ventilation, lack of sufficient preparation surfaces and poorly designed and cheaply made equipment. But, initially, his principal main concern was food safety – well before the Food Safety Act 1990 came into force.

He rewrote the basic hygiene and safety manual into a number of comprehensive manuals, emphasising good practice, with sections on analysing critical control points long before the Food Safety Act's Hazard Analysis and Critical Control Points (HACCP) procedures became common practice; one section looked at eggs before Edwina Currie's involvement while a revolutionary food sampling procedure in units was introduced, now widely practised but then unknown, which would enable alleged cases of food poisoning to be quickly investigated. He was partly responsible for introducing the first self-cleaning vending machine which was bacteriologically risk-free. Training courses – Quality Through Safety and Quality Through Hygiene – were introduced for chefs and general assistants, with multiple question examinations to test their knowledge.

Ultimately, Barnes' influence was extensive. He changed the Christmas practice of buying raw turkey to purchasing ready-cooked turkey breast where all the contamination risk had been removed. Don Davenport, Sutcliffe's managing director, protested that he was de-skilling his chefs; Barnes agreed but replied that he was eliminating risk, which was his target.

Even under the new regime, eggs caused a problem when an orange meringue pie, which had only been flash-heated, caused a major food poisoning outbreak in a Sutcliffe outlet; this led to Barnes being involved in the early days of pasteurised egg yolk, egg white and whole egg. Sutcliffe was an early convert to date-stamping eggs. He banned the use of continuous stock pots, oysters (which put at least one contract at risk) and the re-heating of cooked but incorrectly cooled rice, saying that food poisoning was rarely caused by poor cooking but by poor cooling.

One of his most important acts was to introduce food probe thermometers, now commonplace but then revolutionary – "the only way to fully check temperature, so critical in any food business," he says. A major initiative was to visit suppliers to check their production methods, even visiting Ghana (supplier of tuna) and Thailand (supplier of chicken).

By 1990, when the Food Safety Act was introduced, its measures enforced by Environmental Health Officer inspections, caterers had begun to recognise that they had to take far more serious notice of all aspects of food hygiene than they had before. In Sutcliffe's case, however, the Act's regulations were measures that Bugsy had been preaching for many years.

Constant pressure by the environmental health lobby, regular inspections of food premises, and the fear of litigation have since all been factors in the catering industry's adoption of good food hygiene and food safety practices. No catering company can afford to ignore them. But for Sutcliffe, the Mecca incident in Bristol in 1974 was the turning point.

With a serous-looking David Barnes on the front cover, the 1982 Sutcliffe News promoted the importance of temperature-controlled cooking to all staff. Referring to the temperature, on this copy a wag has scribbled 'Wouldn't think I was that age, would you?' and inked in some some wrinkles.

company to work for. It had a very nice feel about it. It felt like a family business – they only used Christian names, never Mr Harrison."

At the time, the company owned The Amberley Inn, Minchinhampton – now a well respected inn with rooms but then used as the personal watering hole of the local Sutcliffe crowd, probably to the detriment of any profit. It exemplified the free-and-easy atmosphere in the company.

Amorous relationships between company employees became commonplace as they also did between clients and some female employees, and vice versa. This was not just a Sutcliffe phenomenon – executives in other companies also remember examples of sexual transgression.

"For some reason, I think it was far more so in catering than in companies outside the industry," says Jim Cartwright. Perhaps it was because most of the contractors employed large numbers of young women – 'yummy mummies' as another contemporary recalls: "It would be fair to say that a good time was had by all."

Jane Baker found the company environment very free and easy – "very flirty with affairs all over the place, which quite surprised me at the time." This is unlike the more serious, perhaps more professional, atmosphere of GM, where the personalities of Sterling Gallacher and Garry Hawkes tended to run more formal organisations where such goings-on would not have been encouraged – though it is unlikely that they never occurred.

* * *

But in 1973 change was around the corner. The ownership of Sutcliffe had first changed when John Sutcliffe had sold the company to Olympia in 1964. Since the purchase, Olympia had interfered very little except for introducing a new reporting system.

John Sutcliffe and O'Brien had been on the main board since the takeover and throughout Olympia's ownership it had been business as usual.

Sutcliffe prospered, gaining a reputation as a quality catering company with a solid reputation and a growing list of top rank clients such as Allied Breweries, Associated Newspapers, Boots, Bovis, Cadbury Schweppes, Esso and GEC Board meetings were gentle affairs, chaired by John Sutcliffe whose main aim was to get through the business as quickly as possible – "When we come to Any Other Business, say None," he told Verstringhe on his first meeting – before members retired to The Dorchester hotel for the rest of the day.

But Jeffrey Sterling's Sterling Guarantee Trust had just acquired Olympia and, almost without realising it, found itself the new owner of Sutcliffe Catering, a business it knew nothing about.

* * *

Jeffrey Sterling had acquired Earls Court in early 1973 and the chance of buying the neighbourbouring exhibition hall, Olympia, was too good to miss; he was, after all, a property man. He wanted to redevelop Earls Court into a more modern mixed-use exhibition hall with longer-term plans to redevelop Olympia for other purposes. However, any changes that the company had prepared had to be put on hold because of the 1973 economic crisis that engulfed the country and it was several years before Earls Court was modernised. But in buying the two companies to create a new company, Town and City, he had almost unwittingly acquired Sutcliffe. It was a business he knew very little about and what he found could not have pleased him much.

Since 1964, when he sold the business

to Olympia, John Sutcliffe had been left to continue running it almost as if he still owned the company.

Olympia gave Sutcliffe and his fellow directors *carte blanche* with very little control, or corporate strategy, principally because it knew very little about contract catering.

"Why on earth Olympia accepted the paltry returns on their investment, I cannot conceive," says one observer. "There seemed very little coherence or discipline where the subsidiaries were concerned."

During the Olympia ownership Sutcliffe had maintained its structure as a head office with self-contained subsidiary companies. The managing director of each of the nine subsidiaries had the best of both worlds: running it as his own autonomous private company while having the security and image of the group behind him.

Taking full advantage of the cost-plus contracts that were then prevalent, Sutcliffe generated a rolling cash stream and spent it almost as freely on hugely generous expense accounts and on what one insider calls a 'dream car policy' which was better than almost any other company – certainly in the hospitality industry. This included a driver/handyman on the payroll for each of the regional managing directors. Even wives, as well as John Sutcliffe's horses, were alleged to benefit.

Curiously, despite, or because of this free-and-easy approach, senior salaries were chaotically organised. With no personnel function until Peter Davies' arrival as personnel and training director in 1973, there was little if any research into pay and benefits and there was no salary policy. If someone threatened to leave, he (or she) would be valued and the salary would be matched according to their perceived value. There were no systematic salary reviews. On the other hand, there were also few staff

shortages. Sutcliffe was seen as a highly desirable place of employment and the company was generous with both expenses and titles; the word 'director' was handed out frequently which both attracted people to the company for the wrong reason while encouraging existing directors to remain – and confusing outsiders.

With the regional companies operating like autonomous army divisions with their own commanding officer, regional office team and set of accounts, they were seen as personal fiefdoms and head office interfered with them almost at its peril. However, this *laissez-faire* approach was quickly spotted by the new owners. The advent of Sterling Guarantee Trust (SGT) in 1973 soon began to be felt by John Sutcliffe, Mickie O'Brien and others.

SGT got to work to find out how Sutcliffe

Credit Topfoto-UPP

The impact of Jeffrey Sterling – later Lord Sterling – was quickly felt in the company and led to Mickie O'Brien's early departure.

Credit Nobby Clark:Arena/AL

Setting up for a Rolling Stones concert at Earls Court, 1976.

operated, what its strengths and weaknesses were and how they could be enhanced or rectified if need be. An in-house report prepared by SGT people compared Sutcliffe unfavourably with Bateman, GM and others and pulled few punches:

"Sutcliffe is expensively run, it does not use its buying power to earn rebates to the same extent as its major competitors; it has been slow to pick up the lucrative sidelines of its own supply and vending operations; it has probably been less financially aware than its competitors."

The critical report went on:

"Sutcliffe are also badly placed to exploit price partly because of their high reputation for service but mainly because of their relatively weak buying methods and it is estimated that there might be at least another £90,000 [almost £900,000 today] available as bulk discounts, either to enhance profit or, if necessary, to meet price competition.

"Sutcliffe have obvious skill in industrial catering based upon both long experience and formal technical training. In other areas, notably marketing, financial and personnel management, they have not been strong and this may have resulted in their not making the most of their opportunities."

It was not all doom and gloom, however:

"Sutcliffe's major asset is its extremely happy staff, loyal and able management and staff who appear to lack only a better and more detailed objective than the general well-being of Sutcliffe."

The report was deadly accurate and proposed the preparation of a three-year plan which would concentrate on markets and marketing, operations and product, personnel, and finance and administration.

It concluded: "At present, management information is disjointed and not integrated [between the various Sutcliffe regional companies]. Definitions are not always clear, little use is made of comparisons or ratios,

and asset and cash planning are minimal."

Earlier, it had revealed that Sutcliffe's return on sales was 2.2 per cent while Gardner Merchant's was 2.5 per cent and Bateman's was 3.6 per cent.

It was not a document that would have set SGT's pulse racing at the future prospects of its new acquisition. It was clear that it had acquired a company that appeared to be stuck in the 1960s era of easy money and lax controls with little awareness of modern management practices.

* * *

With SGT's increasing (and understandable) interference into its operation, Sutcliffe was losing its family atmosphere and its happy-go-lucky camaraderie.

At the time of the takeover, John Sutcliffe (who died in 1975 receiving – no doubt to his pleasure – only a brief obituary in the Autumn issue of *Sutcliffe News*), was appointed president, an honorary post, and was replaced as chairman by Peter Ford, who quickly moved on to take over a tool company, and then by Christopher Stuart-Smith, a young 34-year-old ex-McKinsey consultant who had joined SGT in 1971. Stuart-Smith wanted to make big changes by implementing the main thrust of the report, introducing the three-year plan, installing centralised group services and trimming down the nine regional companies and managing directors to five ("to improve communications and efficiency," in the words of Ken Graveney, who had now become chief executive) but nevertheless retaining 15 regional offices.

Five profit centres were established – one for each region – which were responsible for controlling revenues and costs "which in turn promotes a spirit of inter-company competition," Graveney told staff in an edition of *Sutcliffe News*. It was an aim

which the SGT report had specifically noted was missing.

"I see my function as perpetuating the principles of the Sutcliffe Catering group evolved during the last 30 years and bringing stability to our present situation," Graveney hopefully concluded, determined not to lose the old Sutcliffe cameraderie.

But it was a difficult time, as he clearly recognised. The regional company structure had not been criticised in the SGT report (indeed, the report had concluded that it had 'probably contributed much to the feeling of worthwhileness and consequent happiness in staff') but the re-organisation was foreign to Sutcliffe's style of regional management. Many thought it stifled initiative and empowerment. More seriously, there was a feeling of a complete takeover.

"What we learned was that when a company buys another company there is a belief that it also buys you as a person, body and soul," Verstringhe sourly told his company's management conference 10 years later.

* * *

No sooner had the acquisition been completed than Brian Smith, who had been with the company since 1958, quit with 80 per cent of his senior team to start his own business (see Chapter 23), and Norman Lazarus, the group's financial director, was fired – "We need the keys to the safe," he was told. Geoffrey Harrison also left to start his own company.

There were others: in the west, Brian Hunter, John Houston, Martin Felstead and Richard Salmon all quit.

Two years later, Marc Verstringhe formed Catering & Allied. Norman Hall, director in charge of the Leeds office who reported to Desmond Blackburn, managing director of Sutcliffe North, threatened to quit and set up his own business; as a peace offering, he was made managing director of Sutcliffe North East, much to Blackburn's chagrin. Ray Worrall, who ran a satellite office in Liverpool, also threatened to quit.

There were other attempted breakaways with some senior people taking Sutcliffe business with them, to such an extent that one of Peter Davies' first acts as personnel and training director was to introduce senior management contracts with restrictive clauses, valid for 12 months (commonplace now), that prevented people from leaving the company with contracts, staff, copying Sutcliffe's policies and procedures or making use of sensitive information, such as supplier terms. Effectively, the contracts gave the company the right to put executives on garden leave.

The breakaways were unsettling for the company and for those remaining in it. On the one hand, senior people left behind had the nagging feeling that perhaps they should also have taken the plunge to make their own way as an independent as people like Chris Hind, Andrew Nelson, William Baxter, Robert Platts, Alastair Storey and Keith Wilson so successfully did later. On the other hand, the breakaways generated more serious competition for Sutcliffe because the new companies knew many of the Sutcliffe clients and the Sutcliffe way of working.

By winning new contracts or, in some cases, offering to run a unit less expensively or by introducing different ways of trading, such as (in Brian Smith's case) returning all discounts to the client, all the major contractors found hungry new independent competition at both the front and back door. At Sutcliffe, the average length of contract retention in the 1980s was seven years; 10 years later the figure had halved.

It was also a time when new employment legislation was sweeping into industry and Sutcliffe was probably not alone in being

A deal too far for Mickie

In setting up Catering & Allied, Verstringhe had negotiated a deal with a company, Halshaw, a Ford dealership based in Halifax and Preston, with the result that it was agreed that a shareholding of 60 per cent 'A' shares should be held by the directors and 40 per cent 'B' shares should be held by Halshaw. To overcome the problem of jeopardising his Sutcliffe pension, O'Brien had persuaded Frank Thomas, a supplier and a friend of Verstringhe, to purchase his shares and provide the financial guarantee that was conditional upon signing the go-ahead for the new company. Catering & Allied was thus launched on September 5th 1975 and the business prospered.

However, two years later, Thomas decided to sell his shares and O'Brien was now able and keen to purchase them. But the agreement with Halshaw stipulated that the A shareholders would have the first right to purchase any shares that came onto the market, and if not taken up by them, then they had to be offered to the B shareholders.

Verstringhe had the unenviable task of telling O'Brien the unpalatable news at a restaurant in Esher – "one of the most uncomfortable lunches I've ever had," he says. Despite O'Brien's protestation that Thomas had agreed to sell him back the shares the agreement with Halshaw prevented such a transaction.

The situation must have festered for many years in O'Brien's mind. In 1988, he wrote a letter complaining about his treatment. Mair Davison, who had just joined the company as Verstringhe's PA, was shocked at its tone but Verstringhe didn't reply and destroyed the letter. "It was better that way," he says. "Mickie had every right to feel aggrieved but there was nothing we could do about it. He must have written it out of frustration."

The friendship was eventually patched up. In 2005, O'Brien, then 83, was Verstringhe's guest at his 70th birthday party. O'Brien wrote a letter of thanks which is kept in a book that he gave to Verstringhe – *From Omaha to the Scheldt – The History of the 47th Royal Marine Commandos*. He died in 2011 aged 89.

Mickie O'Brien died in 2011, aged 89. The front cover of his funeral service shows him in characteristic form, with drink in hand.

unfamiliar with it or even ignoring it. It was to Ken Graveney's credit that he saw the need for expert HR skills persuading O'Brien and Verstringhe that a personnel director had to be appointed which heralded the appointment of Peter Davies.

The company was so unused to the formalities of Contracts of Employment that, to avoid confusion, Davies had them printed on different coloured paper – pink for all staff from area catering supervisors and above, blue for office staff and vending, gold for unit managers and the most senior chefs, and white for hourly paid employees in the units.

"Right through until my retirement in 1996, these colours were referred to when talking about someone's status," he recalls.

As a result of the SGT report proposing the creation of a three-year plan, the slimmed down regional structure began to feel the fat being cut out of the operational teams; at the same time, much tighter financial discipline was being imposed with the appointment of financial and HR directors to each subsidiary company.

A new company secretary, Ron Martin, an SGT appointee, took control of legalities, with particular reference to client contracts. The appointment of Simon Davis began the process of upgrading the company's marketing and sales effort. Within just two years, the easy-going culture within Sutcliffe had changed.

* * *

While Sutcliffe had weathered the storm of the recession and the turbulence of the SGT takeover, in 1975 rumours that it was to be sold had circulated in the industry and the City, though Graveney denied all knowledge:

"We are still in business and we intend to stay so," he told *Catering Times*.

Graveney was right. Sutcliffe was not

for sale but the company soon saw the exit of O'Brien as deputy chairman, a position he had held with Stuart-Smith when John Sutcliffe had moved up to president in 1973.

O'Brien was a leader and, though used to obeying orders from his army days, in the last 30 years he had been giving them, not taking them. A position of joint chairman was not something that suited him; he was used to making decisions by himself. He had experienced personally some of the changes being wrought by SGT and he was not one to be told what to do or how to do it at Sutcliffe. With the culture and management of the company in flux – now more 'long on profits, short on laughs' – he decided it was time to quit.

On one Tuesday afternoon in 1974, O'Brien told Verstringhe that he was taking early retirement and was leaving aged 52; he left on the following Friday with little ceremony. He had guided the company through 20-plus years of growth to some 800 contracts and his personality was imprinted on the company.

The company had not been as profitable as it could have been, as the SGT report had pointedly emphasised, but it had been a happy ship and that was how he had wanted it. With SGT in control, the culture had changed and he wanted no part in the new regime. He had stayed true to his principles. His loss to the business was considerable as he knew so many key clients; his key staff felt his departure just as sharply. Verstringhe felt the upheaval personally.

"When Mickie left, I knew it was time for me to leave, too," he says.

A year later, in 1975, with Kit Cuthbert, who was in charge of Sutcliffe's central London operations, Verstringhe launched his own company, Catering & Allied. Jop Koops, in charge of Sutcliffe's European operations, joined them with O'Brien, now free from Sutcliffe, as non-executive chairman. But this did not work out well.

A still lively Mickie O'Brien, at Marc Verstringhe's 70th birthday party in 2005.

Credit Clive Barda : ArenaPAL

From huge trade shows to the opera: Earls Court was a large contract. Here, Bizet's Carmen is being rehearsed in 1989.

CHAPTER NINETEEN

*Compass – two decades to become
world leader*

Through acquisitions and organic growth, it took Compass only two decades to become a world leader.

While Sutcliffe and Gardner Merchant were undergoing their own transformations, between 1985 and 2005 Compass enjoyed two decades of unparalleled growth. Within five years of Compass going public in 1985, turnover had increased by 71 per cent and profit by 236 per cent; in the next decade, turnover boomed by 3,671 per cent and profit by 297 per cent. Later years saw similar growth, although 2005 was the fateful year that saw the exit of two of the company's principal players: Francis Mackay, the chairman and Mike Bailey, the chief executive.

Mackay was an accountant by training and a highly successful entrepreneur by experience. He knew the contract catering business inside out, having joined Sutcliffe before joining GrandMet and masterminding the Compass buy-out from GrandMet in 1985. He had been involved with Compass ever since.

Bailey was a caterer through and through

and had spent 27 years with GM before moving to the United States – a move which preceded his arrival at Compass in May 1993 as development director and head of the New Famous Foods.

* * *

Bailey had started his career in 1964 at Peter Merchant as a commis chef at the Ford European headquarters in Brentwood, Essex and went on to be district manager at Dagenham and then moved to British Leyland in 1975, by which time John Gardner and Peter Merchant had merged and Bailey had gained the reputation as being GM's motor industry man. He rose through the ranks to become PA to the general manager of the Ford account, Colin Flavell, and was appointed district manager at the age of 22. All his accounts were Ford contracts, the majority being operated 24 hours a day, 365 days a year, with a generous helping of strikes and other industrial unrest into the bargain.

"I learned more about food service finance at Ford than anywhere else," he says.

Aside from finance, Bailey's negotiating

Francis Mackay Credit 2004 Topfoto / UPP

*Francis Mackay – **an accountant by training** and an entrepreneur by experience – oversaw the growth of Compass in its earlier days. By the time he retired, Compass had become **a UK and world leader**, though his departure was not **without controversy**.*

skills were also honed in the environment in which he then worked. In 1975 he moved to Longbridge as operations director at British Leyland, another trouble spot. 'Red Robbo', one of the industry's most notorious shop stewards, was his local union official and he made sure there were plenty of issues to negotiate about. Bailey thought it wise to keep his distance from him as much as he could. Three years later, he was promoted as GM's regional director for the North East based in Sheffield at a time when Stirling Gallacher had moved to Sutcliffe and Garry Hawkes had taken over as managing director. Soon after, Don Davenport, an executive director at GM, joined Gallacher at Sutcliffe.

Both moves shook the company but it's an ill wind that blows nobody any good. Bailey moved into Don Davenport's job and ran the southern half of England as executive director until late in 1984. Serendipity played a hand when Trusthouse Forte acquired Knott Hotels in 1984, a small company in New York which also owned the Westbury

*Mike Bailey: "I felt I was **part of a great** team and I have a huge respect for Francis. He taught me more about acquisitions and **finance** than any other person I've ever met."*

Hotel in London. Knott had a subsidiary catering business that THF's hotel people didn't want to know about. Bailey was asked to go over and run it for GM.

"I jumped at the chance. I had always wanted to live and work in the US so when the opportunity came, I didn't hesitate, even though the business was much smaller than what I was doing back home."

The company was called Trusthouse Forte Foodservices and had recently merged with a US-based contract food service business called Eastern Foods, a deal organised by Graham Smith, a GM veteran who was something of a trouble shooter – "terrific at taking small businesses and installing good standards and systems – and then moving on to something else," says Bailey.

Within six years, GM's US business increased from $40m annual sales to $250m through a combination of organic growth and acquisitions and by 1991 Bailey found himself back in the UK, after being persuaded by Garry Hawkes to return as managing director of GM UK, with Hawkes as chairman. It was not a successful move.

"To be honest, from the moment I arrived back in the country I felt as if I had made a big mistake. And in reality, I had. Garry struggled to let go of the reins and we had a few run-ins over people moves that I wanted to make. Add that to the fact that my wife and family absolutely hated being back in the UK. Life was not good for me." Amid much consternation in the company, after 27 years with GM, he quit and returned with his family to the US.

* * *

Bailey's return to the US was not an immediate success. He joined a small healthcare food service company in Pennsylvania, which was "an absolute disaster". Then, within six month he quit and

was out of work.

"It was the worst moment in my career. I was out of work, living in the US, with a young family. I had a house with a big mortgage in America and a house that I hadn't sold in the UK, which also had a big mortgage. I was in big trouble."

Swallowing his pride, he called Hawkes to ask if he could return to GM, a call that was rebuffed, perhaps not surprisingly in view of the upheaval his departure had caused previously. There wasn't a suitable position for him and GM was about to be engulfed by Compass and Aramark. With this brush-off, he started looking around in the US and the UK. It was Dick Turpin, who had so unceremoniously been ousted from Compass in 1984, who got him into Compass.

"Dick was an old friend and he had a word on my behalf with Chris Bucknell who, by then, was managing director of Compass. I phoned Chris and said that if you're thinking of buying a business in the US, I'll run it for you."

It was serendipity again. When he took control of Compass, after Gerry Robinson and Charles Allen had departed for Granada, Francis Mackay was clear in his own mind about the direction which he wanted Compass to take: into food service (eschewing other support services unless they were intrinsically part of the contract, as they were in healthcare, MoD and remote site contacts); into Europe and wider afield; and into branding. The policy was labelled The Right Direction and its success was predicated on these three principals.

"Our ambition was always to be a global company," he says. Mackay's legendary focus on branding was far sighted; while other contractors were beginning to understand the importance of franchised high street and in-house brands, Mackay had already started his Famous Brands under Compass and was totally focused on developing it.

At the time, Compass was 99 per cent UK-based with 90 per cent of the business in B&I. If it was to grow, Mackay knew the company had to expand overseas and broaden its markets. Bailey flew back to the UK to talk to Compass. He had not met either Mackay or Bucknell before. "I got on with them like a house on fire."

He joined them immediately but initially in the UK, to start the branding business, his family remaining in the US. He had the good fortune to join Compass when it was beginning to gather momentum. "It was a very dynamic and very entrepreneurial company – just as I had hoped."

Much of this dynamism was due to its chairman. Mackay was, in Bailey's words, "a great people person and he loves food" – in most caterers' eyes, the latter being just as important as the former.

In the book *Winning at Service – Lessons from Service Leaders*, which examines the way four service companies, including Compass and Sodexo, had developed over the years, Mackay is described as "the hail-fellow, well-met almost clubby ex-private pilot ('I got too big for the cockpits') has a mischievous sense of humour and loves people". Mackay, for all his joviality, also has a sharp brain. In the same book, he is described as "an outstanding strategist... prepared to make, brave, long-term decisions."

"There's no question that strong retail brands produce higher turnover and profit," he told *Caterer* at the time, and pointing to like-for-like turnover growth of 13 per cent. And the potential, he added, was mouth-watering. "The international food service market is worth £100bn and the bulk of that market is still served by in-house caterers." His enthusiasm for worldwide expansion was amply underlined.

Nevertheless, his opposition to offering a range of other soft services such as cleaning and housekeeping (something that other companies, Sodexo particularly, were beginning to exploit) remained adamant. "Lower margins, different issues," is how he explained it later.

Bailey says: "We were a food service contract business. We never saw ourselves as running a main street restaurant business. We never saw ourselves going that far away from the core guts of the business. We never saw ourselves as a one-size-fits-all business. We didn't want to get into other support services unless we absolutely had to. We decided to stick to our knitting."

This clarity of vision was responsible for Compass' initial success.

When Bailey joined, Compass' turnover was some £350m with one per cent of turnover coming from an Alaska pipeline contract. The disposal of the small private healthcare company, Compass Healthcare, to the management team and a private equity partner in 1995, showed Mackay's determination to stay focused on catering.

* * *

In 1992, Compass bought Travellers Fare, which was big in railway station catering, where brands were extremely important, and Letheby and Christopher, which diversified Compass into catering for a new market of events, race courses and prestige places such as the Royal Albert Hall. To Mackay and his team, it was clear that Compass's growth was intimately allied to its geographic expansion and in the sectors in which it operated.

It was the purchase in 1993 of the non-airline catering business, Scandinavia Service Partner (SSP), part of the Danish-based SAS Airlines, that swept Compass into international airports in nine European countries in one deal; with the purchase came the benefits of the Scandinavian culture and management style. The SSP management was totally focused on brand quality, execution, consistency and customer satisfaction on the basis that if you got these right, profit growth would follow – and with SSP, it did. SSP was an example of good brand management and showed the way for Compass' contracting outlets where consistency remains a challenge even today because of the need for broad menus working across many sectors and with clients who have a habit of wanting things done their way. Brands in contracted outlets were seen as an answer to the challenge of consistency and using the experience of SSP and Travellers Fare management that challenge could be more easily met. SSP was an acquisition that surprised the City but which gave a clear marker for Compass' ambitious expansion plans.

All three purchases demanded branded catering offers and Compass set about expanding the New Famous Foods offer with deals with Pizza Hut and Burger King. The purchase of Harry Ramsden's fish and chip chain gave it a well-known name for railway stations and airports while the Travellers' Fare purchase brought in Upper Crust and Le Croissant Shop brands; Compass created its own Café Ritazza, still a thriving chain though later sold off.

The power of the brands was well illustrated in some research that Compass undertook, which showed that the public perceived Upper Crust to be fourth largest food service brand in the UK, behind only McDonald's, Burger King and Pizza Hut. The finding was nonsense. Upper Crust had only 100 outlets but they were all located in busy rail stations and at Heathrow and Gatwick airports, areas of very high footfall.

"I guess the moral of the story is that reality is one thing but perception is what counts," says Bailey.

Putting the brands into contract environments drove pricing and improved

Credit Topfoto.co.uk

Credit 2004 Topfoto / UPP

Upper crust Credit 2004 Topfoto / UPP

Compass concluded deals with Pizza Hut and Burger King while the purchase of Harry Ramsden's fish and chip chain gave it a well-known name for railway stations and airports and the Travellers' Fare purchase brought in Upper Crust and Le Croissant Shop brands, many of which were sited in rail station forecourts. With Francis Mackay (above right) is Compass director, Roger Matthews.

Not every bid succeeded

Not every acquisition was successful. At one stage, Compass seriously looked at buying Costa Coffee, which was then earning some £15m a year. Red lights started flashing when due diligence revealed few operating systems and each outlet was being run by a family member – "We didn't feel we could get our arms around exactly what we were buying," says Bailey. The talks collapsed in frustration with the result that Whitbread bought it. The rest is history.

"With the benefit of hindsight, we probably should have taken the risk," says Bailey philosophically.

Nor was the bid successful for Compass' deadly rival, Gardner Merchant, which generated such a furore in the industry (see Chapter 15). The acquisition, if it had gone through, would have launched Compass onto the international stage while making it the biggest operator by far in the UK. But the failed bid actually spurred on Compass to expand by other means.

Costa was one company that Compass considered purchasing but subsequently pulled out of the deal.

customer satisfaction and quality at a time when clients were looking for reduced subsidies or even a P&L or concession contract, both of which were much easier to achieve with brands than without.

It was not long before brand names started appearing in some of the larger B&I outlets and in major hospital foyers and other places with a high footfall. Compass' move into retail catering (but not into the high street) was extraordinarily successful. When the M&S Simply Foods franchise was later introduced into motorway catering areas, sales just exploded. Suddenly, Compass was experiencing significant organic growth.

"I remember some of the competition laughed at us at the time, but that was fairly short-lived," says Bailey.

The SSP acquisition in 1993 was the first foray abroad since the abortive Gardner Merchant bid. A year later, in 1994, came the purchase for £300m of Canteen Vending, a struggling vending and catering company in the United States, which had huge but (thankfully for Compass), unrealised potential. It was a deal that Roger Matthews, Compass' finance director (and currently chairman of Mitie) had organised – the first of many – and it sent Bailey back to the States as CEO only 10 months after joining Compass in the UK. He was accompanied by Gary Green who Mackay had promoted to chief financial officer from operations director for Compass' southern region.

The purchase highlighted the critical importance of knowing the business.

* * *

Canteen made about $32.5m EBITDA annually on sales of $1.1bn and was part of a public restaurant company. It was basically a vending outfit but when the restaurant company acquired it some years previously, it had installed its own purchasing staff. It

was clear, in due diligence, that they had no experience of the contract catering business. Canteen had negotiated a great price for Coke syrup but a very high price for bottles and cans of Coke, which it sold by the millions – in fact, outside the supermarkets, it purchased more bottles and cans of Coke than anyone else in the US. But in fast food public restaurants Coke is sold from dispensers using syrup at a much higher margin than bottled Coke. Within weeks, the Coca-Cola contract was renegotiated and Bailey was happy to report back that another £10m had been put on the bottom line. It was an inspired acquisition. The Canteen purchase boosted Compass group turnover by 114 per cent to £740m and profits by 33 per cent to £31m. The turnaround at Canteen took two years. Bailey later told *Caterer*:

"Canteen was a struggling business... Costs had been drastically cut, there had been no capital expenditure and the morale was low. Compass immediately began to invest in the business, reinstating the defunct sales and marketing operations, bringing in new training programmes and spending $70m in the first two years on new vending machines and vehicles.

"It hasn't been cheap but well worth it... Where Canteen had been running a restaurant business with other things added on, we are a food service business. That is all we do."

The US proved a happy hunting ground for Compass and in the next five years, through acquisition and organic growth, revenues rose from $1bn to just under $3bn, with an even headier 280 per cent increase in profits, from $32.5m to $124m.

In 1996, its fortunes were boosted by a deal to feed every IBM employee in America – 34 sites with 74 cafeterias and 2,400 vending machines, worth some $62m in annual revenue or $300m-plus over five years. The contract went on to become a

Your World News

December 2000

Another year of success

In the year in which Compass Group spread its wings still further through its merger with Granada, preliminary figures for 1999/2000 just announced show that the company continues its march of success. Operating profit for Compass Group (including Granada Hospitality businesses) was £928 million (up 2%), with aggregate turnover increasing by 10% to £8, 302 million (£7,306m of which is in foodservice). An interim dividend of 7.4p is expected.

Plans for the demerger are on track and separate listings for Compass Group and Granada (Media) will be made on the London Stock Exchange in February 2001.

Said Compass Group chairman, Francis Mackay: "This year has seen the Group achieve a clear number one position in foodservice, both worldwide and in the UK, supporting our ambition for future growth. Following the demerger from Granada and the anticipated disposal of the Forte Hotels Division, we will continue our foodservice focus, where our prospects for future growth are very attractive."

Compass Group chairman Francis Mackay (left) and chief executive Michael J. Bailey celebrate the new Philips contract – a great boost for the Group and a fantastic job done by Bart Vringer and his colleagues

Philips' extension leads the way for Compass Group

At the end of another significant year for Compass Group, news continues to flood in of major contract gains and extensions from all parts of the business. Among them, **Royal Philips Electronics** has extended its initial three year global agreement with Compass Group for a further three years, one year before the original contract ended. At the time of the initial signing in 1998, the contract focussed on seven countries, with the aim of eventually covering all Philips' worldwide locations. The agreement is now implemented in 15 countries.

Exceeding targets

Said Hans Brons, vice president and general manager Philips' Global Purchasing Services: "When we signed the initial agreement it was the first global foodservice contract

of its kind anywhere in the world. Our aim was to work with a company with the ability to handle the large scale and complex change process and to provide better quality service and choice for the Philips employees. We have decided to extend the agreement because Compass Group has proved its ability to exceed the targets we set." Congratulations indeed to all those involved with Philips.

Excellent News

Michael J. Bailey said: "This contract extension is excellent news for both companies as it will allow Philips and Compass Group to further capitalise on the benefits of the agreement. We appreciate the confidence Philips has in our global scale and local focus. This contract extension and other recent contract gains clearly demonstrates the leading position of Compass Group in the marketplace."

Other major successes include a £40million annual turnover

contract gain for Eurest Sutcliffe to operate the staff restaurants in 427 stores for the UK supermarket group, **Sainsbury's** and the addition of the **Au Bon Pain** brand the Compass Group brand portfolio.

Au Bon Pain is a well-established French-style bakery café brand with over 280 outlets. It is particularly well known in the USA but is also franchised in 6 other countries and is a great addition to our brand portfolio.

New Partnership

Activity in North **America** has also been high, with an international strategic partnership signed between Compass Group and **Levy Restaurants** -- a specialised restaurant and foodservice business holding the leading market share of catering business in the top sporting and convention locations in the US, and a chain of

internationally famous restaurants. Commenting on the agreement, Gary Green president and CEO, North American Division, said: " This partnership is strategically beneficial for Compass Group as we pursue our interest and growth in premium foodservice opportunities worldwide. Together we can have tremendous worldwide impact."

Tripled Market Share

Across the border in **Canada** we have acquired Beaver Foods, a wholly owned subsidiary of Cara Operations, tripling Compass Group's business in the country and giving us the lead position in providing foodservice for education and remote sites. Beaver Foods holds over 1,000 accounts in high

Continued on next page

Staff are told Compass has clinched its contract to feed 110,000 Philips staff worldwide, its first global foodservice contract.

global deal with the addition of European, Japanese and Australian business worth an additional $150m a year.

Four years later, it clinched its first global foodservice contract with Philips to feed 110,000 staff worldwide. A slew of mainly B&I multi-national contracts followed which created huge revenue streams and proved that Compass was becoming a truly international company. They were just a taster of what was to come.

In 1995, expansion turned to Europe with the acquisition from Accor of the French-based Eurest International group for $931m, paying for it with Compass shares using 22.5 per cent of the company's stock and taking on to the Compass board two Accor directors, Gerard Pelisson and John du Monceau, who happened to be a Belgian count. The Eurest deal came at a time when Accor was considering a number of different strategic alternatives and represented something of a coup for French-speaking Francis Mackay.

Mackay had gone out of his way to get to know the Eurest management who held the controlling interest in the company and had been successful in building up a feeling of mutual respect; his fluency in the language also made a huge cultural difference.

The purchase brought Compass into the European arena, adding 60,000 employees with clients throughout the continent, more than Compass' own UK and US workforce combined. A year later, Mackay charmed his way into Eurest France, a separate company though still part of Accor at the time. After a hiccup over an over-hasty press announcement, Philippe Durand-Dagain, Eurest France's CEO and his management team (again holding the majority stake in the company) agreed to the deal which brought in 7,200 people working in 1,200 outlets. Durand-Dagain stayed on with Compass for a couple of years before retiring. But that still

Market leader in US healthcare

In 2001, Compass continued on the acquisition trail. Morrison Management Specialists, the second largest hospital and nursing homes caterer in the US, was taken over for £382m in cash. With more that 475 clients, the company had turned over £534m in the previous year with profits of £45m. Morrison was particularly strong in hospital catering and the new acquisition was a perfect fit for the group giving it a market-leading position in the US healthcare sector and complementing its existing healthcare (mainly nursing home) business.

In 2002, Compass clinched a huge worldwide contract – a 10-year deal to feed the 53,000 employees of Chevron Texaco which was valued at nearly £140m a year. At the time it was the world's largest catering deal though it has been superceded since.

One of the side benefits of both deals was the knock-on effect of bringing Compass into sites throughout the world, thus using them as a platform for expansion into these countries.

left 33 per cent of the share capital of Eurest France in the hands of Sodexo, which was a hangover from the previous ownership by Wagons Lit.

Mackay met with Pierre Bellon, Sodexo's chairman over lunch at Michel Rostang in Paris, and simply said: "We have two choices: either we can fight over the company which will displease both our shareholders, or we can buy your 33 per cent at a fair price and both our shareholders will be pleased." Bellon, ever the realist, agreed.

The two deals were game-changers - so significant that Mackay moved to Paris. In his words, the merger went surprisingly smoothly with no blood on the floor.

In the next three years, he oversaw more heady growth. Through acquisition and joint ventures Compass acquired RKHS in India, KKS in Africa, and GR SDA in Brazil, as well as establishing itself in Australia. It also acquired Restaurant Associates (RA) in the US, a highly unusual purchase for a company so focused on contracting.

RA had been founded 50 years earlier and by the time of the acquisition had become New York's premier public restaurant group, running such eateries as Four Seasons, Mama Leone's and The Brasserie, the city's first

24-hour restaurant. RA was used to train Compass chefs from around the world.

"Who did not want to spend a couple of weeks in New York training in some of its top restaurants?" says Bailey. "Our people were very proud that we owned such an upscale outfit."

Needless to say, it also reflected well in pitches to potential clients.

France's fourth largest caterer, SHRM, and a major operator in the country's healthcare and education sectors, followed the Eurest purchase, blighted a little by internal wranglings between the company's Paris and Marseilles offices – neither of them wanting to communicate with each other – which took three years to resolve. "It was a culture thing," Mackay says stoically.

By 1998, Compass was large enough (with an annual turnover of £4.2bn) to join the top 100 companies in the FT 100 index. It had been an extraordinary achievement for a company that had been rebuffed by Forte in the takeover of GM and was first listed on the Stock Exchange only 10 years earlier.

Two years later, in 2000, came the knock-out blow that sealed Compass's position as the number one contractor in the UK – the merger with Granada and then the

subsequent de-merger (see next chapter). With the Sutcliffe part of Granada now on board – almost as big a prize as Gardner Merchant though without any overseas contracts – Compass took over 40 per cent of the UK contracting market.

Compass' advance into the US market continued with the purchase of Professional Food Service Management (PFM), a small £56m education caterer, and the vending and B&I division of Service America – a £1bn food service and vending company that had been forced into bankruptcy. John Dee, an ex-Aramark executive and a friend of Mike Bailey's, had been appointed CEO with a mandate to 'get it out of Chapter 11'; part of the plan was to slim down the company by selling the B&I and vending business worth some $600m in annual revenues.

Compass snapped it up. One advantage of the Service America deal was that it had a strong relationship with Pepsi which allowed Compass to consolidate its carbonated beverage purchasing, enabling it to pitch major manufacturers against each other. Later, another big US education caterer, Daka International, was taken aboard for £121m.

Compass was attacking the softer underbelly of the industrial feeding market in the United States – the non B&I sector. As in the UK, it was estimated that 80 per cent of B&I contracts were already in contractor hands. The big market had become hospital and education catering which was only 30 per cent penetrated. Yet education by itself was a $14bn market, of which Marriott and Aramark, the two biggest players, had less than seven per cent.

The time was the turning point for Compass. It now owned the two largest vending companies in North America which were quickly merged under one brand, Canteen, which is still the market leader in US vending. Aramark, the only rival, had already announced it was scaling back its presence in vending and Compass became the only national vending business in the US with a double digit EBITDA margin – a position it holds to this day. Vending is more profitable than food service yet, as virtually every client who buys food service also buys vending, so Compass was able to become a one-stop shop. By combining the two services, it was able to undercut its competitors and it frequently did.

"Without a shadow of a doubt, vending was a huge driver of organic growth for Compass," says Bailey.

Acquiring three separate education providers – Canteen, PFM and Daka – gave Compass annual revenues from the sector of $450m and the companies were merged to form Chartwells, a name adopted from the UK business. Steve Sweeny, who came into the company with the purchase of Flik, an upscale contractor, was made CEO after Daka's Alan Maxwell suffered a massive heart attack and died six months after his appointment. Sweeny is still CEO, but now of a business worth £1.5bn. Chartwells is market leader of the US education sector.

During this time, Bailey was in his element. He was in the States; he admired the American 'can do' society and its more casual approach to life. Truth to tell, he also enjoyed having the Atlantic between him and his boss, Francis Mackay, though their relationship could hardly have been more amicable:

"I felt I was part of a great team and I have a huge respect for Francis. He taught me more about acquisitions and finance than any other person I've ever met. But I like being able, within the parameters of good sense, to do my own thing. I've always been very comfortable being accountable for my own results and performance," he says.

The feeling was mutual. Mackay was happy to have colleagues in Bailey and Gary Green who he could trust to expand the

Compass empire in what had become its most important market.

* * *

By 1997, when Mackay had thoughts of stepping up as chairman of Compass with retirement on the horizon, and appointing a CEO in his place, Bailey was approached to take up the position. He demurred. He was happy where he was and didn't want to leave the States which had become his home. Mackay hired Alan Copping, who was CEO of Wembley plc, in preparation for taking on the CEO role, but it was not a successful appointment and within 18 months the vacancy arose once more.

Again, Mackay approached Bailey and offered him the job, this time saying he could run the company from New York, an unusual arrangement for a British-based company. He probably recognised, however, that the travelling involved would eventually take its toll and Bailey would soon be persuaded to come back to run the company from London.

This, in fact, came to pass. "Francis knew that it would get to me eventually," Bailey says, ruefully.

He returned to Europe and Gary Green was promoted to succeed him – a position he still holds today, growing the US business to £8.2bn in 2014, representing 48 per cent of group turnover and making it Compass' most successful geographic sector by far.

"At the time, Compass was in 90 countries, so rapid had been its expansion, and a major part of the job was on the road visiting the various countries and companies that we managed, so to be honest, it didn't really matter where I lived," says Bailey.

But 90 countries demanded a huge span of control and had been driven by the market. Compass needed to be in all the Western countries to be able to service all its

international clients. Its presence in the more exotic countries came at the request of global clients like Philips and Chevron, which had outlets there. "We didn't want to be in Colombia or Angola but VW or Total had outlets there and they wanted us to run their facilities there. So we did," says Mackay.

Compass UK now represented only 17 per cent of the group's total business so the need for Bailey to be resident in the UK was not overwhelming. He settled in Switzerland with an apartment in London. The travelling was easier but it was still travelling because the focus was now on continuing the expansion, controlling the overseas businesses and turning Compass into the worldwide market leader in contract feeding. By then, he had also recognised the need to look more closely at providing full facility management.

When Morrison Healthcare business had been acquired in 2001, only one or two per cent of clients wanted Compass to provide services other than catering; four years later, that figure had climbed to 35 per cent. It was plain that if it didn't respond it would lose out. As a consequence, it acquired Crothall, a specialist US healthcare facility management business which had virtually 100 per cent of the business in acute care hospitals. The combination of the two companies catapulted Compass into market leadership position, a position which it holds today and is still run by Bobby Kutteh who was CEO of Crothall at the time of the merger.

Coming back to the UK after eight years out of the country, Bailey found that standards of catering had improved enormously. Competitively, the market was moving away from cost-plus contracts to nil subsidy, concession catering and profit and loss contracts. It was a time of much change.

This manifested itself in 2000 when Compass and Granada merged and then demerged in 2001 – a move that stunned the City, shareholders and staff alike (see

Chapter 27). Clients, too, were apprehensive. Although the merger turned out to be a huge success, creating a powerful new company that dominated the UK market, shareholder opposition at the time was ferocious which was soon reflected in the Compass share price.

The shareholder opposition needs to be seen in the light of Compass' unprecedented acquisition-driven growth. In 13 years, from 1987 to 2000, revenues had grown from £250m to £5.77bn and it had become an acknowledged world leader in food service. It knew the business inside out. The City and shareholders were aghast at the thought that this kind of growth, which had made it the darling of the financial community, would be endangered by a merger with a company known principally for its media interests and for a handful of acquired hotel brands which Granada had brought to the merger through its recent highly acrimonious takeover of Forte.

The City was strongly opposed to the merger; even if it was able to sell off the various hotel assets, it would still dilute earnings in the meantime and hold back Compass' growth.

The merger so upset the City and shareholders, and so dented the trust in which Francis Mackay and Mike Bailey had been held, that it would be fair to say that the overhang of the deal with shareholders and the City never went away until after they left the company in 2006.

In contract catering terms, the two companies in the UK had been at each other's throats ever since Granada had taken over Sutcliffe in 1993; merging the two companies, for Compass staff at least, brought back vivid memories of the friction that had faced the Bateman and Midland staff two decades earlier when they had merged under Dick Turpin. Gerry Robinson's cut-and-thrust style of management, with its determined

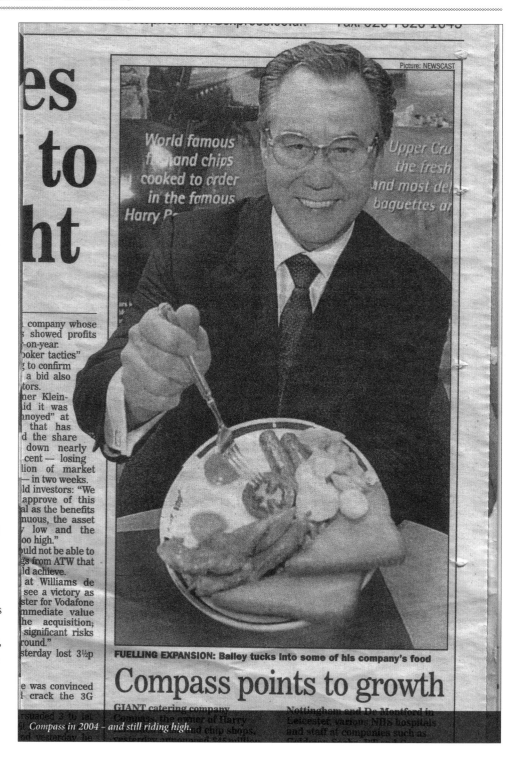

FUELLING EXPANSION: Bailey tucks into some of his company's food

Compass points to growth

GIANT catering company Compass, the owner of Harry Ramsden's fish and chip shops, yesterday announced £45 million

Compass in 2004 – and still riding high.

approach to cost cutting, was but a distant memory, but a memory nevertheless.

With both Robinson and Charles Allen now scheduled to be in charge of the new Granada:Compass merged company, a return to the old cost-cutting days was greatly feared. In fact, it soon became clear that neither would be taking a hands-on role in the new company.

Mackay emerged as chairman with Bailey as group chief executive. It was effectively a takeover of Granada's food service interests by Compass and it was driven by both Mackay and Robinson – the former because Compass was keen to get the Sutcliffe business and, perhaps, to prove something to Gerry Robinson, the latter because Sutcliffe's margins and profit had been driven to the limit and had nowhere to go.

Compass did not discover this until after the merger as due diligence before was confined to what was publicly available.

* * *

The deal was highly complex and structured because it avoided what would have been a £300m tax bill. Compass was only ever interested in the Sutcliffe business, motorway services (a good fit with SSP) and Little Chef (which had potential – never realised – to be used more in the Compass business generally). The media assets of Granada were never of any interest and Forte's large hotel empire was a very grey area indeed. The de-merger of the media assets had to be completed quickly, partly to preserve the tax advantages, but Compass took longer in absorbing the Sutcliffe business and selling off the hotels.

The culture of the two companies was quite different. Granada had grown by a total focus on bottom line; if a manager slipped up in hitting the numbers, he seldom got a second chance before somebody else was wheeled in as a replacement. This led to so many cut-backs and redundancies that people were constantly looking over their shoulder; in consequence, there appeared to be little trust among the senior team.

Compass, too, had grown by both acquisition and organic growth and was certainly bottom-line driven as the results showed, but its purchases appeared to be more strategic than Granada's furious dash for UK growth in the 1990s (Chapter 25), with more focused investment to achieve desired results. Compass recognised that patience was needed before some results came through and having a management revolving door was not something that Mackay or Bailey liked and they certainly did not encourage it.

"The old Sutcliffe company had had a very large infrastructure which is why it made such a good target for Gerry Robinson when he bought it," says Bailey. "The Sutcliffe company that we acquired at Compass was bare bones."

Although it was clear that Sutcliffe would be absorbed into Compass, Don Davenport, Sutcliffe's chief executive and regarded as the most experienced man in the combined company, emerged as CEO. John Greenwood, in charge of Compass UK at the time but never really happy in the role, was moved sideways to make way for Davenport; one of the industry's gentlemen (in both senses of the word) Greenwood subsequently left Compass to join Roadchef but suffered serious health problems and died in 2008.

With Mackay as chairman, Bailey as chief executive and Davenport responsible for the much enlarged UK business, Compass was all set to begin a new era. But for the three individuals, it did not work out quite as favourably as they would have hoped.

Credit 2004 Topfoto/UPP

Gerry Robinson: later, as chief executive of Granada, was one of the driving forces in the merger with Compass.

CHAPTER TWENTY

Gardner Merchant – and the alliance with Sodexo

Gardner Merchant enjoyed two years of independence before forming the alliance with Sodexo.

Gardner Merchant's two years of independence, from 1993 to 1995, was not without incident. Though heavily geared, the company showed that the backers of the buy-out were fully justified in their faith in Garry Hawkes and his team. As if to show his determination to grow the business, in 1994 GM acquired Kielholz Catering in Germany followed by Morrison Hospitality Group based in Mobile, Alabama for $100m and group turnover rose to over £1bn and profits soared to £46.9m. A year later, turnover was £1.2bn and profits climbed to £62m.

It was a period of strong growth both at home and overseas. New contracts were signed around the world including Australia, Japan, Malaysia, Hong Kong and the USA taking the number of outlets to over 6,200 in 20 countries. With 50,000 employees, the company was riding high.

In the restructuring following the buy-out, Hawkes had decentralised, creating new profit centres; in doing so 50 or so middle-ranking managers were offered early retirement or redundancy. The Morrison deal gave the company the opportunity to re-finance its debt at lower interest rates with a small consortium led by Royal Bank of Scotland and it had also tightened up on credit, freeing up £15m of working capital.

Before the buy-out, debtor days had slipped to 50-plus but were later pulled back to around 42 days – each debtor day was worth £1.5m. On purchasing, deals were negotiated directly with manufacturers, all of which increased margins from four per cent to six per cent. There was even greater emphasis on sales training for all staff in a successful attempt to drive customer sales. But even as growth was coming through and the business grew, speculation was gathering pace about GM's next move.

Following approaches from Marriott, Rentokil – the Rat Catchers, as they were called – and others, the fund investors were heartened by the success of the buy-out. But they were not in it for the long-term. Success was encouraging talk of a public flotation, not denied by Hawkes who described the period as an 'interregnum'.

Driven by the indebted nature of the business, a public flotation was seriously considered and was widely trailed in the City with a former senior Barclays investment banker, John Padovan, appointed as non-executive chairman to see it through. If successful (and there was no reason to believe it would not be), it would profit all the investors and place GM into the top 100 FTSE companies, turning what was essentially a privately-owned company into a public corporation with a turnover of well over £1bn. The drawback to such a move, however, was clear: floating the company would make it vulnerable to a predatory bid from Compass, still smarting over its rejection of GM by Forte in 1993 or, indeed, any other buyer interested in taking over what was then the UK's largest contract catering company. Though he would have still preferred a stock market flotation, this was not a prospect that filled Hawkes with delight.

"Any UK organisation would, perforce, have had to rationalise the business and get rid of Gardner Merchant as we know it," he told *Caterer* at the time. It was the key reasoning in accepting the 'Alliance' with Sodexo [although Sodexho did not change its

THE TIMES 2

THURSDAY DECEMBER 24 1992   3X

MICHAEL POWELL

Gardner Merchant profit to soar again

BY JON ASHWORTH

GARDNER Merchant, the worldwide contract catering group that is breaking away from Forte in a £402 million management buyout, is on course for another year of bumper profits.

The group, led by Garry Hawkes, chief executive, and Ian Carslaw, finance director, expects pre-tax profits to climb 10 per cent in the year to January 31, from last year's £33 million. Turnover is topping £1 billion.

Forte shareholders gave the buyout a nod of approval at an extraordinary meeting in London yesterday. For Mr Hawkes, who has worked his way to the top in 30 years with the group, the success of the deal is particularly satisfying. "This is slightly different to the usual five-person MBO," he said. "The deal involves 1,000 of our managers and we are looking at ways of passing benefits on to all our employees."

Gardner Merchant is being sold to a consortium led by CINVen, the venture capital group. Forte is keeping a 25 per cent stake. The management team is taking 8 per cent, rising to 20 per

cent if profit targets are hit. A flotation or trade sale may follow in due course.

Millions of people eat meals supplied by Gardner Merchant each day without even realising it. The group lays on food in venues from Lord Hanson's dining room to Battersea Dogs' Home and provides catering for Wimbledon and other sporting events.

About 45,000 employees serve hospitals, schools, hotels and racecourses in 16 countries. Clients range from Sydney Opera House to North Sea oil rigs. The UK workforce numbers 30,000.

There appear to be plenty of prospects. The group, along with competitors such as Compass and P&O, has not even begun to tap British public-sector institutions such as the National Health Service and government ministries.

Only 38 per cent of British offices currently contract out their catering. Since launching in America in 1978, Gardner Merchant has expanded from 14 to 700 contracts and still has a long way to go.

Buying a company for Christmas: Ian Carslaw, left, and Garry Hawkes head 1,000 managers in the £402 million MBO from Forte

Front page of The Times for Garry Hawkes and Iain Carslaw, the day after shareholders agreed the buy-out from Forte. The company recorded a 10 per cent increase in profit for the year on turnover approaching £1bn.

name to Sodexo until 2008, we have used the current spelling throughout the book].

Sodexo's entrance in the drama was timely. Curiously, its executive board had already resisted bidding for Gardner Merchant at the time of the buy-out in 1993 despite being pressured into it by Pierre Bellon, Sodexo's président-directeur général. The French board was leery of taking on a reluctant management. In Bellon's biography, *I've Had a Lot of Fun*, Patrice Douce, then Sodexo's president, said the board turned down the opportunity: "Gardner Merchant's team was simply not interested in being acquired."

But the times had changed. Approaches by Granada, now under Gerry Robinson's

leadership, were rebuffed but the danger was clear; Granada could directly approach the venture capitalist investors who owned half the shares. Even so. if they had agreed, it is unlikely that Granada would have secured agreement from the other shareholders. Within reason, Hawkes could happily refuse to parley with would-be suitors even if going public with a flotation posed even greater dangers.

However, pressure was mounting. Forte, for one, was keen to sell its 25 per cent share in order to pay down debt and move Forte into new business areas. The venture capital investors could also see a highly profitable exit route. The situation only encouraged

talk of a flotation which began to preoccupy the City. Hawkes and the GM team had to consider the options: the 'interregnum' was just that – a decision had to be made whether to float or to seek a partner either in the UK or internationally. A planned flotation in the autumn of 1994 was abandoned because of economic uncertainties and stock market jitters. It was then that Sodexo re-appeared on the scene.

* * *

Hawkes himself made the move, inviting Pierre Bellon to dinner at Kenley with the idea of forming an alliance which would

Eton College – one of Gardner Merchant's prestige clients.

Pierre Bellon: "It was the British, the Americans or us. We pushed ahead because if we hadn't we would have forever played a bit part in the UK market."

enable GM to continue in its present form but within the French orbit.

"I knew in my heart of hearts that it wouldn't work in the long-term but it was the best way out of the situation," he says. Hawkes' opinion of Sodexo had not changed from the time of their previous discussions when Bellon's board had failed to support his £400m offer for GM.

GM was certainly a prize worth having. Among its prestige contracts were three leading sporting events in the UK – Wimbledon, Ascot and Henley – and such blue chip organisations as BA, BP, Ford, Rolls Royce, Commercial Union, Eton school, Dublin's parliament, the European Commission in Brussels, Sydney Opera House, HSBC and the Jockey Club in Hong Kong. It was the market leader in the UK, Ireland, Holland and the fastest growing food service company in the US. Compared to this list of contracts at the time, Sodexo could boast worldwide revenues of €1.7bn which had grown at an average annual growth rate

of 12 per cent in the previous decade. It was a successful company with growing ambitions on the international stage.

The proposed deal was too tempting to ignore and, for GM, was certainly in excess of what could have been obtained through a public flotation. At £730m it was, indeed, 'a very full price' as one investment banker described it but accepting it would ensure the continuation, with Bellon's agreement, of GM as a separate entity, the continuing employment of its 55,000 employees and the company's name would remain; They were Garry Hawkes's three key objectives.

Hawkes' dinner at Kenley with Bellon was a success and the deal was agreed more or less there and then. He sensed that Bellon was keen to acquire GM not so much because it made Sodexo a major player in the UK and gave it representation in other countries where the French company wasn't present (which was certainly true), but because GM gave Sodexo added size and prestige. Bellon wanted to be big and GM made him big.

In his biography, Bellon says: "It was the British, the Americans or us. We pushed ahead because if we hadn't we would have forever played a bit part in the UK market."

Forging the alliance with GM made Sodexo a world leader in food service management and 23 per cent of its total revenues would now be coming from the UK and Ireland. Bellon's book makes clear that he considered it Sodexo's most important strategic alliance. As far as Hawkes was concerned, it was the deal of the century. Sodexo was willing to pay a premium price for a heavily indebted company.

The meeting was not the first time that the two men had met. GM and Sodexo had discussed some sort of joint venture back in 1990, so complementary were the two businesses while Bellon's £400m bid for GM at the time of the buy-out had only been thwarted by his own board, so the renewed

Did this sow the seeds of doubt?

At the time of the Sodexo bid, GM had over £30m cash in the bank – a sizeable sum though not in relation to GM's total turnover. Although Garry Hawkes and the French were very keen to complete the deal, Sodexo was told at the outset by CINven that the deal would not succeed if Sodexo wanted to retain the cash on the balance sheet.

Iain Carslaw, GM's financial director, who led the negotiations for GM, argued that the £30m had been generated by the investors and it was theirs to do with what they wanted. During negotiations, the French team was told that the cash pile would be used to repay some of the company's bank debt prior to closing the deal; this was formally disclosed though there are doubts that Bellon himself was fully aware of this aspect of the deal. The arrangement had the effect of increasing the value of the company by the amount the debt was reduced – in this case, £30m – and so increasing the share-out to all the investors, including the management.

Some insiders believe that when Bellon realised what his financial team had agreed to it coloured his initial view of the purchase and his subsequent relations with the company's management. "It became a question of trust," says one. The spectre of perfidious Albion began to hover over the deal...

plenty of advantages to the deal. Sodexo was a French company which had made little progress in the UK (it had a small number of healthcare contracts) so there was little or no overlap there, while GM's interests overseas were complementary rather than competitive. Bellon's biography talks of kindred spirits, despite distinctly different cultures, histories and nationalities. "A spirit of teamwork drove the alliance," he writes. And Hans Rijnierse, who was in charge of GM's Holland operation, is quoted as saying that "We were the ones who chose Sodexo rather than the other way round."

It was, in Hawkes' own words at the time, an almost perfect fit. The agreement that GM 'would trade separately and retain its identity, continuing to exist as an entity separate from Sodexo's contract catering subsidiaries' made the deal highly attractive. In the agreement, Hawkes stayed on as chief executive of GM and joined the Sodexo board as joint director-general alongside Patrice Douce. He retained responsibility for GM's existing contracts in the UK, Ireland, USA, Holland, Malaysia, Australasia and Hong Kong – what Hawkes termed the 'anglosphere'. The fact that he was able to remain in charge of an organisation in which he had spent his career, albeit now part of a French-based, global company with a French board to deal with, was an ideal solution to the problem of settling its future. He could help guide it into its next incarnation. He was happy.

* * *

Alliances, however, are not a feature of British corporate life – there are only mergers or takeovers and all mergers end up as takeovers. The Gardner Merchant Sodexo Alliance was predicated on Bellon's belief that "our collaboration will be based on the overriding principle that our two companies will retain their own identities, autonomy

and brands in every country where they have a presence". It was a noble objective and one that, at the time, was happily agreed by both sides; those more attuned to history would have pointed out that such an agreement in the past had never lasted. Indeed, alliance was the same term which was used when Marc Verstringhe sold Catering & Allied to Elior in 1999, and that did not last either. But for GM and Sodexo, the term was good enough for the time being even though it was clearly a takeover in all but name.

Through the deal, Sodexo had doubled in size to over 110,000 employees with sales of €3.3bn, giving it a presence in new markets and making it (at the time) the world's biggest food services company. Sodexo was on its way to achieving Bellon's ambition to be a global player.

The deal comprised £550m in cash and the assumption of £180m worth of debt. The new board consisted of Garry Hawkes and Charles McCole (finance director who had joined in place of Iain Carslaw who had joined CINven) plus any two of Ian Hall (HR director), Alan Reed (managing director UK), John Wares (who was responsible for

Garry Hawkes: "Any UK organisation would, perforce, have had to rationalise the business and get rid of Gardner Merchant as we know it."

bid from the French company was viewed as something of a white knight by the GM team, determined as they were to avoid being swallowed up by Granada or any other rival company. The venture capital investors, too, were willing to sell at the price being offered.

From GM's point of view, there were

most of GM's P&L contracts) and David Ford (managing director) on a rotating basis; four Sodexo executives and three external non-executives completed the line-up. It was also another pay day for over 1,000 senior staff who shared £60m of the proceeds of the purchase; 6,500 other staff were given new share options in Sodexo partly to recompense them for a promise, given at the time of planning the flotation that never took place, that managers would be given discounted shares in GM.

* * *

For the first two years of the alliance, all went well. Hawkes remained in charge of GM but within a French organisation that had a much different way of working than he was used to. The one region where there was some duplication was the US where both GM and Sodexo had an equally strong presence, made more complicated by GM's acquisition of Morrison's Hospitality only a few months before the alliance was agreed. Richard Hutchinson, GM's CEO in the USA, worked with Michel Landel (who was to be appointed CEO of Sodexo group in 2004) to successfully see the merger through with Landel reporting to both Bellon and Hawkes – an awkward arrangement.

The transition from independence to being part of a French-based public company with a global reach was not without some stress. Hans Rijnierse, again quoted in Bellon's biography, said it took some time for everyone to get used to the idea, especially given the cultural divide.

"After more than 20 years of belonging to a UK group, whose corporate culture resembled our own, we suddenly found ourselves to be part of a family-controlled French group that was listed on the stock market."

For Hawkes, however smoothly the

> ## *Vive la différence!*
>
> An article written by Amandine Lanjaret on the FranceInLondon.com website nicely sums up one of the big differences between English and French business:
>
> "In Great Britain, meetings are rather seen like occasions to discuss and take decisions whereas in France people prefer sharing ideas. Most of the time in France these meetings have no impact on the leaders' final decision. This attitude confuses many a British executive who thinks he has reached an agreement, before realising his French business partners took another decision."

---

alliance had been formed, it was certainly a change of culture. He was accustomed to making decisions by himself or in consultation with close colleagues. He was used to the cut-and-thrust of argument, being surrounded by senior people of great talent and with hugely disparate personalities and abilities – certainly no yes-men – who he enjoyed motivating and leading to the huge benefit of the company's growth. He respected his gut feelings which were based on an intimate knowledge of an industry in which he had spent his entire working career. He found Sodexo's more Mediterranean style of management sometimes puzzling, to say the least. One insider, still with the company, describes the French way of working as more technocratic and bureaucratic than would be the case with a British company: more meetings, more discussions and more debate before a decision is reached – even if a decision *is* reached.

The introduction of five-year budgets was also something new, reflecting Sodexo's more cautious, more technocratic approach to business. A new mission statement created some confusion. In Britain a mission statement is short and to the point – no more than 100 words or so; in France it's a 200-page document which outlines all the company's policies and procedures. Sodexo was also, despite being a global company, very French-based and the company took

a French view of the world – one that was prescriptive and involved intense planning with centralised management and control from France. Unlike Compass, which appointed a number of nationalities to the main board as it grew into a global company, even today nine of Sodexo's 13 board members are French with six related to the Bellon family, which still owns 35 per cent of the company.

* * *

Hawkes, an O level French speaker, tried to ride all this change with some equanimity, though not without a good deal of frustration. The lack of a common language caused problems which did not lead to good communications. Bellon himself spoke some English – "Better than my French but that's not saying much," says Hawkes – unlike other board directors many of whom were also non-caterers. Although, there were advisers and translators on hand who attended GM board meetings, such as Sian Herbert-Jones, who became Sodexo's finance director when Bernard Carton retired and David von Simson of Swiss Bank Corporation. Because of the language and cultural differences, communications could sometimes be difficult and confusing. On one occasion, Hawkes bridled when a mistranslation had Bellon insisting that the

I've Had a Lot of Fun

The Sodexho Story

Pierre Bellon

In collaboration with **Emily Borgeaud**

Pierre Bellon's biography: "Everything he promised, he delivered," says Hawkes, but Bellon complains that Hawkes' move to Aramark in the UK left him feeling betrayed.

UK company should implement some plan, whereas, in fact, he was only suggesting implementation. Such confusion did not help relationships. In addition, the Sodexo head office was much bigger than anything that GM had ever enjoyed; it was a completely different environment to that which Hawkes was used to at Kenley or at the Merchant Centre, its London base.

Alliance it might have been called but he had to recognise that GM was now part of a larger concern and one, moreover, based in Paris and run on French lines. He was not his own boss, though he got on well with Bellon personally: "Everything he promised, he delivered," says Hawkes. "He couldn't have been nicer to me and we worked exceptionally well together. The whole board was much more sociable than the Fortes ever were." But that wasn't really saying much, either.

* * *

In the next few years, GM went on something of a buying spree. In 1995 it bought Edinburgh-based Wheatsheaf Catering from Chris Robinson, worth some £4m annually in turnover. In the same year it acquired Tillery Valley Foods, the chilled food manufacturer based in Abertillery in South Wales, for a sum short of £10m, and in 1997 it snapped up three independents – Surrey-based Cadogan Catering with an annual turnover of £4m, which specialised in leisure catering with sites at the RHS at Wisley and Wakehurst Place Gardens in West Sussex; Gilmour and Pether who were caterers to Silverstone; and events caterer Lawson Beaumont, part of the Break for the Border Group, with annual sales of £4m. GM also struck up a partnership with Gary Rhodes to open two fine dining restaurants in London, just to emphasise the company's fine dining credentials (see Chapter 27).

This was all good news but Hawkes was beginning to strain at the leash. He was nearing the end of his career, he was a wealthy man, and he was looking for a new final challenge. In his own words, he had run out of steam. He had been a Gardner Merchant man all his career and had grown up with the company, managed it for both THF and Forte, piloted it through a buy-out, had run it as a major independent and had successfully sold it at a premium price. He had done it all.

"Life's too short," he says. "I wanted to enjoy my wealth – and health."

And inevitably, Sodexo began to encroach on the agreement that had been made when the alliance was formed. Bellon, in his biography, implies that he was never convinced of Hawkes' allegiance to his alliance partner:

"Built on mutual confidence and commitment, an alliance is viable only when its terms are respected by all parties, as was the case in the Netherlands and the US," he writes, noticeably excluding Britain. "But during an acquisition process, how does one assess the managers' willingness to help make the combination succeed?... Unfortunately, the buyers in an acquisition do not usually have the opportunity to audit the managers and management practices of the acquired company."

Was this referring to the decision to use the £30m cash to repay debt at the outset of the deal? It was certainly a dig at Hawkes for, in the next passage, it says:

"Sodexo would be faced with a disappointing experience in the case of Garry Hawkes who, while in office, opposed some of the changes sought by Sodexo. The situation reached its peak in 2000;... Hawkes left the company and moved to competitor Aramark in the UK, leaving Bellon feeling betrayed."

Bellon's account is something of a

simplification of the circumstances that led to Hawkes' departure. The changes were probably inevitable to most observers but in Hawkes' view the agreement drawn up at the time of the alliance had been breached: the loss of GM's responsibility for most of its overseas operations and, even more critical, the loss of the Gardner Merchant name, were changes that directly contravened the spirit of the alliance. They were changes that he could not bear.

* * *

As a postscript to these events, even after Hawkes' departure, it was not all plain sailing for Sodexo. In 2001, UK profits were €102m (£64m); a year later they had crashed to zero after 'accounting anomalies' combined with 'serious errors of management' were found in the accounts, relating primarily to a subsidiary, Sodexo Land Technology Ltd, which was concerned with parks, gardens, sports fields and cemeteries and other land contracts, for which a €33m provision had to be made. The anomalies were never officially explained in detail but insiders have it that Sodexo wanted to see a 15 per cent year-on-year increase in sales and profit. It was a target that most people regarded as unfeasible but Landtech appeared to take it to heart even though the target was an even more unrealistic proposition in grounds maintenance than in contract catering. The company started to sell below cost base even, allegedly, inventing work done. The whole imbroglio was not helped by the loss of some important clients to Aramark after Bill Toner's departure – client retention being a key business measure.

Albert George, Sodexo's director-general at the time, told *Caterer*: "It is not a matter of cash out. It is not a matter of fraud. It's an issue of mis-management." Looking at Price Waterhouse Coopers, he added:

"Our statutory auditors in the UK have not been sufficiently vigilant." Landmark had originally been set up as Taylorplan (Land Technology) Ltd. Taylorplan had been acquired by Marriott in 1996 (after GM itself had rebuffed an approach from Marriott in 1994) but when Sodexo acquired Marriott Food Services in 1997, Taylorplan and the other Marriott subsidiary, Russell & Brand, were handed over to GM to operate.

Albert George took a remarkably forgiving attitude to the whole situation: "Whatever happened, happened. Now the story has closed." Landel promised that the company would bounce back within three years.

So it did – but it was not a good year for Sodexo UK in other ways. Perhaps as a result of the publicity relating to the Land Technology problem, Sodexo was losing hitherto loyal clients. Poor client retention – admitted in *Caterer* as "too weak" – lost business, particularly in B&I, which accounted for 90 per cent of the loss in sales. Turnover dropped from £1bn in 2002/3 to £931m in 2003/4, which sent Sodexo's shares on the French Exchange down by 29 per cent. Poor performance on 20 key contracts, bad debts, asset write-downs and restructuring charges added to the UK woes. Nor did the company give the immediate impression of being firmly in control of events.

David Ford was replaced as chief executive by Mark Shipman who was drafted in from a company acquired by Sodexo in the US, together with his colleague Mark Adams, who took over as finance director. Widely respected, Shipman stayed only a couple of years before he returned to the US because of his wife's health. He was replaced by Francois-Xavier Bellon, Pierre Bellon's son, who quit after only a few months as a result of 'ill health'. Michel Landel took temporary charge until Philip Jansen took over in 2004; Jansen stayed for six years, steadying the ship, eventually becoming head of Sodexo's European operations, until 2010 when he joined Brakes as chief executive. Aidan Connolly, Sodexo's finance director since 2007, was appointed chief executive, but after two years – including some major contract wins and the purchase of Atkins, the design, engineering and project management consultancy – moved on to WorldPay as chief financial officer. Debbie White, an accountant by profession, who had joined Sodexo in 2004 and became chief financial officer, took over as chief executive in 2012 with the aim of boosting revenues from £1bn to £1.5bn within five years – an objective already largely achieved.

Under Jansen, Sodexo UK recovered from the hiatus but it took some eight years to get the new name firmly established; few people in the company ever now refer to Gardner Merchant – and even fewer remember it.

As David Ford had said at the time of the name change, GM had already decided to move into full facilities management as a core service, seeing it as more profitable with bigger margins and greater profits than remaining principally as a food service provider.

For Sodexo, this is something of a pioneering role: in the UK, food amounts to only 44 per cent of total revenues, whereas in the group as a whole it represents 77 per cent. Sodexo Group's 2014 results shows a turnover of €18bn; under Debbie White, the UK and Ireland division contributes €1,483m in turnover yielding €66m in profit at a margin of 4.5 per cent. As a company, it is now fully integrated in the Sodexo way of working. Sodexo itself, though still predominantly French-based with a board of directors largely consisting of Bellon's family and near colleagues, has three US nationals on the 14-strong executive committee, which actually runs the company, as well as two British members – White and Sian Herbert-Jones, chief financial officer – two Belgium nationals and one triple nationality.

The UK company now eschews small contracts; its interest lies principally in integrated contracts for hospitals, MoD and large corporates where it can provide a complete range of support services, including catering, either as a single contractor or as a partner in PFI contracts such as the MoD's Colchester Garrison. Tendering for these contracts has become extraordinarily complex and detailed, each tender involving a team comprising many different disciplines and costing as much as half a million pounds to prepare. The days when Gardner Merchant oiled the wheels by hosting public service clients at lavish dinners at Kenley and other corporate events are long past:

"Now they can hardly accept a cup of coffee," says Phil Hooper, Sodexo's corporate affairs director. It's only one sign of the changing times in contracting.

Debbie White: current chief executive, Sodexo UK – she joined the company in 2007 as chief financial officer, moved to the US in 2008 but returned to the UK in 2012 as chief executive.

CHAPTER TWENTY-ONE

A bit of a bother: Aramark, Garry Hawkes and Bill Toner

Bill Toner arrived at Aramark after Gardner Merchant's injunction was withdrawn and invited Garry Hawkes to be chairman.

By the time ARA moved into Ireland in 2000 in a joint venture with Campbell Bewley, buying a 92 per cent stake in Campbell's £60m a year UK business for £17.2m (and the remaining eight per cent in 2003), it had become the UK's third largest contractor after Compass and Sodexo and the largest contractor in Ireland. Its annual UK turnover of £120m had been boosted by a big interest in MoD catering. It also had a new chief executive.

In 1999, William McCall announced that he would be retiring in the following year and in its search for a new chief executive, Joseph Neubauer, Aramark's president, had set his mind on appointing Bill Toner. Toner, a chef by training, had been a high flyer with Gardner Merchant for over 17 years, ending up at the time of the Sodexo takeover of GM as managing director of B&I. However, two years after the GM/Sodexo alliance was created, Toner found himself caught up in a major *contretemps*.

Garry Hawkes, who was now nearing 60 and wanting to stand down from frontline operations, took up the positions of a non-executive director of Sodexo and chairman of GM. Looking to settle his succession he appointed David Ford, then UK managing director, as chief executive to succeed him with Ford reporting directly to Pierre Bellon, Sodexo's chairman. Toner, seeing his way forward blocked, took the opportunity to accept a handsome offer by Neubauer to replace McCall as chief executive at Aramark. Here was the chance he had been seeking that he couldn't achieve at GM – to have total responsibility for driving a business forward.

This state of affairs, if it had proceeded, would almost certainly have avoided much subsequent anguish. However, just as Toner gave in his notice, and without consulting either Hawkes or Ford, Bellon pleaded with him to stay. He proposed a deal (and assumed both would accept) that Toner and Ford should become joint chief executives. This set in train a period of confusion for everyone. Toner was certainly not of a mind to accept, believing the arrangement was unworkable, while Hawkes, to whom Ford had turned for advice, said that the whole situation undermined Ford's position as the already appointed chief executive. He was also mindful of his own position; after all, he had appointed Ford. The situation came to a head at a meeting of senior executives in September 1999 which was chaired by Bellon. The proposed structure came crashing down when Toner refused Bellon's blandishments to stay on and after an urgent call to Aramark in the US announced he was quitting.

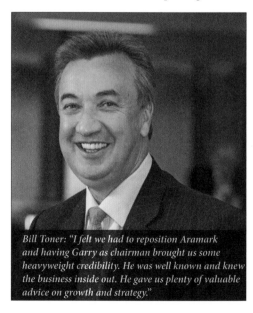

Bill Toner: "I felt we had to reposition Aramark and having Garry as chairman brought us some heavyweight credibility. He was well known and knew the business inside out. He gave us plenty of valuable advice on growth and strategy."

Bellon told him to leave immediately; within an instant Toner had become a hated competitor. Ford remained as chief executive and appointed Nigel Forbes and Richard Muir to run B&I with Vince Pearson running specialist business when Alan Reed retired.

But this did not end the saga. The GM deal with Sodexo had stipulated that GM would retain its name and the operation of all contracts in what Hawkes termed the anglosphere – the UK, America, Northern Europe, Australia, Hong Kong, Malaysia and Singapore. The agreement was that the alliance would, in fact, be run as two organisations but with one shareholder. Hawkes had remained happily in charge of GM within the alliance, though he admits he realised that nothing is ever set in stone forever.

However, in autumn 1997, the merger in the US was sealed between Marriott International's food service and facilities management business (Marriott Management Services) and Sodexo's North American operations, which included all GM's American business. Sodexo Marriott Services became the largest provider of food and facilities management services in North America with over 4,800 accounts and annual sales in excess of $4bn. It was clearly a good deal for Sodexo but it meant that the anglosphere agreement had been overtaken by events. Hawkes recognised the inevitability of the situation when shortly afterwards all GM's overseas contracts, wherever they were in the world, were transferred to Paris. As a result, GM was to be solely a UK organisation with no overseas interests.

In fact, GM and Marriott were not entirely strangers to each other. In 1994, the newly independent GM had rebuffed a takeover approach by Marriott, who wanted to establish a major UK presence. Rejected, Marriott went on to pay full price

Sodexo in the UK

Even prior to the Gardner Merchant alliance, Sodexo had launched a business in the UK exclusively in the hospital sector led by Chris Everden which, although loss-making, generated a £15m turnover. When Vince Pearson joined in the summer of 1994 from Pall Mall Services he led a team including Wilson Barrie to post the company's first profit just as the merger between Sodexo and GM was announced in early 1995.

Pearson was given the opportunity with Reg Awcock to merge all of the combined company's healthcare contracts into one division with three regional directors (Wilson Barrie, Andy Leach and Roy Donaldson). Turnover grew to some £70m by which time Pearson persuaded Alan Reed, who was GM's UK managing director of specialist business, to seek French support for the acquisition of Tillery Valley Foods, the specialist chilled and frozen food manufacturer – a bold strategy which proved highly successful as new PFI hospitals were being built without conventional cooked on-site offers.

The Sodexo/Marriott deal brought in an additional £40m in healthcare as well as key personnel such as Ian Sarson and Andrew Isaacs. Pearson led the healthcare division until 1998 when he was appointed to the UK board looking after healthcare, defence and PFI. Barrie went on to run healthcare and Sarson headed up Sodexo's business in Hong Kong but returned to the UK in 2003 with Compass where he became responsible for the UK business. Pearson was later given education when Tim Cookson left to set up his own company in 2000. The combined £300m business grew until 2003 when David Ford quit as managing director of the UK business at the time of the Land Technology crisis, and Mark Shipman came aboard as his replacement.

Pearson went to Australia in late 2003 but returned in 2005 and with two former GM colleagues (Jim Lovett and Gary Palmer) secured venture capital backing to form a company – Waterfall – in order to acquire Caterplus, a contractor working largely in the residential and care home sector; in 2008, it took over Taylor Shaw based in the North East of England, which took Waterfall into education and school feeding where it continues to operate successfully. With a new investor, LDC, Waterfall's current £70m turnover is planned to reach £100m in the next few years.

Vince Pearson: He was running Sodexo in the UK before the Gardner Merchant/Sodexo alliance.

for Russell & Brand and Taylorplan (with its Land Technology subsidiary – a cause of later grief); Russell & Brand's Tim Cookson was integrating the two companies when Marriott had a change of heart and sold off the US management services division to Sodexo which included its UK operations.

By the time of the Marriott acquisition, Hawkes believed that his time at Sodexo was nearing its natural conclusion, besides which a number of his key people in the buy-out had quit or retired: Ian Carslaw, the finance director, had gone to CINven, Ian Hall was quickly recruited by Toner to Aramark, Bob Cotton went to DCMS as tourism adviser and in 2000 was appointed as chief executive of the British Hospitality Association; others who left included Rod Simpson, head of overseas activities, Graham Smith in charge of Australia and the Pacific Rim, and Alan Reed, the long-time senior operations director. What was left was the strata of senior managers who had been hugely enriched by the GM management buy-out and by the sale to Sodexo which Hawkes and his fellow directors had seen to such successful fruition and for which, he was aggrieved to note, he had personally received so little thanks. Once, when Toner thanked him for changing his life, Hawkes replied that he could count on the fingers of one hand the people who had done so.

Worse was to come, as 18 months later Project Blue emerged: the GM name was to go and the company was to be rebranded Sodexo. This was the brainchild of the UK Sodexo team and Hawkes immediately saw it as a stab in the back. David Ford told *Caterer* the decision was entirely that of the UK team, something that was later repeated by Phil Hooper, the company's UK corporate affairs director in an article for the same magazine. In fact, a name change had been planned in Paris as far back at 1997 by Claudine Pincemin, then Sodexo's group executive, vice president communications and sustainable development, but this had come to nothing at the time.

Why Gardner Merchant became Sodexo

Reasons were put forward for the name change. Gardner Merchant was known as a contract caterer whereas it was claimed that Sodexo was keen to enter the wider support service market and further into Public Finance Initiatives (PFI) contracts; Paul Aitchison headed up GM's PFI activities and the South Manchester Hospitals PFI contract was signed in 1999.

"The name has such a strong association with food service that it's holding back our push in other areas," said David Ford at the time.

In fact, this was only partly true. GM had a facilities management division based within its Kelvin subsidiary which was already beginning to exploit the FM market; this had astonished Pierre Bellon when Hawkes showed him around the company.

Nevertheless, the decision had already been made to broaden Sodexo's offer in the UK by focusing on full facilities management contracts.

With PFI contracts also up for grabs, Sodexo was keen to become a key shareholder member of the Special Purpose Vehicles that organised the projects and see them through to completion. PFI and bundled contracts, particularly in the public sector, were seen as the way forward with healthcare and the MoD leading the way. Colchester Garrison was one such contract.

While the GM name was still regarded as the strongest in the industry – "85 per cent unprompted awareness," says Garry Hawkes – and ditching it seemed like a huge mistake to many and 'madness' to Hawkes, there was little doubt that Sodexo was as keen to get its name as established in the UK as it was throughout the world. It was, after all, a one-brand company and five years had passed since the alliance had been formed. Time was marching on.

For Ford and his team, changing the name to Sodexo was a no-brainer; it was the logical next step. For Hawkes, however, it was the final injustice.

David Ford: "No-one has ever asked me to change the name. We could have waited 10 years before changing it."

Ford told *Caterer*: "No-one has ever asked me to change the name. We could have waited 10 years before changing it. I don't want to preside over a subsidiary where the biggest division is called Sodexo and we are looking like uppity-Brits. I don't find that a tenable situation."

To Hawkes, this made the situation all the worse. Not only was the GM name being changed, which was something against the spirit of the alliance agreement as he saw it but, critically, it was being devised, encouraged and promoted by the UK team, all of them his former colleagues and all of whom had benefited from the largesse of the buy-out and the subsequent merger with Sodexo that he had overseen. He felt it was total betrayal.

"I only sold the company to Sodexo on the understanding that there wouldn't be a name change," he says. "That was the understanding. The French were perfectly happy with the name and they didn't break the alliance. It was broken by the UK directors. They promoted the name change. It was their idea." The change rankles still.

He recognised that the 'sell-out' to the French by the UK team left him with no alternative but to quit, a decision made easier by the fact that Sodexo had been salami slicing his non-executive salary during the last year or so – three times, he claims, to bring it down to the low level of the French non-executive directors.

At the time, there is no doubt that the upheaval was making GM an unhappy ship. David Ford had made management changes which resulted in the departure of some high profile executives including Tim Cookson, managing director of GM's education division, Julian Squire of Primary Management, Howard Colliver, head of vending, and Caroline Black from Kelvin. But it was Toner's defection to Aramark that was seen as the most serious. Sodexo

tried to impose a year's notice on him, denying him work anywhere in the world, although it agreed it would continue to pay his salary and all benefits until the expiry of his contract in September 2000. In January 2000, it launched a High Court action to stop him joining Aramark before September claiming that he was in breach of the contract by already starting to work for the American company in December 1999. A month later, however, the writ was dropped. It was probably unenforceable anyway.

Ford told *Caterer*: "Bill Toner and Gardner Merchant have reached a perfectly agreeable situation whereby GM's interests are protected and Bill Toner can get on with his life." The settlement was that Toner went to the US for six months and William McCall stayed on for a few more months at Aramark to await Toner's return.

* * *

However, this was not the end of the matter. A further blow to GM (now renamed Sodexo) came in July 2000 when Hawkes accepted Ian Hall's invitation to join Aramark UK as non-executive chairman for three days a month. This was a decision that rocked the industry even more than Toner's departure to Aramark six months previously.

Hawkes had never been anything but a GM man, having been courted by many and having stayed steadfast to the company. To join such a high profile competitor so soon after quitting Sodexo was seen as a stab in the back by his former colleagues. In *Caterer*, he denied it was a snub to GM but that was somewhat disingenuous. Toner's decision was one thing; major companies expect senior executives to switch allegiances from time to time. On the other hand, Hawkes' departure to a rival was on an altogether different plane; he had no financial need for the job and it smacked of betrayal. That, however, was

exactly how Hawkes had felt when Ford and his fellow directors had promoted the name change. But even for those in the industry not connected with either company the decision gave an impression of petulance that tarnished a brilliant reputation as an industry leader. For Toner, who had worked for and with him for 17 years, it was something of a coup:

"I felt we had to reposition Aramark and having Garry as chairman brought us some heavyweight credibility. He was well known and knew the business inside out. He gave us plenty of valuable advice on growth and strategy."

Hawkes plays the whole episode down. He says he had fulfilled all his contractual obligations to Sodexo and the alliance, as originally conceived, had irretrievably broken down. The betrayal by his former colleagues on the UK board ran deep. His former HR

The name change from Gardner Merchant to Sodexo was planned and executed by the UK team, led by Phil Hooper, the company's public affairs director.

director at GM, Ian Hall, had already joined Aramark without any fuss and both he and Toner were keen get him on board as a big name, if only on a part-time basis. Besides, the position would be personally usefully giving him the use of an office and secretarial help.

"After 37 years at Gardner Merchant, I needed to be weaned off work gradually," he says. "I had given my all to Gardner Merchant and I owed Sodexo nothing and they owed me nothing. It was not my intention to use my contacts to take existing business away from Sodexo. I was never Aramark's chairman, as such. I was never in charge of Bill Toner. I was really their glorified consultant. They used my name and I attended board meetings and I gave bits and pieces of advice, but I never visited the US and I was never in charge of the operations. In fact, in retrospect, they largely ignored my advice. I never once approached a former Gardner Merchant client and was never asked to."

However, in the hothouse speculation at the time, the industry's negative reaction to his move cannot have been entirely unexpected for someone so politically aware.

What had tipped the balance in his decision to join was Toner's tenacious nature, plus it was a three day a month job that just kept his hand in. He had always admired Toner's driven hard-work ethic: "Clients loved him. He saw Phantom of the Opera with clients 36 times – that's something that goes well beyond the call of duty," he says admiringly. Toner's drive and amazing self-confidence also generated his admiration. "He's very streetwise," he says.

A remark in *Caterer* hints that he saw the position as a counterweight to Francis Mackay's impending merger of Compass with Granada:

"Francis Mackay has done a fantastic job with Compass but he will always be driven by the need to satisfy short-term shareholder value. Aramark in the UK has the power of its American parent behind it but, because it is privately owned, it can afford to take a longer view."

* * *

Hawkes, Toner and Ian Hall were soon to be joined by Dan Wright as managing director of B&I who had been recruited from Catering & Allied at the time of its purchase by Elior, and by Wyn Roberts from Sodexo. The company had been more or less plodding along towards the end of William McCall's tenure and Toner came in like a hurricane with the full approval of Bill Leonard, then Aramark's CEO and second only to Neubauer. He moved the UK headquarters from a miserable office in Reading to an impressive, lavishly fitted-out upper floor in Millbank Tower, a move which was specifically designed to impress clients, something that the Reading office had signally failed to do. He also set about boosting the company's sales efforts, introducing a charm offensive on both existing and potential clients.

"Put Bill in front of a potential client and you'll get a sale," says Dan Wright. "He's so good with people, such a powerful motivator."

Toner also started recruiting new senior people with the result that he drove annual turnover up from £120m when he joined to £400m when he left four years later. In 2000 he had overseen the acquisition of Campbell Bewley in a complicated deal worth some £110m in total to form a joint venture company, Aramark Catering. Four years later he acquired Catering Alliance, with 200 contracts and 2,200 staff and a £50m turnover, for a reputed £20m, saying Aramark had bought "a company with great talent and a proven track record". This

Hawkes was key to the creation of the Edge Hotel School at Wivenhoe on the campus of the University of Essex

acquisition was not so harmonious.

Catering Alliance's three founders, Russell Scandrett, Sean Hagan and Michael Scott, stayed on for a nine-month contractual work-out but, after claiming at the outset that the merger was seamless, left after eight months, together with at least three other senior staff, amid a flurry of recriminations aired in *Caterer*. "It is not unusual that when a change of company ownership occurs some employees will use that opportunity to rethink their own careers and make plans accordingly," said an Aramark spokesman blandly. True enough, but in fact it was Toner himself who was coming to the end of his time at the company.

In October 2004, Hawkes decided that it was time to step down. He had found Aramark 'very American'. He was keen to pursue his interests in vocational training and educational development which were giving him plenty to think about. He had been appointed chairman of the qualifications provider Edexcel from 2000 to 2004 when he became founding chairman of Edge, the organisation dedicated to raising the status of practical and vocational learning. He was key to the creation of the Edge Hotel School at Wivenhoe on the campus of the University of Essex. He thought he had given as much to Aramark as he could. A knighthood in 2009 crowned his career.

Toner regretted the decision to step down: "Garry has made an enormous contribution to Aramark UK over the past four years but has also been a personal inspiration to me since we first worked together 21 years ago," he told *Caterer*. But it took only six more months for Toner to join him at the exit door. Even now, he is not allowed to reveal any specific information on how Aramark conducts its business.

* * *

When he joined Aramark, Toner enjoyed relative independence from the US; a major coup was to win the Barclays Bank contract and there were others of some significance though some in the industry considered they had been gained on unrealistic costings. Nevertheless, he was growing the UK company to its highest-ever annual turnover and probably because of this had been largely left alone by the Philadelphia head office. But the US office kept such tight control over the UK operation that it became an inhibiting factor; this was something which was exacerbated when Bill Leonard quit in 2004 after Aramark floated on the US stock exchange. Leonard knew the business inside out and was highly respected by Toner and others.

All senior people appointed in the UK had to be interviewed and approved in the US; lawyers in Philadelphia inspected all UK contracts (the Barclays contract posed particular problems); US lawyers were deeply involved in due diligence with the Catering Alliance purchase; monthly video conference calls to the US were *de rigeur*. At one stage, head office in the US wanted to introduce systems which were not relevant to the UK operation, one example being appraisal forms that were less effective than the ones already in place. It was as if Philadelphia viewed the UK operation as a satellite of the US company not as a self-operating subsidiary with its own chief executive.

Bill Leonard's departure, and the appointment of his successor, presaged Toner's increasing frustration at the controls being imposed in his words, "by external people who didn't know the catering business". Ravi Saligram, his new boss, had been appointed president of Aramark International in 2003 in charge of all Aramark's overseas ventures; his previous background before joining Aramark in 2003 had been with InterContinental Hotels where he had been chief marketing officer and, latterly, president of brands and franchising. Saligram was based in the US but became a frequent visitor to the UK as did other luminaries from the company and it didn't take long for the relationship between the two of them to come under strain and then to break down completely.

At the time, Dan Wright remembers the company being increasingly uncomfortable: "Bill was under tremendous pressure and it showed. Such a contrast to when he started when he was so gung ho!" Wright himself soon left for a job outside the industry. Six months later the pressure on Toner took its toll; he quit but received a handsome payoff. It was an inglorious end to what had been an exciting six years. "Even if you didn't always agree with them, they were basically very nice people," he admits.

* * *

Toner was succeeded as managing director by a Scot, Andrew Main, who had joined Aramark in 1994 as divisional director for Scotland and off-shore operations; he had previously worked for Kelvin and for Universal Ogden Services which had been acquired by Sodexo in 1997. Appointed managing director of specialist markets in 2000 he was relocated to the US in 2002 as vice president of the business services division and then promoted president in 2003. He returned to the UK as chief executive in 2005 and continues in that position to this day.

Ironically, one of his first acts was to ask Hawkes to act as consultant which he did for two years, largely unrecognised. Yet, even with Hawkes' help, the company found the UK market difficult to penetrate.

The company itself (in the UK at least) is seen as cautious, operating under the radar at a time when competition is fierce and other, smaller companies are expanding rapidly. Over and above this caution, Aramark has a 33-page code of practice, its Business Conduct Policy, which can be accessed on its website and which aims to place the company into the upper reaches of corporate ethical practice. In effect, it stipulates that if the company is to keep a supplier discount, it must tell the client; if it eschews discounts in the UK (some observers believe it does) it would certainly make the UK market less profitable.

There is evidence that this may be the case. In 2011, it told non-food suppliers to cut their prices by 12 per cent – "savings at this level will be essential to secure a long-term relationship" a letter from the chief operating officer, Mark Faulkner, stated baldly. It is true that, at the same time, other contractors were also putting pressure on suppliers, if slightly more discreetly, but Aramark is not a Tesco and the letter sounded a note of desperation.

Nor did a profit warning issued in 2014, which revealed that Aramark's UK annual turnover for 2013 had dropped 12 per cent to £308m from £350m in 2012 (the year of the London Olympic Games) and £341m in 2011, provide much more reassurance. Pre-tax profits for 2013 were down 71 per cent to £2.3m.

Since 2000, Compass has remained the clear UK leader, yet its UK market has declined in importance as other areas of the world – particularly the US – have offered bigger and more rewarding markets (see Chapter 26).

Sodexo has made a conscious decision to expand in the UK via the FM market with over half its UK turnover from support services other than catering. Elior has grown by acquisition. Other companies have emerged largely through organic growth and sometimes in niche markets: ISS in the hospital sector, The Brookwood Partnership in independent schools.

Some of the newer companies on the block: clockwise from top left: Wendy Bartlett, CEO at bartlett mitchell; Caroline Fry, CEO of B&I at CH&Co; Phil Roker, owner director of Vacherin; Kate Martin and Sue Parfett co-founders of The Brookwood Partnership.

The more broadly-based Bartlett Mitchell (one of The Sunday Times 100 Best Companies to Work For) is now a £40m-plus a year outfit while, at the other end of the scale, BaxterStorey has grown twice as big as Aramark in under 10 years and is now the UK's third largest UK contract caterer with total annual turnover (including retail sales) of £550m.

In 2015 the merger between CH&Co, which was only established in 1991, and Host Catermasters Group (HCM) run, ironically, by Bill Toner, created an organisation with an annual turnover approaching £200m – almost two-thirds that of Aramark's – all within four years of Toner joining HCM.

CHAPTER TWENTY-TWO

The emergence of Elior

Sodexo was not the only overseas company wanting to expand into the UK – Elior took a shine to High Table and then four more.

While the alliance between Gardner Merchant and Sodexo was making all the news, another overseas company was making headway in the UK. This was French-based Elior, founded in 1991 by Francis Markus and Robert Zolade.

Both men had started their careers in contract catering in the 1970s working for Jacques Borel International (Borel later becoming better known in the UK for leading a – so far unsuccessful – independent campaign to reduce VAT on serviced accommodation and restaurant meals). Markus became the president of the company's contract catering subsidiary, Générale de Restauration, which was Europe's leading catering contractor, while Zolade was general manager of Borel's contract catering division.

Seeking to expand, Borel entered the hotel business in the mid-1970s with the takeover of Sofitel but the expansion ran into trouble in the recession of the late 1970s and in 1980 he sold it to SIEH, the owner of the Novotel, Ibis and Mercure brands. Three years later, Novotel acquired the rest of the Borel group, including its Générale de Restauration subsidiary. The merged group was renamed Accor.

Both Markus and Zolade remained with Accor building up its new contract catering and restaurant operation until 1991 when Accor decided to sell it off. The two men set up a new company, Bercy Management in order to buy a controlling stake in the Générale de Restauration subsidiary and, with 300 of the subsidiary's managers, they completed the buyout gaining 35 per cent and management control of the business with Accor retaining a 50 per cent equity interest. The two became co-presidents and co-chairmen and set out to build Bercy Management into France's leading contract catering group.

Even from the outset, they had ambitions to become a global player in contract catering. Their first step came a year later, in 1992, when they acquired a minority holding in High Table in the UK, a company which had gained a solid reputation as a top quality contractor in the City. The acquisition,

Robert Zolade and Francis Markus: founders of Elior.

completed in 1995, was the first of a series that established the company in the UK.

High Table

High Table had been launched in 1967 by Chris Ballenden, an ex-infantry major. He answered a small ad in the *Daily Telegraph* and joined Peter Evans Eating Houses, then a well-known steak house chain. Ballenden, like Jack Bateman and the Sutcliffe pioneers

6

DELICIOUS DESSERTS
pastry with perfection

Baked Apple & Calvados Tarte

Guest Chef: Loic-Max Malfait
Sous Chef
Binder Hamlyn, London

Serves 10 (1x8" ring)

Sugar Pastry

125gr Flour
60gr Butter
60gr Caster Sugar
2 Egg Yolks

Almond Cream

250gr Ground Almonds
250gr Caster Sugar
250gr Butter
4 Eggs
65gr Flour

You will also need:

6 green apples 'Granny Smiths'
12cl Calvados
100gr Caster Sugar
Butter for frying

METHOD

For the pastry:

i.   Place butter, flour and sugar in a bowl, and rub together to a crumbly consistency.

ii. Separate egg yolks from whites, and add egg yolks to crumbly mixture and bind together.

iii. Cover bowl and leave aside to relax.

For the almond cream:

Mix together almonds, sugar, butter, and flour, then add your eggs one by one and proceed to mix well.

Then:

i.   Peel and core the apples and slice into fine wedges.

ii. Melt the butter and add in the apples and the caster sugar.

iii. Add the calvados and flame on gas hob. To flame, warm calvados and apples in pan then tilt slightly on heat, to catch light. Reserve the apples after the alcohol has burned off.

iv. Roll out pastry and line flan ring.

v.   Trim edges of flan ring, with a sharp pointed knife.

vi. Place the almond cream mixture onto pastry, and place the calvados apple slices onto the mixture, in a circular arrangement.

Bake in oven at 150°C for 30 minutes.

Melt a heaped tablespoon of apricot jam and glaze tarte to finish.

High Table promoted fine City dining. This apple flan recipe, which appeared in the company's magazine, got the message over in some style.

before him, had had no experience of catering. A change in career direction arose when a friend asked him if he knew of anyone who would be able to take over a suite of City dining rooms for directors' lunches. Of course Ballenden did. He was that person.

He launched High Table with one contract – for the International Paint Company – operating one dining room for 12 executives. He called it High Table after a suggestion from an ex-army chum who was working for J Walter Thompson, the advertising agency; his fee was a bottle of whisky.

Operated initially from a spare bedroom, with his newly married wife Morar as his only (unpaid) employee, and then from a small office above a hairdressing salon in Long Lane, London, High Table grew in spurts 'and a certain amount of luck', but its first major contract was the Hill Samuel Merchant Bank which grew to five sites. After three years Ballenden was joined by Julian Rowe, his former boss at Peter Evans who had since moved to Sutcliffe, and the business grew mainly by operating on a very personal level and under tight financial control. When a new contract became operational, both directors went in every day in the first three weeks to get to know the customers and the client. Even in 1979, when High Table was operating some 40 contracts, one of them visited each site at least once a week.

"A great deal of our work involves the interpretation of what the client needs rather than improving the catering system," Rowe said in an article in *Catering Times*.

Ballenden and Rowe complemented each other perfectly. Ballenden had a military bearing, manner and standards; he was always punctual and had a strong business etiquette. True to his army background, he believed in leading from the front. Rowe was a brilliant foil: a

Happy days at High Table: Julian Rowe, Chris Ballendon, Vicki Wilson (financial director), Chris Davies (director) and Tim West (managing director).

'The bigger you are, the better you are.'

In a service industry, being part of a massive group is no guarantee of efficiency or high quality management. We are growing by being better and more flexible than the big boys.

'If you must economise, there's always vending.'

Some catering companies look on vending as the poor relation. We see it as a genuine option for streamlining services and coping with shifts. And we take responsibility for machine maintenance.

A striking double page brochure promoted Brian Smith's unique qualities

Cambridge graduate with a fine palate and a gentle manner. He was very comfortable with the City folk he was dealing with and he had a strong eye for detail. It was Rowe who was able to ensure the business traded successfully through challenging times.

They were canny operators. Having worked in the restaurant business, they knew all the tricks of the trade. Their accounts system was smart with figures for the previous week produced by the following Tuesday and by 1987 High Table had grown to some 50 contracts with an annual turnover of £10m, catering for such companies as Midland Montagu, the Stock Exchange and Hill Samuel. It had become a caterer of choice in the City, gaining a solid reputation as a boutique operator not only for dining rooms but also staff restaurants.

It was a time when the City of London was expanding and there were plenty of new opportunities for an ambitious operator which is what attracted Tim West, who joined as operations director from Compass where he had been area manager for the City

of London and then regional manager for 100 high profile accounts.

High Table was certainly prepared to move with the times. In 1990, the company introduced TJ's, a specially designed delicatessen developed as a space-saving staff food facility, which offered over 2,000 lines. It was also among the first contractors to obtain Investor in People status. A year later, it caught the attention of Elior, at that time operating as Groupe Elitair, who recognised the potential acquisition as a good entry point into the UK market.

The approach was fortuitous. By then, the two were planning routes to retirement: Ballenden was in his late 50s with Rowe a little younger. After the purchase, Ballenden stayed on as chairman until 1996. A year later Tim West became managing director and the company set about expanding.

In 1994 it acquired Drummond Thompson, a small contract catering outfit with £2.5m of sales based around Manchester which had been launched by the ex-Compass director, David Thompson;

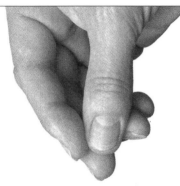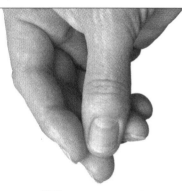

ging director
; available.'

anagement can be
lusive. Especially
1em most.
d Clive Smith are
essible. Ring 0533

'One of our managers
will make regular calls.'

Sadly, it's much easier to
make a promise than to keep it.
However, our 19 mobile executives
service 90 customers with a freq-
uency that makes them part of the
catering team.

'All our managers
are uniquely qualified.'

Starting from the bottom is
splendid but not all cooks make successful executives.
We have distilled an imagin-
ative blend of caterers and managers
with complementary skills.

'Of course we return
all discounts.'

Our clients are guaranteed
every penny of discount available
from the purchase of raw materials.
Our remuneration derives
solely from management fees which
are decided in advance.

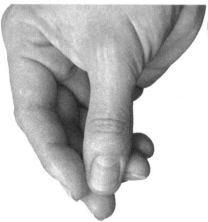

l handle all
g requirements.'

ning and Equipment
kes maximum use of
esources, seeing
to fruition in coop-
Area Management

'We take the responsibilities
off your shoulders.'

Whilst we recognise that
policy decisions will remain with
you, you can rest assured that the
day-to-day running of the oper–
ation will never impinge on your
time.

'Every client receives
a tailor-made service.'

Each of our clients has a
package prepared specifically for his
needs and his budget.
Not a hand-me-down prop-
osal where his requirements are
tailored to fit *our* ready-made plan.

'We look forward to many
years of working together.'

We have become the cat-
ering department for many clients
without seeking formal contracts,
preferring to be judged on current
service and our latest trading
account.

Brian and Clive Smith, father and son, ran the company for almost 30 years before selling to Elior: "The stock market was at its peak – Elior was keen to expand... and we were an excellent acquisition for them."

two years later, Hallmark Executive Catering, launched by John Symonds, a former Compass regional manager, joined the group with some 20 contracts, including Merrill Lynch.

By then, High Table's turnover had grown to £40m with 110 contracts spread beyond London and into some major cities such as Leeds, Manchester and Bristol. West was awarded Food Service Manager of the Year in the 1998 Catey awards and four years later, in 2000, sales for Elior in the UK (still operating as High Table) topped £60m.

Then came a flurry of activity. Elior already owned 20 per cent of Catering & Allied, based in the UK and Holland, and the remaining shares were acquired. Almost simultaneously Brian Smith Catering was purchased and a year later, in 2001, Nelson Hind was scooped up.

Brian Smith Catering

Born in 1925 in Stroud, Brian Smith left the Navy in 1945 as a junior officer and went up to St Catherine's, Cambridge to read history. His only association with food was his mother's health food shop.

An all-round sportsman, young Smith met John Sutcliffe at a social occasion. Smith fitted the bill perfectly because Sutcliffe was convinced that anyone out of the services and good at games would be a good leader. So, coming down from Cambridge at the age of 25, Smith was persuaded to join the fledgling company, Factory Canteens (West of England), based in Stroud, as a trainee manager.

John Sutcliffe's belief in his new young recruit was justified. Smith was almost a workaholic and quickly showed a talent for being an excellent salesman who got on well with people. In 1959, he was promoted to open a new office in Leicester to develop the business in the East Midlands. He

A unique way of working

Much of the success of Brian Smith Catering was due to the way the company operated. A high client-management ratio provided an impressive level of personal service. As a brochure at the time claimed: ' ... a ratio of highly experienced mobile executives to client accounts of 1:5 is generous, not to say unique.'

Another of Brian Smith's mantras was that all purchasing discounts were passed on to the client; in return, it charged a higher management fee. The same brochure claimed:

'We continue to receive our remuneration through management fees alone.

'We are not in the business of raking off commission on bulk food purchases. £5 million buying power attracts solid discounts but we regard them as part of our client service so they are returned to where they belong. To the clients themselves.

'Nowadays, you'll find our philosophy unique.'

It probably was. At the time most contractors were routinely making use of supplier discounts to boost revenues and although some clients were aware of the practice, many were not.

Clive Smith recalls: "Our clients accepted that but many of our competitors just didn't believe us. But it was true. In fact, we had very few written contracts; we just exchanged letters. In our view most contracts are invented by caterers to protect themselves. We didn't feel the need."

gained some significant contracts for Sutcliffe such as Jaguar and GEC (it was at GEC that he recruited a young Marc Verstringhe who was then working at the Lygon Arms Hotel, Broadway in the first stage of his UK career). Smith liked to be left alone to do his job, not suffering fools gladly, and under his leadership the Sutcliffe business prospered. In 1962, on the death of Billy Epsom, who was responsible for the West Midlands, Smith took over the whole of the Midlands area.

Change came 10 years later, in 1973, when Sutcliffe was sold to Jeffrey Sterling's Sterling Guarantee Trust (SGT). With edicts coming down from SGT's head office and a growing centralisation, Smith decided to call it a day. He gave in his notice, together with 10 of his senior colleagues, and launched Brian Smith Catering. It was a remarkable leap of faith.

The new company had some difficult early days. Even so, by 1977 it had consolidated its position, winning some significant new contracts in both the East and West Midlands. It was then that Brian's eldest son, Clive, born in 1955, joined the company. Clive went to the same college as his father at Cambridge, reading modern and medieval languages with the aim of becoming a teacher but found teaching too frustrating. A somewhat reluctant Clive was persuaded to join the business on the understanding that it would only be a two-year stint. On October 1st 1977, at the age of 22, he seriously wondered why he had agreed to join the company, having absolutely no experience of the industry and, thus far, little interest. His father was down-to-earth:

"I could send you off to be a chef, but I can hire a chef any day of the week," he told his son. "What I need is someone who can write fluent English, relate to people and be a salesman." He himself had a way with words and was a stickler for good writing and good grammar, which Clive had inherited.

Clive, with perhaps a tidier mind than his father, recognised the role he could play. Largely learning on the job, and attending some sales and other courses, he taught himself how best to win business for the young company. When his two years were up, he found he had fallen in love with the job – "so I stayed".

By 1984, Smith was turning his thoughts to retirement. He was 59 years old – Clive was 29 – and the company by then was operating some 40 contracts. But Smith had other interests. He was big in Rotary and was a local magistrate and it was clear that he wanted to take a back seat and looked to Clive to take over. Brian became chairman and largely left the business with very little subsequent interference; a few years later he contracted a particularly virulent strain of Parkinson's and died in 1992, aged only 66.

* * *

Under Clive's direction, the business became even more of a family firm. In 1982, his brother, Russell, had come on board. A theology graduate from Keble College, Oxford, Russell was one for living life to the full and was a keen skier but he was at a loss to know what to do on leaving university. A long-standing director of the company (and the brothers' uncle) was Beverley Griffin, general manager of the Savoy hotel, London. He arranged for Russell to spend a year at a hotel in Aix en Provence and on his return, Russell decided to join the family firm and worked his way through the ranks eventually taking frontline responsibility for sales and marketing; however, after marrying a Canadian girl and with a growing family (eventually of five children), he decided to emigrate to Canada. After 13 years with the two brothers in charge, Clive found himself in sole control.

The company, still Brian Smith Catering Services, continued to grow. Moving out of its East Midlands heartland, it won the catering contract at the new BBC White City headquarters and the Cadbury's factory at Bourneville as well as a large number of contracts with Japanese companies, with Clive picking up a smattering of Japanese on the way.

By 1999, the company – by now Brian Smith plc – had reached the crossroads. It was too small to be classed as a big company but too big to be regarded as a small company. With 142 contracts, employing 1,400 people and with a turnover of £28m, Clive saw a difficult future ahead as an independent. Besides, like his father, he wanted to spread his wings and move out of catering. Considering his options, he spent a year negotiating the company's sale to Elior, which was keen to add to its portfolio in the UK after the successful acquisition of High Table in 1991. He judged it the perfect time to sell.

"The stock market was at its peak – it didn't reach the same level again until 2014. We were at a sensitive point in the company's evolution. Elior was keen to buy and expand in the UK and we were an excellent acquisition for them. High Table was strong in the South East and London but we were strong in the Midlands."

Ironically, it was the first time he had used his languages since leaving university and they came in very useful. He stayed with Elior for two years, wanting to make sure the sale bedded in and everybody was treated fairly. At the same time, Elior used his expertise in a European role.

Clive now sits as a non-executive director on numerous boards of SMEs in various branches of the service industry and is also committed to leading two charities. Contract catering is now a memory – "but a very happy one."

Catering & Allied received a highly favourable review of the CDP staff restaurant in the Daily Express.

Marc Verstringhe: At the CDP advertising agency he wanted to get away from mass feeding to something more individual by introducing restaurant standards in staff canteens.

Catering & Allied

Having digested Brian Smith plc, Robert Zolade was keen not to let the grass grow under his feet. He wanted to expand further into the UK so that in size and scope it could rival Compass, Sodexo and Aramark.

Elior had already acquired a 20 per cent share in Catering & Allied in 1995 in an alliance which gave it greater exposure in the UK and Dutch markets; in 2000 Marc Verstringhe finally agreed that Elior should purchase the rest of the company.

Catering & Allied's history and philosophy is well presented in *Managing to Serve* by Sally Heavens and John Child, a case study published in 2002 which is based on the company's approach to management. Marc Verstringhe, its chief executive, formed the company in 1975 with two fellow directors from Sutcliffe, Jop Koops and Kit Cuthbert. He and Cuthbert took control of the UK end of the company while Koops began to win contracts in Holland, gaining seven within a year.

In the UK, the first client was an old people's home but this was followed by five sites for Costain and an outlet of Satchwell Controls, a GEC company. By the end of 1976, Catering & Allied was catering in 10 locations in each country, but it took them 18 months before they turned in a profit – bonuses of between £500-£1,000 were paid to staff for successful leads.

The three took with them the core value which they had subscribed to (indeed, helped create) when they worked at Sutcliffe: total commitment to client satisfaction. There were other values, too: making sure

Catering & Allied held regular meetings of senior UK and European staff.

that employees worked with, not for the company; a desire to be the best in the marketplace; a wish to pay attention to detail; and wanting to have fun.

Verstringhe had no wish to become a contracting giant. In his words, he wanted "to continue to grow whilst staying small" and Catering & Allied built up its reputation as a niche player in high quality staff catering. He also wanted to maintain close contact with clients and customers within a 35 mile radius of head office. The one time when this was extended beyond – into the Chilterns – ultimately turned out

not to be successful with Nigel Anker, its managing director, feeling that the Chiltern company "was not going anywhere" – a view with which the company finally concurred in 1995.

One reason for Catering & Allied's success was its high rate of productivity, calculated by dividing its sales turnover by the number of its employees. In *Managing to Serve*, Catering & Allied comes out top of a list of nine companies with an average productivity per employee in 1998 of £34,391, with Sutcliffe at £30,711, Compass at £25,154 and Sodexo (Gardner Merchant) at £18,290.

Impressive though this is, much depends on how the number of employees is calculated, whether full-time or part-time staff are included and how casual staff are treated. Nevertheless, the company's committed practice of keeping head office small and outsourcing key management functions was fundamental to its success. It led to significant cost savings in the finance, PR and marketing, IT and HR areas. Catering & Allied had a lean head office and it was a lean company.

At the outset, Verstringhe and his team asked themselves the same question that every other entrepreneur who sets out to form his own company asks: What's different about us? What's our USP? Why would a client come to us and not to an established player?

"What we did was to go back to base: to be restaurateurs first and foremost rather than administrators running a large group of canteens," says Verstringhe. "The objective was to provide a service tailored to fit each of our clients' individual requirements... we set out to ensure not only that we got the details right but that we make the whole sparkle... our aim was to grow while retaining the best qualities of a small company."

Catering & Allied had no company uniform – "We always remember we are working in someone else's property," said Verstringhe in an article in *Industrial Caterer*. He was an early protagonist for healthy eating and introduced link manning – another name for multi-tasking – which encouraged staff to turn their hand to a variety of different jobs thus giving them a more interesting work experience as well as leading to reduced costs.

An early contract in 1978 with Collett Dickinson and Pearce (CDP), the advertising agency, set the standard for the company's approach. CDP had designed its own bistro-style staff restaurant which demanded a creative and attractive menu rather than the more prevalent concept of industrial feeding that was then in style. Verstringhe was enthusiastic: he wanted to get away from mass feeding to something more individual by introducing restaurant standards in staff canteens. This proved so successful that, seven years later, the *Daily Express* ran an article on a lunch at the CDP bistro that enabled the writer to argue against a report that had been published on the previous day, by the London Food Commission. The Commission was founded by Tim Lang, professor of food policy at London City University, and the report was highly critical, among other issues, of the standard of industrial catering then prevailing.

No doubt there were quite a few other contracts, particularly in the City of London, that the *Express* could have visited which showed off contract catering at its equally mouth-watering best. In many of them, money was no object. But CDP was a run-of-the-mill B&I contract, well designed but seven years old, that was still providing quality food at a modest cost to its staff. Catering & Allied was fortunate to have been publicly identified with it.

It was also a company willing to learn. When it took over some of the catering for management sites at Ford, which were quality not cost-driven, it found itself on a learning curve. An initial decision not to serve egg and chips and baked beans as a choice from the grill bar had to be overturned in the face of customer resistance; if the customers wanted it, they had to have it. Verstringhe and his colleagues reasoned that it wasn't detracting from the quality of the food being offered but rather it was offering a wider choice.

Education and training soon became a dominating preoccupation.

"It should be a continuous learning craft – hotel school, management, MBA – and then people should keep developing," he said in an article in *Caterer*. He went on the Harvard Advanced Management Program (as did Don Davenport, later) but they were the exceptions at the time; financial and management development in the hospitality industry was not well advanced.

His efforts paid off. In 1978, two years after Catering & Allied was launched, profit before tax was £37,341; this rose to £65,363 by 1982 (over £200,000 today). From then on it went north with some hiccups on the way (a bad debt in 1994 when a client went into liquidation), so that by 1996 and 1997 it had reached £100,000 each year. Some initial finance from the Halshaw Group – a Ford dealership in the north of England, arranged through a director, Frank Thomas who was a friend of Verstringhe's (see Chapter 19) – was paid off within two years. Even more pertinent for the three founding directors and to the Halshaw investment was the 1,600-fold return in 1999 on their initial £20,000 combined founding investment. With 215 contracts and a total turnover in 1995 of £50m, Catering & Allied was profitable and growing.

* * *

During this time, Verstringhe and his colleagues had had numerous takeover offers but by 1995, after 20 years at the helm, all three of the founding investors were thinking of the future; Kit Cuthbert, in particular, being the oldest at 64, was keen to get out. With all the money locked into the company it was necessary to put some equity into it in order to get money out. Verstringhe didn't want to see his creation disappear and was determined to ensure that his management philosophy continued in a new regime. Along the way, he had noticed the way that High Table had been able to continue under its own steam for the last five years after being acquired by Elior and he reckoned that a similar 'alliance' would be the only way that Catering & Allied could ensure the continuity of its culture and core values.

Discussions continued for months before it was agreed to set up a separate holding company, Eurocater, with Verstringhe and Roland Zolande, now Elior's chairman, as joint chairmen of the company. The alliance was designed so that over the course of the following five years it would take a controlling interest in Catering & Allied. The deal meant that Elior injected £1.9m into Catering & Allied which, as the shares became available, gave Eurocater a 25 per cent stake in the company; following further capital injections by Elior this grew to a majority holding in 2000. By the end of the deal, Verstringe had sold the company for 32 times net earnings.

The deal may have been influenced by Elior's impending float on the Paris Stock Exchange. It also wanted to beef up its presence in the UK to be able to compete with its main French rivals – Sodexo (which had, by then, formed its alliance with Gardner Merchant) and Eurest (which had been acquired by Compass).

Verstringhe believed that his 'partenariat' (as he called it) with Elior would last and, indeed, it did until 2000. But by then Verstringhe was not a full-time employee and other board directors, Kit Cuthbert, Jop Koops, Keith Moore and Bob Foster had already retired; Kit Cuthbert died in 2000. Though he remained as co-chairman of Eurocater until the end of 2004, Verstringhe was offered the post of co-president international with Zolade but decided to seek pastures new, now a wealthy man. With Mair Davison (his PA), Verstringhe established the MESV Consultancy and Trust as a voluntary organisation with the aim of bringing education and business closer together.

* * *

Elior had been operating in the UK as Avenance – French for something that is forward looking, courteous or progressive. At the time, Tim West, the chief executive, told staff that the companies hadn't merged, there had been a convergence, a clever way to explain the new arrangement. Indeed, the Avenance name stayed for 10 more years. But, as with Gardner Merchant's alliance with Sodexo, Catering & Allied's alliance

with Elior led to the loss of the company's name. The French word alliance means union or marriage in English, but that's misleading. It is inevitable that one side will gain ultimate control.

Nelson Hind

Two more companies joined the Avenance stable. The first was Nelson Hind. Tim West had been talking to Chris Hind and Andrew Nelson for more than five years about a possible purchase of their company before the £30m deal was finally agreed in 2000.

Chris Hind, a Scouser born and bred, gained his MHCIMA at Liverpool College in 1956; he couldn't afford to go to Hollings College, Manchester. His father died when he was nine which meant he quickly learnt how to look after himself. The tragedy

gave him a certain lifelong chippiness and aggression. He was his own man. After college he spent a few weeks in the kitchens of a hotel in Val d'Isere ("They hated me and I hated them") before coming back to Britain and talked his way into a job with Owen Owen, Liverpool's biggest department store group.

For the next 18 months he moved from store to store as relief chef manager ending up in Liverpool running the chain's largest restaurant. A spell with British Home Stores under the legendary Ralph Coombes followed but, when Coombes quit, Hind went at the same time. In 1971 he joined Gardner Merchant, working as a district manager for Garry Hawkes who was then regional operations manager for the North West under Sterling Gallacher, the regional director. Hawkes impressed him:

On the way Andrew Nelson and Chris Hind won a string of national and regional awards, including the Birmingham Post's Best Business in the West Midlands award – here with Prince Philip.

"Garry was an ideas man. He always had great ideas. He was a free thinker. He thought on his feet, very agile. But he was never a details man."

He admits that Hawkes taught him 'an awful lot.'

"He was a great leader – charismatic."

He also recognised that they both had similar forceful personalities, unafraid of telling it like it is, and liable to clash.

"I once told Garry that his only problem was that he thought he was omnipotent – that he was always right. I guess he might have thought that of me. I remember Garry and Sterling having fierce arguments. We could hear them at it hammer and tongs in the office through the thin office walls. Sterling's Scottish upbringing made him far more cautious and averse to taking risks; Garry was all for risk-taking, and so was I."

Hind was promoted from operations into sales despite being told by the company psychologist that he was far too truculent and bellicose to be a successful salesman – a judgment that the medico might have wanted to revise in the light of Hind's subsequent career. He went back into operations and became responsible for much of the Smallman catering contracts which Gardner Merchant had recently acquired, including BMOC, the catalogue company, and reported to Hawkes, now regional director.

But there was not enough risk-taking. "I was very, very ambitious and I wanted the opportunity to get back into retail catering and run something with some risk," he says.

In 1976 he moved over to THF's leisure division (Trust Houses, with Gardner Merchant, had merged with Forte in 1970) and spent over two years as general manager of the Belle Vue entertainment complex in Manchester under Sir Leslie Joseph. Belle Vue, originally a Forte business, had come into THF after the merger. It was "a

fantastic experience" but his ambition was greater than his ability to solve all Belle Vue's problems.

"It was terribly under-invested and it had been very badly managed when I arrived. It was losing money. The mistake I made was that I thought I could solve all the problems there. I couldn't. Nobody could. I turned a thumping loss into a very modest profit but I eventually told Sir Leslie Joseph that I couldn't do any more. He suggested I went to run the pier at Blackpool but that didn't interest me."

He went back into contract catering joining Sutcliffe in 1979 as operations director for the West Midlands. He was astonished at the way the company was run.

"It was soft – it just wasn't commercial. It was over-managed but it was wildly under-performing. It just hadn't moved with the times. And God, could they drink! It would never happen now but it seemed par for the course then. With hindsight, Gardner Merchant was a far more professional outfit. It took Sterling Gallacher a long time to turn Sutcliffe round after he took it over in 1979 as managing director. I was surprised how long it did take but there's no doubt he changed it for the better and it certainly needed to become professional. He brought much more discipline to the company, clearer reporting, better cost control, and, ultimately, much better profits."

In 11 years at Sutcliffe, he moved from the Midlands up to Scotland, where he was managing director, and then back to Midlands in 1986 when Gordon Wishart, the regional director, quit. In the meantime, he had attended a "very, very intense" senior management course at Templeton College, Oxford, which he thought was mainly theory "and I'm a very practical person", but it gave him useful contacts outside the industry. By 1989 he was running the north of England and was assistant managing director – "a

non-job" – and was clearly heading for the top when he decided enough was enough.

* * *

The urge to take a risk and start up on his own was overwhelming. He took with him Andrew Nelson, his operations director in the East Midlands, whose career Hind had mentored and developed. Gallacher was incandescent when told he was leaving – an indication, perhaps, of Hind's perceived value to the company.

"Sterling went absolutely berserk," Hind says. "He used every expletive under the sun." A profile of Gallacher in *Caterer* in 1987 has him admitting to a short fuse 'and getting a bit uptight at times.' Gallacher's fury had subsided by the end of the week when he had the grace to apologise but Hind was obdurate. He was going to leave. He had seen other start-ups succeed – why not Nelson Hind? Nevertheless, Sutcliffe slapped a covenant on him preventing him from approaching clients, though this was ineffective. The problem that big companies face when senior executives break away is that client loyalty is often to the executive they deal with rather than to the catering company itself. Both Hind and Nelson knew too many of the clients personally to avoid being approached by them once they heard the news of the breakaway, even if they themselves avoided approaching the clients.

In Sutcliffe's case the drain of clients was significant, made worse by a seeming lack of awareness on its part of the dangers this posed. Little effort was made to secure the most vulnerable contracts against the breakaway company's depredations.

Nelson Hind offered what every other start-up offers: personal service, quality food from local producers and tight cost control. Hind ran the operations while Nelson looked after the sales. "My fear was not having enough to do. Instead, the phone never stopped ringing," Hind says.

A £60,000 consultancy with Rolls Royce set them up; a similar arrangement with Nottingham Trent University, wrested from Sutcliffe, further established their credentials. In the first year, they won 10 contracts. Others flowed in and by 1995, when they won their biggest deal (a three-year £1m a year contract to provide the catering at the Felixstowe Dock and Railway Company – another win from Sutcliffe) they had over 90 contracts. On the way they won a string of national and regional awards, including Best Business in the West Midlands. A year later, they turned in a £500,000 profit and were predicting a £30m turnover by 1998. By 2000, turnover had reached £60m, with 2,200 employees, 300 contracts and over £3m profit.

Husband and wife Andrew Wilson and Caroline Vale (later to start up their own company Wilson Vale) were appointed directors to strengthen the team and others were promoted. Hind, now executive chairman (Nelson was managing director) took pleasure in helping out at outlets when he found them short-staffed on visits. "It's amazing how word about this gets around and helps people identify with the company," he says.

It was a period of almost intoxicating growth which attracted the attention of plenty would-be purchasers including Granada (which was then buying up as many independents as it could – see Chapter 25), Aramark, Gardner Merchant and Elior.

When they set up, Chris Hind had a firm objective:"We set ourselves a 10-year target – 10 years and then we would be out. We agreed we'd work like stink and then quit. I didn't want to go on and on. I wanted to build up the company to something decent and then sell it on. Ten years was the target. And we kept to it."

In 1997, a plan to float Nelson Hind on the AIM market by 2000 was publicly announced in a planned attempt to unlock the value of the company to benefit the two founders. The AIM floatation was promoted as the likely scenario but it was also interpreted by others as an indication that the company would shortly be in play and moving out of the hands of the founders. However, Hind told *Caterer:* "I didn't give up my very well paid job and take all the risks of a new company to sell in seven years." The AIM objective lay on the table while rumours began to swirl around the company. Would it float or would it be sold on?

By 2000, true to the original 10-year objective, negotiations were already in place. In fact, Tim West, a personal friend and now running Elior, had been informally discussing a merger with the two founders for a number of years – "It's a regret that we were never able to work with Tim in a business," says Hind.

By then, Nelson Hind was the largest UK independent. It was also highly profitable, had an enviable cash flow and was known as a quality player. As Clive Smith had recognised, in 2000 the stock market was

at a high and business was good but both partners agreed, so eager were the potential buyers, that any trade sale would yield more than launching on the AIM market with all the attendant costs, difficulties and uncertainties. Alastair Storey had already approached the partners with a view to it being the basis of his new company which he was about to launch on quitting Sutcliffe but Chris Hind told him he was wasting his time – adding "you can't afford us".

Hind, who prides himself on being a good negotiator, had also brushed off Granada and Gardner Merchant, but Aramark and Elior were still in play, keen to buy and at a price.

Both partners had already flown over to Philadelphia to talk to Aramark's head office and Chris Hind's discussions with Tim West had been ongoing when he denied in *Caterer* that any talks were underway. "It's news to me. We get these rumours every two or three months," he was quoted as saying, while West said, possibly more accurately: "These rumours have been going round for a while but Nelson Hind has remained doggedly independent both publicly and privately." This was certainly true but neither confirmed nor denied his interest in the

Digby Trout with Marc Verstringhe and John Houston, then managing director of Catering & Allied.

Digby Trout: "Nothing should ever go out to the customer without being tasted."

purchase.

Three months later the deal with Elior was signed and sealed. It had been a Dutch auction. Hind, proving his reputation, had negotiated a £1m increase on Aramark's 'final' offer. Notwithstanding his friendship with West, he was prepared to let it go to the Americans but Elior, keen to win, agreed to cap the Aramark offer.

Ever cautious, on hearing of Elior's enhanced offer, Aramark walked away and Elior won for a reputed £30m-plus, bringing in some big business from outside London including the Rolls Royce head office, NCR, as well as notable independent schools including Charterhouse and Rugby. The deal also gave Elior a foothold in Scotland where Nelson Hind had 25 contracts.

With the proceeds, Andrew Nelson bought a farm near Rutland Water while Chris Hind bought a fine Victorian country house in 17 acres of land on the Staffordshire/Worcestershire border, which he has elegantly extended and improved, as well as buying a number of revenue-earning properties including two office blocks and 11 private houses.

It's all a very long way from his early beginnings in Liverpool.

Justin de Blank / Digby Trout Restaurants

In 1987, Catering & Allied had formed a joint venture with Justin de Blank, an architect turned caterer, who operated a shop in Elizabeth Street selling fine foods and special breads; in addition, he provided the catering at the National Gallery where the standard of food was widely recognised for its quality.

Catering & Allied had already been buying provisions from de Blank's shop and the opportunity arose for a joint tender to cater for the British Museum, a much bigger contract, providing over 1,000 staff meals a day together with the public catering. The contract was a good fit.

De Blank's experience of public catering and Catering & Allied's experience of staff catering were complementary; Verstringhe had also visited the Museum of Modern Art in New York and had been mightily impressed by the quality and scope of the catering there and saw an opportunity to expand his interests in museum and public catering. The opportunity was too good to miss.

He formed a joint company with de Blank, which traded as de Blank Restaurants. Digby Trout, after spending 10 years at Forte and only 34-years-old, was initially appointed as general manager and subsequently managing director.

The venture was a big success, winning contracts at the Science Museum, the Tower of London and the Ashmolean in Oxford. Trout was reputed to be the first man to bring hot food for visitors into museums and similar sites where previously only tea and buns had been available but this was untrue: de Blank had been there before and had paved the way.

The business developed successfully when, in 1992, de Blank proposed to buy out the 50 per cent of the business that was held by Catering & Allied. This was refused but a counterbid by Catering & Allied led to the retirement of Justin de Blank and the appointment of Verstringhe as chairman, a position which he held until 2000, with Robyn Lines (a founder member) and Mike Gilpin as directors.

However, Catering & Allied was reluctant to run de Blank Restaurants because of its

Tim West, chief executive, told staff that the companies hadn't merged, there had been a convergence – a clever way to explain the new arrangement – though only the Lexington brand remains in use today.

Catherine Roe, Elior's chief executive.

niche market success and it did not want to stretch its managerial capacity nor dilute its competitive advantage.

Verstringhe felt that a management buy-out of 80 per cent would enhance its expertise and know-how and add value to both companies. So Trout secured a management buy-in, renaming the company Digby Trout Restaurants, with Trout having 80 per cent of the company and Catering & Allied 20 per cent. Trout was given three years to spread the payments and he successfully shared back office services with Catering & Allied.

Over the next 10 years, Digby Trout traded successfully with turnover reaching £14m by 2002, the year that Elior, through Avenance, emerged as a suitor.

By the time of the acquisition, it was operating well over a dozen major public contracts in London (its catering at Heal's earned it the first store restaurant in the Michelin Guide) and as far afield as the RSC in Stratford. It prided itself on cooking nearly all its products, except bread, on site. It was particularly renowned for its Digby Trout cake displays.

Trout, who was a caterer to his fingertips and was never happier than when behind the counter – "nothing should ever go out to the customer without being tasted" – died in 2012 aged 59 and is much missed.

"Picking is good news," he once said. "It should be very difficult to walk through one of our kitchens without being tempted to pick."

* * *

The acquisitions brought Elior's UK turnover to over £175m, making it the country's fourth largest contractor.

In 2005, Tim West was chairman of the UK operations, at which time, after 18 years, he was looking for something new. He quit to join Lexington Catering, which had been established in 2002 by Mike Sunley, Katharine Lewis and Rachel Lindner, all ex-High Table colleagues.

Lexington prospered to such an extent that the wheel turned full circle in 2014 when Elior acquired the company, now with a turnover of £37m and holding contracts across London and the South East of England, including law firms, hedge funds and creative agencies. Sunley remained as managing director of Lexington and Tim West remained as director and non-executive chairman of Elior UK.

Elior, under West as chairman and Catherine Roe as chief executive, is currently the fourth largest contractor in the UK.

CHAPTER TWENTY-THREE

Facing up to change

Ken Graveney took over as managing director of Sutcliffe in 1975. It was a time of increasing change and growing professionalism.

"Ken Graveney was the nicest boss you could ever have had," says Peter Davies. "Think Biggles. He was utterly charming. He wasn't an intellectual but he was shrewd and street-wise. He was a very good judge of people – a great leader. He absolutely knew how to get the best out of his team."

Chris Page, who was in charge of the West Country company, agrees: "If Ken asked you to step off the end of the world, you would have gladly done it. He was an extraordinary leader."

Graveney had other attributes which made him popular and able. He was, in the words of one contemporary, 'a consummate decision-maker.' He would take his time, consulting widely before coming to a conclusion. As a result, most people bought into the decision.

"He exuded reasonableness and fair play. He was a consensus leader but nevertheless got his own way without apparently angering anyone – a remarkable feat."

David 'Bugsy' Barnes, who became director of environmental services working with Graveney for many years, and who frequently played golf with him, says that he was "superb – a man's man".

"He had a massive personality and everyone respected him. He would often visit a catering unit unannounced and talk to the management, the catering staff and customers."

One of Graveney's first acts on his appointment as managing director was to recruit Simon Davis from Gardner Merchant as Sutcliffe's marketing and sales director. The need for some marketing input had been evident for some time, which Graveney had recognised.

When Jane Baker joined in 1974 – the year before Graveney had taken over from Mickie O'Brien – she had, with all the enthusiasm of a new recruit, introduced a new Sutcliffe corporate identity programme including a new logo, new print and new stationery. She had been given a budget of £1,500 for the project – quite a sizeable sum then for something that few regional directors were convinced was necessary. So it proved.

"We produced some very good ideas, with the folded serviette as the new logo. I think it was the first attempt to unite all the separate regions into one national company and I thought everyone would love the idea. But all I got from the Barons was polite but determined opposition!"

The Barons – the regional managing directors – wanted to do their own thing and were reluctant to accept a national identity. The only proposal that survived was the logo and the Sutcliffe's green corporate colour. In the same way, the Barons gave little credence to the work of Brian Williams as group sales director.

The only surviving proposal was the logo and Sutcliffe's green corporate colour

* * *

Simon Davis joined Sutcliffe a couple of years later, in 1978, and his arrival helped to move Sutcliffe into a far more professional era. He had been a shooting star at Gardner Merchant for 13 years, joining in 1964 after his national service as a second lieutenant, among other duties, catering for 600 officers and men of the Royal West African Frontier Force in Sierra Leone. On demob he joined J. Lyons and worked in Lyons Corner Houses, Lyons Steak Houses and other outlets. It was quite a culture shock.

"I started in the *plonge* – the lowest of the low. A few weeks earlier in the army I was walking around and everyone was saluting me."

He learned the trade, from wash up to restaurant service, getting the kind of grounding for which Lyons had become famous. But he was restless. A couple of years later, in 1964, he phoned John Gardner and spoke to a director, Douggie Logan, saying he wanted to "join the best catering company in Europe". Notwithstanding the fact that he was already working for the country's best known catering company, and despite the fact that he hadn't heard of John Gardner before and didn't know anything about catering in Europe, his confident spiel got him a job. Davis, throughout his career, was never short of confidence.

He ran a few canteens before he moved into sales ("They didn't know anything about marketing then"), where Ron Kirby, a 6ft 6in giant, was sales director. Bowler-hatted and with a neat moustache – "All salesmen then wore bowler hats, a smart suit and a cane," – Kirby was a living legend. His family came from Scarborough hotel stock and he was a caterer to his fingertips.

On his initial interview he didn't ask Davis if he could sell – "he just wanted to know how good a caterer I was". But he gave his staff and his clients immense confidence and Davis found him kind and generous, though not without some temperamental outbursts.

"Once, I submitted a proposal to him for checking and he got more and more agitated and eventually shouted 'Rubbish!' He opened the window, put the proposal on the end of his gold-topped cane and shoved it through the window. The pages just fluttered away. What a man!"

Kirby sent Davis to open a sales office in Bristol. With him went his wife Pat, a manual typewriter, some carbon paper and nothing else. He and Pat drove around South Wales and the West Country listing offices and factories and cold calling clients to win contracts. It was the way it was done then though much the same technique was employed when William Baxter and Alastair Storey (and others) started up 30 years later.

* * *

Davis climbed the Gardner Merchant sales ladder enjoying every minute of it and by 1973 was sales director. One of his initiatives was to involve a high flying industrial psychologist from the London Business School to assist in sales training. But he had already been noticed by Ken Graveney and Peter Davies, Sutcliffe's personnel director, and had been approached a couple of times to jump ship. He was hesitant. Why leave a job you love? It took a further three years before he succumbed in 1980 and finally accepted. He's still puzzled why. Graveney had certainly been persistent: "We're in a mess," he had pleaded. "Come and sort it out. And name your salary."

"I was happy at Gardner Merchant," says

Davis. "I had a good job, good money. I suppose it was a new challenge."

What he found was not what he had expected. "I couldn't believe it. If I had known, I probably wouldn't have moved."

Instead of a head office controlling the company there were eight regional companies, each with its own structure, working more or less independently still without much communication with each other. There was very little sales activity. The company was run by a main board on which sat the managing director of each of the divisional boards headed by Graveney. Davis was given a place on the service board which comprised Peter Davies, Brian Appleton (managing director of the Sutcliffe London company) and Barbara Drew, the company secretary. To his amazement, he initially reported to the finance director, Andrew Brown, though Brown was actually the *de facto* group assistant managing director and had been placed there by Jeffrey Sterling to look after SGT's interests in Sutcliffe.

The regional companies, used to going their own way, weren't keen on co-operating with the new recruit in the same way that Jane Baker had earlier found when she tried to introduce a new corporate identity.

Davis spent his first year working out a strategy and completing a plan of campaign, trying to encourage the companies to recognise that there was more to sales than knocking on doors, sending out letters and expecting clients to turn up at the doorstep. What made clients tick? Why did they contract out their catering? What were they expecting? Who made the key decisions? There was, he was anxious to tell them, much more to influencing people than met the eye.

In effect, Sutcliffe had to embrace the basic principles of marketing – understanding what the client wants and then knowing how best to provide it. Davis was invited to join the Institute of Marketing and the Institute of Public Relations and was made a Liveryman of the Worshipful Company of Marketors as well as a Freeman of the City. He had the idea of engaging Ashridge Management College to undertake some quantitative and attitudinal research towards contract catering in over 60 client companies in order to identify their views on catering policies within their organisation.

In 1981, just when GrandMet was bringing Bateman Catering and Midland together as Grandmet Catering Services, Davis was instrumental in launching *Food for Work*, an 86-page book written by Robert Heller, one of the most respected business journalists of his day and editor of *Management Today*, then a must-read

Food for Work put forward the traditional arguments for providing a staff catering facility and its tone and content were persuasive. It was reprinted in 1986, the same year that Stories Out of School was published, aimed at boosting Fairfield's school catering contracts.

magazine aimed at top managers in Britain's major companies. It was one of the most successful magazines of its day and having Heller's *imprimateur* on the publication was nothing short of a coup; it guaranteed that directors and senior managers who were sent it would read it.

The launch took place in the House of Commons hosted by Charles Irving MP, chairman of the House of Commons Catering Committee, and was followed by full page advertisements in major Sunday papers, the first contract catering company to advertise in them. A year later in 1982, Sutcliffe won the Institute of Marketing's Marketing Award, the only catering company to have won. It was pioneering stuff.

Food for Work put forward the traditional arguments for providing a staff catering facility – namely, that 'a well fed worker works well and paternalism in this area is clearly profitable as well as humane' and its tone and content were persuasive. It was reprinted in 1986, the same year that *Stories out of School* was published, aimed at boosting Fairfield's school catering contracts. This was sent to all Sutcliffe's private school clients and to headmasters and bursars of potential clients.

With a more light-hearted approach than *Food for Work,* with a foreword by Princess Anne and published in aid of Save the Children, *Stories out of School* was a collection of 500 humorous stories by celebrities, including Margaret Thatcher, about schools and their inhabitants. It steered 'a path between the unprintable and the banal', according to the dust jacket and was a vastly entertaining read deserving wider circulation.

Another project developed at this time was *Kitchens by Design* with a foreword by Owen Luder, president of the Royal Institute of British Architects. This well illustrated

booklet identified the importance of well designed kitchens and canteens.

There were other productions. *Design for Catering* was a booklet aimed at changing attitudes towards planning and designing catering facilities, which was produced in conjunction with *Building* magazine. *A Question of Balance,* on the same theme, was produced in association with Colbrook Equipment, Hobart and Moorwood Vulcan.

These publications sold the story of contract catering with the deliberate aim of raising its status as an industry, not just

With a more light-hearted approach than Food for Work, and published in aid of Save the Children, Stories Out of School was a collection of 500 humorous stories by celebrities about schools and their inhabitants. It steered 'a path between the unprintable and the banal'.

Sutcliffe's business. They also aimed to persuade managers and directors that staff catering made a valuable contribution to improving employee relations.

The books hardly mentioned Sutcliffe (to prove their independence, one even quoted Bateman) but as giveaways they had a wide business audience and they certainly helped to raise Sutcliffe's profile in the boardroom and elsewhere, though their impact is hard to measure in terms of contracts gained. At the time, there is no doubt that they helped to change the rather dowdy image that contract catering had acquired. They also helped to push decisions to employ a contractor into the boardroom where previously they had been the responsibility of more junior managers. It showed that catering was not at the bottom of the pile when it came to understanding its relevance in raising worker productivity and improving worker relations. The main message: Sutcliffe, and contract catering, had to be taken seriously.

Davis' efforts acknowledged the fact that, for many companies, catering was a nuisance that they had to bear and try to offload. It was something that Gerry Robinson recognised later:

"For most people, catering is a pain in the backside," Robinson says in his biography. "They just want to give it to someone else to do. Contract catering's great attraction is its quietness. You can just get on with making money in a field no-one really looks at and in a business where both the client and the caterer benefit. They save money and we make it by catering more efficiently."

Davis recognised that bringing in a contractor was more abrogation than a delegation of responsibility; clients who knew nothing about catering were relieved to find that the contractor could organise everything without much, if any, input from them. All the client had to do was to write

the cheque at the end of every month.

In this sense it would be true to say that contracting grew as much by management giving up its responsibility for its workforce and handing it over to the contractor, as through any positive belief on the part of employers in the value of providing a catering service for its employees.

Ken Graveney wrote on Simon Davis' personal copy of *Food for Work*: 'From conception to fruition with my personal thanks'. Stirling Gallacher, who had succeeded Graveney as managing director in 1979, wrote: 'Brilliant – Brilliant. Thank you. Stirling'. Robert Heller opined 'To Simon for tenacity. Bob'.

When asked by Tony Dimambro, Sutcliffe's director of vending, to promote a groundbreaking new microchip credit vending machine with a special key to load money, Davis bought 10,000 crackers from the Tom Smith Cracker company and had them sent with a key to the secretary of every managing director throughout the

country on Valentine's Day with the words 'Your key to the vending machine'. The crackers were in Sutcliffe colours – "Pure theatre," Davis recalls.

"Simon was way ahead of his time," says Jane Baker, who eventually moved over to work for him in the marketing department, organising the PR for the company and the Sutcliffe in-house publications. "He had so many advanced ideas and was so clear on what we needed to do. He recruited Dr Juliet Gray as nutrition consultant and that was a very far-sighted move. At the time he recognised that nutrition was going to be increasingly important. She brought a very important ingredient to the company and she was brilliant with the media. Simon was good at getting the right people.

"I remember Simon arguing that hospital foyers would be good for us to install catering outlets, long before they became a fact. And he also advised us to do the same with the Royal Festival Hall. Look at it now – you can't move for lattes and paninis!

Ken Graveney, and Simon Davis collect the Institute of Marketing's award, presented by David Steel MP (later Lord Steel).

Nutrition rises up the agenda

Simon Davis was forever thinking outside the box. One day he heard Dr Juliet Gray, a consultant nutritionist who was then science director of the British Nutrition Foundation and a regular broadcaster, talk on the Radio 4 *Today* programme. It gave him an idea.

Nutrition had become an area of key public interest, not just in schools; it was becoming increasingly important in catering, too, but Sutcliffe had no expert in the field. Would it not be valuable, from both the PR and operational point of view, if the company could be seen to be *au fait* with the issues involved?

"I always felt that the task of sales and marketing director was to find interesting ways of relating to existing and potential clients," he says, "and I felt that nutritional advice would be useful to our clients and would fit well with our publications."

Dr Gray was quickly appointed as nutrition consultant, particularly in relation to Sutcliffe's new Merton School catering contract and then to the company's school catering arm, Fairfield Catering. It was an unusual appointment for a marketing director but one that showed that Davis was well aware of PR and a need for an expert on hand, even if his operational colleagues were less than enthusiastic.

He recognised the way contracting was going. Clients had to be convinced that contractors could not only provide good, well prepared and tasty food but the food also had to be healthy and nutritious. The role of nutrition and dietetics in industrial feeding had hardly moved on since the war years when the government had been so concerned about the health of the nation and had been encouraged by Magnus Pyke and Jack Drummond to ensure that the food provided by those producing meals for workers was not only appetising but nutritious. Cabbage, with all the vitamin C boiled out, had become a definite no-no but

Dr Juliet Gray was appointed as nutritionist consultant to Sutcliffe.

not every caterer took notice and in some contracts not a lot had changed since the war years. Nutrition was not top of the list of priorities facing caterers in the 1970s and 1980s.

However, as soon as contractors began to win hospital and schools contracts, greater pressure was exerted on them to understand the role that it played and this eventually spilled over into B&I contracts where clients and customers were beginning to demand healthier menus.

Noticeably, Gardner Merchant also took nutrition seriously, with nutritionists based in Kenley. John Forte developed the microbiology laboratory at Kenley which provided services to the whole group and which dealt with everything from foreign bodies to swab testing. A large EHO team under Forte and then John Dyson regularly inspected GM outlets – very rapidly in the event of any suspected 'incident'.

Gray's appointment was at the beginning of a healthy eating campaign which lasts to this day and which had its most public and most successful manifestation in Jamie Oliver's television series on school meals, in which the Turkey Twizzler played such a notorious part.

From the catering point of view, perhaps the more alarming revelation of the programmes was the very poor skill sets of those involved in preparing school meals. The Turkey Twizzler was a manifestation of this skills shortage, the government's decision, under Margaret Thatcher, to remove statutory nutrition standards from the 1980 Education Act, in most observer's eyes, completed the undermining of the school meals service which began under her watch as secretary of state for education.

Children could have chips with everything every day if they wanted, and they did. Such a lack of interest and reduced funding for school meals led to less training in the sector as well as an ever-more rigid control of food costs – hence the use of cheap, processed foods like the notorious twizzlers

In Sutcliffe's case, Gray's appointment acknowledged the fact that school meals represented a key target market. Winning the Merton school meals contract and the acquisition of Fairfield Catering in 1986, a large school meals-based company operating out of Croydon, paved the way. Having a qualified nutritionist on board (if, in reality, for only a day or two a month) told clients that the company was serious about the health of its customers, particularly school children.

Other companies took the same view. Gardner Merchant already had nutritionists operating out of its Kenley head office and specialist school meals providers such as Harrison Catering, The Brookwood Partnership and Bartlett Mitchell have since made great play of their nutritional credentials. More recently, companies, such as BaxterStorey and CH&Co, have hired nutritionists, some on a full-time basis.

At the time when she was appointed as non-executive director of Sutcliffe, Gray's position was publicly deemed to be highly important and her frequent appearances in the media as a well-regarded and trusted commentator on a wide range of nutrition issues, helped to prove the point that Sutcliffe took nutrition seriously. Behind the scenes, it was not quite so positive.

"I think that the operators were ambivalent about my involvement," she recalls. "They recognised the need for nutritional standards but were reluctant to take the necessary steps to introduce them."

Nevertheless, Sterling himself was enthusiastic and arranged for her to check the diets and standards of cooking on some of P&O's container ships. Getting the Sutcliffe catering regions on side was more difficult and she struggled, always doubting her impact, though she remained on the board until 2000, when the Granada takeover swept her – and others – out.

"I think the caterers only marginally accepted me and thought I was a bit of a nuisance trying to interfere in their sphere of expertise. But, really, catering and nutrition are not entirely separate and they can learn from each other. It happens now, but it didn't then."

However, she was able to introduce a healthy eating programme in London which was launched by Edwina Currie MP, then a health minister, and later launched in the North with another big event at the Manchester United stadium which garnered plenty of useful publicity.

Almost every other catering company has since climbed aboard the healthy eating bandwagon and customer demands for healthy food, with escalating rates of obesity and associated diseases in the UK, have since ensured that nutrition has stayed at the top of most caterers' agenda.

Geoffrey Harrison, who had been running Fairfield Catering for Sutcliffe and who had worked with Juliet Gray at Fairfield and previously with the Merton contract, quit in 1994 to start up his own company specialising in education catering. He immediately hired her to advise on nutrition issues. She helped to introduce the company's Eat Well, Live Well healthier catering training programme for all the company's staff. She has remained as a consultant for Harrison

At the height of publicity about food additives, Juliet Gray and Geoffrey Harrison, general manager of Merton school meals service, organised a phone-in to answer parents' queries about additives in school meals.

Catering since then, taking on the title of company nutritionist.

With the abolition of nutrient-based standards, freelance nutritionists have been in high demand in the last decade and every contractor currently claims a commitment to providing healthy, nutritious, sometimes calorie-counted, meals.

The larger groups have teams of nutritionists on hand, widely accepted by those operating at the sharp end unlike in the 1980s when Juliet Gray was initially hired.

Sutcliffe produced a 16-page booklet on the benefits of eating well.

newsbriefs

New beverage vender gives us world first

Sutcliffe have launched the world's first micro-processor controlled beverage vending machine.

It has been researched and developed by the vending team in Bristol, and saves time, money and energy.

"It's the first machine designed *by* caterers *for* caterers", says Tony Dimambro, managing director of the vending department, who points out that he and Paul Pavey, vending manager, started work on designing the new machine (code named The Sutcliffe SG4) because they could not find exactly what they

Tony Dimambro: 'Designed by caterers for caterers'.

The SG4 saves 60% on labour, 30% on maintenance,

least once every 24 hours, stock-take through its print-out facility which controls costs and stocks at a complicated level, turn itself off out of working hours and even ferret out faults and report them visually.

The choice of 33 drinks is selected through a "touch" panel on the smart brown door designed by Mervyn Dawe of the Midlands D&E department. There is also a rosewood version to blend into more sophisticated office environments.

Launched at the Glaziers Hall overlooking the Thames early in June, the Sutcliffe SG4 has been field tested in nine locations and

Sutcliffe SG4: first of its type in the world.

Vending has been dramatically increased in 1982 and that is an indication of our firm belief in

To promote Sutcliffe's new microprocessor vending machine in 1982, Simon Davis sent 10,000 crackers with a key to the secretary of every managing director throughout the country on Valentine's Day with the words 'Your key to the vending machine'.

"His enthusiasm sometimes jarred. He would go into a meeting with his arms whirring and the Barons couldn't really grasp what he was trying to say. They liked him a lot but they didn't really understand him, and that was a bit of a problem."

* * *

Meanwhile, Davis was breaking new ground with his activities and was happy with his achievements. "It was such a fun time," he says. "We had complete trust in each other – nothing like it is today – and the people we worked with were wonderful."

For Peter Davies, the appointment of Davis was "absolutely right for Sutcliffe".

"His personality and flair altered us profoundly and meant we were able to compete effectively on equal terms with our very slick competitors. He brought a breath of fresh air into the company

whereas before we were a very ineffective marketing outfit."

Davis' huge personality was typically exemplified in his love of the river and boating at the Henley Regatta where he was frequently seen poling a Victorian punt with consummate skill, complete with picnic basket and wearing a colourful blazer, white trousers and a straw boater, with an habitual pipe stuck out of his mouth at a jaunty angle.

* * *

But the trust was not entirely mutual and his time at Sutcliffe came to an abrupt end.

In 1986, Jeffrey Sterling appointed Peter Ward as group marketing director and Miles Couchman as group marketing controller. They were two appointments that were unexpectedly imposed from on high; Stirling Gallacher was as unhappy about

their arrival at Sutcliffe as Simon Davis and Jane Baker were, but Davis was not backwards in coming forward, expressing his displeasure at being so side-lined. For a year he made his feelings abundantly clear; nor was Baker happy at the development.

"Simon had done so much for the company," she says. "The way they treated him – and me – was certainly not the Sutcliffe way."

Peter Davies recalls: "It must have been intolerable for Simon to see all the money being spent on outside agencies on campaigns that were really Simon's greatest talent. In reality, Simon had performed his wonders on a shoe string.

"It was a tragedy that he couldn't see a way ahead for himself and Jane in the new regime."

The situation became increasingly acerbic. At close of play on a summer's day in 1988, Davis was told that Sutcliffe didn't need him any more. At the same time, Jane Baker was called into another office and told the same story. They were both stunned. Baker had been with Sutcliffe for 14 years, Simon Davis eight. They were given 20 minutes to clear their desk but Davis didn't even bother to do that.

"What was so upsetting," says Baker, "is that we couldn't say goodbye to anyone. It was a bit like dying."

They were both out of a job. With a wife, two children at private school, a house on a mortgage and no pension, Davis quit the industry entirely and successfully ran a boat hire company on the Thames; after selling it, he then launched, with his wife, a highly successful charitable boat trust on the Thames for the disabled.

Jane Baker went on to a successful career in freelance journalism and teaching creative writing. The two had worked closely together for 10 years and Davis says that he would have achieved nothing without her.

Simon Davis: Davis' huge personality was typically exemplified in his love of the river and boating at the Henley Regatta, where he was frequently seen poling a Victorian punt with consummate skill.

CHAPTER
TWENTY-FOUR

Sutcliffe before Granada pounces

By the end of Ken Graveney's reign, Sutcliffe Catering was coasting along with the same regional company structure.

In 1979, Ken Graveney had been with Sutcliffe for 30 years, as company managing director for several decades and group managing director for four years. It would be fair to say that by the end of his reign, the company, though successful, was coasting along, still with a regional company structure that made it more difficult to manage from the centre.

Although it had strived for profit and had partly succeeded, Graveney was savvy enough to know that change was around the corner and the purchase of Sutcliffe by Sterling Guarantee Trust would inevitably lead to greater demands being made on him than had been made by Olympia.

He had joined Sutcliffe after the war in a different time. He had enjoyed three seasons playing cricket for Gloucestershire (and two more subsequently) and he had lived through the roller-coaster reigns of both John Sutcliffe and Mickie O'Brien. He had seen the company grow and had witnessed the defections of Brian Smith and Marc Verstringhe, two senior men, both of whom went on to create profitable companies in their own right. He had seen the impact of new owners: Olympia Ltd had taken little interest in its contract catering acquisition leaving Sutcliffe well alone, but SGT was a much tougher regime. Change was not yet over. SGT itself would eventually take over P&O, a worldwide shipping, transportation and property company and Sutcliffe would find itself a small cog in a very large international conglomerate wheel.

Nevertheless, with the appointments of Stirling Gallacher as managing director, Peter Davies as HR director, and Simon Davis as marketing and sales director, he had cherry picked key people recognising the huge changes that were taking place in marketing and sales and in business generally. While maintaining the family atmosphere of the company he had introduced Sutcliffe to more modern management practices yet had tried to stay loyal to the priciples of John Sutcliffe and Mickie O'Brien, and to the company itself. Graveney had become as identified with Sutcliffe as Mickie O'Brien and John Sutcliffe himself.

Ken Graveney: by the end of his career, he knew that Sutcliffe was on the cusp of more change and facing increasing pressure from the SGT board.

For those who had joined the company in the 1970s, the experience had been nothing short of a revelation. The army background of the four main participants – Sutcliffe, O'Brien, Horton and Graveney – permeated the company's unique structure. Not only was it organised along army lines, with separate companies representing army divisions, but it was run using army codes and practices.

In the early days, officer 'cadets' were selected twice a year by means of small box number advertisements in the *Daily Telegraph* which attracted young people (almost all men) many of whom had done their National Service and who were used to obeying people in authority without question. These recruits were given quick promotion to director status (this being an army environment) as it was understood that clients naturally wanted to talk to a man not a woman about business matters.

Only occasionally did women break through the glass ceiling and rise above area management. The strata below, however, had to be all-women (another army philosophy) because women – all of them personable and competent caterers as an added bonus – were preferred by clients to run their catering operation, much to the delight of many clients and their Sutcliffe colleagues.

The Sutcliffe senior people had about them the same *sangfroid*, the same larger-than-life approach to business as Dumas' Three Musketeers. 'One for all and all for one' would not have been an inappropriate motto. As one contemporary who lived through it all says:

"If the company had had a heraldic shield, it would have been inscribed with the words 'good fun, good food and good fellowship.'"

Few elite directors of any other company board had ever had the good fortune to indulge themselves in such sport, monetary freedom, gastronomic indulgence and pleasurely licence, and then to sell themselves off to another company, Olympia, and be able to carry on exactly as before. The Olympia deal had been the deal of a lifetime but the emergence of SGT had changed the nature of the company and Ken Graveney knew it.

As befits a Royal Marine and county cricketer, he was a fit and strong man but his back injury, sustained on the Normandy landing beaches, troubled him all his life. By the end of his career, he knew that Sutcliffe was on the cusp of more change facing increasing pressure from the SGT board. His son John says that he was stressed, though whether this was the cause of a triple heart bypass operation which hit him soon after his early retirement is difficult to say. He was taken ill on a flight to America and had to have emergency surgery in Houston. Being wheeled into the operating theatre, he heard the English surgeon mutter: "Graveney? Graveney? Anything to do with cricket?"

Domestically, too, he had suffered tragedy. His first wife, to whom he was exceptionally close, died in an accident on holiday in Spain in 1971; his second marriage (to Jacky Worthington, a Sutcliffe employee) ended in divorce. A third marriage, to the widow of one of his greatest friends who collapsed playing golf, was happily long-lasting. On the death of her husband, Jacquie Richmond had inherited oil wells in the US and when Ken and Jacquie married, the time had come for him to cut the ties with Sutcliffe, move to the US and play as much golf as he wanted in the sun. The strains of running the company, however long on laughs and short on profit it had been, had visibly taken its toll. He was looking tired and drawn. He had shrewdly looked to the future by appointing Stirling Gallacher as managing director of the Southern company and ready to move up to take over the company on his retirement.

In 1979, he retired early, not without regret but looking forward to a long life ahead. When Stirling Gallacher and Peter Davies met him at Heathrow on his first visit back to the UK a few months after his retirement to the US they found him relaxed, sun-tanned, oozing apparent good health. In Davies' words it was a 'miraculous' change. He moved to the US, became a US citizen and lived in retirement until his death in October 2015, aged 90.

It's a cliché, but his departure marked the end of an era. However, his retirement, though hastened by illness, was timely. When Gallacher stepped up as managing director the company was about to move into a far more commercial and more competitive environment.

* * *

James Stirling-Gallacher joined from Gardner Merchant. A Scot who had had Jesuit schooling in wartime Glasgow, Gallacher (Stirling – always used in the industry as his first name – is actually part of his surname) had come up the hard way from catering school (Acton Technical College, later Ealing) then into hotels, joining Peter Merchant as a management trainee. With the merger of Peter Merchant and John Gardner in 1964, he began to rise up the ranks – "The Gardner people thought they were very superior," he says. "The Peter Merchant catering was admittedly fairly basic."

By then, Gardner Merchant had been acquired by Trust Houses, which quickly instigated a report into the structure of the whole group by McKinsey, the management consultants. Other caterers looked on in amazement; for a hotel and catering

James Stirling-Gallacher: he joined Sutcliffe and introduced more drive and direction to a company which he was convinced had a bright future. By the time he retired in 1992, turnover was £358m and profits were £39m.

company to bring in an international consultancy that was wreaking such changes throughout industry generally was a bold step indeed. In the case of Gardner Merchant it resulted in the establishment of regions and Stirling Gallacher, who had been given the job of liaising with McKinsey during their investigations, was a beneficiary, becoming director of the North West region. In 1975 he became managing director, succeeding Leslie Bond who had become a director of THF Catering Services and managing director of Gardner Merchant after joining Trust Houses as head of personnel services in 1962.

For Gallacher, it was a time of increasing concern at the way measures were being imposed from above that cut back on contact time with clients. Within two years of his appointment, he left to join Sutcliffe.

Initially, he had approached Jeffrey Sterling with a view to Gardner Merchant buying Sutcliffe, thinking that the two companies would be a good fit; Sterling had declined the offer but said that if Gallacher ever wanted to join Sutcliffe, he would be very welcome. When the job of managing director for Sutcliffe's south of England region became available, Jeffrey Sterling contacted him. The job was at a lower salary than at Gardner Merchant but Gallacher grabbed the opportunity.

"I was getting choked at Gardner Merchant. Sutcliffe had a reputation for giving good service and I thought I could improve on that." He left, but not without some regrets. He joined Sutcliffe believing he could introduce more drive and direction to a company which he was convinced had a bright future. He was correct. When he arrived, Sutcliffe had some 700 contracts with a turnover of £30m and profits of £600,000 – the long on laughs, short on profits mantra was not undeserved. By 1987, seven years after Gallacher had taken full control, 1,100 contracts yielded a profit of £4.3m on a £110m turnover. By the time he retired in 1992, turnover was £358m and profits (including Spring Grove laundry) were £39m.

At the first meeting held with his senior team, he told them he was leaving a company he dearly loved but not the people who controlled it. He was joining a company he respected.

One of his first acts was to put up a notice in his office: 'I want to hear what you think, not what you think I want to hear.' It was a message he brought from Gardner Merchant where the notice was prominent in his offices there. At least one colleague looked on this notice with some scepticism. "That was crap! If you really told Stirling what you thought, you wouldn't have lasted long." Another senior colleague echoes this view. Nevertheless, at his first meeting with staff, he reiterated his conviction that success depended on the quality of food, of service, of staff – a belief with which few would have dissented.

"If you want to upset me," he said in a later interview with *Caterer*, "then tell me we have fallen down on quality. I would much rather have our services terminated because someone else says they can do it cheaper than if someone says our work is poor."

It was a philosophy that he kept throughout his career with the company.

"We had a good product when I arrived and I began to brighten our image," he told the magazine. "But we didn't want to become too aggressive to begin with, because catering is a very conservative industry. It's like a big ship – it takes a long time to change course... We are not the cheapest organisation in terms of fees but if you charge a good fee and bring home the bacon, the client is more than happy. We build up the business and hang on to it.

You have to bolt the back door."

Bolting the back door meant keeping in regular touch with the clients which was something that Gallacher insisted on. He was proud of the fact that Sutcliffe had a smaller sales force than Gardner Merchant or Compass but had a higher ratio of supervisory management to clients. He liked to keep in touch with clients as often as he could and insisted on managers keeping a record of who they met so he could check that they regularly kept in touch with them. He was a details man. It was vital, he reckoned, that Sutcliffe staff were seen as part of the clients' own management team.

"If you see someone regularly enough, and he trusts you, then you become part of their team," he says.

Gallacher is often criticised for his cautious approach to risk compared to the more venturesome ways of his successor, Don Davenport, who was then reporting to him as director in charge of Sutcliffe's Southern region. Gallacher's style of management was precise and detailed and he had a very small head office team. He knew how to run it properly and he kept a very sharp eye on expenses. "Sterling drove Don mad with his eye always on the bottom line and always wanting to run a very tight ship," says one contemporary. "Don was a very dynamic individual, a bit of a maverick, which Stirling was not. But Don took some handling. He could be very mercurial and could blow up."

Yet Gallacher was making all the right noises as was his profit record. He recognised that merchandising was beginning to rise to the top of the agenda, convinced that contractors had to take a more aggressive approach to presentation if sales volumes were to be increased and profit-making areas enlarged.

"We've got to increase merchandising skills and the business acumen of our

Don Davenport: "I can't think of another business where you get the opportunity at a very early age, to run 15 or so contracts and deal with high-level people in such a variety of professional environments."

catering managers," he told Gillian Upton in an article for *Catering Times*.

One of his best and most far-sighted decisions was to bring Don Davenport aboard who he recruited from Gardner Merchant in 1979 as director for the

London region and who took over from him in 1990 as group managing director. The two were totally different characters but, in their different ways, both made significant contributions to the company.

Gallacher moved up to be chairman of an over-arching company, Sutcliffe Group Services, with Peter Harrison (Geoffrey's elder brother) the catering company's financial director, as his deputy; it was a position which he held until the Granada takeover in 1993.

He stayed on with P&O for a year as special adviser on catering with the company's cruise ships, an assignment that stretched for a couple more years, before finally quitting. He subsequently joined the board of Jerry Brand's Host Catering.

* * *

Don Davenport was chalk to Sterling Gallacher's cheese. He grew up in Essex and London's Docklands – "a pretty unsavoury area," he admits. "There would always be a bunch of kids hanging around who wanted to 'look after' your car." At Buckhurst Hill Grammar he was the only boy to choose domestic science instead of metalwork for which the other boys gave him a hard time, though that was compensated by having attracted plenty of female attention.

At 15 he left to go to Waltham Forest Technical College to train as a chef and by 1960 he was working in the kitchens of the May Fair Hotel and the Trocadero. "In those days you'd just go up to the back door of the kitchen and ask if they needed any help," he told Ben Walker in an interview in *Caterer*. In 1961 he began a two-year management course with Trust Houses and for the next 18 years was a rising star at Gardner Merchant. He never regretted his decision to go into contract catering.

"I can't think of another business where

you get the opportunity at a very early age, to run 15 or so contracts and deal with high-level people in such a variety of professional environments," he told *Caterer*.

By 1979, he was regional managing director for Gardner Merchant's South West division and was persuaded by Stirling Gallacher to join Sutcliffe as managing director of the company's London division, much to Garry Hawkes' irritation. "It was a nightmare," admits Davenport. Nevertheless, he makes no secret of his admiration of Hawkes; for him, he and Ken Graveney were the two most illustrious leaders of the UK contracting industry, to be followed only by Gerry Robinson, with whom he worked after Granada acquired Sutcliffe in 1993.

"Gerry Robinson hated detail. We were accustomed to writing reports inches thick. All Gerry wanted was one sheet of paper, explaining what you were going to do. Churchill did the same in the war. Like him or loathe him, he knew what he wanted and he told you what he wanted. But he let you get on with it. If you didn't agree with him, you were out. And if you didn't produce the goods, you were out. But he was the one person who showed us how to make money in the contracting industry. It was a ruthless pursuit of profit. It's never been the same since."

* * *

With Don Davnport playing a leading role, Sutcliffe remained part of of SGT until 1984 when, in a series of complicated financial machinations led by Jeffrey Sterling, it became part of the P&O group after he injected SGT into the shipping company. This made little difference to Sutcliffe. It prospered under P&O though Sutcliffe barely gets a mention in the official publication which celebrated P&O's 150th anniversary. If *The Story of P&O* is anything to go by, Sutcliffe was a minor player indeed and was

organised very much at arm's length, though Chris Copner, who joined Sutcliffe in 1980 from Peat Marwick, remembers that the company was entirely run for cash.

"The weekly cash flow report was the most important piece of paper of the week."

Nevertheless, it was a delightful company to work for. "No-one was ever rude or unduly demanding. They were extremely decent people."

But they were people who were not averse to selling the family silver.

* * *

Though it attracted a large number of senior people, particularly from Gardner Merchant – Stirling Gallacher, Don Davenport, Simon Davis, Frank Whittaker, Geoffrey Harrison, Martin Waller among others – Sutcliffe also attracted talented people who went on to make a big name for themselves, including Alastair Storey, Keith Wilson, William Baxter and Robert Platts, Chris Hind and Andrew Nelson.

But by 1993 there was a predator at the door in the shape of Gerry Robinson. Having sorted Granada out to his satisfaction, Robinson and Charles Allen turned their attention to Sutcliffe, fully recognising that the company, with its semi autonomous divisions, was ripe for restructuring with potentially highly profitable results.

Before the sale, Sutcliffe was producing margins of three or four per cent; by the time of the Granada merger with Compass in 2000, Sutcliffe's margins were 12.2 per cent (see Chapter 27). However, cutting ever more costs and inflicting ever higher charges on the client eventually affects standards and trust and is unsustainable in the long run. One of the criticisms of the Robinson regime has always been that short-term profit was being sought in preference to long-term gain.

Within an extraordinary few weeks,

Sutcliffe became a Granada subsidiary – to be followed by six years of heady expansion. The takeover, described in more detail in the next chapter, heralded the departure of a number of long-serving Sutcliffe personalities.

The first person to head for the door was Tony Dimambro, the managing director of Granada Vending Services who, with some foresight, negotiated an amicable deal to take private the vending company and related components. Dimambro had recognised that Robinson was not in favour of a catering company manufacturing vending machines. Robinson had, after all, sold off all of Compass' vending interests soon after the buyout) and he realised that it was only a matter of time before the Sutcliffe vending company would also be axed. Dimambro took with him Paul Pavey, his talented young technical director.

The deal was amicably arranged but the next to go caused some consternation. Geoffrey Harrison, then director of Fairfield Catering, with some 90 contracts, which Sutcliffe had bought in 1986 to take the company into school catering, decided to set up on his own.

Harrison had trained as a chef and had worked for both Bateman and Gardner Merchant, spending six years as GM's catering manager at Ford's Dagenham plant, then taking over as district manager in the City of London. In 1980 Don Davenport persuaded him to move into sales and he became sales manager for Sutcliffe's Home Counties division – a bold move for a trained chef. Three years later he became general manager of the schools division and when Sutcliffe acquired Fairfield Catering to expand into school catering he was appointed managing director.

Harrison told *Caterer* at the time of his departure that he was uncomfortable "at the massive cultural change in the group".

"Primarily, their view at the time was to maximise share price but I couldn't see a long-term strategy. I like to have a plan that goes beyond a year," he said.

He quit, taking his personal assistant and Alison Goldie, his former general sales manager at Fairfield, with him. He set up his own company, Harrison Catering Services, specialising in the education sector. It took him three months to get his first contract but the company currently has a turnover of £60m. It was a decision that poleaxed Don Davenport and others:

"Yes, we were very upset at that," he admits. "Obviously, I would have preferred Geoffrey to stick with it and make it work, rather than start up on his own but I understood the motivation."

Indeed, the relationship between Harrison and Davenport was close then and remains so. Harrison subsequently brought his former boss onto his board after Davenport retired from Sutcliffe – a period which, for the new non-exec, was an eye opener.

"It showed how different it was to run a small private company than a large corporate, which I had been used to," Davenport recalls. "In a group you have to have weekly reports, a tightly controlled finance department, forecasts and estimates, budgets and summaries and all the paraphernalia of control. I'm not saying that Geoffrey didn't have control – he did – but the decisions could be made so much more easily and quickly, and there was so much more freedom to develop the business."

Developing a business, however, was Gerry Robinson's forte – and in more ways than one.

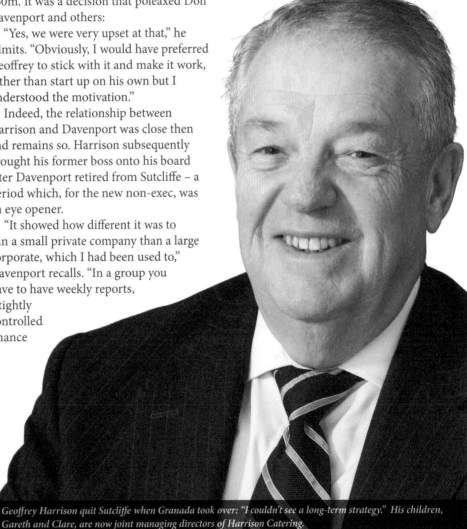

Geoffrey Harrison quit Sutcliffe when Granada took over: "I couldn't see a long-term strategy." His children, Gareth and Clare, are now joint managing directors of Harrison Catering.

CHAPTER TWENTY-FIVE

1990-2000: the decade of headlong expansion

When Granada took over Sutcliffe a decade of headlong expansion followed.

I n 1990, the industry entered a decade of expansion – and no company epitomised this more than Granada. According to the annual survey of the British Hospitality Association's Food and Service Management Forum, turnover across the sector grew from £977m in 1990 to £3.26bn in 2000 with few hiccups along the way. The survey, which relied on returned questionnaires from contractors, estimated that it represented almost 90 per cent of the contract catering industry. This was a fair claim, though the sample of companies, which always included the biggest contractors, meant the base was changing every year as new companies came in and others dropped out, mainly because they had been acquired. In addition, some companies did not provide all of the requested information, so estimates had to be undertaken. Despite these drawbacks, the survey painted an annual picture of the contracting industry that was more accurate than any other resource and showed significant growth as contractors sought to expand in new areas such as schools and education, hospitals and Ministry of Defence, as well as trying to boost footfall and increase take-up in existing contracts.

Turnover: UK contract catering industry, 1990-2000 (£bn)	
1990	977m
1991	1.30
1992	1.49
1993	2.00
1994	2.18
1995	2.26
1996	2.23
1997	2.25
1998	2.65
1999	3.01
2000	3.26

Source: British Hospitality Association, Food and Service Management Survey 1990-2000

During the decade more contractors were looking to expand into areas such as further and higher education.

Introducing the 2001 edition of the survey, Mike Oldfield, the Forum's chairman and a senior Compass director, boasted that contracting had grown "by recognising the importance of satisfying customer needs, greater investment, improved food standards, a more attractive eating environment, better service and improved marketing and merchandising techniques".

This litany of perfection left little to the imagination but what he had written was true enough. Sharper management techniques had improved results, the number of suppliers were being cut to improve discounts generated (they declined by 50 per cent between 1995 and 2000), new ideas were coming through and food service companies were becoming more commercial with branded outlets now an accepted means of selling more meals, while competition had strengthened leading to higher standards.

Oldfield also denied that contracting was stuck in the B&I groove and pointed to the success of contractors entering new markets:

"It's often claimed that contract catering is a mature market," he said. "Certainly it provides a catering and support service for mature sectors of the economy and the biggest market of all – business and industry – is the most developed. Yet while other markets have opened up – healthcare and education in particular – business and industry continues to dominate even though it now represents half of the total market rather than the three-quarters as it did 10 years ago."

It was also a decade of extraordinary growth for the industry's two major companies – Compass and Granada – while Elior was emerging towards the end of the decade as a key player. But it was Sutcliffe,

Mike Oldfield: "It's often claimed that contract catering is a mature market. Yet B&I continues to dominate even though it now represents half of the total market rather than the three-quarters it did ten years ago."

part of Gerry Robinson's Granada group, that set the pace.

When Robinson left Compass in 1992 with Charles Allen to take control of Granada, he had already eyed Sutcliffe as a possible takeover target, but he found on his arrival at Granada that he had more urgent matters to attend to. Nevertheless, the abortive bid for Gardner Merchant, rather than discouraging his ambitions for expansion, only whetted them. He knew that the only other major contractor now in play was Sutcliffe and, in contrast to the clamour of the GM bid – where the management led by Garry Hawkes had been fiercely antagonistic – Sutcliffe fell quietly into his lap. It was a done deal accomplished within a matter of weeks.

Robinson says that Sutcliffe approached him in early 1993 while Jeffrey Sterling, P&O's boss, now a peer, claimed that 'they got in touch within the last two months.' Whoever made the first approach, it was a case of willing buyer and willing seller. Sterling needed cash and wanted to focus on P&O's core cruise ship business, Granada needed to extend its base and balance its activities away from television rental into a cash-generative business that would broaden its revenue spread. Granada's own motorway services network and leisure activities, which Allen was operating, would also benefit from Sutcliffe's purchasing power, while Robinson knew, from his experience with Compass, that he could wring a lot more profit out of the Sutcliffe business once it was under his control.

In March 1993, Granada acquired Sutcliffe for £360m funded by the issue of 42m shares (sold within 30 minutes) and £211m of borrowing. At the time, Sutcliffe had a turnover of £358m and profits of £15m, with a further £2m profit from its vending business, while Spring Grove laundry (included in the deal and soon sold) generated £11m profit; security and other operations brought in a further £1m.

The purchase found favour in the City, partly because investors recognised that contract catering was a business that both Robinson and Allen understood. Granada's share price rose by 20p. It was something of a coup for Robinson as Sutcliffe was an admired contractor. He had snapped it up ahead of any other predator. He knew that it would give Granada a more solid base of cash flow and greater profits, which it needed if it was to get away from its dependence on the declining television rental markets, which then comprised 60 per cent of Granada's business.

It is a simple philosophy but one that must surely have rung alarm bells for Sutcliffe's senior management, for whom the takeover came initially as an unwelcome surprise. Don Davenport, chief executive, only heard about it on his car radio, just before going into a meeting where he was to be told in person. "At least the Gardner Merchant people had had a couple of months to get used to the idea," he ruefully told *Caterer* later.

But the news travelled fast. Robinson's reputation as a ruthless operator at Compass had gone before him – it had been the talk of the industry ever since 1987 – yet here he was, not only on Sutcliffe's doorstep but actually inside the company as the new boss. "It was scary," says Davenport.

Davenport is a key player in the story, with others such as Frank Whittaker, Chris Copner and Alastair Storey.

Whittaker began his career as a chef in the hotel industry before realising that contract catering would give him his weekends free and provide him with more social working hours. "I'd seen chefs who were 40 and looked 60," he says. "I didn't want to go down that route." He joined GM and spent the next 17 years with the company, turning his attention to sales and eventually ending up as sales director based in Kenley. He quit, believing GM was getting further and further away from the market. The closer he got to Garry Hawkes the more he realised the relationship wouldn't work. In 1988 Davenport offered him a job at Sutcliffe.

The other key player in the later story is Alastair Storey. He had left the Scottish Hotel School in 1975 and immediately joined Sutcliffe Hill, the group's Scottish regional company, as a trainee manager in an obscure refrigeration factory in Glasgow. He rapidly moved south to the Midlands and the West Country, becoming managing director of Sutcliffe Catering South East and eventually managing director of Granada Food Services.

Sutcliffe was widely regarded as a reputable company with a good record albeit one that, in the practised eyes of Robinson and Allen, would greatly benefit from a more aggressive managerial approach. Growth had been largely organic. True, it had acquired Fairfield Catering and Catering Guild – the latter "a complete disaster" in Storey's words, "but it was good to cut our teeth on something" – but the heyday of its acquisition trail was still several years into the future.

Organic growth remained the driving force and the senior directors – such as Davenport, Whittaker, who had joined as sales and marketing director; and Chris Copner, as finance director – certainly recognised this.

The Compass buy-out in 1986 had been a step change for the industry generally and the three had already discussed between themselves a possible buy-out of Sutcliffe from P&O. Funding was the problem (the Compass buy-out was only half that of the value of Sutcliffe) but, more significantly,

Stirling Gallacher, who was still the Sutcliffe chairman and on the P&O board, was believed to be opposed to the idea though he later claimed that the board was not receptive to any approach.

* * *

At the time of the Granada purchase, Sutcliffe was still being run in the way that it had always operated – almost as a group holding company with eight operating subsidiaries each responsible for its own geographical area with its own head office, its own specialist directors in sales and marketing, personnel, accounts and purchasing. Each regional managing director still fiercely controlled his individual patch. Although Sutcliffe had bought Fairfield back in 1990, it had been a company happy to grow organically with four per cent margins and no undue strain on its employees.

"It was a pretty decent company and I always enjoyed working for it," says Storey.

Frank Whittaker: "If we had wanted change at P&O, it would have taken years of discussion and negotiation with a final sign-off by the board. But here we were with Gerry Robinson demanding significant change within a matter of weeks. It was a huge breath of fresh air."

"It was very decent towards its employees, and it was strong on training staff. It was a charming, quiet, gentle-as-you-go kind of company. It wasn't commercially aggressive. It could certainly have been more entrepreneurial. I remember we thought we were light in East Anglia, so we just opened an office over there and put in people and told them to get some contracts. It was all a bit haphazard."

It did not take Robinson long to discern that Sutcliffe would be able to unlock a significant amount of extra profit through tighter management and more aggressive cost control. His experience at Compass had already proved the point. It was confidence in his and Charles Allen's judgment that propelled the purchase. Sutcliffe was bought without due diligence within a few weeks of the initial overtures.

As it was already making profit (though much of it not yet realised), the impact of Granada on Sutcliffe was rather more subtle than Robinson's blitz on Compass which had led to the immediate culling of a whole raft of senior management and a total re-organisation. He left Sutcliffe alone to begin with although he insisted that the head office should be relocated to London.

With the acquisiton, Stirling Gallacher quit as chairman and Davenport was appointed chief executive of the newly created Granada Services to Business division – in effect, Sutcliffe Catering. At his first meeting with senior Sutcliffe staff, including Davenport, Whittaker and Copner, Robinson asked them what they wanted to do with the company and where they wanted to go. He then told them to prepare a business plan within the next eight weeks. It was a short meeting and the Sutcliffe team got the message.

"We didn't have one policy instruction from Granada," Davenport said, later – but Robinson's request for a business plan made it clear that he expected change with better margins and greater profit to follow. The plan had to show the way. To the Sutcliffe senior people, the task in hand was more exciting than forbidding.

"If we had wanted change at P&O, it would have taken years of discussion and negotiation with a final sign-off by the board," says Frank Whittaker. "But here we were with Gerry Robinson demanding significant change within a matter of weeks. It was a huge breath of fresh air."

Storey tells the same story: "Suddenly, we were able to do things with the company. I remember saying to Gerry that we wanted to do this and that and he turned on us and said, 'Well, why aren't you doing it, then?' It was like a light bulb going on."

Gerry Robinson's reputation at Granada had gone before him but the senior people at Sutcliffe could only admire his business acumen and his focus.

"He was always very affable," recalls Storey. "He knew what he wanted and knew where he was going. If you agreed something with him, you knew you had to do it and if you didn't there would be trouble. That's reasonable. It was simply good management. Very focused. We found it very motivating."

"Gerry knew he could drive the business much harder," says Copner.

* * *

The Sutcliffe team set about devising a five-year business plan – called the Green Book (the Sutcliffe colour was green and it was in a green folder – John Sutcliffe's racing colours).

"It was a situation completely different to anything we had experienced at Sutcliffe before," says Whittaker.

The plan looked at the most obvious target: the Sutcliffe structure. The eight regional companies were to be dissolved, regional offices culled, specialist departments like purchasing, HR and accounts centralised, while the power of the regional managing directors was to be reduced though the ratio of district managers to

Alastair Storey: "Suddenly, we were able to do things with the company. I remember saying to Gerry that we wanted to do this and that and he turned on us and said, 'Well, why aren't you doing it, then?' It was like a light bulb going on."

Profit Expectation 1993/96

	Profit B/F £m	Natural Company Growth £m	Operational Re-structure £m	Finance Re-structure £m	Company Offices £m	Company Cars £m	Purchasing Discounts £m	PBI/Tax £m	Annual Growth %	Turnover £m	% Return on Turnover
1992/93								16	20	360	4.4
1993/94	16.0	2.0	1.75	1.0	–	–	4.0	24.75	54.7	363	6.8
1994/95	24.75	2.5	1.25	0.5	0.25	0.25	2.5	32.0	29.3	367	8.7
1995/96	32.0	2.75	0.75	0.5	0.25	0.25	2.0	38.5	20.3	370	10.4

By 1995/96 when the plan is fully implemented, the following annual position will result when compared against present trading:

Natural Company Growth	:	£7.25m annual income improvement
Operational Re-structure	:	£3.75m annual cost saving
Finance Re-structure	:	£2.0m annual cost saving
Company Offices & Property	:	£0.5m annual cost saving
Company Cars	:	£0.5m annual cost saving
Purchasing Discounts	:	£8.5m annual income improvement
Total Profit Improvement	:	**£22.5m**

contracts was maintained in order to retain client contact. It forecast that margins would increase from four per cent to 10 per cent (actually achieved in three years) without losing any turnover.

The proposal to abandon the existing regional structure and flatten the middle management, reducing the number of operating regions from seven to five, was a blast of cold air throughout the company. About 50 middle managers were made redundant, followed by a further 140 when the accounts department was centralised in Stockport, saving £3m a year. Further savings of £750,000 were made by sourcing the car fleet from one provider. In fact, Robinson's impact on Sutcliffe was as extensive though less well publicised as his impact on Compass.

Manpower Reduction Programme

This chart shows the planned reduction in staffing levels by job title.

Position	Current	Proposed
Managing Director	8	6
Operations Director	23	13
Sales Director	8	7
Area Manager	123	78
Quality Service Manager	20	4
Human Resource Manager	12	8
Trainers	32	16
Accounts Staff	214	118
Secretarial Support	55	45
Health & Hygiene Inspectors	5	5*
Purchasing Staff	7	7*
Sales Managers	29	29*
TOTAL	**536**	**336**

*It will be noted that investment in these three key positions is being maintained, with no planned reduction in numbers

Proposed headcount reduction over 3 year period = 200

SUTCLIFFE GROUP MANAGEMENT BOARD

1 July 1993

A M Adams (Anthony)	Managing Director, London & East Division
P W Aldrich (Peter)	Managing Director, South West & Wales Division
B D Clark (Brian)	Managing Director, Scottish Division
C C J Copner (Chris)	Group Finance Director
D A Davenport (Don)	Group Managing Director
M L Devlin (Malcolm)	Managing Director, Sutcliffe Ireland
G C Harrison Geoffrey)	Managing Director, Fairfield Catering
A D Hill (Tony)	Group Purchasing Director
C J R Page (Chris)	Group Quality Services Director
H C Richardson (Hugh)	Managing Director, North Division
M J Spiller (Mike)	Group Personnel Director
A D Storey (Alastair)	Managing Director, South East Division
F S Whittaker (Frank)	Group Sales & Marketing Director

After the Granada takeover, the Sutcliffe team produced the Green Book (Sutcliffe's colours were green as was John Sutcliffe's racing colours). The book outlined how the company would be reorganised, where the staff cuts would fall and the profit expectations (with amendments!). The initial management board was also listed, though Geoffrey Harrison soon left.

But it was in purchasing, the area which had yielded so much additional profit for Compass, that the biggest savings were made. Curiously, nearly three-quarters of all Sutcliffe's purchasing was in the hands of area managers. Centralising the operation reduced costs by 20 per cent while a more aggressive approach to charging out costs to clients went straight to the bottom line.

"We were astonished at the benefits," Davenport says.

Anthony Adams, managing director of London and East division, who had spent the nine years of his career as a purser on P&O liners, admits that the takeover did open up new opportunities. "But what happened was an incredible focus on increasing the margins," he says. "Don was being pushed very hard by Gerry Robinson and Charles Allen."

The team had to deliver more profit, be more efficient and make more money out of discounts while reducing HR, training and design and equipment costs.

"Every six months we were given an additional task to make more money,"

adds Adams.

In effect, the strategy proposed by the management team was a repeat of the strategy that followed the Grandmet Catering Services buy-out. The plan was presented to Robinson and Allen at a momentous meeting in Golden Square, Granada's head office, attended by some nine Sutcliffe senior people, Davenport leading. All of them expected to be interrogated on the figures and the new direction of travel for the company. Whittaker recalls:

"I distinctly remember Gerry telling Don

Forward operated 256 outlets in the civil service valued at £17m, employing 1,800 staff, including GCHQ at Cheltenham.

that the floor was his and after listening intently for no more than ten minutes he folded his arms across his chest and looked at Charles Allen, who also had folded his arms, saying to Charles, 'Well?' And we thought Oh God! It's all going down the pan. The body language! The folded arms! I thought it was curtains – next step, polish up the CV. And then Charles started to play with his pen, making it spin like a top. 'I don't think we need to hear any more,' he said. Gerry smiled. 'OK boys,' he said. 'Get on with it.' And they left the room. After only 10 minutes! We were gobsmacked. We thought it was a helluva way to run a company. Very effective, very motivating, very urgent, very scary. We knew what we had to do."

Back at Aldermaston, where Sutcliffe had its head office, Davenport and his team outlined to other directors and managers what had to be done. Some, including Geoffrey Harrison and Mike Oldfield, chose to leave.

"It was such a huge change for us all," says Whittaker. "Sutcliffe had been a company that had been very warm and very cuddly. We were cuddling everyone – clients, employees, suppliers. The Green Book changed everything. Suddenly, we had to become aggressive and assertive and watch everything. Tighter margins were a pre-requisite."

In the first three years of ownership, Davenport and his team saved over £10m in costs, justifying Robinson's conviction that more profit could be wrung out of the company under a more aggressive regime. At the same time, he did not hold back on investment. Computers were installed in every unit and there were never quibbles about bringing in modern equipment. Alex Bernstein, Granada's chairman, told shareholders in early 1994 that Sutcliffe's margins had already improved from under

four per cent at the time of the acquisition to 7.4 per in the last quarter of 1993, which rose to 7.7 per cent a year later. By 1997, margins had risen to ten per cent. The influence of Gerry Robinson and Charles Allen was clearly evident.

"I think we surprised ourselves," says Whittaker, "but we were better rewarded than we ever were under P&O. There were bonuses and good salary increases. Gerry always recognised the merits of a good salary structure, not only at senior level but throughout the structure."

* * *

After the reorganisation, Granada embarked on a string of acquisitions which expanded the size and breadth of its catering operations and made wealthy men of more than a dozen independent operators.

In 1994, it successfully bought up Forward, the civil service catering organisation, for £4.6m in competition with a management buy-out from the Forward team, and also from Compass. Forward operated 256 outlets in the civil service valued at £27m, employing 1,800 staff, including GCHQ at Cheltenham, the Welsh Office and the Register for Scotland.

It was not an entirely trouble-free acquisition. In 1992 it had undergone a Treasury investigation as a result of a lack of financial controls and pension arrangements were a major stumbling block in the negotiations. But the deal went ahead and others then followed.

In 1995, Catering Guild was bought from Gallacher, the tobacco giant, for £5.6m adding 115 contracts and £25m turnover. David Jenkinson, Catering Guild's managing director, stayed on to take charge of the Guild's English contracts (excluding 15 in Scotland and nine in Ireland) which became part of Sutcliffe's South East region. Despite

promises that the contracts would continue under the Guild's name, it was not to be. Jenkinson quit six months later:

"It was clear from day one that we were destined not to grow further as a business within Sutcliffe and after building up the business for eight years, I couldn't stand it any longer," he told Caterer.

He left with three other ex-Guild directors to form Restaurants at Work, which aimed to continue the work of Catering Guild. Unfortunately, it went into administration in 2010 and its assets, consisting mainly of 24 B&I contracts employing some 180 staff, were acquired by BaxterStorey.

In the same year, Granada snapped up Hanrahan In-House Catering, a West of Ireland contractor with 21 contracts and an annual turnover of IR£4m, in what was billed as a merger with Hanrahan retaining its name. The deal brought the number of Sutcliffe clients in Ireland to 145 and its turnover to IR£24m.

Earlier in 1995, Granada had acquired ACMS, a Thames Valley-based contractor from its founder and managing director, Robert Lynch. With 59 (mainly B&I) contracts and a turnover of £8m a year, ACMS was placed under the direction of Fairfield Catering, Granada's education and kosher business run by Martin Waller, who said that ACMS would retain its own identity and client base – "and it is even possible that we could at times find ourselves in competition with Sutcliffe," he told Caterer. Under the terms of the deal, Lynch stayed on for six months as a consultant.

Granada was still very much on the acquisition trail, Frank Whittaker, Sutcliffe's group sales and marketing director, told Caterer: "We were disappointed about Eurest (bought by Compass in 1996) but we are still looking for other acquisitions... Granada is ready for us to do that and the money is there for us to do that." He added: "The

Behind the Forte negotiations

Robinson's interest in Forte had been long-standing. His abortive bid for Gardner Merchant three years previously when at Compass still rankled, though the purchase of Sutcliffe was mollifying.

But Forte was the industry's hotel and catering giant which, Robinson believed, was a prize well worth fighting for with the gloves off, if need be. His experience of dealing with Forte over the Gardner Merchant bid had left him with the feeling that the company was poorly managed.

Gerry Robinson recalls: "We convened a meeting at THF's headquarters in Holborn to discuss the possible merger. There were about 30 people around the table – THF people on one side with all their advisers and us on the other side, with all ours. We had just begun discussions when a lady with a tea trolley came in and started offering everyone a cup of tea, so we had to stop talking as Rocco had said that she was a temp and we couldn't discuss matters in hand in front of her. She wasn't the quickest at the job and she asked everyone individually 'Would you like a cup of tea? And do you take sugar? And do you take milk?'

"It took her 20 minutes to get around the table and we were desperate to get the discussions underway again. The tension was palpable but no-one of the THF side seemed to notice.

"All of us on our side were raising our eyebrows at the length of time it took – here was one of the biggest deals in corporate history being held up by a tea lady determined to do her job. Finally, she served the last cup as she finished her laborious circuit. We nearly convulsed when the chairman asked the assembled company: 'Would anyone like a second cup?'"

Robinson thought it symptomatic of the company though THF would no doubt argue that this was the way a traditional hospitality company should be run.

In his biography, Robinson recalls that three years previously the industry well knew that Gardner Merchant was on the market but Compass had been rebuffed when, by rights, it would have been a better tactic to approach Compass first if only to use it as a stalking horse for later bids and for the MBO.

"In the end, the deal didn't happen. Not only did they not come to us, Rocco wouldn't even answer my phone calls. I wrote, as well, but got nowhere.

"We tried Ken Costa, Forte's adviser at their merchant bank, SG Warburg, but he said there's no point in you bothering because they are so far down the road to a deal and they have an exclusivity agreement with the Gardner Merchant management. And we thought, Christ – what a way to run a sale! Let's have a look at the whole thing. Let's see what's going on here."

John Nelson, then at Lazards, is quoted in Robinson's biography: "The [Gardner Merchant] episode gave me the feeling that Forte was a soft company. It was just badly managed." And he advised Robinson: "This is one for later."

number one slot in contract catering is still our clear vision."

Early in 1996, Granada (through ACMS) acquired Northdowns Catering from its chairman, Kenneth Mayhew, and managing director, Ray Patching. Not for the first time (or the last), in the previous year the duo had strenuously denied the company was for sale. The deal, which added 50 contracts and an additional £5.5m to ACMS' turnover, had been on the cards for several months and well before Granada's ACMS acquisition – hence the earlier rumours. Mayhew and Patching stayed on for six months' consultancy but then retired. Granada considered Northdowns a natural fit for ACMS and the two companies continued to operate as branded names.

One month later, in February 1996, Granada grabbed a share of CCG Services, then the UK's largest remaining independent contractor run by Frank Bell, buying its B&I business, worth £60m in turnover, but not its school meals or international interests which Bell continued to run (see overleaf).

Four months later, Granada bought again – this time Bromwich Catering, a long-established Midlands-based company with 130 contracts and a turnover of £18m, which had its roots in a family company founded in 1837. Frank Jones, its chairman, was 60 and had had 42 years in the industry; he was looking for the best way of assuring the company's future – "I decided that if I could do a deal with Granada, then that was the best way to go," he said. Once again, promises were made to retain the trading name.

"The existing Bromwich team will stay in place and the company will continue to trade as it has done, while we bring it benefits in IT and support services," said Alistair Storey.

Granada's self-confessed appetite for acquisitions became the talk of the industry and reflected the company's determination to buy its way into growth. This is exactly what Robinson did with the biggest bid of his career: his audacious £3.1bn hostile bid for Forte, which he launched in late 1995 and which was successfully completed in early 1996. Described variously as 'vicious',

Frank Bell and CCG

Frank Bell: it was a time of heady growth in B&I and with privatisation Frank saw the opportunities that healthcare, MoD and school meals presented.

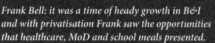

Yes Dining, launched in 1999 with John Wood, quickly won the catering contract at JP Morgan in London which CCG had held before its sale to Compass. Wood had worked for CCG at JP Morgan before selling to Granada.

One of Granada's acquisitions during its decade of heady expansion was the B&I contracts of Commercial Catering Group (CCG).

CCG was founded by Frank Bell in 1964. Born in the Gorbals, Glasgow, in 1932, Bell had a tough childhood; his mother, Agnes, died when he was five. He became an apprentice chef at the Old Grand Hotel, Glasgow, where his father was head waiter, but by 1963 he found himself working at Peter Merchant's Ford contract at Dagenham as catering manager.

The pull of his native roots, however, was too strong to resist. When the job of general manager in Scotland came up with Bateman he grabbed it, delighted to be back in his home territory. Happy to be back and like many since, he soon decided he could do as well working for himself than for someone else. Within a year, aged 30, he launched CCG with his lawyer and partner, Hugh Workman.

Like all such start-ups, it was a difficult time. Operating from a single room office, his first contract took six months to win but by the end of the year he had won three more. It was, in fact, a good time to be going alone, particularly in Scotland. The North Sea oil boom offered opportunities galore and he quickly moved into providing hotel services for the oil and gas fields for construction camps and off-shore. Forming a facilities management company, CCG Contracting Ltd, he began to provide 24-hour catering, cleaning, administration support and medical care.

It was a time of growth in B&I, too, and Bell saw the opportunities that competitive tendering of healthcare, MoD and school meals presented. At one stage, in six weeks the company located, designed, equipped and staffed a central production unit to serve up to 20,000 meals a day for more than 100 schools. The business grew and by 1995 CCG was serving over 200,000 school meals a day, had 8,000 employees and was turning over £100m a year. It made CCG the biggest of the independent contractors.

It acquired Spinneys, though the hospital catering contracts did not stay for long as Bell decided to focus on schools. Needless to say, his success attracted the bigger beasts of the jungle. He was wooed by many of them but refused to sell out for over 30 years until 1999 when he eventually sold CCG's 200 B&I contracts (as well as the name but not the school meals or the oil and gas contracts) to Granada for £40m. It gave Granada a multi-site deal with the Royal Bank of Scotland and its first off-shore contracts – a new market for the company.

Bell renamed the rump of his company Castle View.

Don Davenport at Granada promised to keep the CCG name as a brand on its own – "It won't be merged with Sutcliffe," he said. "We want the company to carry on in the way it has been doing." But it was a stable of brands that was growing by the month and eventually the name disappeared.

Frank Bell became chairman while CCG's managing directors, Peter Kelly and Lindsay Tocher, continued to run the business under Davenport as chief executive. Bell was happy. He had been impressed by the way Granada had handled the Sutcliffe and Fairfield acquisitions.

The loss of the B&I contracts, worth some £65m a year in turnover, considerably reduced earnings and profit for the rest of his company but what remained was significant. Castle View's oil and gas contracts were worth some £30m a year and school meals enjoyed an annual turnover of £40m – "It's still going to be a tight margin business but there's growth potential in state schools if you can manage costs and get good purchasing agreements," he told *Caterer*.

Bell sold to Granada because some directors wanted out "and I wanted money to expand", he told *Caterer* in the same interview. "What we got from Granada for the B&I contracts sorted things out and cleared all the debts. We owe nobody now. We're turning over £75m and we're on the move." In fact, the jewel in the crown had to be sold because the company's bank had decided it didn't want to support CCG any more.

That 'move' in 1999 was back into B&I but an experience of losing a bid to Leith's for the Edinburgh International Conference Centre because he had no experience of high street catering led him to believe he needed some commercial profile if he was serious about expanding. In 1997 he opened YES, a high street restaurant in Glasgow; at the same time, the restaurant gave him the idea for Yes Dining. What he planned was a new niche catering contracting business in a very crowded market.

In fact, Yes Dining, which he launched in 1999 with John Wood, quickly won the catering contract at JP Morgan in London, which CCG had held before the sale to Compass; Leith's, another Compass subsidiary, handled JP Morgan's directors' dining which Yes Dining also won.

Wood had worked for CCG at JP Morgan before it was sold to Granada. JP Morgan turned over £3.5m and Yes Dining's turnover was £8m in its first year, presaging its 11-year period into B&I and local authority catering.

But the growth of the new company was not on the scale that CCG had back in the 1970s; there was more competition for one thing and although Yes Dining's open book accounting had its attractions to clients – "They know we have to make a profit and we'll tell them how much" – by 2005, when Woods left, although having 20 contracts including the GLC and Allied Irish Bank, the company made a pre-tax loss of £5,725 on turnover of £5.1m. Yes Dining was clearly struggling.

In 2002 Bell had already slimmed the company down by selling off his profitable school meals subsidiary, Castle Independent, which was generating turnover of £30m a year, to Compass for £16m, but it took another five years before Yes Dining was sold to the somewhat inappropriately named Bright Futures Group (BFG).

This was a company with ambitions which had floated on the PLUS market in 2008; it was already in contract catering with two trading subsidiaries: Restaurants at Work and Jill Bartlett Company.

At the time of the takeover, Yes Dining was trading with an annual turnover of £4.5m but the business was struggling to make a profit because of the brutal competition. The final straw came when 45 other contractors turned up at a bidders' day. BFG was a clean way for Bell to get out but still have some interest in the business as a major shareholder.

Chris Mitchell was brought in as managing director of BFG, with the idea

of merging the three companies into one, thus saving on overheads and streamlining the business, but with the recession still impacting the industry the timing was all wrong; the banks took control and Restaurants at Work and Jill Bartlett were forced into administration (and then into BaxterStorey's hands), leaving Yes Dining as a standalone company.

Mitchell told *Caterer* it was "an awful name. What does Yes Dining mean, anyway?"

"We had a complete rebranding, the management team completely changed and it was effectively a brand-new start up for us all."

At this juncture, looking around for investors, Mitchell successfully completed an MBO with Luke Johnson, the former Pizza Express chairman, acquiring a majority stake in the company. Yes Dining was swiftly renamed the Genuine Dining Co – a company which continues to this day as a successful and award-winning niche contractor.

Meanwhile, Frank Bell, now aged over 70, had gradually been handing over the day-to-day running of Castle View to his sons though he still played an active part in the business. In 2002, Martin Bell took over as managing director.

Now out of catering contracting altogether, almost 50 years after Frank Bell created CCG working out of his front room, Castle View continues as a successful privately-owned group of businesses comprising sports and leisure facilities management, food production, procurement and catering management systems, working with the NHS, Great Ormond Street Hospital and 27 local authorities.

Frank died of cancer in 2011.

'acrimonious', 'opportunistic', it was all those things: a no-holds barred assault on a family company that had become an emblem of British hospitality even though the family had Italian roots.

Three years had gone by. It was only after the furore of Granada's highly publicised bid for LWT in 1994 that Robinson again turned his attention to Forte. The timing was near-perfect. Forte's results were reflecting the effects of the Gulf War against Iraq; pre-tax profits had slumped from £215m in 1990 down to £61m and then had climbed back only to £127m by 1995. The company was also facing questions from City analysts and rumours abounded that Forte was now in play.

* * *

Robinson and his team poured over the Forte business, analysing the accounts and inspecting every outlet. This even involved Don Davenport and Frank Whittaker who were asked to look at the Little Chef, motorway service and budget hotel divisions of the Forte empire. The specific aim of this analysis was to be able to announce to the City that over £120m-worth of savings could be generated by a Granada takeover of Forte. The eventual conclusion of this remarkably detailed analysis was that the savings were achievable and that Forte was indeed 'soft'.

Robinson was amazed at Forte plc's lack of preparedness. "You would have thought they would have reasoned that as Granada's name was being mentioned and we had results coming out in a few days, they had better be on the alert, just in case," he says in his biography.

Robinson's early morning courtesy call to Rocco, which found him shooting on the moors and unobtainable, has found its way into corporate legend. For Rocco, it was certainly a public relations disaster that did

little to help his subsequent defence of the family business which was now imperilled by a powerful marauder at the gates – one which Robinson believes Rocco should have seen approaching.

The eventual acquisition of Forte for £3.87bn has been well documented elsewhere. What followed was Robinson's well-tried and tested tactic of selling off unwanted bits of the company (Granada was committed to £2.1bn of asset disposals at the outset – principally Forte's hotel brands) and improving profit margins by introducing the programme that cut costs by the £120m which had been part of Davenport's and Whittaker's remit. It also showed, more generally, that he and Charles Allen were not afraid of tweaking any lion's tail even if, in their opinion, Forte had been more like a dozing cat.

This huge deal, however, did not slow down Granada's push into contract catering. Even if the prize of Gardner Merchant had eluded them, Robinson and Allen remained determined to build up Sutcliffe into a contracting giant. In one year, in 1997, it acquired 3 Gates, Shaw Catering, Baxter & Platts and Pall Mall – four thriving independent contractors.

The first, in January, was 3 Gates, founded in 1996 by David Walker and Mike Greaves and based in Warrington. The company had 60 contracts in the north of England worth some £6m annually.

Only a day later, Granada announced it had acquired Shaw Catering, a company that Jim Cartwright, an ex-regional director of Compass, had originally bought and had built up to 220 contracts worth some £23m annually – "A very healthy business, financially well run, with some very good clients and a lot of client loyalty," says Storey. Cartwright and fellow directors Peter Bland and Mike Latimer stayed on for a year as part of the deal but went on to create Cygnet

Catering (which was sold to Compass in 2011) before Cartwright launched another company, Dine Catering, which is still prospering (see Chapter 28).

In June, nearly 10 years after resigning from Sutcliffe to set up their own company, William Baxter and Robert Platts sold their business back to Granada for £15m – a high price for an outfit with a £23m turnover, but one that Storey claimed was worth it: "The reason we bought them is that they are a very high-quality niche player," he says. With clients such as Whitbread, Price Waterhouse and the Financial Times, Baxter & Platts had some high profile outlets and the company had been named Food Service Caterer of the Year in 1996.

But Granada's acquisitiveness was beginning to worry clients. Independent caterers, though still numerous, were clearly being picked off by the major contractors and this was narrowing client choice alarmingly. Those that had purposefully chosen a small independent possibly on the grounds of personal service were suddenly finding that they had a different and perhaps unwanted contractor on their doorstep. This was the main reason why Granada had decided to keep the names of its acquisitions as a separate business and to ensure that the owner and other key personnel remained in post, though in many cases, this was not successful. Even William Baxter had to admit that there were sensitivities, "especially where a client may have replaced Granada with us. But people buy people, generally, and those people are staying in place".

Caterer even interviewed Chris Scott, director of facilities management at Whitbread, who told the paper that he would have preferred Baxter & Platts to remain independent.

"Clearly one of the benefits of working with a smaller independent company is that we can influence the service and the value for money directly with the top man." He added: "It might be more difficult to deal with Granada at that level."

Baxter stayed on with Granada until 1999 though Robert Platts retired earlier to Guernsey on the grounds of ill health.

In fact, the growing plethora of brands was causing some internal confusion and angst at Granada. Whittaker found that much of his time was spent in arbitrating disputes between the various sales forces, many of whom were simultaneously wanting to win the same client.

In June 1997, Granada acquired its fourth prize – the non-cleaning interests of Pall Mall Services from Davis Services Group. With 57 contracts and turning over £40m in healthcare, Defence and B&I, including Moorfields Eye Hospital and RAF Lyneham, Pall Mall had experienced some well publicised industrial relations issues and in the previous year had reported a pre-tax loss of £163,000. It was pertinent that Granada told *Caterer* that its own excellent industrial relations record would be 'a core benefit for the Pall Mall business.' The business was absorbed into Granada's specialist divisions – healthcare, defence and ACMS.

With its four acquisitions during the year, Granada had bought almost £100m worth of turnover; it was growing fast but it was another nine months before it took control of the available 49 per cent stake in Quadrant, the Post Office caterer in a £70m joint venture. Competition for this prize had been strong, "very detailed and very competitive", says Storey. But it was a prize worth having, giving Granada 446 staff restaurants serving 55,000 meals a week. David Bate, formerly managing director of Sutcliffe's South West region, was appointed Quadrant's managing director.

A few months later, in April 1998, came Reading-based Capitol Catering, with 65

contracts in the South East turning over £10m annually. Founded in 1990 by Ian Tritton and Gordon Haggerty, the company remained an independent within Granada, with both signing a deal restricting them from starting up another contract catering business within two years. Tritton took a long sabbatical and Haggerty moved to Summit but in 2002 they decided to re-enter the market, with Derek Warman as finance director, to form a new company, Accent. Tritton said he wanted "to come back and do it better". He took a back seat and Haggerty took over as managing director until his early death from leukemia, aged 60, in 2014; Accent continues to thrive as an independent.

Summit Catering was also in Granada's sights but before that, in June 1998, it acquired Carlton Support Services, a Cheshire-based contractor with 65 contracts and a turnover of £13.5m formed in 1992 by former in-house catering managers at ICI led by managing director John Salisbury. Later, in November, Customised Contract Catering (CCC), with 40 contracts and turning over some £4.5m a year, fell into Granada's lap. The company was originally named MDA Food Services when it was launched in 1992 by its two founders, Mike Day and Lou Willcock, but changed its name to CCC when it merged with the Aspen Group in 1997, taking on Richard Adams and Martin Felstead, the founding partners.

In late February 1999, Granada completed lengthy negotiations to buy Summit for £6.5m. Its founder, Chris Richards, had repeatedly denied the company was for sale 'at any price' but, with over 100 contracts and a £15m annual turnover, it was an irresistible target. "Summit has a very strong contracts base and is a natural fit for our current business," Storey told *Caterer*. He said it would continue as an independently

managed business. Richards stayed on as chairman but Granada brought in Graham Alston, managing director for Sutcliffe's Thames Valley region, as its new managing director.

The Summit purchase brought Granada's annual contract catering sales to over £800m. For the company the decade had been a period of unabated growth though it lost contracts as well as gaining them. Since 1984 there had been various reorganisations of the business as it absorbed the new acquisitions; overseas interests, retail, Ministry of Defence and vending interests were also contributing but under different management to the Sutcliffe business. In 1993, Don Davenport had moved over from managing director of Granada Services to the Business division (effectively Sutcliffe), then to Granada Hospitality, and two years later became chief executive of Granada Restaurants with responsibility for Little Chef and Travelodge. Storey had taken control of the Sutcliffe business.

Along the way, Granada had lost a few experienced players. Geoffrey Harrison had already quit. Rick Holroyd and Nick Howe followed in 1997 to set up Holroyd Howe. William Baxter and Robert Platts left in 1999 and Mike Smith quit as managing director of Baxter & Platts three months later in 2000, joining Baxter to form Baxter Smith.

Perhaps the biggest defection of all was Alastair Storey, who resigned in March 2000 as managing director of the Granada Food Services division to launch Wilson Storey with Sutcliffe's then finance director, Keith Wilson.

What had hastened the latter departures was the impending merger in 2000 of Compass and Granada. It was a deal that worried the City as much as Granada's takeover of Forte a couple of years earlier but it was one that was to create the world's biggest food service provider.

CHAPTER TWENTY-SIX

*Granada and Compass:
merger of the giants*

The merger between Compass and Granada upset the City – but it paved the way for a global leader.

In the six months to March 2000, contract catering profits for Granada (the former Sutcliffe business) were up by 11 per cent to £59m, while Compass' global turnover for the same period was up 12.1 per cent to £2.6bn and its pre-tax profit had risen 15 per cent to £90.7m. Compass was the bigger catering company because of its extensive overseas interests while Granada brought in large hotel brands – Le Méridien, Posthouses and Travelodge – but these were secondary and needed to be off-loaded. The prize for Compass was Sutcliffe Catering, Fairfield Catering and Granada's defence and hospital catering interests.

The announcement was lauded as a significant business opportunity by both companies, but the City regarded it as a dangerous gamble. The two companies were considered strange bedfellows. Granada was a UK-based media company albeit with significant (but new-found) hotel assets acquired in one of the City's most hostile takeover battles, and Compass was a highly focused and well regarded catering company with no interest in other sectors of the hospitality industry and with publicly stated ambitions to move onto the international stage.

The announcement in May 2000 explained that Granada (value £12bn) and Compass (value £6bn) would merge and then de-merge six months later into two separate companies. Despite the behind the scenes work that had been going on for months, the announcement took the markets by surprise – never a good outcome – and the Compass share price paid for it, dropping 47p or 15 per cent on the day. Granada's price plunged even more: 39p on the first day and another 42p the following day. It was not an auspicious start for one of the stock market's biggest deals.

The reaction of the City was worrying to both Gerry Robinson and Francis Mackay, the key players. The deal had been extensively worked and re-worked, the arguments had been thrashed out and for them it was a brilliant and extraordinarily tax-efficient way of establishing a major catering company while spinning off one of the country's most prominent television broadcasters.

One factor behind the deal was that retirement was on Robinson's mind. He wanted to leave Granada in good order and not be subject to a hostile takeover after he had left. He was keen to see the company's media interests hived off into a separate company, while Mackay was keen to acquire Sutcliffe and the other catering interests. The only part of Granada that neither party wanted was the multiplicity of Forte hotels, although, again for tax reasons, this was not made clear at the time.

Given these objectives, it took no great leap of imagination for both to look favourably on a merger with each other; Gerry Robinson and Charles Allen knew all about Compass, which was their old stomping ground where they had made their original fortunes, while Mackay had forged Compass into one of the most highly rated companies in the FTSE 500. A direct sale of Sutcliffe alone had already been ruled out as it would have generated an unacceptable £1.2bn capital gains tax bill. It was entirely because of the tax complications that the two companies had decided on the merger and subsequent de-merger – "It's more complicated to do this than sell off the media business, but it's much more tax efficient," admitted a Granada spokesman publicly. The proposal would leave Compass Group plc with all the hotel and catering interests and Granada Media plc with all the broadcasting interests.

Both companies were profitable: Robinson's and Allen's legendary cost-control techniques had seen to that at Granada. Sutcliffe, in particular, had been subjected to enormous cost pressures and it was difficult to see how further profits could be generated from the company without inflicting damage on it. It was one reason, no doubt, for Robinson's enthusiasm for the deal.

"We had stripped every cost that we could out of the system," says Frank Whittaker, "and there was no way to increase revenues organically." Alastair Storey, who quit just before the merger took place, describes it rather more vividly:

"If we had stretched the operating resources much thinner, we would have disappeared. The company was like a donkey flogged to death and haemorrhaging on the side of the road."

Clearly, Sutcliffe's margins, later revealed at 12.2 per cent, were astonishingly high and unsustainable.

Meanwhile, Compass was well on the way to its rapid expansion across the globe and Mackay realised that the planned merger would help catapult it into UK dominance, achieving significant cost savings and purchasing leverage and, at the same time, giving it extra weight to achieve further international stardom. Nevertheless, the complexity of bringing the two companies together and then de-merging was almost overwhelming. It had not been achieved before and all kinds of questions were raised internally: What would Compass do with

A tabloid newspaper was produced for Granada and Compass staff explaining the purpose – and benefits – of the merger.

the hotels? How would the City take it? Would the two companies merge easily? How would the clients take it?

At the outset, Citibank, Compass' lead adviser, prepared a preliminary paper and outlined the options highlighting one major area of concern for Granada: if not Compass then who? Remembering the acrimony that the Compass abortive bid had caused when it sought to acquire Gardner Merchant in 1992, Mackay was initially wary about the idea of merging with a major competitor which had such a plethora of other interests, though he recognised that it would be a huge step towards realising his ambitions for Compass. No doubt, too, he was wary of Robinson who had already been in talks with Aramark before Compass had been approached but the talks had come to nothing. Mackay thought that Aramark, still ambitious, might propose a similar arrangement to the one he was considering with Granada. Recognising a formidable competitor in Joe Neubauer, the CEO of Aramark – "tougher than any we had in the market at the time" – he certainly didn't want Sutcliffe to end up in Neubauer's lap.

However, both Robinson and Mackay were too experienced not to recognise the key advantages of their proposed deal: the opportunity to bring about efficiencies in terms of area and divisional management of the catering operations (in other words, redundancies and significant cost savings), as well as hugely boosting Compass' purchasing power. Some £70m worth of savings was suggested. With a greater share of the UK market – over 40 per cent – it was a chance to ease the pressure on margins which Granada had pushed to the limit. From Robinson's point of view, it would create a broadcaster that could happily expand in the media environment without the encumbrance of catering and leisure interests.

The hotels were the sticking point. With the Forte merger, Granada had acquired the mid-market Posthouse chain, the international Le Méridien group, the traditional Heritage chain of olde-worlde coaching inns (the basis of the original Trust Houses empire), as well as a handful of major London properties including the Cumberland and Strand Palace hotels and the budget-end Travelodge brand – well over 400 properties and many located outside the UK. In normal circumstances Compass would never have considered purchasing them, nor did it have the slightest interest in retaining them. The objective was to maintain Mackay's focus on catering. At the time, however, this could only be hinted at: "We will undertake a review of the assets as soon as the merger is completed," said a spokesman guardedly; he promised an announcement on the fate of the hotels only after the merged companies had completed a strategic review. The statement did not encourage the City but there was a good reason for it.

"If we had decided to sell them before the strategic review and before the transaction had been completed, and had started the sale process at the time of the transaction, we would have undermined the deal, which could have generated a £300m tax charge," Mackay says.

Mackay and Robinson stood firm against the resulting clamour most strongly expressed by Commerzbank, which had been following Compass' progress for a number of years. The bank complained that the main benefit of the deal was to free up Granada's media operations without any debt while offloading onto Compass a large number of hotels from the Forte takeover that Granada could not sell. In view of the rapidity with which Compass offloaded them, this did not turn out to be a very valid objection but it was real enough at

the time. Indeed, one overlooked advantage of the deal was that it led to a significant capital injection into Compass of about £4bn without any equity discount. For the company to get hold of that amount of capital would have created a significant dilution of the equity base. At the time of the merger, however, the success of these disposals was in the future and analysts were downplaying a favourable outcome.

* * *

The clamour against the proposed merger persisted. Commerzbank complained the deal lost Compass its pure play status of being a focused contract catering company to one that was now saddled with a disparate clutch of hotels. Worse was the £3bn of debt. The nub of the concern was that highly-rated Compass, with very little debt, would be weighed down by Granada's slow-growing hotels and its significant debt pile. Granada had also starved the hotels of significant capital investment which made them even less attractive as an investment. Dresdner Kleinwort Benson described it as a merger for merger's sake and slapped a reduce recommendation on Compass shares, down from buy. There was also some disappointment in the marketplace that the lingering hope that Granada would make an outright bid for Compass and pay a premium for control had disappeared. Although, it was recognised that the merger would create significant purchasing and some revenue benefits from the roadside operations (Granada Roadside Catering was later rebranded as Moto), it was not a deal that the stock market considered had been made in heaven.

The market's misgivings continued to be expressed as Mackay and Robinson operated an immediate charm offensive on the City, explaining the benefits and advantages of the merger and the proposed de-merger, one of which was the planned cost savings of £70m. Some investors took advantage of the fall in the share price to buy in, while those (a minority) who didn't approve sold out, leaving a shareholder base that approved of the deal.

"We knew 40 per cent of the shareholders of the two companies were the same institutions but there was concern by the remaining Compass shareholders that the large asset base that Compass was now taking on was about to coincide with an imminent recession – some of them subscribed to the seven-year economic cycle and we were in the seventh year at the time," says Mackay.

"It was also true that some had consciously not invested in Granada and here we were taking them into it. Not surprisingly, they didn't like it. We did argue that retaining the hotels was a good option because more than half of the turnover was restaurant sales and with our experience of branding, we could make the sites more of a destination and significantly increase their profitability. In fact, this had been a market sector for Compass even before the Granada merger."

This argument tended to ignore the fact that the restaurant sales were far less profitable than room sales and much of the Forte profit had been generated by the rooms.

However, staff were told in *Your World News* the benefits of the merger: "It widely extends our existing business across the globe, giving us further opportunities for organic growth. It also takes us into new market sectors of hotels and motorway and roadside catering, with their opportunities for cross-selling and extending our brand portfolio."

Even Mackay explained: "The combination of the hotels and foodservice businesses will be a key advantage in our future successful growth."

But this was never the planned outcome. Compass certainly intended to retain Sutcliffe in order to make the combined company by far the dominant caterer in the UK, but the hotels were always superfluous to requirements.

The plan was to create a holding company, Granada:Compass, with Robinson as chairman and Mackay and Allen as joint deputy chairmen. Mackay and Mike Bailey were responsible for the catering and hospitality part of the business while Allen ran the media company; he lost little time in expanding. The day after the merger was completed on 27th July 2000, he acquired United News and Media's television interests for £1.75bn.

By the time the de-merger was completed, on 1st February 2001, two separate companies had been created: Compass Group, worth £7bn, with Mackay as chairman, Bailey as chief executive, Andrew Lynch as finance director, and Don Davenport as CEO of the combined Compass/Sutcliffe businesses; Granada Media was chaired by Allen. Robinson became a non-executive director of Granada and a consultant to Compass with a view to retiring at the end of 2003; he earned £6m from the deal and a further £3.5m acting as a Compass consultant until October 2003. Allen earned £4m, plus £2m in pay and shares over the next 18 months.

* * *

UK Margin Analysis – Compass and Granada Food Services 1998/99

Compass				Granada Food Services		
Sales (£m)	PBIT† (£m)	Margin (%)	Segment	Sales (£m)	PBIT† (£m)	Margin (%)
304.1	17.1	5.6	Business & Industry	630.7*	78.2	12.4
71.7	5.9	8.3	Off-shore & Remote	-	-	-
51.1	1.8	3.5	Healthcare	78.7	9.1	11.6
82.4	5.7	6.9	Education	66.0	9.6	14.5
131.0	17.0	12.9	Rail	-	-	-
43.0	2.6	6.1	Airports	33.0	5.4	16.2
12.5	(0.2)	-	Shopping Malls	-	-	-
6.0	0.4	7.2	In-store	44.0	2.2	4.9
5.5	0.2	2.9	Leisure	-	-	-
-	-	-	Ferries	21.0	1.9	9.1
96.0	4.9	5.1	Sports & Leisure	6.0	0.9	15.8
3.2	0.5	15.0	Vending	-	-	-
7.4	(0.02)	-	Cataforce	-	-	-
15.9	(0.08)	-	Design and Planning	-	-	-
-	(0.66)	-	Central overheads	-	-	-
830.4	55.1	6.6	Totals	879.4	107.3	12.2

*including Defence turnover of £45m.
†PBIT is after deduction (for Compass) of all direct costs and overheads including allocation of shared overheads such as financial services and business systems (also for Granada including finance, HR, marketing and sales but excluding Stockport accounts office).

Bill Vickers: The merger was surprisingly smooth, though it was very difficult to shake off old loyalties

The early disposal of the hotels was an immediate step. Not surprisingly, only three months after the creation of Granada:Compass the promised strategic review concluded that the hotels were, after all, expendable – a conclusion that was, no doubt, influenced by the continuing slump in the group's share price which the hotels were dragging down. The announcement that they would be sold as soon as the de-merger was completed in the spring of 2001 was received with approval in the City: it was, after all, one of the main criticisms of the merger in the first place.

"A sale of the hotels would definitely be positive for the shares," said one analyst, Tony Shepard at broker Charles Stanley. "There's no convincing logic to any synergy."

In the event, in 2001, three of the hotel brands were successfully sold off – Posthouses to Bass for £810m, Heritage Hotels to Macdonald for £235m and Le Méridien to Nomura for £1.9bn – the latter a premium price. Three Forte London

Signature hotels went to various bidders for a total of £315m (because of landlord issues, the Strand Palace remained with Compass for some years). Later, in 2003, Travelodge and Little Chef were sold to Permira (formerly Schroder Ventures) for £712m. As with all good decisions, one deal brought about its own luck. The sale of Le Méridien was completed in July 2001, just before 9/11, which created a slump in the worldwide hotel industry. "Something of the guardian angels about that," says Mackay, happily.

The sums netted over £3.9bn which gave Compass the capital to write down debt and expand into the USA, the engine room of Compass' success which is still growing today at some eight per cent a year under Gary Green, who is widely regarded as a key player in Compass' later success.

At the same time, a huge effort was undertaken to merge the Compass and Sutcliffe catering operations. The same challenges reared their head as they do with all such heavyweight mergers: how to amalgamate two different company cultures though they were not as widely dissimilar as Granada's takeover of Sutcliffe back in 1993. Both companies had been through the Robinson cost-cutting/margin-improvement regime even if it had been seven years since Robinson and Allen had left Compass. Would Sutcliffe's more aggressive approach to margins impact on Compass' clients? Which company personalities would win through and which would lose out? How would the new company be structured? How to maintain staff morale? How could the sales teams be best coordinated? How to integrate the different accounting and IT systems? Above all, how to keep the clients on side?

At the outset, an integration team was established with, on the Compass side, Trevor Briggs (managing director of specialist operations), Mike Burton (HR

director) and Bill Vickers (marketing services director); on the Granada side were Mike Spiller (personnel and training director), Chris Rayner (HR director) and Frank Whittaker (sales and marketing director). The individuals were chosen "for their high credibility and perceived fairness... with past experience of acquisitions, re-organisations and change management." Although Granada's Don Davenport had already been signposted as the new head of the combined UK contract catering businesses – called Compass Hospitality – it was clear that Compass would end up in the dominant position.

Mike Bailey told *Caterer* firmly: "There's no doubt that Compass management and culture will be the leaders in the situation."

One problem quickly emerged: By the time of the merger, Sutcliffe was operating on a margin of 12.2 per cent. In the words of one expert, "no contract catering company in the world has ever successfully operated at such a high margin, and never will".

John Greenwood: one of life's gentlemen.

They were unsustainable and even Robinson must have recognised there was no more organic growth to be squeezed out of the company. The merger with Compass had, in fact, been a necessity for Granada. With margins at almost twice that of Compass which, even at 6.6 per cent, were above the industry norm of 3-4 per cent, the merger with Compass was a safe harbour for Granada in what would have become a very turbulent sea if it had not gone ahead.

Something had to give. Yet merging the two companies was surprisingly painless. Although there were job losses, the integration committee, reporting to Davenport, took less than a year to amalgamate the two businesses to the satisfaction of most.

"The merger was surprisingly smooth, though it was very difficult to shake off old loyalties," says Bill Vickers.

Whittaker claims that communication was the key. The integration team had a very wide brief. It had the responsibility of recommending the future organisational structure of the combined company, the job roles and the names of the most suitable people for these roles. In short, it was to take the best from both companies in terms of people, ideas, systems, processes, communications, brands and purchasing. But there was understandable concern among senior staff about who would win through and who would lose out, as redundancies and some office closures were seen to be inevitable. An early casualty had been John Greenwood, Compasss CEO, whom Davenport had replaced. Greenwood, one of life's gentlemen, moved to Roadchef as chief executive until 2004 but had serious health issues and died in 2008.

A 16-page document examined each sector of the business, highlighting the key questions to be answered. Bailey admits that the two food service businesses operated

very differently. "But, to be honest, nothing that we could not resolve fairly quickly."

"The main reason it went well," says Whittaker, "is that we communicated with everyone." Even so, he noticed that the styles of management were different, Compass being the more cautious and keener to set up a meeting to resolve an issue whereas Sutcliffe's style had always been more urgent – "load, fire and aim afterwards" is how he describes it.

"We had been Gerry-ised for the last seven years and we had grown up in a very commercial environment," he says. "Gerry's impact on Compass was in the distant past. And there were turf wars as the various sales teams fought out their new sphere of activities. My main job was keeping the sales teams from each other's throats."

As part of the re-organisation, Peter Aldrich, Sutcliffe's managing director, was appointed managing director for corporate accounts, while Nigel Dunlop, previously Compass' operations director, became managing director of B&I and leisure. Trevor Briggs moved over to take charge of specialist markets for the combined company, including education, healthcare, MoD and local authority catering. Tony Monnickendam, at SSP, took over other retail outlets, Chris Copner remained in charge of Granada's Little Chef and Travelodge divisions as well as the motorway service areas and Harry Ramsden's, while David Mortimer, Granada Restaurants' commercial director, became finance director. Mike Burton, HR director at Compass, took over HR responsibility for the combined group. Mike Oldfield, who had moved to Compass from Sutcliffe at the time of the Granada takeover, was appointed business relations director charged with implementing a comprehensive client and customer satisfaction programme – an indication

that maintaining good client relations was seen as a top priority; he was also charged with developing the company's vending and FM businesses.

By and large, Compass Hospitality was more or less evenly balanced with both Compass and Granada/Sutcliffe top people in place. One reason for this was that many of the key players had known each other for most of their careers and had even worked with each other in the past. "There's a no question that that made life easier for us all as there was mutual respect," says one who was deeply involved.

* * *

By mid-2001, Compass was set fair for the future. Indeed, in the next four years the company experienced extraordinary growth. Mackay, always the great visionary as Copner calls him, had set his sights on worldwide expansion to which Bailey, Don Davenport and the senior team subscribed in no small measure. The driver was growth and the main focus was overseas.

In 2000, Beaver Foods was acquired in Canada for £142m followed by Au Bon Pain, a north east US mainstream coffee and sandwich brand, for £77m. In 2001, Atlanta-based Morrison Management Services was purchased for £397m, providing food, nutrition and dining services to healthcare and senior living communities throughout the US – the company has since grown to more than 18,000 food service workers as well as 15,000 employees in over 900 outlets. An FM provider, Crothall Healthcare, currently serving 1,200 healthcare clients in 41 states, was bought in the same year for £138m.

Compass then entered into a joint venture with Abu Dhabi National Hotels to operate its extensive catering interests in the Middle East, providing facility management

Credit TopFoto/UPPA

The SSP franchise agreement with Marks and Spencer Simply Food outlets was extended to over 40 shops.

services in the UAE, Egypt and Qatar. Before the year was out, Compass had purchased the Swiss-based Selecta Group, a large European vending services operator, for £361m.

It was a heady round of international acquisitions. In 2002 came the purchase of Seiyo Foods, a long-established food service provider in Japan for £337m; Seiyo now operates nearly 2,000 outlets with over 24,000 employees. In the States, Compass bought up Bon Appétit Management Company, an on-site restaurant company based in Palo Alto, California providing full food service management to corporations, universities and specialty venues, now with more than 500 cafés in 33 states. It then cleared an EU Commission enquiry for a 60 per cent stake in the purchase of the Italian-based Onama Group, for €127m, now Italy's largest restaurant chain. The rate of expansion resulted in Compass eventually operating contracts in 98 countries.

The company became a darling of the City, though some critics were beginning to wonder whether there was too much froth in the expansion: was it concentrating too much on top-line growth and ignoring underlying profitability? It also entailed a huge span of control which, by 2005, had begun to look as if it was just getting too unwieldy to handle

At home, the SSP franchise agreement with Marks and Spencer Simply Food outlets had been extended to over 40 shops and a couple of acquisitions had been made – the 60 or so B&I contracts in Frank Bell's CCG company and, in 2004, the small-time Emerson Hewett, founded in 1995.

By the end of 2004 and into 2005 the bubble burst. Davenport, who was 62 and had successfully steered Compass through the merger with Granada as CEO, announced that he had been considering retirement for a long time and now was the time to go. With the departure of Davenport went Clive Grundy, HR director, and Ron Morley, the Group company secretary. Davenport's departure was something of a turning point. He had been one of the driving forces in the merger of UK enterprises and his influence on the company had been significant.

"Don is so focused," says Anthony Adams. "He's so helpful. You don't *not* ever listen to what he has to say." A man of great charm, drive and experience, he had been largely instrumental in ensuring that the merger of Compass and Granada had worked so smoothly.

"He was such a dominant figure and his departure marks a complete change of culture," opined the oft-quoted Chris Stern, the food service consultant, in *Caterer* at the time. It was certainly true that change was around the corner.

In Davenport's place stepped Peter Harris, an old Compass hand and chief executive of the subsidiary ESS Support Services in the Middle East. Davenport's retirement had led to the decision to merge Compass' UK and Ireland division with the Middle East and Africa in a wider attempt to cut costs by reducing its eight operating divisions to four. Running the two divisions was a big step up for Harris.

At the same time, Compass was undergoing a business review that was attempting to save £50m in overheads by 2006. It announced its intention to sell SSP – highly lucrative but capital-intensive – on the grounds that it wasn't a main core business. The pressure was on to boost profits when the opposite happened: a trio of warnings over 18 months slashed £66m off operating profits and, at one time, cut the share price by 34 per cent.

* * *

In many ways, the cause of these warnings was outside the control of Compass. The transfer of military and off-shore accounts to other parts of the world had cost £18m; the demise of Peters Food Services, one of the group's leading distributors, cost £13m in transferring the business to Brakes, while a decision to cut payment terms from 90 days to 55 days required an injection

Compass hits a UN scandal

Eurest Support Services (ESS) and a registered food supplier to the UN was accused of bribing a UN official to improperly obtain confidential information concerning a three-year contract to supply food and water to UN peacekeepers in Liberia. It was alleged that nearly $1m was paid out. The two companies that lost out to Compass on the deal were Es-KO, a Monaco-based international FM provider, and Supreme Foodservice AG, based in Switzerland.

It was a serious charge that hit the headlines of the nationals on both sides of the Atlantic and had the potential to significantly derail Compass' ambitions, certainly in the US, if not handled properly. The company was suspended from the UN's list of suppliers and the damage could have easily escalated without some immediate action.

Compass brought in Freshfields, its law firm, and Ernst and Young, its accountants, to investigate the allegations. It was a smart move that took some of the PR heat out of the situation. "Investors should not underestimate the impact of scary headlines," one City analyst was reported saying. "There is still a huge amount of uncertainty surrounding the ESS fiasco."

This uncertainty did not last long, however. Freshfields reported back to the board. The investigation, involving conference calls some lasting eight to 10 hours in Bailey's recollection, was concluded quickly. That there was seen to be some truth in the allegations was reflected in the instant dismissal of Peter Harris, who had only just succeeded Davenport, and two others – Andy Seiwert (sales executive) and Doug Kerr (operations manager). Harris had overseen the ESS business for some years and had been instrumental in building it up; it was an unfortunate end to a blossoming career at Compass but it emphasised the company's determination to get the scandal off the front pages.

However, there was still the question of compensation. The lawsuits brought by Es-Ko and Supreme claimed they had lost $600m by losing out to Compass; this figure was dismissed out of hand as bearing no relation to the value of the UN contracts involved. But the allegations were referred to the UK's Serious Fraud Office and to criminal Federal investigations in the US, as well as wider investigations into procurement by the US Congress and the UN. Compass recognised it had to get the whole sorry saga put to bed as soon as possible. Despite the fact that the outcome of the investigation revealed that nobody had benefited from the contract win, it was clear that the Compass team was in possession of information which helped them win the bid. Ironically, the contracts generated an operational loss for Compass in the first few years of operation.

The court cases could have dragged on for years just as BP's (far bigger) Gulf of Mexico oil rig disaster only too clearly showed a decade or so later. Compass didn't fight the allegations, a procedure that would have been difficult to defend anyway as the main participants had been fired, but it didn't admit liability either. Deciding that discretion was by far the best route forward, it paid a confidential settlement, widely assumed to be £40m. It was the cheapest and most effective way of climbing out of a very deep and dangerous hole.

Richard Cousins, who by then had succeeded Bailey as chief executive, was quoted as saying: "We believe it is in the best interests of the business and shareholders and good management to avoid the uncertainties and costs associated with prolonged litigation. My focus is on the future and this settlement is a major step in putting the matter behind us."

of £100m in capital. Further warnings revealed profits were down by £24m because military contracts in the Middle East had been downgraded as soldiers switched to peacekeeping roles – high risk premiums in combat zones could not be imposed. In addition, £9m extra cost was incurred in boosting its sales and marketing effort in the UK.

At the same time, Compass was caught up in the perennial problem of supplier discounts which opened up the whole question of purchasing transparency just at the time when clients were becoming more astute in monitoring costs by employing more experienced purchasing specialists and bringing in consultants to advise them. The issue was beginning to influence clients in their choice of caterer, which posed a danger to Compass, being the UK's largest.

"Clients are less receptive to the large corporates as they think they are being ripped off," Jonathan Doughty (now with Turpin Smale) told Caterer. Chris Stern, quoted again, was reported as saying: "You're going to see far greater involvement of client's purchasing departments and formal procedures." It was fair comment.

Cost-plus contracts, which had set the industry on its way to prosperity in the 1950 to 1980 era, were looking vulnerable as clients began to query how caterers were charging out the ever-rising food costs and other costs. Were the clients benefiting from the discounts being obtained? Would not a fixed price contract serve the client's interests better? Subsidies were under pressure, too. Some companies had already trumpeted the fact that they passed on all supplier discounts to clients. Jerry Brand, when at Russell & Brand, claimed to be first to do so, but Brian Smith was a much earlier proponent. But an admission by Compass that supplier discounts, in one form or another, remained a significant revenue stream, unsettled the City though it came as no surprise to other caterers.

With the third profit warning, despite strenuous counterattacks by Compass, came a growing chorus in the City for Bailey's resignation. "The management team are fully aware of investors' priorities and are totally focused on generating free cash-flow and delivering improved return on capital employed," a spokesman claimed. Mackay had already announced that he would retire in 2006 but neither his, nor Mike Bailey's position had been helped by two other events that crashed over the Compass bows in the same year.

* * *

The first was a series of programmes on television aired in 2005 by Jamie Oliver, the celebrity chef, which centred on the state of the country's school meals. There had already been much criticism of them and Oliver, seizing the moment, attempted to highlight their poor nutritional value. In doing so, he wanted to encourage local authorities to improve standards. This meant more realistic costings and much better training of cooks. One particular menu item, which had become something of a staple in schools, was particularly criticised: the Turkey Twizzler. Notwithstanding the fact that most children

actually liked them, Oliver turned the Turkey Twizzler into the food of the devil. Compass, more than any other company, was caught up in the furore; it had been serving them in its school meal contracts though it was by no means the only caterer to so do. Unfortunately, it was named in the programmes. As education catering was worth £25m a year, the danger was all too obvious and the impact was real and the response immediate.

Georgina Parkes, of Scolarest, Compass' school meals subsidiary, told the *Daily Mail*: "Turkey Twizzlers will be removed from all our menus. Across the vast majority of schools we have not been serving Turkey Twizzlers for more than three months but in a handful of cases the client requested the product was kept on. We recognise consumer concerns over the product and regardless of client preference, we will not be serving them any more." She added, not very believably: "We don't regard this as a knee-jerk reaction to Jamie Oliver's

Credit David Loftus

Jamie Oliver's 2005 TV programmes highlighted the difficulties faced by school meals providers – and led directly to more government funding.

PA Photos/TopFoto

A young looking Jamie Oliver in a television discussion with prime minister Tony Blar at the height of the Turkey Twizzler row.

programme, although he has had some influence in us putting the final step in place."

Even so the upshot was that the sale of school meals declined as children brought in packed lunches. "The school dinner issue has had an impact," admitted Paul Kelly, the Compass spokesman. "There is less uptake in terms of kids buying meals." Even Bailey admitted the same at the next Compass AGM.

Bernard Matthews, the manufacturer of the spiral shaped goodie, was unrepentant: "We have been unfairly treated over a turkey product which is the least fatty of all meats," David Jolly, its managing director, told *The Independent*. "We were picked out by Jamie Oliver because everyone has heard of Bernard Matthews, yet we are a company that has been responding to health concerns for years and going down the low-fat route. A Twizzler has much less fat than a sausage." It also had only 34 per cent turkey meat.

Compass' decision to remove them immediately from menus softened the potential damage that might have been inflicted and, in fact, the Twizzler story only reinforced Oliver's nutritional message which galvanised the government into announcing an immediate £280m increase to pay for better ingredients in school meals. A School Food Trust to advise schools and parents on healthier meals was also established with a budget of £60m (part of the £280m).

It was not all bad news. Jamie Oliver's programmes had been one of the most successful television campaigns in history, benefiting children and caterers alike: the children got better meals and the caterers were able to increase meal costs to a more sensible level.

Compass was able to brush off the Twizzler saga relatively quickly, inflicting little lasting damage, saying it would not bid for any school meal contract for under 55p per meal, but just when the saga was abating it was hit by the second crisis – the UN scandal (see panel on previous page) which no international company would ever want to have to deal with.

For Bailey, the events had been deeply troubling. He and Mackay had steered Compass into one of the biggest food service companies in the world with a turnover of £11bn. However, the events of 2005 had proved too much for either to realistically survive; Mackay's replacement, Sir Roy Gardner, was already in the wings. Bailey recognised that his position would continue to cause press comment.

"The scandal had happened on my watch," he says. "I decided to call it a day and take early retirement. It was best for me and best for the company. Roy Gardner exerted no pressure. Quite the reverse. He asked me to stay but leaving was the right thing to do and the reality was that the shareholders wanted to see a change. I was very disappointed to end on such a sour note but such is life. When you take the top job, you take what goes with it, good or bad."

His departure left a hole in the company. Gary Green was recalled from the US to help out the UK business following the Peter Harris debacle and it was decided that Briggs, director of specialist markets for Compass, should be put in charge of UK and Ireland. Green returned to the US shortly afterwards where he remains in charge of Compass' highly successful US operations. Richard Cousins was appointed in 2006 and had a month's handover before Bailey left in May 2006. With the US generating 48 per cent of Compass' £17bn revenues, commentators believe that Green is one of the industry's most admired – and largely unsung – operators and has been key to the company's subsequent success.

Richard Cousins was particularly critical of the previous regime's headlong growth and lost no time in rationalising the extent of the Compass empire.

Credit Gary Lee/UPPA/Photoshot

Sir Roy Gardner succeeded Francis Mackay as Compass chairman and appointed Ian El-Mokadem to succeed Mike Bailey – a controversial appointment.

Gary Green – head of Compass' US operations – widely recognised as one of the industry's most admired operators.

In the last decade, Green has been responsible for driving Compass to be the largest food service provider in the US with an annual turnover of $15bn – a remarkable achievement. The US now accounts for almost half the company's total turnover.

* * *

Neither Roy Gardner nor Richard Cousins had any experience of the catering industry but they were highly experienced businessmen with successful track records behind them. Gardner had been with British Gas since 1994 and was involved in splitting the company into two parts, becoming chief executive of Centrica plc. Cousins came from BPB plc, the world's largest manufacturer of plasterboard. Under his leadership, he had taken the company

into the FTSE 100, increasing its market capitalisation from £1bn to £4bn before selling it to the French-owned Saint-Gobain for £3.9bn.

Both set about steadying the Compass ship. Cousins was particularly critical of the previous regime's headlong growth and lost no time in rationalising the extent of the Compass empire, recognising that growth had been at the expense of profitability and non-existent cash flow (Compass currently operates in 50 countries). In the UK, SSP, together with the motorway service areas now operating under the Moto brand, had already been sold off by Mackay and Bailey for £1.82bn – a price that exceeded City expectations; the sale included an airport concession business in the US, Creative Host Services. They had also taken the decision to sell the European vending company Selecta. But other businesses were also sold, including Restaurant Associates/Patina and Krispy Kreme, together with European in-flight and rail catering and the Italian motorway services business. In 2007, Selecta finally headed for the exit; operating about 150,000 vending machines in 22 countries, a German private equity firm, Allianz Capital Partners acquired it for £772.5m. The disposals began to reduce Compass' exposure to a more manageable number of countries and allowed it to return money to shareholders and reduce net debts – two actions that pleased the City. "All round, it is a good outcome and Compass can now focus on the challenges facing its core business, such as falling subsidies, rising competition and food quality issues," one analyst was quoted in *Caterer*.

Under Cousins' successful stewardship, which continues to this day, Compass did exactly that and the blip in profits in 2005 became a distant memory. True, the appointment by Roy Gardner of Ian

El-Mokadem (known as Elmo) as chief executive of UK and Ireland, caused a stir. El Mokadem had joined Centrica, Gardner's old company, in 1997 as head of gas competition and later became managing director of One.Tel, a subsidiary of Centrica. His pursuit of a policy of highly centralised control, which took more and more power from the regions, began to encourage an exodus of highly talented people.

To many Compass old-timers with a catering background he seemed not naturally drawn to catering and food service, bringing in many new people who appeared to have little interest in food. He changed the company's culture. "I don't want food development meetings, I want business development meetings," was a frequent refrain.

One of his most public acts was to withdraw from the BHA in a well publicised press statement without telling Bob

Ian Sarson succeeded Ian El Mokadem as managing director.

Cotton, the chief executive, beforehand, thus causing maximum damage to the association. All this was anathema to many in the company. His four-year tenure at Compass also coincided with a downturn in its UK fortunes, as the table on the following page shows. UK group turnover in 2006 was £1.97bn but by 2010, when he was succeeded by Ian Sarson, who had been with Compass for many years, it had slid to £1.78bn at a time when, over the same period, group turnover had risen

from £10.8bn to £14.4bn – entirely from international (principally US) growth. Since 2010, UK turnover has been amalgamated with that of Europe and Japan.

In just over a couple of decades, Compass had burst from its UK base to become a truly international group. Cousins' impact on the business has been profound. Under him, the growth of Compass continues apace. In 2014, turnover was £17bn with an operating margin of 7.2 per cent. For the company, it has been a remarkable

journey – not without its stumbles on the way – but no-one who worked for Midland or Bateman Catering in 1981 could have foreseen that the result of that merger would be a global giant.

As a footnote, the departure of Mackay and Bailey did not see the end of their careers. Mackay came back into catering by launching Grayson Hospitality Associates and Grayson Restaurants in 2008, recruiting a slew of disaffected Compass talent including as chairman, Philip Nash from

At a private ceremony in Lord Forte's London house, Mike Bailey and Francis Mackay return the THF name to Lord Forte and Rocco – Bailey subsequently named his new operation in the US Trusthouse Services Group after the company that gave him his first job.

Compass' fine dining division, Restaurant Associates (RA). Chris Pearce, who worked under Nash, became operations director, Ron Morley as company secretary, Rowena Edwards as managing director of Grayson Restaurants, and David Cheeseman as chief executive. Graysons subsequently sold its education business to The Brookwood Partnership, which led to the departure of most of these operators but the company continues successfully to this day with a new team and with Mackay as executive chairman.

Bailey returned to the US in 2007 – "a no brainer" – and with the help of a private equity partner, Gryphon Investors, purchased three small caterers under common ownership in Charlotte, North Carolina, which had $100m turnover in the education and healthcare sectors between them. It was the start of a second career. He renamed the company TrustHouse Services Group after the company which gave him his first job.

The TrustHouse Forte name had actually been owned by Compass following the hostile Granada takeover of Lord Forte, but after the dust had settled the name was given back to an ailing Lord Forte and Rocco by Bailey and Mackay at a small private ceremony in Forte's London residence. Rocco, however, had no intention of ever using the Trust House name again, saying it carried too much baggage following the acrimonious Granada bid.

It was partly in homage to his old company that Bailey decided to resurrect the name for his new US business. Trusthouse Services now trades in all 48 mainland states in the US and is in the list of top 10 US foodservice companies. By the end of 2015 it had a turnover of $700m. In 2013, Elior took a controlling interest but Bailey continues as its chairman – not bad for a retirement project that started in 2007.

Compass Group turnover and profit, 1986-2014

	UK turnover (£m)	Group turnover (£m)	Operating profit before tax (£m)
1986	228.6 (7.8* £15.9†)	228.6	8.4
1987	254.6 (11.0* 27.1†)	254.6	16.8
1988	276.9 (14.8* 34.7†)	276.9	24.7
1989	343.0 (26.8* 54.0†)	343.0	31.9
1990	352.7 (40.3*)	352.7	38.4
1991	320.9 (56.0*)	320.9	38.1††
1992 (GM bid)	345.1 (56*)	345.1	40.0
1993	382.2 (56*)	497.0	46.8
1994	456 (68.7*)	917.9	62.8
1995	494.0 (69.7*)	1,506	91.2
1996	597.7 (15.0*)	2,651	143.8
1997	668.2	3,703	179.5
1998	746.6	4,213	216.5
1999	813.2	4,814	254
2000	1,200	5,770	309
2001	2,877	8,716	676
2002	3,160	10,617	533
2003	3,060	11,286	797
2004	3,033	11,772	775
2005	1,982	12,704	711
2006	1,957	10,815	508
2007	1,931	10,268	529
2008	1,926	11,440	659
2009	1,829	13,444	877
2010	1,782	14,468	989
2011	Combined with Europe	15,833	1,016
2012	Ditto	16,905	856
2013	Ditto	17,557	802
2014	Ditto	17,058	1,217

* Contribution of Compass Healthcare (sold in 1996 for £20m)
† Contribution of Rosser and Russell
†† including £3m sale of Rosser and Russell
Profit figures are operating profit for company and subsidiary undertakings.

Compass' Junior Chefs Academy is a unique training programme designed to attract and develop young talent through the sponsorship of Saturday morning cookery schools at colleges throughout the UK. Since the programme began in 2003, approximately 3,000 teenagers have graduated nationally, including Scotland and Ireland. Seen here with Albert Roux are some of youngsters on the programme.

CHAPTER TWENTY-SEVEN

Celebrity chefs boost the image

By the 1990s, contractors began to use celebrity chefs to boost their quality image.

In 2004, Aramark joined forces with Roy Ackerman, the restaurant entrepreneur, to set up Parallel, a new hotel and leisure division that teamed up with chef Brian Turner to open restaurants in some top class hotels, first at the Crowne Plaza NEC and then at the Millenium Hotel, London.

The move reflected the eagerness with which caterers had been trying to upgrade their image as well as their standard of food and service, even though clients dining in any one of the City boardrooms would hardly need reminding that the quality of contractors' food could, at its best, rival that of the finest West End restaurant.

However, the caterers felt they needed something else to convince clients that their catering wasn't just about providing sausages and mash and other popular favourites for the staff restaurant – one of the reasons why Garry Hawkes had opened Kenley years before. They wanted to promote their ability to provide a five-star food service for the most discerning client and customer. If they could ride the newfound wave of interest in high quality cooking that was beginning to emerge in the UK in the early 1990s, and which manifested itself in the award of Michelin stars to an increasing number of British-run restaurants, they believed they could gain (and retain) more business.

Much of this interest in food was being fuelled by television programmes featuring celebrity chefs such as Gordon Ramsay, Gary Rhodes, Rick Stein and others, so companies naturally looked to them to help them enhance the skills of their chefs and create new menus and dishes for their clients. An additional and not inconsiderable

Credit 2000 Topham/PA

Albert Roux and Prue Leith join in the celebrations when Compass bought Eurest in 1995. Eurest was then part owned by Accor. Left to right: Francis Mackay, Gerrard Pellison (chairman of Accor who joined the Compass board), Albert Roux, Prue Leith and Alain Dupuis (responsible for Accor's catering business who also joined the Compass board). Dupuis died in 2014 while working on an orphanage he had founded and supported near the Cambodian capital, Phnom Penh.

bonus was that the caterers would be able to bask in the reflected glory of the chefs they hired. With a celebrity name on board, they could legitimately boast that they had top flight chefs to go with their Michelin-starred ambitions.

The new names were also able to encourage some of the higher-end clients to upgrade their staff restaurants to even higher standards.

The move started in 1993, when Compass acquired Roux Restaurants from the brothers Albert and Michel Roux, renaming the acquisition Roux Fine Dining. In the same year, it acquired Leith's – Prue Leith's £15m catering business which she founded in 1960 and which led to the opening of her Michelin-starred restaurant in 1969 (not included in the deal) and continues as a Compass brand today.

Prue Leith did not join Compass but Albert Roux stayed on as a consultant, eventually joined by his son Michel Roux Jnr. The partnership continues and has proved to be highly successful in terms of raising Compass' reputation as a caterer capable of providing fine dining for the public and for clients – a 10-year contract for Michel Roux Jnr to front the Roux at Parliament Square restaurant in conjunction with Compass' Restaurant Associates was signed in 2009; under the contract, RA also operates the Royal Institute of Chartered Surveyors' staff restaurant with menus created by Le Gavroche, the Roux family restaurant.

Three years later, in 1996, Gary Rhodes left the Greenhouse in London's Mayfair, where he had been making a big name for himself, to join Gardner Merchant with a view to opening his own restaurant but under the GM aegis – City Rhodes. The move came at a time just after the GM sale to Sodexo.

Garry Hawkes' primary aim was to set Rhodes up so that he could put a little gloss on GM's image as a provider of mass catering

Compass acquired Leith's – Prue Leith's catering business – in 1993.

Gary Rhodes with Garry Hawkes: City Rhodes attracted plenty of publicity, receiving a Michelin star and much praise for the quality of its food. It also helped raise the game of many of Gardner Merchant's own staff, who spent time working in the restaurant's kitchen.

and both were enthusiastic about the idea.

City Rhodes was to be a GM restaurant that provided high quality, Michelin-starred food. This would provide the best possible venue to entertain existing and potential clients, as well as being a venue for some staff training. Bill Toner, then GM's director for London and who knew Rhodes well, was given the task of managing the enterprise from scratch.

The restaurant was created out of a former conference centre within premises that were GM's London office, The Merchant Centre in Shoe Lane, between Fleet Street and Holborn. The deal surprised many, including the landlord, who tried to extract a higher rent from GM by claiming that the 'user clause' in the lease, in referring to a conference centre and fine dining, did not extend to a first class restaurant. The issue got as far as legal proceedings being issued but GM was determined to go ahead; it eventually struck

a deal that saw the landlord amend the lease and also invest in upgrading the office areas. Toner and Rhodes were gung-ho about the enterprise.

It was an opportune move. Rhodes had been making a name for himself in television and with books. For him to join forces with Gardner Merchant raised some eyebrows but Gary Crossley, writing in *Caterer*, said that it was hard to see how either side could possibly lose from the deal:

"The biggest winner of all, however, is the contract catering sector. Some of Gardner Merchant's rivals may not see it that way but the transfer of the biggest name ever to move into contract catering will have a profound and lasting effect."

This was, perhaps, an overstatement but City Rhodes attracted plenty of publicity, receiving a Michelin star and much praise for the quality of its food. It also helped raise the game of many of GM's own staff, who spent

time working in the restaurant's kitchen. As a marketing and profile-raising exercise it was judged a success but it never made money and was highly capital intensive, incurring significant fitting-out, marketing and running costs – and operating losses. All of these were borne by GM with Rhodes receiving a salary and an incentive fee. For GM, however, its ownership was inevitably overshadowed by Rhodes' own personality and his ability to garner media publicity, which he did very successfully.

Another Rhodes restaurant followed, this time in an unpromising location in Dolphin Square, London, which opened in May 1998. Despite gaining a Michelin star, this was never commercially successful. Further expansion came with a public restaurant in Jenners store in Edinburgh, followed by a brand of brasseries – Rhodes & Co – which launched in Edinburgh and Manchester in 1999 and at Gatwick Airport. However, none of these was a success either and when Sodexo undertook a strategic review in 2002, it concluded that the venture with Rhodes was not a core part of the business and should end. The losses were too heavy to be sustained and all but the Dolphin Square restaurant were closed down.

"From Sodexo's point of view, it wants to concentrate on industrial catering rather than fine dining outlets," Rhodes told *Caterer* at the time. He put a brave face on it: "We've had a fantastic relationship – it's proved itself with the Michelin stars and six years is a pretty good track record."

Nevertheless, after Rhodes left, Sodexo hired Anton Edelman, who had just retired as chef de cuisine at the Savoy hotel, to oversee the Dolphin Square restaurant, on which it had the lease, renaming it Allium; he also became principal chef of Directors' Table, the company's fine dining division for B&I clients in London, again with a mission to develop the skills of Sodexo's chefs.

Edelman remained chef patron of Allium at the Dolphin Square Hotel for four years until 2006, when it closed for redevelopment. At the same time, he quit as principal chef at Directors' Table. Two years later he was snapped up by Elior's Digby Trout, as consultant chef, an arrangement that has lasted to this day.

Rhodes was not idle. A few months after quitting Sodexo he joined Compass in a partnership with the company's Restaurant Associates division that saw the opening of two Rhodes restaurants in the Cumberland Hotel in London, Rhodes W1, which gained a Michelin star within a year of opening, and Rhodes W1 Brasserie, as well as Rhodes 24 in Tower 42 in the City of London. This partnership was long-lasting with Compass being able to point out to clients that it was associated with a number of top-flight celebrity chefs – Rhodes and the Roux brothers.

Restaurant Associates, with a Brasserie Roux outlet, was hired to provide the food and beverage operation at the Sofitel at Heathrow Terminal 5 when it opened in 2008 but this contract was later terminated and taken in-house. With Rhodes, too, the arrangement began to run out of steam though it had a good 10-year run. Rhodes was increasingly looking abroad to develop his ideas, particularly in the Middle East. Talking from the United Arab Emirates in 2013 when it was announced the contract with Compass was not being renewed, he told *Caterer*: "I've probably spent more time here in the past year than I have in England." The Cumberland took over the operation of the two restaurants and Tower 42 is now operated as City Social, again in conjunction with Restaurant Associates.

Nor did the Aramark deals with Roy Ackerman succeed. They fell apart, as did the agreement to run the Refettorio restaurant in the Crowne Plaza – City of London, in

In 2015, Sodexo announced that Raymond Blanc would be partnering the company in its contract at the Chelsea Flower Show.

conjunction with chef Giorgio Locatelli, which included Bar 606, café and takeaway Benugo, in-room dining and conference catering. The £3m turnover venture was an attempt by Toner to replicate his experience at City Rhodes but the venue was probably not suitable and did not succeed. Within a year it was closed by Simon Titchenor, who had joined Aramark.

"Fundamentally, the contract wasn't working for either organisation," he told *Caterer*. "The food and beverage operation is an essential part of the hotel and it made sense for them to run it directly. We were happy to pass control over to them. It was an amicable agreement."

* * *

These few failures, however, did not weaken the allure of using celebrity chefs but it channelled their interest more practically into training staff rather than running a commercial restaurant. Companies found that a celebrity chef is able to inspire staff in a way that normal training schemes find difficult, while having a big name on board also impresses potential clients.

As far back as 1996, Emerson Hewitt, a small consultancy launched a year earlier by Stuart Emerson and John Hewitt, both former Sutcliffe managers (acquired in 2004 by Compass), engaged Pierre Koffmann as a consultant. Koffman, whose three-Michelin star Tante Claire restaurant had received numerous fine dining accolades, was engaged to train Everson Hewitt chefs in his kitchen as well as providing help with menu planning. The deal meant that Koffman could spend the majority of his time at his restaurant but, as Everson himself said: "Having an alliance with someone of his quality and standing in the industry is very good for us."

Aramark, too, later set up deals with both Gordon Ramsay and Marcus Wareing to improve food standards with workshops, mentoring and coaching to help with chef training. Wilson Storey Halliday hired John Campbell, and Baxter & Platts looked to Michael Caines to improve staff skills; at the time of writing, BaxterStorey, the successor company of both, uses four top names: Campbell, Mark Hix, Tom Kitchen and Nigel Haworth as chef consultants, as well as Fred Sirieix of Galvin's in Park Lane. Sirieix coaches front of house teams, 'bringing Michelin-star quality to our fine dining and hospitality', as the website says.

In 2011, Toner, now running the Host group, signed up the two-Michelin-starred chef Andrew Fairlie to train and mentor Host chefs at Gleneagles. Four years later, in July 2015, Sodexo signed up James Tanner, owner of four restaurants in Plymouth, as an ambassador for the company's independent schools business, Independents by Sodexo. In the same month, Raymond Blanc announced he was partnering with Sodexo Prestige in its contract at the Chelsea Flower Show to serve breakfasts, Champagne receptions, lunches, teas and private dinners. For Blanc, it is an appropriate partnership. "From the garden my gastronomy is born," he said rather grandly. "I truly look forward to designing a space, menu and experience that will delight our guests."

The demarcation between contract catering and commercial restaurant operations became further blurred when Alastair Storey of WSH announced he was working with Monica Galetti, a judge on BBC's *MasterChef: The Professionals* and the former sous chef at Le Gavroche, to launch her own restaurant in London. "As a business, we will always look at new opportunities to develop and create exciting new food concepts... we are delighted to be working with her to launch this new

venture," said Storey.

In 2002, CH&Co (when it was Charlton House) went one step further and hired David Cavalier as full-time food innovation director; he stayed on for 11 years, becoming director of food. Cavalier was a Michelin-starred chef, running his own restaurant, Cavalier's, when he joined the company. He resigned in 2013 to launch his own hospitality consultancy business.

CH&Co had gained immeasurably from Cavalier's skills and experience but his time there had taken him out of public view. "Charlton House had become all-consuming and that was all I've become known for," he told *Caterer*, announcing his departure. Cavalier had been a well known name when he joined; his 11 years in contracting had allowed his name to all but disappear.

Clearly, the advantages and disadvantages of celebrity chefs working with a catering company have to be finely balanced but their appeal to the contractor remains.

In 2002, CH&Co (when it was Charlton House) hired David Cavalier, then a well known celebrity chef, as full-time food innovation director; he stayed for 11 years, becoming director of food.

City Social now occupies Gary Rhodes' former haunt at Tower 42. The restaurant is overseen by Jason Atherton, in conjunction with Compass' Restaurant Associates.

CHAPTER TWENTY-EIGHT

An industry of entrepreneurs

Contract catering is an industry of entrepreneurs, many of whom have made personal fortunes.

Bill Baxter is one of the industry's most accomplished salesmen, a master at putting the client at ease and selling him the goods. He wanted to go into architecture but the five-year course and two-year RIBA apprenticeship stretched too far into the distance for an ambitious young man who was keen to go places. Instead, he went into hospitality – "I've always liked meeting people and I like food," and signed up to the three-year HND course at Westminster College where he met his wife Fiona and married her in his final year, a union that has lasted.

He joined Sutcliffe immediately after leaving college as assistant manager at Blue Circle Industries' head office in Victoria and then spent a further six months at Aldermaston where eventually the workforce rose to over 1,000. His area supervisor was Robert Platts and they struck up a friendship, partly based on a shared passion for fishing, that has lasted all his life.

Bill Baxter and Robert Platts struck up a friendship partly based on their shared love of fishing.

Within two years, at the age of 23, Baxter found himself as an area supervisor in charge of over 16 sites, the youngest in the company's history, and working all hours of the day and night. Once, he fell asleep at the wheel of his car, bumped the car in front and, opening the door, knocked over a motor cyclist who was just about to overtake. He took aboard the message and tried to limit his working week but he was then made area manager for the Thames Valley region in charge of 50 sites. It had been a meteoric rise but, at the age of 25, he and Platts, aged 31 and by now best mates, decided that working for themselves would be more profitable than working for Sutcliffe.

"We thought about going into the hotel business, even thought about opening a fish farm, but we eventually decided to stick to what we knew best – contracting. Besides, it needed very little capital," he says.

They walked into Don Davenport's office, Sutcliffe's managing director, and told him they were quitting. Davenport spent five minutes trying to dissuade them and the next 40 minutes giving them advice on how to make a success of their new venture.

He needn't have bothered. In 1997, the two sold the company to Granada for £15m.

***

Bill Baxter's story is typical. Contract catering has created more personal wealth in the last 40 years than any other sector of the hospitality industry even though the term millionaire doesn't quite have the caché that it had 20 or more years ago when most of the fortunes were made. Significantly, it has done so largely without the need for any investment other than time, effort and total commitment; no start-up has required the capital outlay that even the smallest hotel or commercial restaurant demands. All that is required is an office (frequently the front bedroom), a telephone, a persuasive manner and endless optimism. From Roland and Bruce Webb at Midland Catering, Jack and David Bateman, John Sutcliffe and the Taylors who sold up in the 1960s and 1970s, to the many who came later, success was the result of initiative, drive and an ability to grasp and exploit opportunities.

The list is long: Bill Baxter and Robert Platts, Frank Bell, Jerry Brand, Jim and Ian Cartwright, Chris Hind and Andrew Nelson, Rick Holroyd and Nick Howe, Clive Lindley, Brian and Clive Smith, Ian Tritton, Marc Verstringhe, to name just a few. Contracting is a remarkable success story of entrepreneurs creating wealth out of almost literally nothing. With minimal upfront capital, they grasped the opportunities to their own advantage with an undying faith in their own abilities, a hunger for success and an unlimited commitment for hard work. And, of course, they had the good fortune to be in the right place at the right time.

This last attribute should not be overlooked. Luck plays a part in most business success stories and for these individuals their wealth was largely generated by the need of a small handful of public companies – GrandMet initially but Granada most notably – to use the success of others to consolidate their presence in the industry. GrandMet, for example, made rich men of Jack Bateman and the Webbs; the buy-out of Compass led by Gerry Robinson and Francis Mackay created their personal fortunes. Later, the buy-out of Gardner Merchant from Forte and its subsequent sale to Sodexo made millionaires of 12 senior directors and, thanks to the distribution of the spoils, made many others lower down the hierarchy far wealthier than they could have ever dreamed possible.

As Chapter 25 highlighted, Granada in the 1990s, in a wild and frantic rush to become bigger and yet bigger, spent millions swallowing some 15 independent companies spawning as many as 20 or so millionaires in doing so. Elior, in buying up half a dozen independent companies, similarly created a clutch of very wealthy individuals.

No other sector of the hospitality industry, indeed, of industry generally outside IT, has come near to rivalling the success of contract catering as a generator of personal wealth for so many. And in the case of a few, the sun has shone twice. Both Bill Baxter and Jim and Ian Cartwright each created a follow-up company, successfully selling their second enterprise on some years later (Jim Cartwright, with his son Ian, is currently in his third incarnation).

Yet the pace of acquisitions, which so enlivened the 1990s, has slowed down. Granada's frantic dash for growth in the 1990s was unique and is unlikely to be repeated by any company in the present day.

Granada principally fed the hunger for growth by acquisition in the 1990s but has itself disappeared and those remaining are now more cautious, more aware. An acquisition today has to have a more significant purpose than just adding top line growth – it must open a way into a new sector (as was Compass' purchase of Cygnet Catering which consolidated its presence in education catering or Sodexo's purchase of Atkins, which gave it new skills and expertise in hard FM services). Host's merger with CH&Co in 2015 was a merger of two independents which recognised the advantages of trading as a bigger enterprise, and no doubt there will be more of this kind of amalgamation but, in the UK at least, major companies are now more determined to grow organically than by headlong acquisition. The dash for top line growth is over.

This is the story of some of the industry's most inimitable entrepreneurs who made it through the good times of the 1990s –

to emerge, still going strong 20 years later.

***

Jim Cartwright, Midlands-born and still with a Brummie accent, began his career as a cook at the Belfry Hotel (now combined with the PGA Centre & Golf Course near Sutton Coldfield) and then went to Birmingham College of Food under the legendary Louis Klein for two years. A spell as a cook working the liners with P&O followed but in 1966 he took a shore job in hotel management, believing a sailor's life and domestic bliss were incompatible. He had met Alison, his wife, at Birmingham College and they both joined Bateman at the same time in 1968, Alison for the second time. In the next 18 years Jim was promoted to catering manager, area manager, general manager and divisional director, while Alison quit and raised the family: Stuart born in 1970 and Ian two years later.

"Bateman was a great company to work for," he recalls. "Very friendly. Very organised. It brought out the best in people. We thought we were the best and no other company could touch us."

The merger with Midland Catering came as a shock but as a regional general manager based in Loughborough he relished the challenge of bringing the two cultures together in the East Midlands. When Dick Turpin re-organised the company and the Compass name emerged in 1983, he found himself divisional director for the North working for Tony Coles. Two years later came Gerry Robinson's whirlwind entrance into the industry and Cartwright was the only Compass director to survive. In fact, with John Kane (the company secretary), he was one of only two Compass officers for a short period. It was the beginning of a revolution.

He admires Robinson's *chutzpah* and recognises that his impact on the industry,

in terms of operational efficiency, driving margins and personal wealth creation, was enormous. "Gerry taught us how to make money in contract catering," he says. "We were really only playing at it before he came along."

Not many people would disagree, though some might query how it was achieved.

Although Jim was in a senior position in charge of 1,000 units and 10,000 staff in the north which included Northern Ireland and Scotland, in a company run by wildly ambitious people who were clearly going places, the temptation of going it alone proved too strong to resist. From his position in the north, he could see that there were plenty of opportunities for a new boy on the block.

"I thought it was time to go it alone. I could see the opportunities," he says. "In fact, I remember Pat Lichtensteiger, when at Berni Inns on a trip to Manchester, saying to me, 'Why don't you try and do it for yourself, Jim?'"

Two years before, he had tried to interest Compass into buying a security company based in Glasgow, Strathclyde Security, to add to Compass' extensive security operation in the north. It was on the market for £1.4m but Gerry Robinson wasn't interested and the idea was shelved. But then Strathclyde ran into big trouble. It came back suggesting a price of £500,000 which, again was rebuffed. Recognising that the company was in dire trouble with the tax authorities and was facing receivership, Jim and two others personally offered £50,000. Still in employment with Compass, he took a 20 per cent private stake in the company with Colin Beasley, who had previously sold his cleaning company to Compass taking up 60 per cent, and David Robertson, previously Cartwright's divisional security manager taking the final 20 per cent. But Strathclyde, unbeknown to the new owners,

had an overdraft of over £300,000 which the Clydesdale Bank wanted reducing dramatically. Nothing daunted, Cartwright produced a business plan, which the bank saw as a cheaper way forward than receivership and which promised a vastly better result. The business survived, with all the debts paid off and the three sold it in 1988 for £750,000 plus a deferred payment of £250,000.

The success was tempting and his family urged him to strike out by himself. He took the advice. He had his eye on Shaw Catering, a small company with 12 contracts based in Liverpool. Started by Charlie Shaw, an ex-Gardner Merchant man who was more interested in spiritualism than catering, the company was in trouble but the opportunities were obvious. To finance the deal, he put in £60,000 of his 20 per cent share of the Strathclyde Security – although the purchase price of Shaw was only £50. He took with him Peter Bland, George Hallam and Mike Latimer who were working at Compass at the time; they all invested in the company. Sue Wainscot, also from Compass, joined as personnel director once profits began to be generated. At a meeting of the families, Cartwright told them bluntly: "No guarantees. We're all in it together. We sink or swim together." They swam.

***

Robyn Jones was another from Compass who decided to break away. She had first joined in East Anglia in 1981 straight from an OND course at Buxton High Peak college; it was just at the time of the merger between Bateman and Midland and she was appointed as a graduate trainee in a Midland Catering contract at a boarding school in Cambridge. After six weeks she was chef/manageress at Stoke College, Suffolk, a boarding school for 250 children. Two years on, she jumped ship

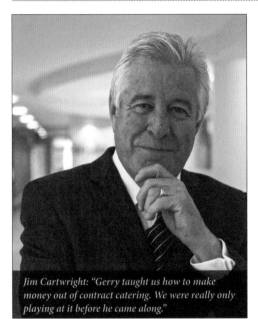

Jim Cartwright: "Gerry taught us how to make money out of contract catering. We were really only playing at it before he came along."

and joined Gardner Merchant as catering manageress at WH Smith's head office in London and then at Westpac Banking before moving on to the Potato Marketing Board for a two-year spell as catering advisory officer. A year at High Table as an operations manager preceded her return to Compass in March 1988, in charge of 22 contracts in the West End, which later increased to 33. She took the plunge in 1989 when she was asked to set up a new contract catering arm of Higgs and Hill, the construction company. The timing, however, was all wrong. Now married to Tim, an accountant and with two children, but with the recession beginning to bite, her new employer pulled the plug on the venture and in 1990 she found herself out of a job. It was a hard struggle:

"My confidence went to the floor but Tim said, 'If you're ever going to do it on your own, now's the time' – so I took his advice."

She set up an office in her back room using an old wallpaper pasting table as her desk, grabbed the phone book and started cold calling. She named her new company

Charlton House – "I didn't want a corny name. I wanted the name to have style and sound credible." It took her three months to secure her first client – The Guide Dogs for the Blind Association, a training centre with accommodation. It was small time but it was her first win and it set her on her way.

***

The search for the first contract is always the most testing time. For Bill Baxter and Robert Platts it took six months, entailing visits to towns by the three of them (Bill's wife Fiona had joined them) to check out what factories and offices there were and then cold calling them on the phone.

"Robert and Fiona were crap at selling so it was left to me do the sales calls," Baxter recalls, cheerfully.

The partners were getting seriously worried about their future, both having big mortgages and no income, when they landed their first contract, the Halifax Building Society offices in Hemel Hempstead, catering for 50 staff and worth £50k in annual sales. At last, they had put down a marker. It enabled them to show potential clients that though they were small they weren't just aspiring caterers. The next contract came two months later, Amersham International, the medical products group based in Little Chalfont with three big sites, which was the first public company that Margaret Thatcher privatised. It got them even more firmly on their way. Catering for some 750 people, it was worth £700,000 in annual sales.

Both contracts were gains from other caterers and Baxter was beginning to prove his point, if only to himself and his partners: the business was there if only you looked hard enough for it. He knew, at the outset, that the secret of any success would be building up a close relationship with the client and always promising his personal

attention – something that the majors could never promise.

***

Good salesmen and operators build up personal relationships with clients. In the 1980s and 1990s catering contracts were often appointed by the company chairman or managing director rather than through today's more formal procurement processes. Those at the sharp end took care to generate and maintain close contact with the client: retention was the key objective. Some even became close friends, being feted at sports and leisure events and given hospitality, often lavish, in order to seal the bond, though this is less prevalent today and non-existent in public sector contracts. In those days (and even today), a client's loyalty was often more to the individual salesman or manager than to the company itself. It was these personal relationships with the client that encouraged some to start up their own company by taking established clients with them. Not every independent did this – Bill Baxter, Alastair Storey and Clive Smith vehemently deny any poaching – but certainly it was commonplace.

***

Jim Cartwright had little compunction about using his contacts to win new contracts when they came up for renewal. His four ex-Compass directors knew their territories like the back of their hand and big wins such as Scottish Widows, Land Rover, British Rail, all gains from Compass, came along. The company began to gain traction, winning more and more business from other contractors. At the time, Jim was chairman of the BHA's Contract Catering Forum (later renamed Food and Service Management Forum) which negotiated, on behalf of the sector, with the government on key issues, such as TUPE and VAT on agency contracts.

"We won a few battles there which benefited the entire industry," he says.

Nine years later, in 1996, with Shaw now operating over 250 contracts, Granada offered to buy the business. It was an opportune time – one of the directors was keen to retire with his share of the winnings and there was plenty to share out "The money was mind-boggling," says Cartwright.

The four original partners became millionaires overnight, although the taxman took his 40 per cent.

A central production unit, which was part of Shaw and which had been feeding British Gas employees, didn't go with the sale to Granada, however. Instead, it formed the basis of Cartwright's next enterprise – now in partnership with his son Ian, Cygnet Catering Limited. For three years Jim and Ian set about building a network of food vending supplies, delivering and filling food vending machines all over the country.

***

The turning point for Robyn Jones was in 1992 when her company won the contract for Sony. It signposted Charlton House as a major player and 23 years later, Sony is still a client.

"Guide Dogs was nice but Sony was a huge gain for us," she says. "It's a building all steel, glass and marble and it enabled us to do our thing there. The main reception has a very prestigious feel and winning it set us on our way. We could show it off to potential clients and it was definitely our big break."

She had always promised that once she had won three contracts that would be it. "But I just got bored with three and we just kept it growing and growing and growing. Somehow, we'd found a niche in the market that favoured us – and we made sure we

kept it personal. That was always our secret." Promoted as a bespoke service, all her clients had her personal contact details. If they didn't like something, she could quickly sort it out.

One development that helped was the decision to become one of *Caterer's* Adopted Businesses. "That raised our profile no end – it was incredibly helpful." Within two years, the company won the Booker Prize as Best Young Business and Best Caterer, which further established its credentials; it began to be seen as one of the up-and-coming independents with a great reputation and able (and keen) to offer the kind of personal service that the most demanding clients needed: Robyn lived the business 24/7. Her husband Tim gave up his accountancy job in 2000 and joined the company as chairman.

***

With only two contracts but with undying confidence in his sales ability, Bill Baxter won the company's third contract, Prudential Assurance at Welwyn Garden City, worth £100,000 and catering for 150 people selling, as always, on a commitment to provide freshly cooked food combined with good relations with the client, staff and suppliers. It was nothing new but his enthusiasm and drive made it plain that the new company was young, enthusiastic and out to succeed.

"We sold the dream. They could see who we were. They could see the whites of our eyes. They knew they would have our personal attention," he says.

"This business is all about relationships. If you can convince the client that you, personally, will ensure that his every need is satisfied, and you'll do everything in your power to make him happy, then you can win the business. Presentation is all important."

By the time Baxter & Platts was sold for £15m to Granada in 1997 it boasted 130

(mainly cost-plus) contracts and employed over 1,500 people. Along the way Robert Platts encountered serious health issues and in 1993 was diagnosed with MS although he continued to put his all into the business. In the following four years, Baxter took on more of the day-to-day operations and the contracts kept coming in. In 1997 the company won the Food Service Operator of the Year in the annual Cateys.

***

In 2006, 15 years after Charlton House was established, and with 150 contracts and with an annual turnover of £57m, it won the Food Service Caterer of the Year award at the annual Cateys. A year later it made its first acquisition, taking over Chester Boyd, which had been founded 14 years earlier by Charles and Liz Boyd to cater for the Butchers' Company. With a turnover of £10m at 14 venues, including the Naval and Military Club and some prestigious City Livery Companies, Chester Boyd had 240 staff and was valued at somewhere north of £5m. "It was a lot of money," Robyn Jones admitted wryly. Charles Boyd stayed on to run the company which was operated as a separate division.

The merger brought Charlton House into high-end City and Club catering, though Charles left as chief executive in 2009 to run 8 Northumberland Avenue, a large-scale function venue within a short walk of Trafalgar Square in which he had an interest.

A year or so later, Tim and Robyn made the decision to change the name to CH&Co; it was long in the making.

"Charlton House was a good name," says Tim Jones, "but we had acquired Chester Boyd, which was operating as a separate company, and we thought it better to keep Charlton House as the B&I brand and rename the group CH&Co. It was a

Robert Platts (left) with Bill Baxter being presented with the BDO Stoy Hayward Business of the Year Award by Denis Healey, the former Chancellor of the Exchequer in 1995.

big decision but we felt we had to stick to the courage of our convictions."

***

Ironically, in all the time Baxter and Platts had spent building up the business, the partners had never considered selling – indeed, Bill Baxter's one mild regret today is that they actually did sell out.

"With hindsight, I would have liked to have built up Baxter & Platts into something really big but the offer from Granada was too good," he says. "They approached us and it came out of the blue and we were surprised at the amount they offered. So we decided to cash in. At the time, I had no idea how to value the company." The deal meant that they joined Granada to run Baxter & Platts – "which suited us fine" – but three months later Robert Platts retired to Guernsey.

Baxter stayed on as chairman of the company, which continued to trade as Baxter & Platts but it was no surprise that he would hanker after setting up his own company again. At the age of 37, he still enjoyed

working in an industry that had already given him a successful lifestyle; like Jim Cartwright, he just wanted the freedom and creativity of his own business again.

In May 2000, just at the time of the Granada merger with Compass, he decided it was time to start afresh. He teamed up with Mike Smith, his managing director at Baxter & Platts, to form BaxterSmith at exactly the same time that Alastair Storey (by now Sutcliffe's managing director) and Keith Wilson (Sutcliffe's financial director) also decided to go it alone. Indeed, at the time, there was a suggestion that the four of them should combine to form one company. Baxter thought long and hard about this but decided against it – "There were too many people involved and they all wanted a piece of the action. It would have been too complicated and we would have got in each other's way."

It was all perfectly amicable. BaxterSmith and WilsonStorey emerged as two new companies created out of nothing, little realising that they would merge four years later.

***

In 2010, CH&Co ventured into retail catering by acquiring 50 per cent of the high street café group, Apostrophe; by 2012, when it took full ownership, it boasted 23 sites in London, Heathrow and Gatwick. Selling a wide range of freshly baked pastries, sandwiches, salads, soups and desserts, all prepared on site, Apostrophe had gained a loyal following for its award-winning coffee and hot chocolate. The acquisition enabled CH&Co to offer a successful high street brand in the B&I, visitor attraction and corporate entertainment markets – a move that replicated the success that Compass and others had enjoyed with branding.

"The joint venture offered new horizons for CH&Co commercially and a wider choice for clients," said Tim Jones at the time. "It's time for us now to take the next step."

That step was to restructure the company. They kept Charlton House as the B&I brand and Chester Boyd as a City event caterer; Lusso was created to provide fine dining service to the City of London and beyond and Via360 provided clients with a high class front of house service, while Ampersand provided bespoke catering to clients such as London Zoo and Historic Royal Palaces.

***

Once the limitation clauses with Granada's purchase of Shaw had expired, Ian and Jim Cartwright decided to go back into contract catering, initially with a small acquisition which was based in Stoke-on-Trent. They also transformed the central production unit from supporting the vending industry with food to supporting school meals. The move came before Jamie Oliver's television attack on school meals but the two had already recognised that the standard of food being delivered to schools left much to be desired.

Setting up a new company. At the creation of BaxterSmith, seated left to right (on Baxter's sofa at home): Bill Baxter, Claire Parkinson (sales director), Jane Stallard (finance director) and Mike Smith.

Cygnet Catering eventually operated over 60 vans, run on biofuels, which delivered chilled food as far afield as Bournemouth and South Humberside.

Then came the Turkey Twizzler episode, which more or less forced the government to decree that every primary and secondary school should provide a hot meal – this despite the fact that 60 per cent of the schools didn't have a kitchen in which to prepare any kind of meal, had no budget to buy the equipment, and no skilled staff to cook the food from scratch. The answer was a chilled food service and the Cartwrights recognised that Cygnet's CPU was the answer.

Based in Nottingham with over 40 staff, Cygnet was already providing quality food for the company's B&I clients and the vending service. Cygnet then launched the service to the schools sector. Blast chilled dishes were delivered overnight by 60 refrigerated vans to schools as far afield as Bournemouth and South Humberside, eventually producing some 25,000 meals a day. The system met all existing and foreseen nutritional standards and provided finishing and service staff at point of service.

It was a highly successful operation, gaining numerous best practice awards and soon attracted the attention of others. Compass was keen to develop its local authority school meals business and saw that greater investment in an already efficient CPU would help its expansion in the sector. Investment was needed in the CPU anyway and Ian and Jim realised that it was a good time to sell so that they could concentrate more on their B&I contracts. While Jim, with directors Ian Gill and Hazel Bygate, had been expanding Cygnet, Ian, with directors Steve Kyffin, Zoe Green and Stephen Griffin, had been expanding the company's activities in contract catering, trading as Compact Catering, the name taken from an earlier acquisition. At the time of selling Cygnet, Compact had a turnover of around £14m.

***

Join Cygnet Catering for our school meal promotion 7th June - 11th July

Through competitions, Cygnet set about encouraging more and more young children to take a daily meal.

Once again, Bill Baxter, now partnered with Mike Smith, started their new company, BaxterSmith, with no contracts – "On principle, we took nothing from Sutcliffe" – but in the next four years he again proved his salesmanship by growing annual turnover from zero to £35m. He proved, for the second time, if proof was ever needed, that he was no ordinary salesman.

At the same time, Alistair Storey had finally decided to quit Granada to join the band of caterers who were creating their own companies – "I understand his decision and we all wish him every success in the future," said Davenport, his chief executive at Sutcliffe at the time, perhaps a little wryly.

"I thought, why am I working here when I can do it better myself?" says Storey. With a mortgaged house, wife and five children, no money and no clients, it was a brave decision.

"I had no bad feelings about Sutcliffe and no interest in taking any contracts," he says. Instead, he and Keith Wilson set up an office in Gerrards Cross and spent their time cold calling – "soul destroying," he says – until they landed a contract with La Brioche Dorée, the French retail bakery outlet, to roll out the chain in the UK which started to bring in revenue. The big break came when they acquired Halliday Catering, a company founded in 1985, on a £20,000 redundancy package paid to George Halliday on his departure from Compass where he was a regional director. He and his wife Linda, a personnel specialist, had spent 10 years building Halliday Catering but George died suddenly of a heart attack in 1995 playing squash. Linda successfully continued with the business with Nigel Anker and by the time of the merger with WilsonStorey in 2000, it was credited as the largest independent in the business, bringing in 70 contracts. WilsonStoreyHalliday (WSH) was established.

A year later, WSH acquired Houston and

Church, a small Berkshire-based enterprise run by John Houston (there never was a Church on the basis that two names sounded better than just one) with 24 contracts and an annual turnover of £7m. In 2004, Caterlink, the Kent-based contractor with a £10m turnover in healthcare and education, was snapped up.

Both BaxterSmith and WSH were on a roll but by 2004, the four key players – Bill Baxter, Mike Smith, Alastair Storey and Keith Wilson – were all coming to the conclusion that a merger would have its advantages; a bigger company, a bigger board of directors

and like-minded individuals would catapult them into the big league. Baxter and Smith sold to WSH and the combined company became the largest independent in the UK with a turnover of £80m.

Alastair Storey was enthusiastic. "We thought it offered a great fit for our business," he says. "The strength of our combined management allowed us to grow significantly but still to provide a service to our clients that is led personally by the company's owners."

The WilsonStoreyHalliday name was abandoned in favour of BaxterStorey as

the service operating company though the holding company is still Westbury Street Holdings (WSH). The company began to exploit its commitment to green issues, fresh food, the environment and other social and environmental causes. Its website, in fresh and vibrant colours, is one of the most attractive in the contract catering sector.

***

In 2010, the transformation of Charlton House to CH&Co, while creating a new name in contract catering, set tongues wagging. Was it being readied up to be sold? It was clearly an inviting prospect. The company had a great reputation, some 100-plus clients and an annual turnover of £75m, making it a highly attractive acquisition, but Robyn Jones rejected the suggestion when it was broached to her by *Caterer* in 2011:

"We live and breathe the business together," she said. "We've been married 25 years and in business 20 years. The business and our lives are completely interlinked. Why would we spend all that money [rebranding] just to sell up? It cost us a fortune."

Tim Jones added: "All you have to do is to look at what we're doing to see that we're not selling. The rebranding was for a purpose and that purpose was not to sell the business."

In the next four years they were true to their word, gaining Historic Royal Palaces (estimated to be worth £60m over five years), Thames Water, Virgin Atlantic and once again retaining the Sony contract. Turnover rose to over £90m by 2013. Then, in 2015, Robyn's deteriorating health (she had been fighting MS for many years) coincided with Bill Toner's approach, which proved irresistible.

***

Linda Halliday: the big break came when WilsonStorey acquired Halliday Catering, a company founded in 1985 on a £20,000 redundancy package paid to George Halliday; his wife Linda had taken the business forward after George's death.

After leaving Aramark in 2005, Bill Toner

had spent five years out of the industry. The experience had left some scars though the payoff had been generous and it enabled him to play plenty of golf and live in Scotland for a while. It was not until 2010 that he ventured back into the business as non-executive chairman of Jerry Brand's company Host Contract Management (HCM). Brand, however, was more interested in developing his software company Caternet and Toner became chief executive of HCM with Brand taking on the role of non-executive chairman. Toner effectively took over the business.

In 2012, he made the company's first acquisition, buying Couture, the £5m-a-year concession caterer, retaining its brand name as a division of Host; in the same year, Juice for Life, a £2m turnover business trading as OJs, took Host into leisure and heritage sites. A year later, Style Services came on board – a Hertfordshire-based contractor founded in 2007 by John Rathbone, Ruth Fenton and Jim Walker, worth an annual turnover of £1.9m. In 2014 came the biggest acquisition so far: Catermasters, established by chefs Nigel Johnson and Richard Moody in 1989, which itself had grown by acquisition – first of In House Catering in 2008 and Bite in 2013. The merger created a new business – Host Catermasters Group (HCM) – boosting turnover to £60m and "pushing it into a different league, creating a more rounded organisation with specialists in multiple sectors of hospitality," said Toner at the time. Along the way, Host had won a £10m five-year contract at Salford Royal NHS Foundation Trust and a £16m eight-year contract at the Spectrum Leisure Centre in Guildford, a gain from Compass.

In 2015 came the opportunity to merge with the much larger CH&Co, which stunned the industry. CH&Co was regarded as a highly desirable acquisition and Toner had been fleet-footed to land the

In 2015 came the merger of Host with the much larger CH&Co to create a near-£200m business that retained the CH&Co name. Bill Toner became CEO while Tim and Robyn Jones became chairman and founder respectively. Sadly, Robyn died soon after the merger was announced.

prize, creating a near-£200m business that retained the CH&Co name. Toner became CEO, while Tim and Robyn Jones became chairman and founder respectively. Toner had quietly established himself as one of the new entrepreneurs, while Tim and Robyn, two of the most successful entrepreneurs in the business, began their exit from the stage. To much sadness in the industry, Robyn died in September 2015, only a few months after the merger, and her interview for this book, but the CH&Co name lives on as a fitting memorial for her.

***

In 2007, BaxterStorey bought up Holroyd Howe, founded 10 years earlier by Nick Howe and Rick Holroyd. This added 100 contracts worth £40m a year in turnover, thus creating two more millionaires. Holroyd Howe's B&I contracts were absorbed into BaxterStorey while Holroyd Howe became the company's independent school business – a focus on one market that, according to Storey, has proved to be "brilliant". In the same year, the café-to-restaurant group Benugo came on board. It was an inspired takeover but "a bit stupid really, because it was a bit stressful – but it worked really well," Storey told *Caterer*. It was a young business with great possibilities but frustrated by lack of capital. Modelled on a New York deli where, in the words of Ben Warner, its founder (brother Hugo was also there in the early stages), the concept had a warehouse feel – "the colour comes from the abundance of food instead of strong graphics and mission statements." The chain started with one store in Clerkenwell in 1998; by the time of its purchase it was operating five retail units across London including such venues as St Pancras Station and the V&A.

The acquisition took BaxterStorey into the retail arena but also acted as a foil for the

Outside Preston Town Hall, Ian Cartwright hands over the keys of a minibus that Dine Contract Catering sponsored for the Duke of Edinburgh's Award scheme to HRH The Earl of Wessex, chairman of the Award's council.

B&I business. Even in its early days, Benugo had managed to gatecrash some B&I sites but now it had the opportunity to be installed in some of BaxterStorey's bigger sites where BaxterStorey offered the catering and Benugo provided the coffee bars, each brand helping to sell for the other. The purchase also enabled it to enter the venues market. By 2009, Benugo's turnover had grown to £22m and then to £50m in 2012. By 2014, with over 12 restaurants and shops and in over 50 catering sites, Benugo upticked its turnover to over £70m and now spearheads WSH's foray into retail catering. Its key role helps in joint pitches to B&I and other clients.

"The days of subsidies are becoming fewer," Ben Warner told *Caterer* in an interview in 2012, "and you've got to have a commercial arm to your business to succeed. I don't think caterers can develop a commercial proposition on their own. It's incredibly difficult."

WSH took another tilt at the retail market

in 2014 when it acquired Searcy's, the event and visitor centre caterer, for some £20m. Operating at 20 sites, including the Champagne Bar at St Pancras Station and at Westfield Stratford, Searcy's gave WSH an entry into the lucrative events market.

Notwithstanding the purchases of Caterlink, Holroyd Howe and Benugo, growth by acquisition is not entirely to Storey's liking and 80 per cent of BaxterStorey's growth has been organic.

"Generally, I'm not very keen on acquisitions," he told *Caterer*. "It's just a culture clash. You end up with clients who didn't choose you and team members who didn't choose you and for whom you've been the enemy... You've got to feel the cultures are quite similar in order to do it."

From the start, Bill Baxter stayed on as deputy chief executive under Storey; Smith was appointed joint managing director, a position he held until 2008 when he stepped back from day-to-day management to

*The Champagne Bar at St Pancras Station: WSH **took** another tilt at the retail market in 2014 when it acquired Searcy's, the event and visitor centre caterer, for some £20m.*

concentrate on business interests outside contract catering. He quit in 2010. Baxter remained as deputy chief executive until 2012 when he retired at the age of 50, one of the youngest and one of the most successful catering entrepreneurs of his generation. He retained a major financial stake in the business.

"I felt it better to leave the company when I did. It was probably time, anyway," he says. In truth, relations with Storey, though still immensely cordial on a personal basis, were beginning to show signs of strain in the business.

"We each had ways of working and we both have strong ideas and views. That's natural. Alastair was the boss and I've run two companies where I was the boss. So we naturally have different approaches, different ways of working. It was time to move on."

Moving on meant more time as chairman of Hospitality Action (for which he was awarded a CBE in 2010 for services to the catering industry and the Lifetime Achievement award at the 2014 Cateys), leaving him more time for fishing, charity works and his farm in Wales which has over two miles of salmon fishing rights on the River Wye.

Alastair Storey remains chairman and chief executive and is still looking for growth – "We like growth; growth is fun, isn't it? It keeps our ideas fresh. I don't imagine business is a holding pattern." He created Boxford Investments, an umbrella company, after a refinancing in 2013 which brought in some private equity via a specialist investment company, ICG, but management still controls 85 per cent of the business, WSH UK and Ireland controls the trading brands. Storey knocked Jamie Oliver off his perch as *Caterer's* choice of the most influential man in the hospitality industry in 2014 and remains one of the industry's most successful entrepreneurs, now running

A modern, themed staff restaurant for a client in Manchester of Dine Contract Catering .

a business employing 12,000 staff and worth some £550m in annual turnover.

***

When Tim and Robyn Jones began to talk to Toner, despite their protestations in 2010, they had been alive to the possibilities of a merger for some time. They wanted to determine the long-term legacy of a company that they had built up over 25 years; the deal also came against a backdrop on increasing competition where, inevitably, mid-size companies were merging to compete with the largest competitors.

"We're starting to see more consolidation in our industry," said Tim at the time of the merger, "some of which is through new entrants to our market and we want to be leading this, because there are only

so many opportunities to build on this scale. We're now represented across a wider range of hospitality sub-sectors than either company was before, which also gives us the operational scale on a national basis to compete more effectively."

It was the classic case of bigger is better and stronger.

***

After letting Cygnet go to Compass in 2011, Jim took a back seat and Ian took over the running of the company. He abandoned the Compact name, rebranding it Dine Contract Catering, and expanded successfully from B&I into care homes, further education and universities, expanding from its northern heartland into Scotland, the Midlands and the south. The company, a keen supporter of

apprentice training, was recognised as one of the top 10 companies in service and retail in the Sunday Telegraph's Top Apprenticeship Careers List 2015. It also supports the Duke of Edinburgh's Award scheme, sponsoring a minibus in 2015 for the charity.

"The work of this brilliant charity links back to the ethos of our own company – to help provide young people in catering with the tools, knowledge and confidence they need to forge a successful career in the future," said Ian Cartwright at the handover.

The company now operates 200 contracts and employs over 1,000 people. With an annual turnover of £30m, profits have trebled in the three years since the rebranding – sure evidence of the confident touch that Ian – a fitness fanatic who completes Iron Man contests – continues to bring to the Cartwright business interests.

For Jim, the journey from a 15-year-old apprentice at the Belfry to a successful catering entrepreneur, including industry recognition with the FSM Lifetime Achievement Award in 2014, has not been without its hiccups. "We lost over £1m in one deal," says Jim wryly, "but it's been a fabulous ride and with a little bit of luck, it's not over yet."

***

From 1970 to the beginnings of the 21st century, when the number of acquisitions began to tail off, the contract catering industry enjoyed three decades of extraordinary opportunity that offered rich rewards to those who had the foresight, the ability, the courage and the tenacity to set up their own enterprise.

Contract catering, a term disliked by many in the business – "It's a complete misnomer," says one of them, Alastair Storey. "We are competing with the high street. If we don't get that as an industry, we are missing a trick" – is now a £4bn-plus industry with the capital requirements of an industry a tenth of its size.

Many, such as Storey (BaxterStorey), Geoffrey Harrison (Harrison Catering), Bill Toner (CH&Co), Ian Mitchell and Wendy Bartlett (Bartlett Mitchell), Kate Martin and Sue Parfett (The Brookwood Partnership), Jim and Ian Cartwright (Dine Catering), Patrick Harbour and Nathan Jones (Harbour and Jones), Mark Philpott, Clive Hetherington and Phil Roker (Vacherin), Alison Frith (Artizian), Sue Johnson (ABM Catering Solutions), Trevor Annon (Mount Charles) are managing companies that continue to thrive and prosper; there are plenty of others who could be added to this list. How they will develop in the future is yet to be determined but there is no doubt that they are among the entrepreneurs of today and tomorrow.

Jim and Ian Cartwright: Since Jim's semi-retirement at the sale of Cygnet, Ian has been responsible for the company's successful development of Dine; a fitness fanatic, he competes successfully in Iron Man contests.

CHAPTER
TWENTY-NINE

What of the future?

Contract catering has survived a century of turmoil but the future should hold no fears.

The UK food and service management industry (in modern terminology but still contract catering to many) is dominated, as it always has been, by a small number of large companies: Compass (by a mile), Sodexo, Aramark, Elior and BaxterStorey, with independents such as CH&Co, Dine Contract Catering, The Brookwood Partnership, Bartlett Mitchell, Wilson Vale, Artizian and others, successfully growing steadily. In 30 years, British-based Compass has become the world's largest food service company with a global turnover of £17bn; in 15 years BaxterStorey (£550m annual turnover) is now the UK's fourth largest contractor, though a big slice of that is generated by retail catering. The two examples highlight the opportunities that the industry has presented to entrepreneurs. Compass' growth illustrates what can be achieved on the international stage while the emergence of a host of smaller independent caterers in the UK, some operating as boutique-style operators and many on a regional basis, continue to show what can be achieved in the domestic market.

In the companies already created there is ample evidence to show that the industry will continue to harness the powerful entrepreneurial spirit that Jack Bateman, John Sutcliffe and others so amply demonstrated all those years ago. Today's entrepreneurs are following in illustrious footsteps but, in doing so, are they likely to meet the same challenges as the industry's founders faced? Looking back might give us a clue to what these challenges might be.

One thing is certain: it is not a static industry, nor will it remain so. We have only to look back at the rough and ready catering of the early pioneers to appreciate the extraordinary improvement in food standards which has swept through the industry even in the last 20 years. During the war and in the immediate decades following, caterers were concerned with putting food on a plate at the lowest possible price and still making money out of it. There was little pretence at sophistication.

Despite the vast improvements in catering in the 1980s onwards (and even before in major City boardrooms), staff feeding got itself a bad name which has taken years to shake off. When, in the mid to late 1980s, high street brands in the shape of Burger King, Pizza Hut and others began to emerge as staff restaurant offerings, together with brands created in-house or acquired on the way, there was plenty of scepticism in the industry. Many thought, and maybe still do, that brands have only a minor role to play. It is true that they aren't the answer to every problem but their introduction certainly signalled a change in attitude. No longer was it just a question of providing a traditional hot meal at the least possible price and at the greatest profit.

Staff feeding is now in competition with the high street if not physically (though it often is) but psychologically, too. At the popular end, branded restaurant chains have emerged in the high street, offering a staggering variety of cuisines at reasonable prices. At the other end, talented chefs, who are increasingly difficult to recruit, have led the way in raising food quality (and prices). New styles of food and so-called healthy alternatives continue to be 'invented', even as fish and chips, pies, curries, burgers and pasta remain cherished favourites. Today's

Staff feeding is now in competition with the high street, if not physically (though it often is) then psychologically. New styles of food and so-called healthy alternatives continue to be 'invented' even as fish and chips, pies, curries, burger and pasta remain cherished favourites.

wraps, burritos and snack pots are a long way away from yesterday's sandwich, yet three billion sandwiches are still sold through shops every year according to the British Sandwich Association – M&S and Prêt à Manger no doubt in the lead and both are rivals for the caterer's pound, it should be added.

The point about this particular revolution is that it is not yet played out and never will be. The restaurant sector, by far the most dynamic in the UK hospitality industry, harnesses new ideas, new concepts, new tastes every year. Contractors are rarely able to follow these trends as soon as they appear but they will always need the skills, the talent and the foresight to continue to respond to what is a constantly changing commercial marketplace.

This challenge has been successfully met so far though it has taken time and there has been no instant revolution. The canteen has become the staff restaurant: posher, more refined, cleaner, more attractive, more reflective of what is available in the high street, more aligned to the changing needs of its customers. The vast staff canteens, so familiar in the 1950s and 1960s that could easily feed a thousand in one sitting, have largely disappeared and have been replaced with staff restaurants which are typically smaller and usually brighter and specifically designed for the purpose, decorated to appeal to the modern diner. Marc Verstringhe's wish to make the canteen a *restaurant at work* as far back as the early 1980s still reflects the urge of most caterers to raise standards to those of the best commercial restaurant, enabling the eating environment to meet the more discerning, more selective, more demanding needs of clients and customers, all of whom are becoming ever more conscious of price and value.

New cuisines, new tastes, new methods of cookery and service have been accompanied by the introduction of grab and go and other snack items from smaller outlets, even kiosks. Compass' first Lunchtime Report in 1990 suggested that workers spent only 26 minutes on their lunchtime break – not a new finding to those caterers who can remember having to serve a three-course meal to several thousand hungry workers in one 20-minute sitting in some of the old-time factories. But time pressures at work continue apace. In many offices, workers take advantage of what is available as quickly as possible, so the style of catering in many outlets has changed to one that is increasingly casual and informal; in city centres there are plenty of eating places on the high street eager to poach the staff restaurant's business, given the chance.

None of this will change. Indeed, this customer-led revolution will exacerbate the pressure on those providing food at work. With subsidies declining, caterers will have to fight even harder to retain the loyalty of their customers and thus justify their existence. It is a never-ending race to the top.

***

Client attitudes, too, have changed, but to the contractor's advantage. In sharp contrast to 50 years ago, corporations today want to concentrate on their core expertise. It would be unthinkable for Bloomberg, Coca-Cola, Google and others, who have tended to set the pace in providing the most enlightened facilities for their employees, to want to organise these facilities themselves. The same now goes for many other businesses. With plenty of companies able and very willing to organise all the facilities an organisation requires, at a higher standard and, often, at a lesser cost, why not stick to your core function and outsource what is not core?

Thus, for caterers, the opportunities are huge although the challenges are just as formidable.

Even by the 1980s, clients were beginning to demand more from the caterer than a plate of food. The cost of providing the space and facilities for a catering service began to weigh heavily on corporate balance sheets, not helped by recessionary times. In order to satisfy this more challenging environment, contracts began to move from a simple cost plus/management fee basis, on which the early caterers made their fortune, to the more demanding fixed price contract; some then became profit and loss, concession or total risk contracts. If a caterer can make money out of an outlet, some clients reasoned, why

subsidise it at all?

Canny clients reckoned that the benefit would not only be financial. By reducing (or withholding) the subsidy the caterer will have to rely entirely on the quality of the food is provided, how well it merchandises and prices it and how satisfied customers are for what it provides. In other words, without a subsidy, the caterer is forced to up its game or it risks losing the contract by customers voting with their feet. All things being equal, few contractors would quibble with that. But even in 2010 (BHA's latest figures) there were still over 4,100 cost plus contracts although this was down from 5,656 in 2001. At the same time, fixed price contracts in 2009 numbered 10,553 and there were 1,887 P&L

Investment by catering contractors in client premises, by number, 2001-2011					
Year	£0-£25,000	£26,000-£50,000	£51,000-£100,000	£101,000-£500,000	Over £500,000
2001	1,503	328	228	145	80
2002	1,390	130	97	41	7
2003	776	172	96	41	7
2004	725	159	91	70	5
2005	318	119	79	49	16
2006	152	75	61	33	15
2007	135	95	34	39	9
2008	102	78	34	31	4
2009	90	43	21	54	19
2010	131	42	38	49	12
2011	164	46	27	36	6
TOTAL	5,486	1,287	806	588	180
Investment assuming	£12,500	£37,500	£75,000	£250,000	£600,000
Investment	£73.1m	£48.3m	£60.4m	£147m	£108m

BHA's Food and Service Management Surveys

contracts, including concession and total risk contracts. Clearly, the end of the cost plus contract is not yet in sight but its future in the next 20 or so years must surely be in doubt for some clients.

With so many catering offerings available to workers locally, the question arises, and will arise even more in the future, whether a staff restaurant is actually necessary anyway. Why try to re-create a high street environment in client premises when there are plenty of cafés, restaurants and coffee bars locally? Why indeed?

Here we come back to the original benefits of offering a catering facility in the first place: it is a means for the wise employer not only to provide food and sustenance but an opportunity to give something back to the workforce, an opportunity for employees to network and bond with each other, an opportunity to reinforce the message to employees that they are working in a caring environment. A catering outlet can be the most visible evidence of how the employer values its workforce. And not every high street is so conveniently close as to tempt people out of their office, nor is the right food always available in the right place at the right price. The argument for retaining a staff dining facility remains positive. But changes are afoot.

***

The best contractors have largely become work associates rather than mere suppliers. They are now seen as having a beneficial impact on the quality of life of the people they cater for, touching every employee at least once a day (in some cases three times a day) in the millions of meals they provide. As a result, increasingly, the success of catering will be measured on outcomes rather than on just buying in services. Food in hospitals will be judged on how well it has helped

Michel Landel: "If a company's employees take fewer sick days, we're probably doing a reasonable job... if they're losing weight, perhaps it's because we're offering more healthful food in the cafeteria."

Healthy eating has become a key trend of modern catering outlets.

patient recovery; school meals will be judged on how effective they are in keeping children attentive throughout the day; corporate clients will judge the effectiveness of the food the caterer provides by how well it aids worker retention and job satisfaction.

It is perhaps significant that for Sodexo, 'Quality of Life Services' is as prominent on the company's website as the Sodexo name itself – in fact, it appears directly underneath the name. Michel Landel, Sodexo's chief executive, in an article in the *Harvard Business Review,* wrote that Sodexo's primary purpose today is to "deliver only services that directly improve the lives of individual people... even though it is client organisations... that foot the bill.

"If a company's employees take fewer sick days, we're probably doing a reasonable job... if they're losing weight, perhaps it's because we're offering more healthful food in the cafeteria."

Later, Landel describes catering on remote sites where there is a high risk of workers becoming overweight and or having alcohol problems.

"We put together a programme to help individuals better manage their diet and exercise, both on-site and during home leave... It's a pretty extensive service package and a not inconsiderable investment for the client, but companies have found that it pays off in reduced absenteeism and improved productivity."

Such an approach – not limited to Sodexo it should be noted and adopted, if not quite so self-consciously, by many others – drives caterers into ever closer partnerships with clients, hopefully yielding mutually beneficial results.

To some extent, this has coincided with requests by clients for a financial investment by the caterer to upgrade and improve the catering facilities, sometimes by as little as £25,000 or less but in some cases by over

£1m, typically in exchange for a longer contract. This is an attractive trade-off for some caterers, tying them even more closely to their client. Most of the larger companies have cautiously agreed to this though many smaller independents do not have the necessary financial resources, nor the desire, to go down this route. As can be seen on the previous pages, between 2001 and 2011, according to the BHA's FSM surveys, over £440m was invested by caterers in client facilities. This is not an inconsiderable investment for a sector that claims it is almost cap-ex negative. Nor does this figure include any PFI involvement. It is interesting to note, however, that the investments have gradually declined in the later years. Nevertheless, the need for some investment in client premises, in an industry traditionally averse to capital expenditure, will continue to arise as caterers are increasingly viewed as partners, not merely suppliers.

Another future influence on contractors is the use of social media. Major hospitality and food companies now monitor social media on a 24-hour basis, assiduously noting comments made by customers and clients. Sodexo has two people full-time on this task for its contracted meals service. The company has found that it is now commonplace for customers to use their mobile phone to check on dish availability before they decide to use the staff restaurant. In the same way, reaction to what's provided can be immediate; 10 tweets praising a meal can be good, 10 critical tweets can highlight a problem. Instantaneous value judgments by customers are the stuff of life for the high street restaurant; it is often forgotten how often these judgments can be made about food at work – and are now publicly broadcast. Caterers ignore them at their peril. Tweets become external quality control measurements but can never replace

In many outlets, the standard of food and presentation in today's staff restaurants match (and may surpass) that of commercial restaurants on the high street – as in this restaurant at Sky Television's campus at Osterley where Gather & Gather provide the catering.

Elior's One Under Lime: Elior provides a variety of catering at the Lloyd's building in the City of London, including a wine bar on the basement floor.

internal controls which remain critical.

Thankfully, too, contract catering has attracted many more women into its senior ranks than ever before – and continues to do so. Not only are there successful women entrepreneurs running their own companies (the late Robyn Jones, Sue Johnson, Wendy Bartlett, Sue Parfett, Alison Frith are just some names that immediately come to mind) but major groups, too, have broken the glass ceiling with such appointments as Debbie White at Sodexo, Catherine Roe at Elior and Caroline Fry at CH&Co. It could be claimed that contract catering is setting the pace for the hospitality industry as a whole in its enlightened employment of women in top jobs – and for the entrepreneurial opportunities it offers them.

In all these trends, food standards must continue to keep pace with customer needs.

The variety of food offered will become more extensive and standards will improve further. Those canteens that have not already become restaurants at work will need to look at their offer; those that do not improve their environment and enhance their offer will certainly lose out in the long-term. Yet having suggested that some B&I units in city centre locations are vulnerable to high street competition, the B&I market remains strong. B&I represents about half the total number of outlets and over a third of the number of meals provided by UK contractors – but this has fallen since 1991 when it represented 75 per cent of outlets and half the number of meals. That's quite a change in two decades but it reflects the changing structure of British industry rather than any downturn in demand for catering services.

B&I successfully accommodated the massive changes in the structure of British industry in the 1960s and 1970s, not entirely without damage, but it remains a happy hunting ground for any caterer eager and able to provide a service that chimes with the needs of increasingly demanding customers and ever-cautious clients. The need to service specialist markets, such as schools, hospitals, even B&I, will witness the continuing evolvement of specialist companies or, at least, well defined divisions within broader-based caterers. There are plenty of examples here. New clients are opening up who need bespoke services which caterers can happily provide but this can pose a danger for the larger groups.

Personal service remains a significant attraction for clients and is the key factor in the success of most independent caterers. Global clients will (almost) always choose a global caterer but other organisations will choose to hire a caterer who can promise to provide personal attention at all reasonable, and sometimes unreasonable, times. It is significant that every start-up described in this book in the last 20 years has succeeded by promising – and delivering – a level of personal service that larger caterers find more difficult to provide.

Because of their more complicated hierarchies, corporate groups have to work much harder to ensure that clients get the level of personal service they think they deserve. The skill and talent of the caterer's local representative is the key factor in client retention. Many a catering contract has been won on promises of personal service by the caterer and many a client lost because this was never delivered. Maintaining client relations at all levels remains critical and any caterer that heedlessly denies this should take careful note.

Even today, there is one well-known industry leader who claims he has more

Sodexo's Knead St Deli: a fully branded commercial retail offer, which acknowledges the need to keep pace with the demands of today's customer.

friends who were former clients than former colleagues, so diligently did he succour his client relationships.

There are other things to note. Despite the merger of HCM and CH&Co in 2015, much of the recent growth of established companies in the UK has not been through acquisitions. Compass, many years ago, set itself up as an international player and only acquired Cygnet Catering's school meals business in 2011 in the UK to consolidate its penetration of the sector. Its development in the UK in recent years has been largely organic. It has purchased no UK catering business since Cygnet. Similarly, Sodexo acquired Atkins in 2011 to broaden its range of services in the UK facilities management sector – another strategic purchase – though both companies continue to seek acquisitions in other parts of the world. Neither company, nor others such as Elior, Aramark or BaxterStorey, are likely to consider expensively buying a business which it reckons it could create itself under its own steam.

***

Of course, this does not preclude all mergers or acquisitions. Undoubtedly there will be opportunities which are just too tempting to resist on the part of both buyer and vendor, but the heady days of the Granada/Sutcliffe buy-fest in the 1990s (see the list of takeovers in the appendix), when it purchased 15 companies and some £350m in turnover in a decade of acquired growth, will surely not reappear in the foreseeable future. Mergers and acquisitions will be cautiously strategic rather than a headlong rush for market dominance, so the chance of making future millionaires of current operators is reduced though by no means eliminated. It's just that the present day caterer needs to be more realistic.

Of course, the industry has not been blind to the opening up of new sectors of the economy. The Ministry of Defence has contracted out all of its UK catering provision with Sodexo, Aramark and Compass chiefly because the contracts are so big and comprise such a wide range of support services. In-house provision is fast disappearing in most other public sectors except the NHS and, to a certain extent, education, although the government's current (2015) position to provide a free school meal for all infant primary children has proved to be a boon, particularly for those contractors with access to a central production unit which can provide chilled food that needs reheating on premises without sufficient kitchen facilities. Even in the NHS, contractors have gained more than a toehold and, with ever tightening budgets, NHS hospitals will inevitably follow private hospitals into contracting out their catering provision, although there remains much internal NHS opposition.

Tight cost controls and low budgets, however, will always make NHS catering provision a challenge for even the most cost-obsessed caterer. A food charge for patients (under discussion for years but never likely to be introduced) would dramatically change the hospital catering landscape, pouring more money into the system but adding almost unbearable pressure on caterers to provide food immune from criticism – tough, indeed, in a hospital environment. If patients have to pay for their food, they will be even more demanding.

Both the NHS and education are big sectors, however, some contractors are making a success of specialising in these markets and will continue to do so, but ever higher standards of performance at less cost will remain a constant demand.

Colleges and universities, with high levels of footfall, represent a new and attractive sector, lending itself particularly to snacks and the sale of grab and go items; the turnover at its outlet in Brunel College, London, is the highest in the entire UK Subway chain. And all the while, contractors are being tempted to join the melee of providers on the high street. BaxterStorey with Benugo and Searcy's has bought up two well known high street brands. Will others follow? Maybe – but cautiously. Compass bought Travellers Fare in 1992, merging it with SSP, its airport and retail brand in 1997, but exited in 2006 when it sold SSP. Both Compass and Sodexo dallied with Gary Rhodes for a time (see previous chapter) but not primarily with a view to creating a branded restaurant chain.

Caterers remain leery of challenging the high street brands in their own territory, and wisely so. Sticking to low risk catering is always likely to be more profitable than being caught in the complicated web of high risk, high cost commercial restaurant operations, though Alastair Storey is clearly willing to give it a go. Nevertheless, caterers are already catering for the public in places like the Historic Royal Palaces, museums and leisure attractions where concessions have been granted. Catering in these outlets represents 10 per cent (150m) of all meals provided by contractors, a significant increase on the 62m meals served in 1991. Concession catering at football stadia and other sporting events remains highly attractive.

Nor is catering now the only provision. As soft FM beckons with an almost alluring charm, other avenues open up. Cleaning, reception, housekeeping, gardening, security and other support functions have now become commonplace services to be provided as part of the catering service. Sodexo in the UK, as we have already seen, now regards itself as primarily an FM rather than a catering provider.

***

But in meeting the competition, established companies have to acknowledge that there are new kids on the block. These are not just the smaller start-ups that can unexpectedly win a prize contract through some unforeseen but critical advantage which may be as simple as a chance meeting with a potential client on a golf course (and that personal telephone number). This has always been a danger. FM companies, some well-known overseas such as Mitie, ISS and Serco, have moved into catering. How quickly they will develop in the UK is not clear but there is no doubting their determination.

Traditionally, clients have viewed the catering service as the most skilled of all the support services; as a result, the caterer has tended to be engaged first before being invited to undertake the other, less skilled support services required. Will this work the other way? It has in the US where Aramark is widely regarded as an FM provider with a strong catering offering, in much the same way that Sodexo is now becoming viewed in the UK (catering represents only 40 per cent of Sodexo UK income). But can FM companies build a sufficiently strong track record to be accepted as a caterer? Almost certainly yes – and traditional caterers will need to be wary here. Of course, it's possible that a catering and an FM company can combine by pitching together for different parts of the business, though this did not work when CH&Co joined a consortium of providers for a short time. Some clients may well be willing to accept this but the advantage of outsourcing is that the fewer suppliers you outsource to, the better; one point of contact for the client makes for much easier management and control.

And no longer is catering purchased by the personnel or works manager. Full-time purchasing departments are the norm, often aided by consultants who are former contract caterers themselves. Tenders are becoming increasingly more demanding and more costly to provide; those for major public service contracts need teams of professional people, each tender costing a six-figure sum. Such a commitment precludes all but the largest companies from tendering, despite promises and some (very little) action by the government to open up the tendering process to smaller companies. High value public sector contracts mean that caterers have to be highly resourced in finance and manpower even to be able to quote and this will not change. As a consequence, a large sector of the market will continue to be effectively out of bounds for the smaller independent.

Cost clearly remains the key factor in the provision of any catering outlet but there is some understandable belief that clients tend to obsess too much about costs while ignoring the benefits which are clear but impossible to identify on the P&L account. It is these benefits that need to be universally promoted. Catering is certainly a relatively high cost function in food, staffing, space requirements and equipment. It also demands investment by caterers in staffing and training. Latterly, caterers have recognised this, opening cookery schools, introducing apprentice schemes and, as a previous chapter has showed, hiring talented chefs to help them raise their culinary game. More training is being undertaken than ever before. These investments will have to continue in order to encourage more young people to adopt the industry as a recognised career. But looking back over the last century, more or less the period of this book, the industry's past success is clear and evident. It has been a roller-coaster ride in which companies have been launched, developed and have been successfully transformed into new entities through merger and acquisition, while new entrepreneurs have emerged, young and talented, who immeasurably broaden the industry's range and scope. The opportunities remain though the competition is tougher and the clients are more demanding.

In a century of turmoil, the industry has steered a successful course, sometimes hesitantly, to its present size and dominance, primarily by its ability to accept change, meet customer demands and take risks. If it continues in the same way, with the same talent and commitment, the future should hold no fears.

Presentation is all – choice at the Financial Service Authority in Canary Wharf, a bartlett mitchell contract.

APPENDIX

Takeovers and mergers

In the 1990s and later, contract catering was a particularly fertile area for takeovers and mergers. Compass, Sutcliffe, Granada, Gardner Merchant and overseas-based companies such as Aramark and Elior were all keen to acquire successful independent companies in order to build mass and a meaningful profile; at the same time, many independent owners were willing sellers. In turn, some of the purchasers were, in their turn, taken over. Gardner Merchant was itself the result of a merger and was the subject of a takeover by Sodexo. Both Bateman and Midland were acquired by Grand Metropolitan in the late 1960s and Sutcliffe succumbed to Granada in 1993 which, itself, merged with Compass in 2000. So mergers and acquisitions became part and parcel of everyday life in the industry and they helped make many people wealthy individuals indeed. Although mergers and takeovers have continued into the present era, they reached their zenith in the 1990s and heralded a major consolidation of contract catering, as the list here (which we do not claim is comprehensive) indicates.

Acquisition	Acquiring company
Major companies – pre 1990	
Sutcliffe Catering	Olympia Group (1961)
Peter Merchant	John Gardner (1964)
Taylorplan	Marriott (1965)
Russell and Brand	Marriott (1966)
Bateman Catering	GrandMet (1969)
Midland Catering	GrandMet (1970)
Sutcliffe Catering	Sterling Guarantee Trust (P&O Group) (1973)
Domco Food Service (UK)	Hamard Catering
Smallmans	Gardner Merchant (1975)
Four Square Vending	Gardner Merchant (1977)
Thwaites and Matthews	ARA (1980)
Kelvin Catering	Gardner Merchant (1983)
Spinneys	CCG (1986)
Breakmate Catering	Sketchley (1986)
Hamard Catering	Compass (1986)
ABM	Lindley Catering (1986)
Compass	Buy Out from GrandMet) - £163m (1986)
Sketchley/Breakmate	Gardner Merchant (1987)
Fairfield Catering	Sutcliffe (1990)
Northern Caterers	Stuart Cabeldu (1990)
Hall Ellison	Sutcliffe Catering (1990)
1991	
High Table	Elior
1992	
CMS	Sutcliffe
Travellers Fare	Compass
Letheby and Christopher	Compass
Stuart Cabeldu	ARA - £5m
High Table	Elior
Catering by County	Sutcliffe
1993	
Gardner Merchant	CinVen - Buy out
Sutcliffe Catering	Granada - £360m
Leith's	Eurest
Eaton's Exclusive Catering	Compass
1994	
Forward Catering	Granada - £4.6m
Caterskill	Eurest
Drummond Thompson	Elior
1995	
Gardner Merchant	Sodexo - £780m
Roper Catering Events	ACMS
Caterskill	Eurest
Catering Guild (Gallacher)	Granada - £5.5m

1995	
Hanrahan In-House Catering (Ireland)	Granada - IR£4m
ACMS	Granada
Taylorplan	Marriott
1996	
Northdowns	ACMS (Granada)
CCG (B&I)	Granada
Bromwich Catering	Granada
Wheatsheaf	Gardner Merchant
Russell and Brand	Marriott - £16m
Payne and Gunter	Compass
Shaw Catering	Granada
Tillery Valley Foods	Gardner Merchant
Link Partnerships	Campbell Bewlay
Hallmark Executive Catering	Elior
1997	
National Catering Leisure	Compass
Baxter and Platt	Granada
Pall Mall Services	Granada - £8.4m
Cadogan Catering	Gardner Merchant
Lawson Beaumont	Gardner Merchant
3 Gates	Granada
Marriott UK	Gardner Merchant
BET/Initial	Rentokil
Universal Ogden	Sodexo
Shaw Catering	Granada
Caterwise	Campbell Bewlay
Effective Partnerships	Campbell Bewlay
MDA Food Services	Aspen Group (merger to form Customised Contract Services)
Hallmark Executive Catering	High Table
1998	
Quadrant (Post Office Catering) 49% stake	Sutcliffe
Capitol Catering	Granada
Red Ball Group, Brighton	Compass
Customised Contract Services	Granada
Hunters	Campbell Bewlay
1999	
Brian Smith Catering Services	Elior
Catering & Allied	Elior
Summit Catering	Granada (1999 - £6.5m)
Ring & Brymer (Gardner Merchant)	Chester Boyd
2000	
Halliday Catering	Wilson Storey
Granada	Merger with Compass
Nelson Hind	Elior

2001	
Campbell Catering	Aramark
Campbell Bewley (45% stake)	Aramark - £13m
Houston & Church	Wilson Storey Halliday (WSH)
Compass (de-merger from Granada)	
2002	
Digby Trout	Elior
Castle Independent	Compass
2004	
Cater Link	WSH
BaxterSmith	WSH renamed BaxterStorey
Emerson Hewitt	Compass - £2/£3m
Catering Alliance	Aramark - £20m
Just Deli	OCS Group - £7m
2005	
Lindley Catering	Sovereign Capital Partners - £14m
Buckley Support Services	Almond Catering - £1m+
2007	
Holroyd Howe	Baxter Storey
Caterplus	Waterfall
2008	
Taylor Shaw	Waterfall
2010	
Yes Dining	Bright Futures Group (BFG)
2011	
Cygnet Catering	Compass
Yes Dining (BFG)	Luke Johnson (Genuine Dining Co)
2012	
7 Day Catering	Servest Group
2013	
Bite Catering	Catermasters
Grayson Education	Brookwood Partnership
Lindley Group	Centreplate
2014	
Host Management	Catermasters (merger 2014 to form HCM Group)
Quartet Catering	Dine Contract Catering
Inn or Out	Aspire Hospitality
Inn or Out (Aspire Hospitality)	Bartlett Mitchell
Lexington	Elior
Searcy's	WSH
2015	
CH&Co	Merger with HMC (CH&Co name retained)